T0342325

THE BANKS DID IT

THE BANKS DID IT

An Anatomy of the Financial Crisis

NEIL FLIGSTEIN

Harvard University Press

CAMBRIDGE, MASSACHUSETTS

LONDON, ENGLAND

2021

Library of Congress Cataloging-in-Publication Data

Names: Fligstein, Neil, author.
Title: The banks did it : an anatomy of the financial crisis / [Neil
Fligstein]
Description: Cambridge, Massachusetts : Harvard University Press, 2021. |
Includes bibliographical references and index.
Identifiers: LCCN 2020050258 | ISBN 9780674249356 (cloth)
Subjects: LCSH: Financial crises—United States—History—21st century. |
Banks and banking—United States—History—21st century. |
Mortgages—United States—History—21st century. | Global Financial
Crisis, 2008–2009.
Classification: LCC HB3725 .F55 2021 | DDC 330.973/0931—dc23
LC record available at https://lccn.loc.gov/2020050258

For Heather

Contents

Illustrations

Figures

Tables

Preface

The financial crisis that began in the United States in 2007 created the most intense economic downturn in the United States since the Great Depression. The crisis not only engulfed the United States but also quickly spread to banks across western Europe. The ramifications of this crisis and the recession that followed are with us today. Not surprisingly, from the first moment of the crisis, scholars and journalists attempted to make sense of what happened. The search for the "cause" of the crisis brought about an avalanche of books and papers on the subject. Many were journalistic accounts, some were memoirs, and still others were books rushed to press by economists, political scientists, and sociologists. Andrew Lo, a financial economist, reviewed twenty-one of these books in 2012 and declared, "No single narrative emerges from this broad and often contradictory collection of interpretations, but the sheer variety of conclusions is informative, and underscores the desperate need for the economics profession to establish a single set of facts from which more accurate inferences and narratives can be constructed" (Lo, 2012).

Unfortunately, many years on, we are not anywhere near a "single set of facts," nor is it clear what those facts might be. The causes of the crisis include a great many contradictory things. Some have argued that government regulation caused the crisis by forcing banks and the government-sponsored enterprises to make subprime loans to poor people (Wallison, 2015). Others have argued that too little government regulation permitted the banks to take on too much risk (which is at least part of the theory of the Dodd-Frank Act) (Acharya et al., 2009). Still others have argued that there was regulatory capture of the Federal Reserve, the Treasury Department, and the Securities and Exchange Commission. Bankers could do whatever they wanted while regulators cheered them on (Johnson and Kwak, 2010). Others blamed the real estate bubble whereby consumers and speculators drove up the price of housing to unreasonable levels (Schiller, 2015). The crash of prices was inevitable, and that crash, when it came, precipitated the crisis.

One of the original and more sophisticated stories focused on the chain of firms involved in the sale of mortgages to homeowners, the packaging of these mortgages into securities, and the sale of securities to investors. This theory suggested that perverse incentives existed such that those banks who originated risky mortgages passed on those risks to unwitting investors. The banks did not care if the loans were bad because they had no intention of holding on to them (Ashcraft and Schuermann, 2008). Other accounts favor blaming the complexity of the financial instruments: an insufficient understanding of the risks inherent in those instruments caused both investors and bankers to be too optimistic about the riskiness of the financial instruments being created (Furfine, 2014; MacKenzie, 2011). Another version of this argument holds that the credit rating agencies were similarly ill-informed and overly optimistic, thus rating too many mortgage-backed securities "AAA" (Rona-Tas and Hiss, 2010). This rating made those investments appear to be super safe and encouraged many investors to hold them.

Financial economists have focused on the moment whereby banks actually began to go out of business, beginning in the spring of 2007 when Bear Stearns defaulted on its loans. They interpret what happened as a lack of liquidity on the part of banks (Brunnermeier, 2009; Gorton, 2010). While the banks held significant investments, they were not able to sell them fast enough to provide additional cash to cover the money they had borrowed to buy them. When they tried to sell them, they found there was little market for them. The literature attributes this liquidity crisis to banks funding their long-term investments, like buying tranches of mortgage-backed securities, by using short-term loans. This argument has several variants, primarily focused on the organization of the repo market, the asset-backed commercial paper market, and the money markets, or what is collectively referred to as the "shadow banking" system.

One other explanation was to shift the blame to countries around the world who were running high positive current account balances, often because of the US chronic trade deficit. Foreign banks had cash to invest, and they chose to invest it either wittingly or unwittingly in American mortgages (the explanation proposed by no less a figure than Ben Bernanke, chair of the Federal Reserve Bank). This explanation implies that the housing bubble was caused by foreign banks that had to park their cash somewhere. In essence, this explanation neatly shifts the blame from Americans who took out those mortgages and American bankers who sold the mortgages and created and sold mortgage-backed securities to foreign banks. Those banks with so much cash to spend made cheap mortgages too attractive for unworthy home buyers to pass up and thereby pushed the housing bubble forward.

Finally, some have argued that the entire crisis was simply the result of the greed of bankers trying to make as much money as possible (Akerlof and Schiller, 2009). The sophisticated version of this argument focuses on executive and trader compensation. Here, the argument implies that bankers were rewarded most for making the risky deals by originating subprime mortgages and creating risky securities made up of these mortgages. Such deals paid off handsomely for the bankers, who generated high profits, but ended up putting the banks at long-term risk (Bhagat and Bolton, 2014; Crotty, 2009).

All of these explanations seem plausible. But they can't all be true. Part of the problem is that each explanation sets itself up as the one real cause of the crisis. It proceeds from the view that if the favored variable had somehow been recognized and changed, the entire crisis could have been averted. One of my advantages in having taken so long to work through the many elements of the crisis is that I have gotten some perspective on these events.

There have been two major problems with the literature as it has evolved so far. First, the banks have oddly not been a significant part of the story. Instead, the causal story has tended to focus on regulators, the individuals who bought mortgages, financial instruments, CEOs and traders, and capital flows. The firms that created modern finance and the many markets that made up the industry at its demise have rarely received sustained analysis. My purpose is to put the banks front and center in the analysis and show how they evolved, morphed into new markets, and took advantage of opportunities that barely existed even thirty years ago. The title of this book is *The Banks Did It* because I want to show that the banks played the critical part in the construction of what happened. They created new products and industries and pioneered the models underlying the new financial services. Banks watched one another, copied one another, and built entirely new kinds of organizations and markets. They also interacted with regulators and, for the most part, convinced regulators that what they were doing was both innovative and efficient. In the end, the world that the banks constructed and their role in making money from it are at the core of what happened.

Second, the most important idea missing in extant accounts of the crisis is that the banks formed a system. At the core of that system has been the relationship between the government and the banks in the making and remaking of the market for mortgages in the United States. In fact, the history of this relationship, which shows that the government and the market have been joined at the hip since at least the 1930s, opens up a view for an alternative political economy. The story of Americans getting mortgages for their homes is really a story of how politicians gladly put into place a system that produces the stable opportunity for homeowners to acquire mortgages and the opportunity for banks to thrive by producing a myriad of financial products to serve them.

That system has gone through four crises in the past ninety years. Every time, the system gets reconstructed, mostly by the government picking up the pieces and trying to ensure that Americans can get mortgages. The crisis of 2007–2009 was followed by just such a reorganization. It is impossible to understand what happened without connecting the dots between what citizens have wanted (more mortgages) and what politicians delivered. The complexity of the market over time shows the back-and-forth of the government's role in creating, stimulating, and regulating the provision of mortgages by banks. Banks have responded to these opportunities by taking advantage of what the system has given them to earn high rates of growth and enormous profits.

But the system that existed was not just about government regulation and oversight of the mortgage market. The underlying structure of how people get mortgages, who provides them, how capital is raised to fund them, and who ultimately the investors are requires deep analysis. The fact that the market for mortgages, the making of securities, the expansion of shadow banking, and the market for trading those securities were connected is critical to understanding what happened. Indeed, one of the problems that the regulators faced in the summer of 2008, as the system came unhinged, is that they lacked a thorough understanding of exactly how the markets were connected. While I admire the fact that Federal Reserve Chair Ben Bernanke and Secretary of the Treasury Hank Paulsen helped saved the world banking system from collapse, I believe that their theory of how the system worked was ad hoc at best. To this day, the people in charge of regulating our financial system do not really grasp its system-ic character. Now, of course, a great deal of that system is gone, blown away by the crisis. But the system that has emerged in its wake (which I describe in the conclusion) is still a system and one fraught with many problems.

Why has this kind of understanding been so difficult to grasp? Regulators tend to be bankers or economists, many of whom were trained as relatively narrow specialists. One group of these specialists, who dominated the Federal Reserve, were trained as macroeconomists. They viewed the economy as a set of sectors with varying rates of economic growth that in the aggregate produce GDP. In analyzing the impact of changes in a particular sector's growth, the critical facts for their analyses were the relative size of the market and its potential for directly impacting some other sector. For example, if housing construction went down, then one could expect that certain related durable goods markets, say the market for toilets, would experience a downturn as well. This meant that they tended not to see the deeper connection between the housing market and the financial markets. So, in the spring of 2008, they saw the foreclosure crisis that was brewing in the subprime mortgage market as relatively contained because it was "only" a $200 billion market, missing that the entire banking system in the economy was wrapped up in the production of mortgage-backed securities.

The other group of experts were trained in financial economics. Their orientation was to understand the role of the financial markets in the economy. They were focused on arguing that financial innovation would make the financial system more efficient by creating financial instruments that would bring together people who had money to loan with people who had a need to borrow. The 1980s witnessed a flowering of financial innovation that garnered praise for its promotion of new financial instruments to control risk and put money to the best possible use. In the 1990s, financial economists also promoted the idea of banks becoming financial conglomerates. They wanted to break down the barriers between retail, commercial, insurance, and investment banking and allow banks to participate in whatever markets they deemed profitable. These ideas were seen as bipartisan, and both political parties embraced financial innovation and deregulation as good for the economy.

These perspectives made it difficult for regulators to analyze what was occurring in the mortgage market from the early 1990s. They never paid much attention to or cared to understand how the system worked and the nature of the risks that were being taken. For much of 2008, macroeconomists were reassured that the difficulties were not substantial and would be contained without damage to the larger economy. Financial economists were convinced that what was going on was good for the economy. Neither group was oriented toward unpacking how Main Street (consumers buying mortgages to purchase homes) and Wall Street (the largest and most systemically important financial institutions) became fused. This book attempts to lay out the steps that the government and the banks took to produce this market. It did not have to happen this way—but it did.

Tracking out the critical moments when new banks and new markets emerged is crucial to laying out the basic facts of what happened. My main tactic in this project is to approach what happened historically. I want to show how the various pieces of the puzzle came together over time. The aim is less to understand the ultimate cause of the crisis and more to make sure that we have all of the pieces in place and can set them in motion. There is evidence that many of the factors that scholars and journalists have so far discussed played some role in the crisis. But how those factors fit together is poorly understood, if understood at all.

This does not mean that I am giving up on causal analysis altogether. I believe that it is possible to evaluate whether the causal stories that have been told make sense of what happened. My intention is not to just reconstruct what happened but to set what we know against many of these hypotheses about how people think things were working. So, for example, there is little evidence that the government-sponsored enterprises were the cause of the subprime crisis. Those organizations were not allowed to sell subprime mortgages until 2005, and by then the market was well developed and dominated by private banks. Indeed, they were quite late to the party and had little effect on what was going to happen. Moreover, private banks were the issuers of most of the securities based on subprime mortgages. There is similarly little evidence that everyone was passing the risk on to the next guy. The evidence shows quite clearly that the biggest banks involved in subprime mortgage lending were issuers of bonds and purchasers of those same securities. The important stylized fact is that when the end came, all of the largest banks in the country were holding such bonds, and most of went out of business, were forced to merge, or were substantially reorganized under pressure of the Federal Reserve.

For me, the craziest thing to explain is the most obvious: how did the savings and loan industry, with its emphasis on loaning locally and holding those loans, end up becoming the mortgage securitization industry centered on Wall Street and exotic financial instruments? How did mortgage securitization become the core way to make money not just in the American financial system but in the world's financial system? Putting it another way, how did Main Street end up being taken over by Wall Street? And how did the global market for securities get taken over by the market for American mortgage securities?

The story as it really happened is quite complex. But it is explicable, and the truth, to the degree that I have grasped it, is stranger than any of the stories that have been told. As the outcome of both crises and opportunities, the system was created with little intention. The government actively organized the market. But how they did so changed as the situation changed. The regulators and policymakers were pragmatic in their orientation to ensuring that Americans could buy mortgages. They gave little thought to the kind of system that had been constructed, and they used organizations and institutions at hand to try to make sure that mortgages were always available. As such, many of the endpoints had little to do with the beginning. Banks were only interested in finding markets to replace those that no longer had growth or proved profitable. That they all eventually became the same bank is the result of their collective realization that mortgage origination and securitization were so profitable that becoming organized around them was what the most successful banks were doing. It is therefore not surprising that bankers, regulators, and scholars never saw the true nature of the system (and still don't!). They did not appreciate all of its moving parts and how those parts came together.

This book is directed to making sense of that question.

THE BANKS DID IT

A LONG, STRANGE TRIP

The Great Recession that began in the fall of 2008 was caused by a series of complex and connected events. These events were lined up like a set of dominos. The housing market began to turn down in the beginning of 2006 as house prices peaked and began to decline. By early 2007, this caused an increase in foreclosures, particularly for homeowners with subprime mortgages who were unable to refinance their mortgages and thus could not continue to pay their mortgages. Over the next year and a half, the securities based on these mortgages came under increased scrutiny. The value of these securities began to drop, and it became increasingly difficult to sell them. This was a problem because most of these securities were bought using borrowed money. The contracts for borrowing that money included clauses that required financial institutions to put up more capital if the securities lost value.

Many large financial institutions began to run through their capital, either because they had to repay the loans or because they had to increase their collateral. Since no one knew which banks held these securities, beginning with the collapse of Lehman Brothers on September 14, 2008, a full-blown panic effectively closed down the markets for short-term borrowing (what is called "shadow banking") in the United States and abroad, especially in western Europe. This meant that many large financial institutions did not just experience a liquidity crisis (i.e., the inability to raise cash quickly enough to cover what they needed to add to that collateral) but were actually insolvent (i.e., bankrupt), as the cash they had quickly ran out as they had to pay back their borrowings and were not able to sell assets to pay off their debts. In the fall of 2008, the massive restriction of access to short-term borrowing caused nonfinancial corporations to lay off workers, and a recession ensued in many of the advanced industrial countries.

It is useful to remind ourselves what policymakers and economists were saying about the problem as US house prices began to decline in early 2006 and home foreclosures took off in 2007. While the signs of a housing bust were mounting, regulatory authorities were not particularly concerned that a larger economic crisis was brewing. In a speech given in Chicago on May 27, 2007, Ben Bernanke, chair of the Federal Reserve, said, "Given the fundamental factors in place that should support the demand for housing, we believe that the troubles in the subprime sector on the broader housing market will be limited, and we do not expect significant spillovers from the subprime market to the rest of the economy or to the financial system" (Bernanke, 2007).

Bernanke's view was shared by most of his colleagues and the academic economists who were frequent contributors to discussions of the subprime market and Federal Reserve policies. For example, at their annual summer meeting of central bankers from around the world held in Jackson Hole, Wyoming, in the summer of 2007, Frederic Mishkin, at that time a governor on the Board of the Federal Reserve, remarked, "Problems in the subprime market have led to investors reassessing credit risk and risk pricing. Fortunately, the overall financial system appears to be in good health and the U.S. banking system is in good position to withstand stressful market conditions" (Mishkin, 2007).

As the housing market continued to deteriorate in the fall of 2007, the economics profession began to take notice. GDP growth estimates for 2008 were adjusted from somewhere around 3.5 percent to a consensus of about 2.5 percent, while expected unemployment rates were increased from 4.5 to 4.8 percent. These judgments and estimates did not foresee that the housing crisis would bring the financial system to its knees or that it would begin the most serious economic downturn since the Great Depression. How could they have been so far off? The economists making these predictions were making their best guesses based on their analysis of the significance of the housing downturn to the larger economy. The housing sector accounts directly for about 5 percent of GDP and indirectly for another 10 percent. Given the size of the market, macroeconomic models showed that even with a serious housing downturn, the effects on the larger economy were thought to be muted.

I think it is safe to say that the people who were in charge of trying to understand the mortgage crisis and how that crisis might spill over into the financial services industry were the people in the best position to understand how the housing market and the financial markets were connected. They held important positions in the government and business, and they had the training and access to information to know what was really happening. Yet they were all clueless about what was about to happen. What were they missing?

The Banks Did It

The main thesis of this book is that it is impossible to understand what happened unless one studies what the banks themselves were doing. While this seems obvious now, in almost all of the accounts given by the Federal Reserve and the economic regulators, these financial institutions and their strategies to make money were not the focus of attention. Financial institutions are subsumed into an industrial sector (i.e., the mortgage industry) or, even more generically, the markets (referring to financial markets that include the sale of stocks, bonds, derivatives, and other financial products). The goal of this kind of analysis was to understand the impact of adverse changing circumstances within a particular market on the wider economy. So, for example, when subprime mortgagors began to default on their loans in 2007, the main argument was that these defaults were relatively inconsequential in terms of the size and breadth of the financial markets, and even less significant for the larger economy.

The goal was never to make sense of why the banks had given out so many subprime loans in the first place and what that meant about the way the system worked in order to assess the potential broader impacts of these foreclosures on the financial system. This meant the regulators never even tried to understand how connected the mortgage market had become to the financial markets and how mortgages were the raw material that was driving investments being made by banks in most of the developed world. While the story I told in the first two paragraphs of this chapter is now more or less accepted by regulators and economists as an account of the crisis, it is still only a description of what happened. It is my assertion that until we drill down into what the banks were doing to make money and how they had come to do it, we will not really understand how the dominos were lined up in the first place, such that they were arranged to fall and produce the crisis. Without understanding the banks as a system whereby the links within and across financial markets are explicated, one has no chance to make sense of how and why the crisis happened.

But what are the elements of making sense of such a system? Any approach to understanding what banks were doing has to begin with the basic facts of American banking. Finance has a long history of boom-and-bust in the United States stretching back into the nineteenth century. New products, new firms, and new markets are produced. But eventually, financial markets overreach, and chaos ensues. Usually, the economy is then plunged into a recession or depression. The government steps in and helps markets and banks reconstruct themselves so that lending and borrowing can resume. Usually the banks left standing play an important role in this reorganization. The cycle then begins anew.

To make sense of this kind of dynamic, one needs a set of concepts that rec-ognize three facets of the way that markets are organized in modern capitalism (Fligstein, 2001). First, one needs to understand that governments and markets are by definition co-constituted. That means that large-scale modern markets cannot exist without the extensive intervention and active engagement of gov-ernment. Government helps establish the rules of the road and gives firms the ability to build stable market structures. Governments frequently underwrite innovation and often provide the road map to new products and services. In the case of the mortgage market, the government innovated the conventional mortgage in the 1930s and mortgage securitization in the 1960s. Government regulation is not an alien invasion into the marketplace but rather a prerequisite for a market economy to function.

The alternative to government action is not a perfect market but rather re-al-world markets thoroughly sullied with collusion, fraud, imbalances of power, and production of substandard or dangerous products and prone to crises due to excessive risk taking. In the case of mortgage finance, there has been a long history of government involvement in trying to make mortgages widely available to the American public. For example, during the Great Depression of the 1930s, the government helped the banks recover and provided the architecture to de-fine how mortgages could be obtained that helped provide an increase in home-ownership from about 43 percent of the population in 1940 to 63 percent in 1965.

The second facet is that the real-world political economy hinges on the rec-ognition that such market arrangements are not innocent but the outcome of power, both political and market power. They are the product of power struggles between firms, industries, workers, and government within particular markets and in the political arena. Stable markets can be characterized as containing in-cumbent-challenger structures whereby the largest firms set and use the rules of the game to reproduce their dominance while challengers figure out how to survive (Fligstein, 2001). In the United States, where firms have tended to have more market share and political power, this has generally meant that incumbent firms have been able to shape the political governance of their markets, thereby reinforcing their market power. In the case of financial markets since 1980, the largest and most politically connected banks have gotten the government to give them the kind of market rules they wanted.

Finally, the natural state of markets is dynamic. Emergence, stability, and moments of crisis and transformation are natural life-cycle events in markets. Governments may help to initially produce the conditions for the emergence of new markets, provide the architecture to stabilize existing ones, and manage cri-ses to limit damage and facilitate recovery. Government can innovate products, facilitate exchange, and provide investment in new technologies. But firms are ultimately the ones who influence how the market works and what is produced. They make investments; innovate products, processes, and organization; and work to create incumbent-challenger structures where some of them dominate. They are the ones who figure out how to make money. This means our story needs to pay attention not just to the formal institutions governing markets but also to what banks were doing and why they were doing it.

Making sense of the business models of financial institutions is at the core of understanding what caused the crisis. While the rules governing markets are pertinent to an understanding of what happened, they do not explain how banks and markets were actually organized. This requires knowledge of the history of the mortgage market, the rise of securitization, and later the creation of the market for nonconventional mortgages (which include adjustable-rate, subprime, Alt-A, home equity, and jumbo loans). Without this knowledge, it is impossible to make sense of why the crisis was so large, so deep, and so unseen. Without tracing the history of the business models of financial institutions, we will fail to understand why the banks were so vulnerable in 2007–2008. It was the banks who made loans to individuals. It was the banks who took those loans and created mortgage-backed securities (MBSs), sold those securities, and held on to many of those securities as investments And it was the banks who used the short-term credit markets (shadow banking) to borrow money to make all of this possible.

There are three important puzzles about the crisis that can be answered only by making sense of the system of mortgage securitization and the business models of the banks. One puzzle involves two competing narratives that purport to explain what happened. The first narrative focuses on the idea that at the core of the financial crisis was the originate-to-distribute model of banking, which pushed banks to make riskier and riskier loans to people with bad credit. This idea implied that those who originated the loans did not care about the ability of the buyer to pay back the loan because the originator sold it to someone else, who was going to turn it into a security. That person also did not care about the quality of the loan, since they sold it on to its ultimate unwitting customer (Ashcraft and Schuermann, 2008). According to this narrative, the increase in foreclosures that caused the devaluation of the securities was directly the result of financial institutions lending to people with worse and worse credit, people who they knew were not going to be able to pay back their mortgages.

The problem with this narrative is that it directly contradicts the other main account of the crisis, with which I opened the chapter and which most analysts now agree fits the facts. In the fall of 2008, the largest banks held large amounts of mortgage-backed securities that they were funding by using the short-term credit markets (shadow banking). As they needed to put up more collateral to keep these loans, they found that the decreasing value of the securities meant that they rapidly experienced a liquidity crisis. When it turned out no one knew what the securities were worth, this turned into the banks being insolvent (Brunnermeier, 2009). These two stories are obviously contradictory. Were financial institutions passing on the bad securities to unwitting buyers, or were they selling them to themselves? If they were buying these securities themselves, why was this happening?

A second puzzle is why financial institutions did not stop producing both mortgages and securities as the housing market slowed and foreclosures rose. One logical thing for the banks to have done as the mortgage market declined in 2006 was to shut down their origination businesses or their securitization businesses. They would have taken some losses, but they could have pivoted to businesses where they were making more money. In the case of commercial banks, they could have focused on their retail banking and credit card businesses. Investment banks could turn to their roles as traders of securities, advisers on mergers, and underwriters of corporate equity and debt. They would have had to shrink in size and profits, but they would have lived to fight another day. Instead, as we know, they continued to look for mortgages by lowering credit standards and increasingly committing mortgage and securities fraud. They continued to buy and hold large amounts of mortgage securities as investments.

Finally, the question of why the crisis was so deep and spread so quickly across the population of financial institutions in the United States and parts of Europe remains a mystery. The crisis spread almost instantaneously to Iceland, Great Britain, the Netherlands, Germany, France, Switzerland, and Luxembourg. Curiously, it failed to spread to Japan and the rest of Asia, and most of the developing world was unaffected. Most financial crises in the postwar era have shown a flight away from risky settings, such as from developing countries to less risky ones, like the United States and Europe. But this crisis started in the United States and spread to a few European countries in a matter of months.

These puzzles can be resolved only by looking more closely at what the banks were doing and why they were doing it. The narrative I construct is more complicated than most of those out there. But it has the great advantage of helping make sense of the main dynamics of what happened and posing satisfying answers to these questions.

What Were the Banks Doing?

The most interesting and important fact that emerges from this book is that on the brink of the crisis, most of the largest financial institutions in the country were involved in producing many kinds of products for the mortgage markets: prime, subprime, jumbo, interest-only, adjustable-rate, and home equity loans. Even more intriguing, most were both originators of those loans and issuers or underwriters of mortgage securities, sellers of those products, and many were among their own best customers. Moreover, their integrated businesses were funded mostly by borrowed money. Industrial organization economists describe this type of organization as vertical integration. Here, mortgages can be viewed as the raw product that is turned into securities. These then are sold to other financial institutions or held on one's own account as an investment using borrowed money.

In essence, the largest of the savings and loan banks, commercial banks, mortgage banks, and investment banks, which were previously divided by market and customers (and by statute law before the repeal of the Glass-Steagall Act in 1999), had by 2007 become the same bank. They did this because it was good business. It is easy to forget how profitable the banks were during this period and how much individuals working for those banks were making for themselves. At its peak in 2003, the mortgage market was almost $4 trillion. Even after the conventional refinancing market began to dry up in 2003, the mortgage market remained around $3 trillion until 2007. During this period, the financial sector of the US economy produced almost 40 percent of all of the profits in the entire economy in 2003 with about 10 percent of GDP and 7 percent of the labor force. Good business indeed.

This crucial fact about how banks were vertically integrated and what it meant to their organizations and performance is missing from all existing accounts of the crisis. Why is it so important? The banks were locked into a system of making money that worked incredibly well from 2001 to 2004 and pretty well from 2004 to 2006. Before 1990, the banks tended to be specialists in one kind of product. But over time, banks began to realize that lucrative profits could be made by capturing profits at every part of the securitization process. Banks who were mortgage originators realized that making and selling securities was a good business. They decided to become issuers and underwriters in order to make money off of the production of the securities. They opened trading desks and bought and sold securities for their own accounts. Once the investment banks saw that their suppliers had become competitors, they felt compelled to buy up mortgage originators to guarantee the raw material for their securities production businesses. By 2006, four of the five large investment banks, Bear Stearns, Lehman Brothers, Merrill Lynch, and Morgan Stanley, had invested in mortgage origination. Only Goldman Sachs never sought out closer ties to mortgage originators.

This vertical integration explains a lot about how the crisis proceeded and provides answers to our puzzles. While there was a great demand for mortgages and high returns to be had from mortgage securities, financial institutions had money pouring in (and out) from every pore. The CEOs of these institutions were seen as heroes, and everyone working in the industry was making money. Once financial institutions became dependent on a supply of mortgages to make, buy, and sell mortgage-backed securities, it became difficult for them to adjust their business models when the housing market began to turn down in 2006.

Instead of pulling back from the market when the housing market turned down in 2006, all of the financial institutions who had business models based on the integration of mortgages and mortgage securitization doubled down and continued to seek out mortgages even as the quality of those loans deteriorated. By the end, eleven of the thirteen largest financial institutions in the United States either went bankrupt or were reorganized in the fall of 2008 because they were so locked in. Their entire business model was predicated on making money from mortgages and mortgage securitization, and their organizations were set up to efficiently buy, process, and hold mortgage securities based on borrowed money. Even if managers had wanted to change, abandoning those models would have meant a complete overhaul of those organizations, and that simply was not going to happen quickly. But managers were unlikely to do this no matter what. They had made huge amounts of money off of their vertically integrated business model. Moreover, their main competitors were in the same position, so backing off the business model would have seemed like surrender to other firms and potentially would have left money on the table. This was something that aggressive managers were not likely to do.

In hindsight, it is easy to see how impossible it was for the banks to figure out what to do, as the entire organization of the bank was predicated on the throughput of mortgages. It was a management consultant's nightmare: a business model that was printing money as late as early 2006 turned, in eighteen months, to one that led the largest banks in the country to insolvency. One of the things that we know is that most of the banks kept desperately chasing mortgage origination as long as possible in order to keep their securitization machines running. This resulted in making loans that were worse and worse over time. They got so desperate that they routinely began to commit mortgage fraud in order to secure mortgages to package into securities. Not surprisingly, foreclosure rates were highest for loans issued in 2006 and 2007, and the securities based on those mortgages were the most likely to be downgraded in value.

The vertical integration of banks also explains why banks turned to sell mortgages to people with worse and worse credit over time. Over the period 2001–2008, in order to keep their business models intact, financial institutions had to continue to find mortgages. My metaphor here is thinking about the mortgage stream as the nutrients for the financial community to thrive and prosper. As long as there was a steady supply of mortgages, financial institutions had the nutrients they needed to grow and be successful. From 2001 to 2003, interest rates were quite low. This set off a refinancing wave that drove the mortgage market from $1 trillion in 1999 to almost $4 trillion in 2003.

But eventually, these nutrients (conventional mortgage refinances) dried up. This meant that the community of financial institutions who had gotten rich and fat during the refinancing wave with their vertically integrated mortgage securities pipelines needed a new source of nutrients. They found these in Alt-A, jumbo, subprime, home equity, interest-only, and adjustable-rate mortgages and packaged these products into securities to continue to grow their businesses. But, by 2005–2007, even these mortgages began to dry up, and financial institutions had to pursue people whose credit was even worse. The problem of the deterioration of loan quality was caused not by an originate-to-distribute model but instead by the need of vertically integrated banks to continue to originate mortgages to produce securities, which they would then sell and buy on their own accounts.

This need for mortgages also explains why banks were pushed toward predatory lending and securities fraud. There was an apocryphal story that was widely reported in 2009 about an out-of-work carpenter who lived in Fresno, California, who had the previous year made less than $20,000 and was given a $450,000 mortgage. Few at the time asked why banks would do this. But, consistent with the analysis presented here, banks were so desperate to secure mortgages for securitization that they were perfectly willing to lend to people who they knew were not going to be able to pay back their loans. This resulted in loans that were substandard being packaged into securities in order to keep the business running. By misstating the degree to which the loans that were going into these securities were problematic, financial institutions committed securities fraud. While fraud was not a core cause of the crisis, it was a symptom of how financial institutions would go to every possible length to keep their securitization machines going.

Once banks had invested in origination businesses, securitization and trading, and buying and holding on to securities as investments on their own accounts, they were committed to making profits at all parts of the process. They could not escape the system they had created as prices for homes decreased and mortgages started to be foreclosed on. They continued to need mortgages to fund their securities businesses. But as the value of the securities that banks held came into doubt as foreclosures rose, the largest vertically integrated banks came under financial pressure. The securities they had were being funded by short-term debt, and they needed to find more collateral in order to keep those loans. This meant that all of the banks who were involved in all phases of the industry found themselves facing the same financial duress. Because all of the largest banks were implicated in multiple parts of the mortgage market by 2007, they all experienced severe financial distress at the same time. When in the fall of 2008 Lehman Brothers went bankrupt, the panic spread immediately to the holders of the commercial paper for all of the largest banks, all of whom were obvious suspects for having exactly the same problem as Lehman Brothers. In essence, all of the largest financial institutions had ended up with the same business model. When that model proved untenable, they all went down together.

The American banks were so profitable that their counterparts in other developed countries, particularly in Europe, could not help but notice. Indeed, some of these banks became directly involved in the origination and securitization of mortgages (such as Barclays, HSBC, and Deutsche Bank). Others became major borrowers in the ABCP market in order to purchase mortgage securities (such as ABN Amro, ING, Dresden Bank, BNP Paribas, Rabobank, and Fortis). They saw that the American banks model of borrowing money to buy AAA-rated mortgage securities was highly profitable and relatively low risk. They dove into the US market. Foreign banks purchased $1 trillion of mortgage securities between 2003 and 2007, mostly made up of nonconventional mortgages.

When the American banks experienced the pullback from the ABCP market in 2008, all of the European banks who had heavily invested in mortgage securities or who were involved in mortgage securitization in the United States immediately fell victim to the same forces. The swiftest spread of the crisis was to countries where these banks who had gotten the deepest into the American mortgage securitization industry were located. They were illiquid and then insolvent. Their governments had to bail them out, and these countries faced a financial meltdown followed by a recession. By understanding what the banks were doing and how they formed a system, we can understand the links between the events leading to the crash.

Why Did Mortgage Securitization and the
Vertical Integration of Banks Emerge?

This raises the question of why all of the banks converged on the mortgage securitization business as their main source of profit and the vertical integration of that business as their business model. One only has to go twenty years earlier to the world of 1988, to find that savings and loan, commercial, mortgage, and investment banks were more specialized in particular businesses, smaller, and focused on different customers. Most of the customers who wanted to buy houses went to locally owned and managed savings and loan banks. These banks took in funds from the community, sold mortgages locally, and held on to the mortgages until the house was paid off or sold. Most households used the services of commercial banks for checking, savings, and loans for things like paying for home renovation, college, and cars. Commercial banks also focused on small and large businesses that came to them for banking services and loans. Only the largest corporations used the services of investment banks to issue corporate debt or engage in producing new stock issues. All of the investment banks were small and were organized as partnerships, not publicly held corporations, and their activities were concentrated in Manhattan where the stock and bond markets were located.

Understanding how this fragmented financial system ended up focusing on mortgages, and more specifically mortgage securitization, is one critical piece of making sense of what happened. This requires delving into the history of the mortgage industry to understand how both crisis and opportunity shaped the business models of financial institutions. The process by which the mortgage securities industry emerged is a story that spans over five decades, with many twists and turns. Almost no one in the world of 1975 and very few in the world of 1985 would have predicted that mortgage securitization was ever going to become the dominant way that Americans would finance their mortgages. Literally no one would have predicted that it would become the dominant business of all of the largest financial institutions and the central product around which the financial markets would be organized.

To understand the crisis of 2007–2009, one needs to step back and understand the coevolution of home financing between the public and private sectors since the 1960s. Until the 1980s, this process was relatively straightforward. Individuals would find a house. They would go to their local bank (most likely a savings and loan bank) and apply for a mortgage. The bank would agree to lend the funds and then hold on to the mortgage until it was paid off or the house was sold. During this historical period, the largest holders of mortgage debt were savings and loan banks. The laws and rules that governed this process were forged during the Great Depression of the 1930s.

Since the 1980s, however, this process has become increasingly complicated. Under the mortgage securitization model, the borrower goes to a lending company (frequently a bank, but not exclusively) that is called an "originator" because they make the initial loan. Unlike the original savings and loans banks, these companies use the mortgages as input into mortgage-backed securities. The "originator" makes their money from the fees that homeowners pay to get their mortgages and from selling the mortgages to issuers or underwriters, who turn the mortgages into securities. If originators hold on to the mortgages, then they are unable to lend money again, and their ability to generate fees goes away. So, they turn around and sell the mortgages, thereby recapturing their capital, and move back into the market to lend.

The mortgages are then packaged together into a legal device called a special purpose vehicle, which creates a subsidiary company whose entire assets consist of mortgages. This is used by issuers and underwriters to create a legal entity to create the bond. Issuers and underwriters are usually investment or commercial banks. This vehicle turns the mortgages into a security that pays a fixed rate of return based on the interest rates being paid by the people who buy houses. The financial institutions who make these special purpose vehicles divide the mortgages into what are called "tranches," which are claims on the cash flow generated by mortgage payments. Tranches have different amounts of risk, and the interest they pay depends on that risk.

Bond rating agencies consider the mortgages in a security in terms of their risk of either prepayment or foreclosure. They then assign a rating to each of the tranches of the bond based on a model that predicts how likely the mortgagors in the tranche are to stop paying their mortgage. The highest-rated tranches (AAA) have the least likelihood of failure, and the lowest-rated (BBB) have the highest rate of failure. These bonds are sometimes referred to as mortgage-backed securities (MBSs), residential mortgage-backed securities (RMBSs), collateralized debt obligations (CDOs), or MBS-CDOs. In this way, investors can buy tranches of bonds that pay a higher rate of return if they are more risky or less risky bonds that pay a lower rate of return. The special purpose vehicles are managed by servicers, who act to collect the monthly mortgage payments and disburse them to the bondholder.

In the world of the early 1990s, each of these transactions could have been undertaken by a different bank. But by 2007, most financial institutions were involved in almost all phases of the securitization process. The main exception was the servicing industry, which remained the domain of more specialist firms, although most large banks also did some of their own servicing. Circa 1975, mortgages were owned mostly by local savings and loan banks and were highly geographically dispersed. By 1993, most mortgages migrated to a few square miles of Manhattan, where in the offices of the major banks and government-sponsored enterprises (GSEs) they were packaged into special purpose vehicles. They then were redispersed to investors all over the world and serviced from a few locations. Investors are a heterogeneous group. The largest investors in these securities are the GSEs who hold on to lots of MBSs. But MBSs are held by banks, mutual funds, and private investors here and around the world.

The interesting question is, how did we move from a world where the local buyer went to their local bank to get a loan to one where most of the mortgages in the United States are now packaged into MBSs and sold into a broad national and international market? The push away from the savings and loans model of mortgage origination to the mortgage securitization market is the story of the crisis in the business model of the savings and loan industry. The savings and loan industry came under severe financial pressure in the 1970s. Savings and loan banks asked the government to try to save them by removing the rules that had previously governed interest rates and deposit insurance. The federal government complied and deregulated the industry in the hope that savings and loan banks would survive. Savings and loan banks then entered businesses where they had less expertise and made risky loans. By the late 1980s, a huge percentage of them had failed. Many had been looted by executives who took advantage of the lax oversight to try to feather their own nests.

This disaster created the opportunity for a new form of mortgage market to emerge. It will surprise most readers that the origins of mortgage securities and the complex financial structure we just presented were not invented by the financial wizards of Wall Street but instead were invented by the federal government. It is probably even more surprising that this set of inventions dates back to the 1960s. The federal government has been involved in the mortgage market to some degree since at the least the 1930s. But the roots of the modern industry begin in the 1960s.

Quinn (2019) shows that the idea to create mortgage-backed securities began during the administration of President Lyndon Johnson. The Democratic Congress and president had three goals: to increase the housing stock for the baby boomer generation, to increase the rate of homeownership, and to help lower-income people afford housing. Quinn presents evidence that the Johnson administration did not think the fragmented savings and loan industry was in the position to provide enough credit to rapidly expand the housing market. But federal officials interested in expanding homeownership did not want the government to get in the business of supplying and holding on to mortgages. Because of the Vietnam War and the Great Society expansion of Medicaid, Medicare, and other social benefits, the government was running large and persistent debts. An expensive housing program where the government provided funds for mortgages would add to the deficit, because the government would have to borrow money for the mortgages and hold those mortgages for up to thirty years.

If the government was going to stimulate the housing market, the Johnson administration would need to do it in such a way as to not add to the federal deficit. This caused them to reorganize the Federal National Mortgage Association (later known as Fannie Mae or Fannie) as a quasi-private organization, called a government-sponsored enterprise or GSE, to lend money and hold mortgages. They also created a new entity, the Federal Home Loan Mortgage Corporation (Freddie Mac or Freddie) to compete with Fannie Mae. Both Fannie Mae and Freddie Mac eventually became publicly held corporations with the assumption that should problems emerge with the securities issued by these entities, the government would intervene to protect investors. The government also created a government-owned corporation to insure those mortgages against risk of default, the Government National Mortgage Association (Ginnie Mae or Ginnie).

But taking these mortgage entities private and thereby taking their transactions off the books of the federal government was not the only innovation of the Johnson administration. The government also pioneered the creation of mortgage-backed securities (Sellon and VanNahmen, 1988). The government did not want the GSEs to ultimately hold the mortgages because this would limit how many mortgages they could originate. Instead, it wanted to use the capital the GSEs could raise to fund the mortgages and then offer the mortgages to investors as bonds. These bonds would be seen as backed by the "full faith and credit" of the federal government and therefore would be considered as low risk as treasury bonds. The GSEs began in the 1970s to offer and guarantee the first modern mortgage-backed securities (MBSs). These bonds were then being sold directly to investors by the GSEs or through investment banks (Barmat, 1990). The first mortgage-backed security was issued on April 24, 1970, by Ginnie Mae (*Wall Street Journal*, 1970).

The private MBS market barely grew in the 1970s. There were several issues. The savings and loan industry continued to have control over the bulk of the mortgage market where they took deposits, lent money, and held on to mortgages. But potential buyers of mortgage bonds were skeptical of buying mortgage-backed securities because of prepayment risk. The problem was that if you bought such a bond, people might prepay the mortgage before the end of the mortgage term, and bondholders would get their money back before they made much of a profit. This was made worse by the fact that mortgage holders were more likely to refinance houses when interest rates were falling, thus leaving bondholders with money to invest at interest rates lower than the original mortgages (Kendall, 1996).

This problem was ultimately solved through cooperation between the GSEs and the investment banks. They created the system of tranching, described above, in order to let investors decide which level of risk of prepayment they wanted (Brendsel, 1996). But there were also legal and regulatory issues involved in the packaging of bonds (Quinn, 2019; Ranieri, 1996). The most important was the problem of turning a mortgage into a security. The issue of a loan originator selling the mortgage into a pool of mortgages required changing the tax laws. The Tax Reform Act of 1986 cleared the way to the rapid expansion of the MBS market.

The demise of the savings and loan banks was a fortuitous collapse that in the end hastened the growth of the MBS market. The general economic crisis of the 1970–1980s produced very high interest rates. Savings and loans banks relied on individual deposits for most of their funds. The regulation known as Regulation Q fixed the rate that savings and loan banks could pay on these deposits. Savers began to flee those accounts, and the savings and loan industry faced the crisis that they could not raise enough money to make new loans. Moreover, they were holding on to a large number of mortgages that were priced at very low interest rates. Congress responded by passing the Garn-St. Germain Act. They repealed Regulation Q and allowed the banks to pay whatever interest rate they chose. They also allowed the banks to make riskier investments while still guaranteeing very large deposits.

The banks responded in several ways. First, they began to sell their mortgage holdings at a great loss in order to raise capital. These mortgages were repackaged into MBSs by primarily Salomon Brothers (Lewis, 1990). They also began to pay high interest on interest rates on government-guaranteed bank accounts. They then made very risky investments including many in commercial real estate, which helped create a commercial real estate bubble. This caused their ultimate demise (Barth, 2004).

As the savings and loan industry collapsed, the question of how Americans would get mortgages became a political issue. The obvious solution to the problem was to push for the rapid expansion of the GSEs and the mortgage securitization process as the main mechanism by which mortgages were financed. The MBS market grew enormously in the late 1980s and the early 1990s as the savings and loans banks collapsed. In 1980, the GSEs had issued only $200 billion of mortgages. This grew steadily to a peak of $4 trillion in 2003. As late as 1978, the savings and loan banks held almost 65 percent of the mortgage debt in the United States. But beginning in the late 1970s, their market share plummeted. By 1990, less than 15 percent of mortgages were held by savings and loans. By 1990, 50 percent of mortgages were being packaged into MBSs. The GSEs also held on to 10 percent or so of the mortgages as investments. Thus, the GSEs were involved in the ownership and securitization of 60 percent of US mortgages.

The GSEs acted as middlemen in making the mortgage securitization market. They would buy mortgages from mortgage originators such as commercial banks, savings and loan banks, and mortgage wholesalers and brokers. They would then secure the services of one of the five investment banks to act as the underwriter of the bond and to help sell the bonds once they were produced. Many of these MBSs would end up in the investment portfolios of commercial and savings and loans banks. This is because the mortgage securitization process had allowed individual mortgages whose risk was difficult to assess to be packaged into bonds that had high ratings (AAA in many cases) and the implicit backing of the federal government. Banks could borrow capital cheaply to hold these bonds, and they were viewed as close to riskless. Since these bonds typically paid higher interest than US Treasury bonds, they made great investments.

When the mortgage securitization industry began to take off in the late 1980s, many of the commercial and investment banks were reluctant to participate in the creation of MBSs. Indeed, the GSEs at the beginning had a hard time convincing the other banks to participate. But by 1993, banks of all kinds began to realize that the new model for mortgages had replaced the savings and loan model. This created a huge opportunity to enter a large and lucrative business. The residential real estate market contained a huge number of transaction possibilities. Mortgage securities were safe investments that paid high rates of return, returns that appeared to be backed by the government. By 1993, mortgage, commercial, investment, and the remaining savings and loans banks pivoted to find a role in the new securitization structure. This usually meant acting as an originator, wholesaler, broker, issuer, underwriter, trader, or investor. By virtue of the fragmentation of the industry around 1993, no one controlled very much market share of any of the markets except for the GSEs. But this was about to change.

The Rise of Vertical Integration, 1990–2001

It is useful to describe how the different kinds of banks found a niche in the emerging mortgage securitization industry being created by the GSEs. Making and selling securities was one of the basic businesses of the investment banks. While initially they were slow to enter the business, they realized the opportunity was huge when Salomon Brothers began to make huge profits on MBSs during the mid-1980s. All of the investment banks started divisions to participate in this new market.

The mortgage banking business where banks specialized in originating mortgages was in its infancy when the GSEs replaced the savings and loans with the mortgage securitization model. Banks who were trying to compete with the savings and loans for mortgages had a difficult time doing so. But when the GSEs began to aggressively purchase mortgages in order to create their new securities, these banks seized the opportunity to become suppliers to the GSEs. Mortgage banks would raise capital to broker loans by selling through real estate agents or would buy loans from others who originated them. They would then turn around and get their capital back by selling these loans to the GSEs. Eventually, the largest of these mortgage banks spread their activities to other parts of the securitization industry.

One industry that came to be important during the 1990s for participating in origination, securitization, and investment were the commercial banks. The commercial banks were faring no better than the savings and loans banks during the 1970s and 1980s. Davis and Mizruchi (1999: 219–220) show that commercial banks lost their core lending markets to other financial entities during this period. Corporations stopped going to banks for loans and instead went directly to the financial markets to raise money. Consumers stopped putting money in savings accounts in banks and began to invest in money market funds and a wide variety of stock and bond mutual funds. "Nonbank" banks such as GE Capital made "industrial" loans, while the financial arms of the automobile companies such as GMAC took over the auto loan business. In the mortgage business, mortgage brokers and lenders ate into the traditional business of savings and loans banks and commercial banks as they provided mortgages for securitization for the GSEs (Kaufman, 1993). Dick Kovacevich, CEO of Norwest, a large regional commercial bank, said, "The commercial banking industry is dead, and we ought to just bury it" (James and Houston, 1996: 8).

Commercial banks began to search out other market opportunities. They began to look in two directions. First, they wanted to diversify by entering more lucrative businesses such as investment banking and the buying and selling of stocks, bonds, and insurance. From the mid-1980s, the commercial banks pushed to undermine and circumvent the legal strictures that kept them out of these lucrative businesses, namely the Glass-Steagall Act (Barth et al., 2000). Their central argument was that such regulations were obsolete because market changes had blurred the lines of financial services.

The Federal Reserve, the regulatory authority for commercial banks, supported them in this effort (Hendrickson, 2001). The Federal Reserve adopted very lax standards in enforcing the legal barrier between investment and commercial banking. They took the position that as long as less than 50 percent of the business of commercial banks was involved in investment banking activity, there was no violation. Not surprisingly, commercial banks entered into various kinds of investment banking during the 1990s. In 1998, Citibank audaciously purchased Traveler's Insurance (along with its brokerage firm and investment bank), making the bet that the last regulatory barrier, the Glass-Steagall Act, would be repealed. Afterward, the Clinton administration and Republicans in Congress did just that with the passage of the Gramm-Leach-Bliley Act of 1999. With the repeal of Glass-Stea-gall, any financial firm could freely enter any financial industry. While the passage of the Gramm-Leach-Bliley Act was important, it is clear that it was only the end-point of a process that had already been going on for at least a decade. This led to a flurry of bank mergers and the creation of large financial conglomerate firms, which saw themselves no longer as lending institutions but as diversified financial services firms (Hendrickson, 2001; Barth et al., 2000). Kaufman (2009: 100) shows that between 1990 and 2000, the ten largest financial institutions increased their share of the total banking assets from 10 percent to 50 percent.

The second important change in the commercial banking industry during the 1990s and early 2000s involved a shift in their basic business model. During the 1970s and 1980s, banks tried to build relationships with their customers in the hopes of selling more banking services to individuals and corporations. But by the early 1990s, commercial banks, which had seen their customers migrate to other finan-cial firms, changed their view of customers. Instead of viewing their main business as being about building relationships with customers through the selling of loans, they began to see their industry as about charging fees for services, much as invest-ment banks had long done.

The most important fee-generating business quickly became the origination and securitization of mortgages. This is because customers for mortgages were charged a large number of fees to engage in a transaction. The sale of those mort-gages to special purpose vehicles and the production of MBSs also generated fees. Finally, the selling of those MBSs generated fees as well. It is not too strong to say that the creation of the mortgage securitization market by the GSEs saved the commercial banking industry. DeYoung and Rice (2004) document these changes across the population of commercial banks. They show that income from fee-related activities increased from 24 percent in 1980 to 34.8 percent in 1990, 35.9 percent in 1995, and 47.1 percent in 2003. This shows that commercial banks were moving away from loans as the main source of revenue well before the repeal of the Glass-Steagall Act. The largest sources of this fee generation in 2003 were, in order of importance, securitization, servicing mortgages, credit cards, and investment banking (DeYoung and Rice, 2004: 42). Not only were commercial banks increasingly dependent on mortgages for their fee-based profits, but they also began to change their asset base toward GSE-issued MBSs. Banks would originate mortgages, sell them into GSE pools, and then borrow money to hold on to the MBSs. Real estate accounted for 32 percent of commer-cial banks' assets in 1986, increasing to 54 percent of assets in 2003.

The joint effect of these two institutional shifts—the deregulation of financial service boundaries and resulting conglomeration on one hand, and the reorientation from loans to fee revenue on the other—was that different types of financial services firms all coalesced around mortgage finance as a core business. Within the mortgage finance business, banks began to integrate either backward into mortgage origination or forward into mortgage securitization. The main reason that banks began to integrate was that they realized that there were opportunities to earn profits at all points in the chain from origination to investing. But some of the integration was defensive as well. As originators decided to build their own securitization platforms, they began to keep more and more of the mortgages they originated in-house. Those who were involved only in the securitization business found themselves in increasing competition for existing mortgages. This pushed those who wanted to do securitization to own a mortgage originator or have an arrangement with an existing company.

We see this integration occur among all kinds of banks. By 1999, Bank of America, Citibank, Wells Fargo, and JPMorgan Chase (all commercial banks) had shifted their businesses substantially from a customer-based model where individual households and firms were the main target for their financial products to a fee-based model centered on originating mortgages, creating securities, and selling and holding mortgage securities. While all of these banks had been mortgage originators, they decided as part of their push into investment banking to become create mortgage securitization businesses and trading desks.

Countrywide Financial started out as a mortgage broker, while Washington Mutual Bank was a savings and loan bank. Countrywide Financial entered origination, securitization, and trading. Washington Mutual quickly entered securitization beyond its traditional business of making mortgage loans. On the investment banking side, Bear Stearns was a pioneer in integration when they entered the mortgage origination business by setting up lender and servicer EMC in 1993. Lehman Brothers, another investment bank, was also an early mover into the mortgage banking business, acquiring originators in 1995, 1999, and 2003 (Currie, 2007). Industrial product lenders GMAC and GE Capital moved aggressively into the market for originating mortgages and eventually into issuing and underwriting MBSs (Inside Mortgage Finance, 2009).

By 2000, a new business model had emerged in the mortgage market. The market for mortgage securitization was still centered on the GSEs for the conventional market. But banks of all kinds had over the course of the decade moved to increase the scope of their businesses by entering into all of the transactions in the market. The product mix of the financial conglomerates that were centered on mortgage finance meant that the largest banks were all becoming the same bank.

The final part of the story of the 1990s concerns the beginnings of the market for nonconventional mortgages. In the world of 1985, the number of products available to consumers to finance mortgages was quite limited. The main product was the conventional mortgage, which required households to have a 20 percent down payment, a mortgage amount limited to 30 percent of their monthly salaries, and a credit score above 650. In return, households got a fixed interest rate payment, usually for thirty years. They could, at any time, pay off the remaining loan amount without penalty. The high interest rate period of the 1970s and 1980s had introduced an adjustable-rate mortgage into the mix of products. But most mortgagors preferred the conventional mortgage because of the certainty it provided.

Households who had poor credit or could not come up with the down payment were simply unable to buy a house. It was also nearly impossible to access equity in a home to use for household expenses. Beginning in the early 1990s, small consumer lenders such as Associates First Capital, Beneficial Finance, and Household Finance started to experiment with lending money to households with impaired credit, those who could not put down a down payment, or those who wanted a home equity loan. The subprime business grew from $37 billion in 1990 to $62 billion in 1995 to $130 billion in 1999. These mortgages came with both higher fees and higher interest rates. By the mid-1990s, this business began to attract the attention of the larger banks. In 1999, Citibank, Washington Mutual, Bank of America, and Countrywide Financial joined Household Finance (which was bought out the next year by HSBC, a large British bank) as a top five producer. The business had grown to $130 billion.

Other market segments developed during the 1990s in much the same way. The home equity loan business where households could borrow money against the equity in their homes was a $20 billion business in 1990, $44 billion in 1995, and $75 billion in 1999. Early on, it too was dominated by many of the same lenders in the subprime market, such as Beneficial Finance and Household Finance. But by 1999, Citibank, Lehman Brothers, Countrywide Financial, and Bank of America were among the top five lenders in making home equity loans.

Many households were living in housing markets where price appreciation during the 1990s had sent housing costs through the roof. This meant that while they might have had good credit scores and were able to afford the monthly payment, coming up with the down payment was very difficult. The GSEs decide whether or not to purchase a loan to package into a security based how much they determine is the maximum a person can borrow. This limit became a barrier to households in high-priced parts of the country on both the East and West Coasts. So, banks began to offer a new product, what became known as a jumbo loan, where the person has good credit but needs to borrow an amount above the conventional conforming loan limits. Traditionally, the interest rates on jumbo mortgages have been higher than for conforming mortgages.

That market for jumbo loans grew dramatically from $88 billion in 1990 to $135 billion in 1995 and finally $315 billion in 1999. It too became dominated by the largest banks, with Washington Mutual, Countrywide Financial, Bank of America, Lehman Brothers, and Wells Fargo being the top five producers in 1999. Finally, adjustable-rate mortgages, which had existed at an earlier date, grew in importance as well. In 1990, $128 billion in adjustable-rate mortgages were originated. In 1995, this rose to $232 billion, and in 1999, it was $318 billion. By 1999, Washington Mutual, Lehman Brothers, Bank of America, Countrywide Financial, and Bear Stearns were the top five originators.

By 2000, the broad outlines of the mortgage securitization industry could be discerned. The largest financial institutions in the country were originating and securitizing a large number of loan products. They were buying and selling the securities based on those products. Most of them could be characterized as integrated producers. The proliferation of mortgage products produced new opportunities for both households and financial institutions. The business model of the modern financial institution was to produce in all segments of these markets and to invest in the securities produced by those segments. Not only had these markets grown in size, but the largest banks held large market shares in many of these markets. The mortgage industry was a $1.0–1.5 trillion industry by the end of the 1990s. It is this structure that was in place when the 2000s opened with a serious recession and the Federal Reserve dropped interest rates. This created a once-in-a-lifetime opportunity to expand their businesses, and in three years, the industry grew from financing $1.0 trillion in 2001 to $3.8 trillion in 2003.

The Great Expansion of Mortgage Securitization and the Eventual Crisis, 2001–2008

By the turn of the twenty-first century, the mortgage-backed securities business was increasingly dominated by a smaller and smaller set of big players. The largest commercial banks, mortgage banks, and investment banks had begun extending their reach both backward to mortgage origination and forward to underwriting and servicing. But it is important to note that through the early 2000s mortgage finance was still dominated by the prime conventional sector, and the GSEs were the mainstay of that market. The standard model of the mortgage market for conventional loans circa 2000 was that a mortgage originator, even if it was a commercial or investment bank, would sell the mortgage to one of the GSEs.

The GSEs would purchase the services of an underwriter to turn the mortgages into MBSs. The GSEs would then either have the underwriter sell the MBSs or buy them for its own account. Frequently, the GSEs also used outside servicers for their loans when packaged. Many of the banks that did business with the GSEs were large commercial banks. They would sell the mortgages they had originated to the GSEs and then act as underwriters for the bond process. They would then frequently buy the MBSs and hold on to them in their own investment portfolio. They would borrow money to buy those bonds, thereby freeing up their money to go out and make more loans.

An astute reader would wonder why the banks sold their loans to the GSEs at all. After all, if the purpose of vertically integrated production of MBSs was to make fees, bringing in a middleman would dilute those fees. To understand why some fees were foregone, one needs to understand the role of the GSEs in the market. The GSEs essentially served two purposes. First, because they bought the mortgages and packaged them into MBSs, the eventual buyers of the bonds felt that at the end of the day, the federal government stood behind the integrity of the bonds (Ranieri, 1996). This meant the bonds could get high bond ratings (often AAA) because it was assumed that if some problem ever arose, the federal government would bail out the GSEs. Second, the commercial banks and other entities who bought these bonds were able to borrow cheaply because of the high quality of the bonds. Buying mortgaged securities that were issued by the GSEs also meant that their asset portfolios looked much less risky. In essence, the GSEs performed the magic act of turning mortgages with varying degrees of riskiness into almost riskless investments that could be financed with money borrowed on the best terms. If commercial or investment banks acted as the underwriters or issuers for the GSEs, they continued to get the fees associated with securitizing mortgages.

The central role of the GSEs in the mortgage market had been changing throughout the 1990s as nonconventional mortgages grew as a share of the market. The GSEs were legally restricted in their ability to issue MBSs for nonconventional mortgages, and the increasing growth of that market gave financial institutions the incentive to enter into underwriting and issuing their own MBSs. From 1990 to 2003, the share of conventional mortgages as a total of all originations remained high, about 70 percent. But beginning in 2003, this changed, and by 2006, 70 percent of loans were nonconventional. In 2005 and 2006, the peak years of the nonconventional market, financial firms issued $1 trillion of nonconventional MBSs, up from only $100 billion in 2001. This shift in the market brought the integration process into its final phase. In essence, because the GSEs could not package MBSs from nonconventional loans until 2006, a lucrative opportunity opened up for financial firms. They seized this opportunity and made spectacular profits as they rode the market up.

Beginning in 2001, the overall mortgage origination market began to take off, increasing from $1 trillion a year in 2001 to almost $3.8 trillion in 2003. The main cause of this massive expansion in mortgage originations was the low interest rates put into place by the Federal Reserve in the wake of the stock market meltdown in 2000. These low interest rates had several effects, which worked to produce massive growth and profits for integrated banks. Low interest rates brought in customers to refinance and buy new houses. This produced a massive influx of mortgages that could be securitized. Thus, the fee-based businesses of originators expanded rapidly.

But the creation of these securities required that buyers exist to hold on to them. Given the rapid increase in their availability, one is led to ask, who wanted so many of these securities and why? The low-interest-rate environment also affected investors, as it meant that the safest securities, US Treasury bonds, paid very low returns. This caused investors to seek out safe investments that paid higher returns. This phenomenon was affecting not just American investors. Investors from around the world, most notably Japan and western Europe, were seeking out higher returns on safe investments as well. The investment they all discovered was American MBSs. The demand for AAA-rated MBSs in a low-interest-rate environment was nearly infinite. Banks who had integrated made massive amounts of money originating mortgages and made even more as they sold the securities that they created to investors, who had insatiable appetites for their products.

The same banks that originated and securitized mortgages were also likely to see that holding on to some of these securities would allow them to reap large and safe profits as well. For example, commercial banks had been investing in MBSs since the early 1990s. Financial institutions turned to the short-term credit markets, which have become known as shadow banking, to borrow money cheaply to buy MBSs. Here, they would borrow money using the MBSs as collateral for that money, often a portion of the same MBSs they were themselves producing. If they borrowed money at 2–3 percent and held MBSs that paid out 6–7 percent, they could make payments on their loans and essentially make money on the difference. This explains why in 2002–2007, the quantity of MBSs held by all financial investors except for the GSEs increased dramatically (Fligstein and Goldstein, 2010).

What remains to explain is why the nonconventional market took off in 2004. After a record year in 2003, the mortgage securitization industry experienced a supply crisis in 2004. In 2004, the drop-off in new mortgages was severe, with monthly origination volumes declining over 70 percent from $200 billion in August 2003 to under $60 billion a year later. Several factors were at play, including a slight uptick in interest rates from their historic lows. But the foremost cause was that the 2003 refinancing boom had run its course. Of the $3.8 trillion of new mortgages written in 2003, $2.53 trillion (about two-thirds) was attributable to refinancing as borrowers took advantage of low rates.

The precipitous drop in mortgage originations posed a major source of concern for industry actors given that the dominant business model was based on high throughput. Interest rates were still relatively low, and there still existed a large demand for MBSs from investors. Moreover, originators had grown their operations and needed new markets for their suddenly excess capacity. As an editorialist in the Mortgage Bankers Association trade newsletter wrote, "Mortgage originators who geared up their operations to capitalize on the boom now face a dilemma. Given a saturated conforming market that is highly sensitive to interest rates, where can retail originators turn for the new business, they need to support the organizations they have built?" (*Mortgage Banking*, 2004).

Concerns about the raw mortgage supply reverberated down the value chain. Barclays Capital researcher Jeff Salmon noted in May 2004 that "the recent dearth of supply has caught the [secondary] market off guard" (*Asset Securitization Report*, 2004b). If the financial industry was to keep the mortgage securitization machine churning, firms would somehow need to find a new source of mortgages. Industry actors quickly sought to stabilize their supplies by collectively settling and expanding the market for nonconforming loans.

Countrywide Financial was one of the most successful beneficiaries of this shift, and they became a model that other firms emulated in order to profit from nonprime lending. Their annual report boasted, "Countrywide's well-balanced business model continues to produce strong operational results amidst a transitional environment. Compared to a year ago, the total mortgage origination market is smaller as a result of lower refinance volume. This impact has been mitigated by Countrywide's dramatic growth in purchase funding and record volumes of adjustable rate, home equity, and nonconventional loans" (Countrywide Financial, 2005).

The rapidity with which the main players reoriented toward nonconventional lending and securitization after 2003 is dramatic. By 2005, the nonconventional mortgage market had been rapidly transformed into the core business for the largest financial institutions in the country. Nonconventional origination and securitization turned out to be enormously profitable. According to a study by the consulting firm Mercer Oliver Wyman, nonconventional lending accounted for approximately half of originations in 2005 but over 85 percent of profits (*Mortgage Servicing News*, 2005). Commercial banks, mortgage banks, and investment banks learned to profit from nonconventional MBSs in multiple ways simultaneously, earning money from both fees on MBS production and investment income on retained MBS assets. They could fund both the production and the investment with cheap capital, which meant enormous profit margins.

In sum, the shift toward nonconventional markets was caused by both a crisis and an opportunity. The crisis was the decline of the prime market for mortgages that began in 2004. The opportunity was the realization that originating, packaging, and holding on to nonconventional MBSs was likely to result in higher returns than prime mortgages. The absence of the GSEs in these markets allowed integrated firms to capture all the fees at every step. The riskier nature of the mortgages allowed the issuing and underwriting firms to charge a higher percentage fee for the more elaborate financial engineering that these non-agency-backed MBSs required. The resulting MBSs also paid out higher returns, as riskier loans had higher interest rates attached to them. After 2003, the large banks grew these formerly marginal niche segments into a multitrillion-dollar-a-year business.

The reader should by now understand why the banks were unable to shut down their securitization machines when house prices stopped rising and mortgage origination slowed. They had grown so fast and were so profitable that their entire business models and organizational structures were based on the throughput of massive numbers of mortgages. As conventional mortgages dried up, they rapidly expanded the nonconventional mortgage market. When that market was exhausted, they continued to look for customers and issued mortgages to any household, even those with poor credit and little chance to pay back the mortgages.

One of the ways they were able to do so was by massively expanding the supply of adjustable-rate mortgages so that poorly qualified customers could buy homes with artificially low payments for one to three years. They also took low-rated securities that they could not sell and repackaged them into new securities, which allowed them to create more AAA tranches. When what appeared to be changes in the competitive conditions got bumpy, they pushed harder to keep their market shares by making riskier and riskier loans and producing more and securities of dubious quality. They stayed the course in the hope they would weather the storm.

One reason that regulators have had such a hard time understanding what happened was that when the end came, it was not because there was an obvious failure of the entire business model of vertical integration. The part of the business model that failed was the banks borrowing to invest in MBSs. The proximate cause of the crisis was that banks found themselves holding on to large amounts of MBSs that they were not able to liquidate at prices that would allow them to pay that money back. What regulators have failed to consider is why the banks were holding on to such a significant amount of MBSs in the first place.

This occurred only because the banks had been committed to vertical integration. They might have been able to unload some of those securities as prices fell if all they were doing was selling off investments where they were losing money. But since they were committed to the production of mortgages and MBSs, they were unlikely to do anything to sell off the MBSs they held, because their business models were predicated on keeping the process going.

In essence, the degree to which this business model of banks had joined the fortunes of the housing market to the fortunes of the financial market was invisible to the regulators. That these two huge markets were now integrated through the activities of the biggest and most important banks in the country meant that the unwinding of the housing part of the model did not warn regulators of the dangers in the financial markets. Similarly, the troubles of some of the banks, such as Bear Stearns, were not easily traceable to their positions in the housing market. Bear Stearns appeared to be a simple case of traders who had borrowed too much money and could not cover their investments. The size of the connection and the high degree of leverage in the system meant that when the end came, it quickly spread across the largest integrated banks.

Plan of the Book

The rest of this book elaborates and explores the basic argument laid out in this chapter. There are a number of themes that will animate these chapters, some of which have been developed here but several of which will come to the fore in our analyses. First and foremost are the links between government policies and regulation and the structuring of the market. The story of the mortgage market can be told only in the context in which the regulators sought to provide the highest levels of homeownership possible. Almost all of the policy changes in the mortgage market were justified by increasing the ability of households to get mortgages, which has been a central goal of public policy since the 1930s. Second, while I have touched on the globalization of the crisis, I have not spent much time explaining how that happened. The market for mortgage securitization in the United States increasingly became part of financial globalization. Between 2001 and 2008, foreign investors bought $1 trillion of MBSs, mostly nonconventional mortgages. Many foreign banks came to participate in the production of mortgage securities, and a few became vertically integrated. The rapidity with which the crisis spread from the United States to select countries followed the path of those banks that were most involved in the US securitization market. In this case, financial globalization was ironically about banks around the world investing in the individual mortgages of American households.

Chapter 2 explores the emergence of the market for mortgage securitization. The chapter begins by considering how the savings and loan banks came to dominate the mortgage industry in the wake of the Great Depression. One of the key features of the structuring and functioning of the savings and loan business model was its dependency on the government. After World War II, the savings and loan banks' business model proved to be an amazing success, raising the rate of homeownership from about 43 percent on the eve of World War II to 63 percent in 1965. The bad economy of the 1970s and 1980s undermined the efficacy of the model. The government tried to intervene to help the savings and loan industry regain their footing. That story, where the deregulation of the banks resulted in their collective collapse, is one of those political economic stories that seem to disappear when scholars and regulators discuss market innovation. I also document how the GSEs came to create the market for mortgage securitization by working with both the government and the investment banks to create financial products that would be attractive to investors. Eventually, this new model replaced the savings and loan industry.

Chapter 3 takes up the vertical integration of the mortgage securitization market during the 1990s. I provide an overview of how and when different kinds of banks entered various markets and provide an account of the rise of the non-conventional mortgage market as well. The market for mortgage origination became more concentrated in all market segments over the decade. The percentage of mortgages originated that were securitized also increased, reflecting the integration of origination and securitization. I provide evidence that the banks were large investors in the mortgages they originated and securitized. On the eve of the twenty-first century, the business model of all the largest banks had converged around the origination and securitization of mortgages and buying them as investments. Countrywide Financial pioneered the vertical integration model and the market for nonconventional mortgages. I show how other banks followed Countrywide's lead. To illustrate how this worked in different kinds of banks, I provide four case studies of banks who pioneered vertical integration within different banking markets: Countrywide Financial (mortgage bank), Bear Stearns (investment bank), Washington Mutual (savings and loan bank), and Citibank (commercial bank).

Chapter 4 introduces the topic of financial innovation. Most people think of innovation primarily as new products. But scholars argue that innovation consists of not just products but also processes and new forms of innovation. The goal of this chapter is to document all three of these forms of innovation in the emergence of the mortgage securitization industry. The innovations to create mortgage securitization were breathtaking. They required whole new kinds of organizations (the GSEs and later the vertically integrated banks), whole new sets of regulations and regulators, and the linking of disparate markets that came to supply inputs in the process of producing mortgage securities. This integration required the creation of a huge number of new processes to originate mortgages and turn them into securities, including the computerization of applications, credit scores, and tranching. Finally, there was an explosion of new financial products, including new kinds of mortgages as well as new kinds of securities and other financial instruments. All of this was part and parcel of what financial economists saw as a massive wave of financial innovation in the 1980s. At the core of this wave was the process of securitization. While not all financial innovation was restricted to the mortgage securitization industry, mortgage securitization was at the center of this huge expansion.

Chapter 5 presents how the nonconventional mortgage market evolved from a small niche market dominated by what is often thought of as predatory lenders to a large market that eventually eclipsed the conventional mortgage market in 2004–2007. The story of the nonconventional mortgage market (including home equity loans and subprime, jumbo, and adjustable-rate mortgages) begins in the 1990s. By 2001, these were already large markets. When the refinance boom ended in 2003, banks turned aggressively to the nonconventional mortgage market. Eventually, that market began to dry up, and banks found themselves having to chase mortgagors with worse and worse credit in order to keep their securitization machines going. I show that they aggressively pursued the model of integration until the bitter end.

Chapter 6 considers how the crisis came about in the United States and how it spread around the world. I describe the general breakdown of the banks in 2007–2009. I return to my innovators of the vertical integration model in the 1990s and provide an account of the collapse of Bear Stearns, Countrywide Financial, Washington Mutual, and Citibank. One of the most striking aspects of the crisis was that within weeks, many of the world's largest banks were insolvent and in need of bailouts from their governments. This chapter presents evidence that the main cause of the direction and timing of this collapse was the participation of banks in many countries in the MBS-CDO market. Many foreign banks, such as HSBC, RBS, and Deutsche Bank, had become originators and securitizers just like their American counterparts. Others, such as Credit Suisse and Rabobank, bought massive amounts of securities. I show that between 2002 and 2007, foreign banks increased their ownership of mortgage securities by over $1 trillion, mostly securities based on nonconventional mortgages.

Chapter 7 takes up this question and provides an account of why there was so much mortgage and securities fraud. We know that mortgage and securities fraud increased dramatically, particularly after 2005. But there are few explanations of why this is the case. While the nonconventional mortgage market kept the vertically integrated banks going from 2003 to 2005, after 2005, it became difficult to find even mortgages for people with impaired credit. As competition for mortgages increased, more and more mortgages were originated through mortgage fraud. Mortgagors were encouraged to lie on their loan applications, with the complicity of banks. These mortgages were then packaged into securities, thereby causing banks to commit securities fraud. Chapter 7 shows that the banks most likely to commit mortgage and securities fraud were those who were vertically integrated.

Chapter 8 considers why the Federal Reserve missed the oncoming crisis. By analyzing the transcripts of the meeting of the Federal Reserve Open Market Committee, I show that this happened for two reasons. First, there was a kind of positive bias inherent in every meeting. That means that there was a tendency to downplay or dismiss bad news. Second, and more importantly, the use of macroeconomic analysis made it difficult for the Federal Reserve to see the connections among the origination market, the house price bubble, and the growth of the securitization market. This inability to understand the systemic nature of mortgage securitization led the Federal Reserve to underestimate the risk to the wider economy of the overall downturn in housing prices that began in 2005. Chapter 8 documents how, as late as the collapse of Lehman Brothers in September 2008, the Federal Reserve was as worried about inflation threats to the economy as it was to a possible banking crisis.

Chapter 9 explores three themes. First, it describes how the financial institutions have been reorganized since the financial crisis. The large banks have become financial conglomerates, fulfilling the dreams of banking economists in the 1990s. The ten largest banks owned $12.2 trillion in assets in 2018, fully two-thirds of the assets of all US banks. These banks now participate in nearly every financial service market. Most of these banks were reorganized during the financial crisis, including buying or merging with scores of failed banks. Second, I consider what regulators can do to avoid the next crisis. The Federal Reserve responded aggressively and successfully to the systemic crisis that unfolded before them in 2007–2009. But they clearly missed the depth of the crisis and the interconnectedness of markets. I propose some ideas as what might be done. Finally, I consider how the financial crisis has opened up the politics of thinking about the relationship between government and business. The past forty years has been dominated by neoliberalism, the idea that government should not actively intervene in markets. But my analysis shows the limits of that kind of thinking. It suggests it is time to reconsider how we think about government and markets.

Conclusion

One of the great business stories of the 1980s and 1990s was financial innovation. At the core of this period of innovation was the idea of securitization. The innovation was seeing that any asset that generated a cash flow could be turned into a security that could be sold to an investor. This meant that the holders of the asset could immediately translate that asset into cash, while investors would take on the risk of the investment. This innovation led to another insight. Risk should be bought and sold to investors who were sophisticated enough to understand what chances they were taking. Those who wanted more risk got higher returns, and those who needed certainty accepted less. The 1990s then witnessed an explosion of financial instruments of all kinds. All of these instruments worked to allow investors to pick and choose their portfolio of investments in a way that was not possible earlier.

There were two important effects of all of this, from the perspectives of the economics profession and the regulators of these instruments. First, risks would end up with people who understood them and priced them in a way that reflected their concerns. Second, the growth of such innovations would lead to more credit being available to more households, businesses, and governments. Financial innovation would allow sophisticated investors to price risk, manage their portfolios responsibly, and invest in new kinds of risk. The explosion of these products was taken as evidence that they were fulfilling both functions and doing so in a way that worked to the benefit of everyone.

While there is certainly some truth to this analysis, it makes the mistake of generically equating financial innovation with the control of risk at the level of entire markets or the economy. My story about the mortgage securitization industry offers a cautionary tale about financial innovation. While the creation of new financial instruments proved useful to expanding homeownership and allowing homeowners access to some of their home equity, it also helped create a business model that connected risks in the provision of mortgages to risk in the financial system as a whole. The fact that banks combined these two markets meant that the risks to the financial system were multiplied given the huge size of the mortgage industry. It is to making sense of how and why this happened that I now turn.

2

FROM MORTGAGES TO
MORTGAGE SECURITIZATION

Homeownership has defined what it means to be a middle-class American since the 1920s (Megbolugbe and Linneman, 1993). As a result, politicians in both the Democratic and Republican Parties have favored policies that promote homeownership. In practice, this has meant that the evolution of the housing market has been deeply entwined with the history of the welfare state in the United States since the Great Depression (Prasad, 2012). Everything to do with government policy has consistently worked to try to favor homeownership. The government standardized mortgages by creating the rules that define a conventional mortgage as combining a low down payment (20 percent or less) for a long fixed term (fifteen to thirty years) with a fixed interest rate. It has helped underwrite the financing in the housing market directly in the case of the Federal Housing Authority and the Veterans Administration Home Loans and indirectly through the government-sponsored enterprises (GSEs). The interest deduction for home mortgages has provided a substantial tax break for middle-class Americans and promoted homeownership. The explicit policy purpose of creating the GSEs was to draw more private capital into the private housing market to increase the rate of homeownership.

But this has not always been a smooth ride. Indeed, the history of government intervention into the housing market is a story of a burgeoning crisis and collapse of the banks and other financial institutions that were dominating the market for mortgages followed by a government attempt to resurrect the market. Republican and Democratic presidents and Congresses dominated by both parties have always ridden to the aid of the housing industry in its moment of crisis. This has happened four times since 1930: during the Great Depression of the 1930s, in the first crisis of the savings and loan banks in the 1970s, during the collapse of the saving and loan banks in the 1980s, and during the takeover of Fannie Mae and

Freddie Mac in the wake of the financial crisis in 2008–2009. Each of these re-forms has been proposed by some set of banks in the existing banking communi-ty. Those who successfully lobbied for their alternative got rules changed to favor their business model. In return, the government has made sure that when the banks began to fail, a new set of rules would be in place such that most Americans who had enough income have been able to buy a home by getting a mortgage.

In this chapter I take up how this process worked from the Depression until the rise of mortgage securitization. There are three parts to my story. First, the chapter begins by considering how the savings and loan banks came to dominate the mortgage industry in the wake of the collapse of the banking system during the Great Depression. At the behest of a trade association representing the savings and loan banks, the government oversaw the reorganization of the mortgage market by creating the Federal Home Loan Board, which acted as the regulator for the sav-ings and loan system. It created depository insurance for account holders, making it safe for them to deposit their funds. It put ceilings on interest-bearing accounts to stifle competition between banks for those funds. The government defined the modern conventional mortgage, thereby providing guidance for mortgage terms. These changes restored the savings and loan banks and made them the principal mechanism by which Americans got mortgages. After World War II, the savings and loan banks' business model with the help of the government agencies promot-ing housing proved to be an amazing success, raising the rate of homeownership from about 43 percent on the eve of World War II to 63 percent in 1965.

The second part of my story takes up the fall of the savings and loan industry. Essentially, the bad economic times of the 1970s with high inflation and low eco-nomic growth undermined the business model of the savings and loans. High interest rates due to high inflation made the savings and loans unable to continue to borrow money at low interest rates. It also meant that households had a harder time buying homes that were inflating in value and could not afford either the higher down payments or the bigger monthly payments. At the behest of the in-dustry, the Carter and Reagan administrations intervened by changing the rules by which the banks could borrow and invest. For a few years, it appeared as if the savings and loans might be stabilized. But by the mid-1980s, it was clear that this had been built on risky lending, and the new business model began to fail. When the end came, there was a massive bankruptcy of the industry.

The third part of the chapter tracks the rise of the mortgage securitization industry. I document how the GSEs came to create the market for mortgage securitization by working with both the government and the investment banks to create financial products that would be attractive to investors. It took fifteen years to produce the modern MBS. It required the use of financial innovation around tranching the bonds. But equally important were changes in the tax laws that allowed mortgages to become securities and allowed investors to hold them without negative tax implications. Investment banks, led by Salomon Brothers' executive Lewis Ranieri, in cooperation with officials who ran Freddie Mac, were able to get Congress to pass legislation making the securities more attractive to investors. These changes occurred mostly during the presidency of Ronald Reagan with the enthusiastic help of Congress. When the savings and loan industry collapsed, the GSEs stood ready to organize the market for mortgages.

By the early 1990s, the crisis of the savings and loan industry had given way to a new way for Americans to get their mortgages. The mortgage market was now firmly joined to the financial markets because of mortgage securitization (Hendershott and VanOrder, 1989). This meant that mortgage lenders of all kinds had access to capital markets to fund their activities. It also meant that a new product, the mortgage security, became a major source of profits for those who made, sold, and bought the new bonds. It was the joining of mortgages to the financial markets that propelled financial innovation through the 1990s and the growth and profits of that sector. The GSEs occupied the center of the mortgage market because of the assumption that the federal government would bail out any problems in the market for GSE-issued bonds. Their products became known as agency-backed bonds, and their safety and returns mimicked those of government securities, reflecting their privileged status in the market.

It is fascinating that a Republican president, George H. W. Bush, oversaw one of the largest expansions of direct government action to organize a private market. Moreover, this takeover was little noticed by the public, the media, or Congress. Had the GSEs not taken the main role in organizing the market for mortgages, the public would have been unable to easily secure mortgages to buy homes. But the massive shift in the way mortgages were funded was little noticed as long as people could continue to get mortgages. Ironically, this more direct intervention was never perceived by the public as government intervention or ownership because it was so well hidden. Part of the subterfuge was to allow the GSEs to become publicly listed corporations while still maintaining the assumption that if there was a problem, the government would be there to bail the holders of MBSs out. When the crisis hit in 2008, the government did its part, and the GSEs came under direct government ownership and control.

The Rise of the Savings and Loan Model of Mortgages

Figure 2.1 presents a graph showing the pattern of homeownership in the United States from 1900 until the eve of the Great Recession in 2008. One can see that

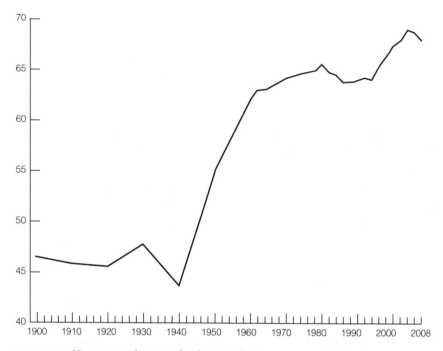

FIGURE 2.1 Homeownership rates for the United States, 1900–2008. Data source: US Census Bureau.

early in the century, ownership rates fell from 1900 to 1920, rose in the 1920s, and then fell in the Depression of the 1930s. The most remarkable change in home-ownership occurred between 1940 and 1965, when ownership rates increased from about 43 percent to 63 percent. Rates remained in that range until the mid-1990s, when they rose from around 63 percent to almost 69 percent at their peak. In the wake of the housing crash, rates have fallen back to their post-1965 historical normal level of about 64 percent. Obviously, the most important aspect of this figure is the dramatic rise in homeownership after World War II and ending in the 1960s.

Ownership rates were already almost 45 percent at the turn of the twentieth century (of course from a much smaller population base and including many people who owned farms). While many homes were self-financed, households frequently needed financial help to build homes. During the nineteenth century, there were few banks, and most of them would not lend to consumers for building homes. This meant that people who wanted to build houses had to seek out other methods of finance. The first organizations to offer housing finance in the United States were called terminating building societies. They were founded in 1831 and modeled after British building societies (Lea, 1996).

Middle-income households would pool their funds in the terminating building society and agree to loan each member the money to build a house. The members would contribute to the fund until sufficient funds were built up to lend. The order in which the money to build was lent was based on members offering to pay a higher interest rate in order to build earlier. When the last home was built and paid for, the society would be dissolved. The ability to create such societies required places where people knew each other well, had long time horizons, and trusted that they would get their turn.

These building societies were the basis for what would later become the modern savings and loan banks (Haveman and Rao, 1997, 2007). By the mid-1850s, building societies began to accept new members and thus not dissolve when the original members had built their homes. Members were also allowed to remove their funds when they had finished building if they chose to do so. The next important step was for the building societies to begin to accept deposits from individuals who did not want to build a home. These deposits were usually placed in accounts where they could not be removed for some period. These accounts were a forerunner of modern time deposit accounts. This meant that the funds available to build and be repaid would not be removed suddenly. It also had the effect of separating the depositors from being involved in the lending process. As a result, building societies turned to professional management to monitor savings and the loan processes. By the turn of the twentieth century, a version of the modern savings and loan bank was in place (Haveman and Rao, 1997).

Other types of mortgage providers also emerged in the nineteenth century. Mutual savings banks were originally founded to provide outlets for lower-income people to have savings accounts. To protect their accounts, depositors were also the owners of the bank. These banks began to enter the mortgage market in the 1850s and surpassed the building societies as the largest provider of mortgages until the 1920s. Their business model was to take deposits from savers and lend to borrowers who wanted to build homes. Life insurance and mortgage companies also began to offer mortgages on a national basis. Their business model was to use local agents to make and service loans rather than build a national organization. These local agents would find the borrowers and take monthly mortgage payments.

The mortgage companies also pioneered private mortgage bonds. These were based on a model introduced in Germany whereby investors with capital would invest long term in a set of diversified mortgages (Snowden, 1995). The main investors in these bonds were insurance companies in the northeast and investors in Europe. These bonds resembled modern mortgage-backed securities. In the 1890s, there was a financial crisis in the United States, and these bonds failed en masse. Snowden (1995) attributes this collapse to investors having had little information about the underlying mortgages in the bonds. He also suggests that their lack of regulation meant they were riskier than similar bonds in Europe. This event eerily resembles the MBS meltdown of 2008–2009. Many of the national mortgage companies that pioneered these loans disappeared by the early 1900s. The national mutual savings banks met a similar fate. They depended on agents from around the country to monitor the ability of the mortgagor to pay back the loan. In a series of scandals, it was revealed that homes around the country had been appraised at too high a value.

Commercial banks generally stayed out of the market for mortgages in the nineteenth century. They viewed their main concern as providing loans to small businesses. They also tended to view mortgage lending as risky because capital was committed for long periods of time. But beginning in the twentieth century, they began to enter the market. By 1914, 25 percent of their loans and 15 percent of their assets were in real estate (Snowden, 2010).

The mortgage market, until the Great Depression, was not well developed. Mortgages were unevenly available in every part of the country, as capital did not easily flow to the places that needed the funding for housing the most. Different types of firms dominated in different markets (Lea, 1992). Mortgage terms were not standardized. Many loans required mortgagors to put 50 percent down on a home. They also had variable terms, some running as short as two to three years and the longest-term mortgage running ten to twelve years. Building and loan societies tended to have the best offers. Their mortgages would run ten to twelve years and would allow borrowers to take loans out up to two-thirds of the house value. Mutual savings banks tended to have mortgages that ran for five years with a balloon payment due at the end (Morton, 1956). The mortgagor had to either pay the remainder of the mortgage or refinance the mortgage. Commercial banks tended to have the shortest-term mortgages, reflecting their desire to not tie money up for long periods.

Figure 2.2 documents who held nonfarm residential debt from 1895 to 2005. As a result of the difficulty of finding a mortgage and the need to put down a large down payment, 41 percent of households owned their homes in 1920 but only 40 percent of these were mortgaged (Snowden, 2010: 7). Before 1920, between 40 and 50 percent of these mortgages were provided by individuals or other noninstitutional investors. The 1920s was a period when homeownership increased. The share of the market taken up by savings and loan, mutual savings banks, and commercial banks rose to meet this demand and increased their share of mortgages from 50 to 65 percent. Private mortgage securities reemerged to help finance homes and took almost 10 percent of the market. On the eve of

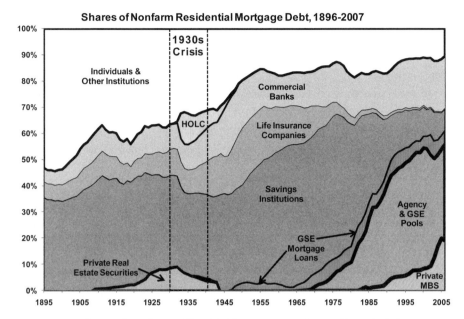

FIGURE 2.2 Shares of nonfarm residential debt, 1895–2005. Source: Kenneth A. Snowden, "The Anatomy of a Residential Mortgage Crisis: A Look Back to the 1930s," NBER Working Paper 16244, figure 2. Used by permission of the author.

the Great Depression, the share of mortgages held by institutions increased to a little over 65 percent (Snowden, 2010: 7).

There was a proliferation of business models for the various parts of the industry during the 1920s in what would now be called financial innovation. Each of the participants in the booming real estate market had a different way to fund mortgages and mortgage products with very different characteristics. For example, during the 1920s, a bond market that funded a pool of mortgages reemerged. This time, the market that evolved created bonds that would own businesses that would develop particular tracts of land. Private mortgage insurance, which had sprung up earlier, now grew rapidly to support the growing private market for mortgages. Mortgage issuers of all varieties used the insurance to protect their mortgages.

Unfortunately, when the Great Depression hit, the mortgage industry was particularly vulnerable to the economic downturn. The 1930s witnessed the collapse of the entire banking system (Bernanke, 1983). As businesses went bankrupt, people were laid off, and unemployment rose to almost 25 percent. The drop in economic activity meant that banks had loans that stopped performing, many of which were based on assets that were rapidly losing value. The housing market was particularly hard hit. As people lost their jobs, they could not pay their mortgages, and many just abandoned their homes. This left banks with outstanding loans based on homes whose value had dropped dramatically. Not surprisingly, banks failed at a high rate. Commercial banks were hit by losses in both their loans to business and their loans for homes. Savings and loan banks found themselves with defaulted loans. Grebler et al. (1956: 477) estimates that they lost $5 billion between 1930 and 1933. As a result, it is thought that nearly a thousand homes a day were foreclosed on from 1930 to 1937. Half of the twelve thousand building and loan associations disappeared between 1929 and 1941 (Kendall, 1962: 76–77).

The buildings and loan model, the private mortgage insurance industry, and the private bonds markets all collapsed. Many of the buildings and loans associations were privately held and owned by their customers. This meant that they were not subject to the same laws as the commercial banks. Moreover, many of these associations had put their capital in accounts in commercial banks (Green and Wachter, 2005). When those banks went bankrupt, those funds were nearly impossible to recover. In spite of their apparent insolvency, it was not easy for such organizations to go bankrupt. Given that they also held mortgages that were ten to twelve years in length, the wind-down of these organizations took years. These problems also discredited the building and loan model of creating mortgage pools to fund housing. People who had entered these pools were likely to have lost all of the money they put into the organization and, for those whose houses were foreclosed, their houses as well. This meant the end of this model for providing mortgages.

Private mortgage insurers had sprung up in some states. These firms offered insurance policies against defaults on mortgages. They were regulated by state insurance boards. Herzog (2009) provides evidence that there were fifty of these companies in New York alone. He also shows that between 1930 and 1934, the entire industry went bankrupt. Part of the problem was that investigation of these failures showed that private insurers did not do their due diligence as the housing market heated up through the late 1920s. They sold policies to anyone, as they were more interested in collecting premiums than they were in making sure the borrower was able to pay the mortgage. The scandal created a huge distrust in this kind of insurance, and the New York State Legislature held hearings on the matter and recommended that the industry be made illegal (Snowden, 2010: 18). As a result, private mortgage insurers did not return to the market until 1957 (Herzog, 2009: 3).

As mentioned above, the mortgage bond reemerged during the 1920s. Most of these bonds were created to build particular projects. Bonds would fund the projects, and once they were built and sold, the bondholders would be returned their money. The amount of these bonds grew dramatically during the 1920s (see Figure 2.2). Snowden documents how these projects massively failed during the Depression (2010: 14). It is estimated that 80 percent of the bonds in Chicago, Cleveland, and Detroit failed. Half of all the bonds issued during the 1920s defaulted (Snowden, 2010). These bonds were also the subject of hearings. The US Congress passed legislation allowing closer regulation of the industry by the Securities and Exchange Commission (Halliburton, 1939: 46–93). The single-project bond industry was never able to overcome this downturn, and it disappeared as a form of real estate financing (Koester, 1939).

In response to the Depression, the entire banking system became the subject of regulation. In a series of pieces of legislation, each of the parts of the now-almost-bankrupt system came under some new form of regulation. At the state level, governments worked to maintain protection for banks that were located within their borders (Kroszner and Strahan, 2005). At the national level, this regulation pushed banks to define themselves as commercial or investment banks. It also set rules for loans and solvency and provided deposit insurance (Sellon, 1990).

After the Great Depression, banks were restricted in the rate of interest they could charge on all types of deposit accounts. Under Regulation Q of the Banking Act of 1933, savings accounts were capped at 5.25 percent, and time deposits were limited to between 5.75 and 7.75 percent, depending on maturity. Paying interest on checking accounts was outlawed. These regulations were intended to prevent interest rate wars whereby banks would offer higher and higher rates to obtain deposits. In order to encourage mortgage lending within local communities, however, thrift institutions were allowed to offer deposit accounts interest rates 0.25 percent higher than other banks (Sherman, 2009; Sellon, 1990; Gilber, 1986). It should be noted that from 1934 until 1965, Regulation Q interest rate ceilings were above the average interest rates in general and thereby had little effect on what was actually being paid (Gilber, 1986: 17).

The federal government implemented several other emergency measures to respond to the mortgage crisis. Congress passed the Federal Home Loan Bank Act in 1932 (Ewalt, 1962: 87). Ewalt (1962) presents evidence that the United States Building and Loan League (USBLL), a trade association for the savings and loan banks, played a significant role in this creation by lobbying for the legislation for over a decade. The structure they lobbied for worked to the benefit of those banks and against the more traditionally organized buildings and loans. The act created the Federal Home Loan Bank Board (FHLBB), which was organized on a regional basis with twelve banks. These facilities began to help member institutions in early 1933 to help refinance the loans of distressed homeowners

(Ewalt, 1962: 66). Of the eleven thousand building and loan associations, only thirty-nine hundred joined. These associations became the core of the modern savings and loan industry and ended up holding 92 percent of all savings and loan assets by 1950 (Ewalt, 1962: 97).

The Home Owners' Loan Act of June 1933 represented a second federal emergency response to the mortgage crisis. The act authorized the Home Owners' Loan Corporation (HOLC) to offer new loans to homeowners who were delinquent on existing mortgages (Harriss, 1951). The HOLC opened four hundred offices throughout the country and employed twenty thousand people to process loans and appraise properties. It ended up writing new loans on 10 percent of the owner-occupied homes in the United States. These loans reappraised the value of the homes to reflect the depressed prices around the country. Lenders could hold on to the refinanced mortgages, or they could sell them to the HOLC. Either way, the HOLC allowed many households to stay in their homes with more affordable mortgages (Harriss, 1951).

The FHLBB was given authority in the Home Owners' Loan Act of June 1933 to establish a system of federally chartered savings and loan associations. Two elements of the model ensured that members of the federal savings and loan industry would be structured and behave differently than traditional building and loans. First, federal savings and loans offered new kinds of contracts: share savings accounts instead of membership dues and direct reduction loans to replace the fragile share accumulation loan plan. Second, federal charters erected new barriers to entry so that small, part-time associations would never again represent a competitive fringe. About six hundred federally chartered savings and loan banks emerged and joined the FHLBB (Ewalt, 1962).

The final element of the industry's transformation was the creation of the Federal Savings and Loan Insurance Corporation (FSLIC) enacted in the 1934 National Housing Act. The government had earlier passed legislation creating the Federal Deposit Insurance Corporation (FDIC). That organization helped provide insurance for the savings and checking accounts of people who put money in commercial banks. The savings and loan industry realized that if they wanted to get deposits from local citizens, they would need to offer similar protection. The FSLIC made it safe for depositors to put their money into savings and loan banks.

The National Housing Act of 1934 created the Federal Housing Administration (FHA), which took a different approach to federal residential mortgage policy (Ewalt, 1962: 138–144). The FHA had two main activities. First, it created the FHA mortgage insurance program, which was designed to encourage commercial banks and insurance companies (competitors of savings and loans) to increase their presence in the mortgage market by providing mortgage insurance for lenders. Second, the FHA created a loan program that created the modern conventional mortgage. They specified down payments and loan limits as well as fixed terms and interest rates for mortgages. The idea behind giving the FHA these powers was to make sure that credit would flow to parts of the country where savings and loan banks were not able to raise enough capital to keep up with demand for mortgages. These features soon attracted commercial banks, life insurance companies, and mortgage companies to the program.

In practice, the FHA played two important roles in the postcrisis residential market (Jones and Grebler, 1961: 40–44; Klaman, 1959). First, federally insured mortgages became the dominant instrument that was used to aid the interregional transfer of mortgage credit. Second, these loan programs were used to finance the activities of large merchant builders because they provided advanced commitments for permanent financing during construction. This meant that FHA financing was used extensively to finance the expansion of the multifamily housing stock.

By 1940, the shape of the modern savings and loan industry was in place (Prasad, 2012). Government regulators had created a world where local households would put their money into savings and loan banks that guaranteed the safety of their deposits. These banks would use those funds to loan local households' money to buy homes with fixed-rate mortgages that required a 20 percent down payment and a fifteen- to thirty-year term. The banks would hold on to the mortgages until they were paid off. Banks had Regulation Q, which provided a ceiling for the rate at which they had to pay for funds. This meant that there was little competition between banks for the deposits of savers. In sum, households with relatively small down payments could buy houses with reasonable payments and know how much they would be paying over the course of the mortgage. This became the major source of house financing in the United States until the 1980s. Their share of mortgages was around 60 percent at the peak of the industry.

But the government also created its own direct model of intervening into the housing markets. By providing deposit insurance for commercial banks and creating the FHA, the government made sure that incentives were in place for these banks to lend to homeowners as well. The FHA defined the conventional mortgage in the late 1930s, and it quickly became the standard for both the savings and loan and commercial banks. The FHA helped low-income households buy homes directly by loaning money. FHA loans could be marketed through commercial and mortgage banks. The FHA also provided mortgage insurance to commercial and mortgage banks to facilitate buying.

The last piece of the New Deal legislation to consider was the creation of the Federal Home Mortgage Association, eventually known as Fannie Mae, in 1938. The organization's explicit purpose was to provide local banks with federal money to finance home mortgages in an attempt to raise levels of homeownership and the availability of affordable housing. Fannie Mae was supposed to create a liquid secondary mortgage market and thereby made it possible for banks and other loan originators to issue more housing loans, primarily by buying FHA-insured mortgages. Until the 1970s, Fannie remained quite small. There was not much market to buy mortgages, and Fannie was the main buyer in that market.

With the end of World War II in sight, Congress passed the Servicemen's Readjustment Act of 1944, informally known as the GI Bill. Included in the GI Bill was the invention of the Veterans Administration mortgage insurance program. This program allowed veterans returning home to obtain mortgages with very low down payments. The program was intended both to reward veterans and to stimulate housing market construction. The FHA also sought to stimulate housing construction by substantially liberalizing its terms. In 1948, the maximum term of a mortgage rose to thirty years (from an initial maximum of twenty years). In 1956, the FHA raised the maximum loan-to-value ratio to 95 percent (from an initial maximum of 80 percent) for new construction and to 90 percent for existing homes.

One interesting question is the degree to which the creation of this stable structure can account for the huge growth in homeownership in the postwar era. It is obviously difficult to untangle the large set of factors that explain the rise of homeownership. For example, once the basic institutional infrastructure to fund homeownership was in place by 1940, it did not change much. Thus, one can compare homeownership rates before and after the 1930s and conclude that the government interventions made a great deal of difference. But it is useful to try to separate the contributions of each of these innovations to explain the nearly 60 percent increase in homeownership over two decades.

The academic literature shows there is a good empirical case to be made that each of these reforms had a significant effect on homeownership rates. Chambers et al. (2013) show that about 21 percent of the increase was due to changes in mortgage terms. Fetter (2011) makes a plausible case that around 20 percent of the increase was due to shifts in policy by the FHA and the VA after the Second World War to encourage homeownership. Grebler et al. (1956: 243) present data showing that the share of mortgages in the United States provided by the FHA and the VA rose from 0 percent in 1935 to 44.1 percent in 1952. Rosen and Rosen (1980) show that about 20 percent of the increase was due to the tax deductibility of interest paid on mortgages. Taken together, this implies that the aspects of government policy that can most easily be measured account for up to 60 percent of the increase in homeownership from 1940 to 1965. The models used in this work correct for increases in education, income, economic growth in the postwar era, all of which had an impact on people's ability to borrow money.

I note that there are several features of what happened that are not easy to measure. The government created the legal and regulatory conditions for a stable mortgage market to emerge. The expectations of everyone in the system were built on the knowledge that at the end of the day, the government was committed to mortgages being available. Because of depository insurance, savers knew their deposits were now safe in banks. This stability had a cognitive aspect as well. Mortgage providers had a standardized product they could easily price because of Regulation Q. The savings and loan industry had a well-known business model by which they could borrow from individual households at a relatively fixed rate and make a profit loaning money. Figure 2.2 shows that between 1945 and 1975 the savings and loans increased their share of mortgage debt from about 35 percent to 50 percent. The FHA and the VA played their part by stimulating property developers and providing money to individuals to buy houses. The tax incentives for mortgage interest deduction meant that renting was not much cheaper than owning. As the economy grew in the postwar era and people had more disposable income, the structure was in place for them to buy houses with affordable mortgages (Prasad, 2012).

The Fall of the Savings and Loan Industry

The savings and loan model depended on reliable payment of a relatively low and fixed rate of interest for deposits to allow a somewhat higher but fixed rate of interest for mortgagors. The underlying economic conditions beginning in the 1960s and worsening in the 1970s saw increasing levels of inflation accompanied by increases in interest rates. This high rate of inflation was accompanied by slow economic growth in an era characterized by the term *stagflation*. This created a set of interrelated problems for the business model of the savings and loan banks. Inflation meant that house prices were going up, but potential borrowers' incomes were not rising to keep pace. Moreover, rising interest rates also made it more difficult for borrowers to afford mortgages. Together, it meant that demand for mortgages was dropping. Inflation also encouraged savers to look to earn more interest on their deposits. So, even if there were people who wanted to borrow, savings and loan banks found it impossible to provide a low and fixed interest rate to borrowers to secure enough money to lend. This made the business model of the savings and loan banks untenable.

The first sign of trouble came in 1965 when for the first time since the Great Depression, the deposit ceiling set by Regulation Q proved to be too low. Most analysts have attributed this to a tightening of the credit markets in the United States caused by high levels of economic growth during the 1960s and high levels of government borrowing to fund government deficits (Gilber, 1986: 27–29; Lea, 1996; Barth, 2004). In 1966, Congress decided to make the interest rate ceilings proposed by Regulation Q binding. The rates were set to make commercial bank ceilings lower than savings and loan ceilings and thus to keep attracting deposits to the savings and loan banks. The rationale was that by setting rates, competition between the banks for funds would lessen. But throughout the late 1960s and into the 1980s, instead of increasing their deposits, savers began to find more high-yielding financial instruments and slowly took their deposits out of savings and loan banks. The emergence of mutual funds, time deposits, and money market funds in the 1970s drew off even more potential deposits.

The worst was yet to come. Throughout the 1970s, inflation was high and economic growth was low. Interest rates were high, and as a result, the savings and loan banks were being pincered by the high cost of obtaining funds in the face of a declining and troubled housing market for new mortgages. When the Federal Reserve began to raise interest rates dramatically in the late 1970s, the business model of the savings and loans cratered. Not only was it difficult to raise funds because of Regulation Q, but mortgage rates rose dramatically and the market for new homes declined dramatically. The net worth of the entire industry approached zero, falling from 5.3 percent of assets in 1980 to 0.5 percent in 1982 (Sherman, 2009). Not surprisingly, the savings and loan banks began to fail as a result of this pressure. By 1982, the number of saving and loans that were insolvent rose dramatically (Brumbaugh et al., 1987). The FSLIC was ill equipped to deal with the prospect of widespread insolvency. According to some estimates, bailing out all the insolvent institutions in 1983 would have cost the FSLIC around $25 billion, but the fund held only $6.3 billion in reserves at the time.

This suggested that the industry was basically bankrupt. From the historical record, it is clear that neither the regulators nor Congress wanted to face the fact that the FSLIC could not bail out depositors. The savings and loan industry lobbied hard to give it another chance by changing the nature of regulation and allowing it to change its business model (Romer and Weingast, 1991). Two pieces of legislation were passed. President Carter signed into law the Depository Institutions Deregulation and Monetary Control Act (DIDMCA) of 1980. The legislation established a committee to oversee the complete phaseout of interest rate ceilings within six years, thereby repealing Regulation Q. Depository institutions would be allowed to offer accounts with competitive rates of return in the market. The act also increased federal deposit insurance from $40,000 to $100,000 per account. This meant that large depositors could safely put money into savings and loan banks at high interest rates knowing that their deposits were insured if the bank failed.

The Garn-St. Germain Depository Institutions Act was passed by Congress in late 1982. This legislation had as its primary goal the partial deregulation of the savings and loan sector. It expanded the scope of activities permitted to thrift institutions, and it broadened the type of assets that they could hold. It also relaxed regulatory accounting standards to allow thrifts to write down their low-interest mortgages and sell them without having to pay taxes.

The theory behind these two pieces of legislation was that they would buy the industry time to right themselves without having to resort to a costly bailout of depositors by the government. It would give the savings and loan banks time to shift their business models in order to meet the competition for deposits and allow them to make more risky investments to increase their profits. This theory has been described by policymakers and policy analysts after the debacle of the collapse of the industry as "massive gambling for resurrection" (see Calavita et al., 1997; Romer and Weingast, 1991). Of course, the banks were not gambling with their own money: their deposits were protected by insurance, and at the end of the day they knew the government would make sure depositors were bailed out.

Throughout the 1980s, Congress resisted efforts by regulators to intervene even after it became obvious that the newly deregulated savings and loan banks were not succeeding. This made the eventual bailout, when it came, even more expensive. The FHLBB, representing the interests of the savings and loan banks, was on Congress's side and helped resist the reorganization of failed banks. They used the term *forbearance* as a way to describe how savings and loans should be given a chance to restore their profitability (Romer and Weingast, 1991; Calavita et al., 1997; Sherman, 2009).

By the mid-1980s, it looked as if the prospects for the savings and loans were looking up as bank failures decreased from 252 in 1982 to 41 in 1984 (Brumbaugh et al., 1987). Between 1982 and 1985, deposits flowed in, and the savings and loan industry underwent a rapid expansion as Regulation Q was phased out and savings and loan banks offered high interest rates for new deposits. Investors saw potential for profit in the new investment powers granted to thrifts and invested in condominiums and other commercial real estate. This meant that the investment portfolios of savings and loan associations shifted away from traditional home mortgage loans into higher-risk loans. From 1981 to 1986, the percentage of savings and loan assets in home mortgage loans decreased from 78 percent to 56 percent. There was a great increase in investment in commercial real estate development and other risky investments such as junk bonds.

But much of this improvement was illusory. The ability of the savings and loan banks to hide their real financial conditions from regulators and to have the support of the FHLBB and Congress protected them from oversight (Brumbaugh et al., 1987). In a deregulated industry with poor supervision, the competition for deposits spiraled out of control. Many institutions attracted capital by offering large brokered deposits at above-market rates. This meant that in order to justify these rates they had to make risky investments. Most of these investments failed to pay off. Also, in a deregulated industry where banks were playing with other people's money, fraud became rampant. By 1987, it became apparent that the industry was in a disastrous financial situation (Tillman and Pontell, 1995).

There are two stories out there, both of which have some truth to them. The first story is that the terms of the deregulation created the crisis. Banks were given the ability to pay any interest rate that they wanted on deposits insured by the federal government up to $100,000. This meant that in order to attract capital, they had to raise interest rates. To justify such high interest rates, they needed to make risky investments. This narrative emphasizes that the government failed to regulate the industry sufficiently to make sure that bank executives would not behave in a recklessly aggressive fashion. Some have viewed these executives as needlessly reckless, others as incompetent investors. The scholars who have this viewpoint argue that depository insurance and lax regulation caused the crisis (Barth and Bartholomew, 1992). The idea is that the government acted here as enablers to an industry filled with ex-alcoholics who could not resist a free drink.

One obvious problem with this story is that the lobbyists for the savings and loan industry put an enormous pressure on Congress to go along with the reforms that led to the ultimate demise of the industry. They kept that pressure on in the mid-1980s as things went from bad to worse. Given the members of Congress all had savings and loan banks in their districts, it is hard to imagine that they would have willingly pulled the plug. By blaming the government alone, critics forget that the industry lobbied long and hard to maintain their privileges. Using the language of addiction, the banks and the government were codependent, at the very least.

The second story is that the lax regulatory environment brought into the industry players who had a different economic agenda: looting (Akerlof et al., 1993; Calavita et al., 1997; W. Black, 2005a). The idea of looting is that executives cross over from engaging in risky investment behavior, which is not illegal even if it endangers the health of the firm, to behavior that is oriented to transfer money to the executives by engaging in transactions that show no possible prospect of profit (W. Black, 2005b). This included making fraudulent loans that would not fail for several years, thereby making the firm look profitable. It could also mean using kickbacks or making loans to friends or relatives in other banks at favorable terms and having them reciprocate.

There is evidence that in the wake of the deregulation of the industry, many of the savings and loan banks turned over their ownership to new management (Calavita et al., 1997). These managers saw the opportunity to rapidly expand the size of the bank by offering high-interest-rate deposits. But in this story, the main reason to expand the size of the bank was to feather the nest of the executives who were in control. This brought these executives to engage in fraudulent lending in order to make the bank look more profitable than it was and to allow executives to pay themselves bonuses and use company funds to support lavish lifestyles. Calavita et al. (1997) document how these various schemes worked. Most of these fraudulent schemes took place in Texas and California, the epicenter of the eventual meltdown of the savings and loan banks. It has been estimated that between 11 and 44 percent of the losses in the crisis were due to fraud.

The collapse of the savings and loan industry brought the government into action once more. As hundreds of institutions failed, the FSLIC fund was overrun with claims. In 1987, the Government Accountability Office declared that the fund was insolvent by at least $3.8 billion. Congress responded with legislation that recapitalized the fund with $10.8 billion over the next year. However, troubled institutions continued to fail over that time, and more drastic action was required. In 1989, President Bush signed into law a bailout plan for the savings and loan industry. The Financial Institutions Reform, Recovery, and Enforcement Act (FIRREA) abolished the FSLIC fund and transferred its assets to the FDIC. The FHLBB was abolished, and a new institution, the Office of Thrift Supervision, was created to regulate savings and loans.

It was also in this piece of legislation that the Resolution Trust Corporation (RTC) was created to dissolve and merge troubled institutions. Between the FSLIC and the RTC, the federal government resolved the failure of 1,043 savings and loan institutions with total assets of $874 billion (in 2009 dollars). The total thrift industry declined from 3,234 to 1,645 institutions, a decrease of almost 50 percent. After all the dust had settled, the savings and loan crisis was estimated to cost taxpayers around $260 billion (W. Black, 2005a). I remind the reader that if Congress and the Reagan administration had bit the bullet in 1983, the bailout would have cost around $25 billion.

The Rise of Mortgage Securitization

The disaster of the collapse of the savings and loan industry could have been much worse. The collapse could have led to American households being unable to finance their homes at all. But if one examines Figure 2.1, one can see that even as the industry was collapsing, homeownership rates remained steady. This meant that from the point of view of American households, the crisis was alarming but not very consequential for the economy or the ability of citizens to get mortgages. Indeed, the collapse of the savings and loan industry affected GDP growth by less than 0.3 percent per year from 1985 to 1993 (Caprio and Klingebiel, 1996) and did not cause a recession. The recession of 1990–1992 was caused by a combination of factors that included the tightening of monetary policy, the Gulf War, and a decrease in consumer spending (Walsh, 1993).

The main reason that there was not a more substantial crisis, particularly in the ability of households to get mortgages, was that an alternative set of institutions was already in place to take the market over from the savings and loans. Whether one views this outcome as luck or serendipity, the GSEs and the burgeoning mortgage securitization market rapidly took up the slack of the failed savings and loans (McConnell and Buser, 2011). This process accelerated beginning in 1985, and the new business model for getting mortgages was solidly in place by 1993. Figure 2.2 documents the rapid decline of the savings and loan banks and the rise of the GSEs and the commercial banks as the providers of mortgages in the United States over this period. The GSE share of mortgages rose from around 10 percent in 1980 to 35 percent in 1990.

The rise of mortgage securitization meant a huge transformation in the identity of the businesses that came to dominate the mortgage industry. The collapse of the savings and loan industry meant that there was an opportunity for a whole new set of firms to rise and dominate the mortgage market. This was a revolution, not just in how mortgages were to be funded but in who were going to be the dominant players in doing the funding. The savings and loan collapse produced the conditions for a multitude of new market niches to form. It is to this story that I now turn.

The basic business model of the savings and loan banks was to borrow and lend funds locally. But even during the Great Depression, the government worried that the savings and loan industry would be unable to provide enough capital to satisfy the demand for housing. The main issue was that capital that would be made available for local mortgages might be unevenly distributed across the country. This would leave some parts of the country starved for capital and others flush. The FHA and Fannie Mae were established to create a national market for capital to be used for mortgages all over the country. They would do this by seeking out other kinds of investors in the housing market in order to ensure that capital might flow to parts of the country that were underserved by the local savings and loan banks. As can be seen in Figure 2.2, these investors were mainly insurance companies and commercial banks.

The FHA played three important roles in this process. First, it was instrumental in defining a conventional mortgage, allowing the production of a standard product. Second, it provided mortgage insurance to buyers in order to attract investors. This insurance meant that the government acted to guarantee that the mortgage would be paid off no matter what, thereby guaranteeing that investors would not lose their money. Finally, it originated mortgages using borrowed money. It was particularly effective at providing funding for mortgages for multifamily housing from 1945 to 1960.

Fannie Mae was created to operate what was called a secondary market for mortgages. Its job was to find investors to buy the mortgages that were insured by the FHA. In doing so, they took on a role as an intermediary between mortgage originators and mortgage investors in the market for conventional mortgages backed by insurance from the FHA. Mortgage originators could be savings and loan banks, commercial banks, mutual savings banks, or local mortgage brokers, while investors were mainly commercial banks and insurance companies.

Fannie Mae's activities were relatively small scale from 1938 until 1968. In practice, it mostly bought loans that the FHA had originated and held on to them as investments, using money it borrowed to fund them (Sellon and Van-Nahmen, 1988). However, one can see the nascent outlines of the modern GSE in its organizational design. The creation of a secondary market where mortgages would move from the hands of originators to investors with the oversight of a government-backed agency would be the same modern role played by the GSEs. There were, of course, two big differences between the modern GSEs and their forerunner. Until 1970, the product that was exchanged in this secondary market was individual households' mortgages, not MBSs. Moreover, this system was never intended to replace the savings and loan banks. Instead, it was viewed as a way to supplement the actions of the savings and loan banks by making sure capital would be made available to parts of the country that might have been capital starved. But by 1993, the GSEs and the market for mortgage securitization had replaced the originate-and-hold model of the savings and loans.

It is useful to put the problem of the availability of capital for different kinds of investments into a larger perspective. If one conceives of all available capital in a society, then it follows from standard economic theory that if left unimpeded, it will flow to investments that pay the highest return on a risk-adjusted basis. Economic theory also implies that if there is a strong demand for capital across sectors in a society, interest rates will rise. There were several forces driving up interest rates for investment capital in the 1960s. The 1960s was a period of sustained economic growth, meaning that businesses were busy borrowing money to fund their activities. There was also an active merger movement going on where companies were borrowing money to buy up the shares of other companies. This meant that borrowing capital in the private economy was relatively expensive.

At the same time, the Johnson administration oversaw one of the greatest expansions of government expenditures outside of wartime in American history. The government increased the size of the social safety net by increasing spending on welfare and on health insurance for the poor and elderly (Medicaid and Medicare). They were also involved in an escalating war in Vietnam. As a result, the government was running large budget deficits, which it was funding by borrowing money. The only way it could attract funds to do this was by paying higher interest rates. There was very real worry that the government was potentially crowding out business investment. The demands of both business and the government for capital had to affect funding for mortgages.

Investors looking for investments could buy government bonds or invest in corporate bonds or the stock market. Small savers had less access to these markets, but as interest rates rose, they found ways to move their money into more lucrative investments such as stock mutual funds, money market funds, and time deposits. The first attempt to stem the flow of funds from small savers out of savings and loans came in 1966 with the imposition of an interest rate cap on savings accounts using Regulation Q. But this ultimately proved unsuccessful, as the savings and loan and commercial banks forced the government regulators to allow them to introduce financial products that paid higher, market interest rates as consumers found ways around these limits. In spite of the attempt to contain small savers, money market funds, checking accounts that paid interest, and time deposits grew rapidly over this period.

The Johnson administration was worried that as the baby boom generation aged, the savings and loan banks' credit crunch would mean that getting a mortgage would become more and more difficult (Quinn, 2019). One idea was for the government to increase its role in the housing market by not just providing mortgage insurance but also directly originating mortgages. But given that the Johnson administration was already running a large budget deficit, they were reluctant to go to Congress to ask for a new, expensive social program aimed at housing. If the government became the lender for households by borrowing money from the private sector, the money lent would add to the budget deficit. Quinn (2019) documents how the political discussion about how to finance housing was mainly focused on avoiding increasing the budget deficit.

In response to this dilemma, in 1968, the Johnson administration, working with Congress, passed the Housing and Urban Development Act. The basic idea was to create the GSEs. The GSEs would issue bonds to raise private capital to fund mortgages outside of the federal budget. This ingenious idea would in one fell swoop potentially solve all of the problems of providing more funding for housing. The act split Fannie Mae into two organizations (Quinn, 2019). Functions considered essential to the government were incorporated into a new government agency, the Government National Mortgage Association, or Ginnie Mae. This new agency was authorized to guarantee MBSs issued by approved private companies for mortgages already insured by the FHA or VA. Thus, the new bonds would have two kinds of governmental guarantees. First, the FHA and VA had insured the loans going into the MBSs, and second, Ginnie Mae would guarantee the return of principal and interest (D. Black et al., 1981).

The rest of Fannie Mae was turned into a GSE. A GSE is a financial services corporation created by the United States Congress. They operate to enhance the flow of credit to targeted sectors of the economy such as housing and to reduce the risk to investors and other suppliers of capital. While the GSEs can sell shares in the public markets, they are assumed to be backed by the government. In the case of the housing GSE, not only could Fannie Mae borrow at rates close to that of the federal government, it was also allowed to have a high degree of financial leverage. Quinn (2019) shows that Fannie Mae was not given a debt-to-equity ratio.

In practice, Fannie Mae operated mostly to promote a secondary mortgage market by continuing to use its relationships with mortgage companies, commercial banks, pension funds, and insurance companies to raise capital and fund mortgages and MBSs. They would buy mortgages from originators using borrowed money, turn those mortgages into bonds with the help of investment banks, and sell those bonds to investors. They would also hold on to some of those bonds for their own accounts. The investors for the bonds were frequently commercial banks who might have been the originators of the mortgages. By selling the mortgages to Fannie Mae and having them turned into bonds with the backing of the US government, commercial banks took the risk out of holding on to mortgages as investments. Of course, this was true not just for those who had sold the mortgages to Fannie Mae in the first place but for all investors. In effect, the US government absorbed the potential of a great deal of mortgage market risk but conceded the profits to private shareholders.

In 1970 Freddie Mac was created using the same model as Fannie Mae. It was created under the FHLBB. While Fannie Mae confined its activities to mortgage companies, commercial banks, and insurance companies, Freddie Mac was viewed as the GSE who would help savings and loans create MBSs. The savings and loan industry preferred to work through the FHLBB rather than with Fannie Mae, who had traditionally been aligned with their principal competitors—mortgage companies, commercial banks, and insurance companies that purchased FHA- and VA-insured loans. This allowed savings and loan banks to also reduce the riskiness of their mortgage holdings. Freddie Mac took the lead in the issuance of MBSs throughout the 1970s, while Fannie largely stuck to portfolio lending until the 1980s (Sellon and VanNahmen, 1988).

The GSEs were set up to pioneer the modern mortgage-backed securities industry. This produced a set of innovative ideas. The basic notion was to expand the secondary market for mortgages by having the GSEs shift from just brokering investment in mortgages by issuing mortgage insurance to issuing bonds. Given that the market for government and corporate bonds was large and deep, issuing mortgage-backed bonds would be a way to attract some of that capital to mortgages. The idea of a mortgage-backed security implied that instead of investors buying an individual mortgage where a default might occur, they bought a security where the risk of default was spread across a group of mortgages. This made the number and type of investors who might be interested in purchasing such bonds expand dramatically.

The bonds would be registered with the Securities and Exchange Commission, like all other government and corporate bonds. They would be rated by the credit rating agencies, who would examine the riskiness of the underlying mortgages in the bond and provide a rating for the bond. At the bottom of all this was that at the end of the day, the bonds were backed by the government, and this meant that their odds of failure were equivalent to the odds of US Treasury bonds failing. From the point of view of investors, mortgage-backed securities would pay a higher rate of return than US Treasury bonds because of the interest rates paid for by the mortgagors and would be nearly as safe. Investors seeking safety and high returns would be rewarded by MBSs, a clear win for investors.

In practice, this also meant that the cost of capital for the GSEs to fund these bonds would be near to what the federal government paid for funding US Treasury bonds. This gave the GSEs a huge advantage over anyone else wanting to create a secondary market for mortgages. It could borrow more cheaply than anyone else to buy mortgages, borrow more cheaply to hold on to those mortgages for its own accounts, and sell those guaranteed MBSs to private investors to make higher returns on those bonds because of their cheaply obtained capital. Theoretically, if all of this worked, capital would flow more readily into the mortgage market, thereby lowering mortgage rates for individual households. Thus, if the savings and loans could not raise enough capital to provide mortgages for the baby boomers, the GSEs would step in to supplement the market and make sure mortgages were available at the cheapest rates. This meant a win for consumers.

Setting Fannie and Freddie up as private corporations effectively took the GSEs out of the federal government's yearly budget process. The money they borrowed and the bonds they held, bought, and sold would not show up on the government's balance sheets as assets or liabilities. They would not contribute to the national debt. This was true in spite of the fact that the GSEs started out as corporations totally owned by the government. Eventually, the shares in the GSEs were sold to the public, allowing them to become privately owned. When they began to sell shares, this allowed them to raise capital to expand their activities in the securitization market. From the point of view of politicians, the Johnson administration and Congress could be seen as doing something about the housing issue. At the same time, they would be doing it in a way that did not increase the budget deficit or the government's debt. Finally, this produced a clear win for politicians (Quinn, 2019).

From the very beginning, the GSEs had both defenders and detractors. Defenders of the GSEs saw them serving an important function by bringing capital into the mortgage markets and thereby promoting the policy goals of homeownership. These defenders saw a great advantage of using private capital to fund mortgages and at the same time providing homeowners with easy access to credit. Others (mostly economists) saw that by linking the mortgage market to the larger financial markets, the overall efficiency of both markets would be enhanced. Capital would now flow more readily to where it had the highest returns and whatever risk investors were seeking out. Investors could now diversify their portfolios of stocks, corporate bonds, and government bonds to bonds based on mortgages.

Detractors saw the GSEs as intrusive in the mortgage market and against free-market principles. The government-based advantages of the GSEs meant that their low cost of capital prevented competitors from participating in the lucrative market to produce securities. It also guaranteed the GSEs an oligopoly by which they could ensure themselves higher-than-average profits based on their implicit pledge of government backing. Detractors of the GSEs also saw that they meant that the savings and loan banks were at a distinct disadvantage if the GSEs could offer households mortgages at lower cost.

The GSEs and the creation of the MBSs seem like logical ideas that provided a win-win-win for lots of constituencies (except for the savings and loan banks and free-market ideologues!). The first mortgage-backed security was issued by Ginnie Mae in 1970. Figure 2.3 presents an announcement of that event in the *Wall Street Journal*. But the creation and rise of the GSEs was not assured. Indeed, it took fifteen years before the GSEs actually began to be a significant force in the mortgage market. There were a number of problems. First and foremost, no one had ever tried to bring Wall Street bankers and Main Street bankers together in such a large market. They had very different cultures, were enmeshed

First Ginnie Mae Bonds Set For Issue in May; 3 Maturities Planned

Initial Offer to Be $400 Million With Minimum Denomination $25,000; Buyers Called to Talks

By a Wall Street Journal Staff Reporter

PALM SPRINGS, Calif.—The first issue of mortgage-backed bonds guaranteed by the Government National Mortgage Association will be offered in late May.

Woodward Kingman, the association's president, told the California Mortgage Bankers Association convention that the initial issue, to be offered by the Federal National Mortgage Association, will amount to approximately $400 million and will include bonds of three maturities. One-fourth of the issue will carry a 12-month maturity; 50% will carry a five-year maturity; and 25% will carry a longer maturity.

The Federal National Mortgage Association supports private home building by acquiring mortgages insured by the Federal Housing Administration or backed by the Veterans Administration. Under the 1968 Housing Act, Fannie Mae has become a Government-sponsored, privately owned corporation, and the Government National Mortgage Association has taken over its previous task of aiding Federally subsidized housing programs.

Four firms will serve as managing underwriters for the issue: First Boston Corp., Merrill Lynch, Pierce, Fenner & Smith Inc., Morgan Guaranty Trust Co. and Salomon Brothers & Hutzler.

The guaranteed securities, representing investments in Fannie Mae-held mortgages, will have all the characteristics of regular bonds. Interest will be paid semiannually, with principal paid at maturity. The bonds will be issued in bearer or registered form and will be transferable at the Federal Reserve Bank of New York. Minimum denomination will be $25,000.

The mortgage bonds, designed to attract new investment to mortgages, are in addition to Ginnie Mae's mortgage-backed "pass-through" securities, which provide for a passing through of principal and interest as collected from pooled mortgages to investors.

Mr. Kingman said investment officers of state and local pension funds, along with pension trust officers of major banks, have been invited to Washington by the Housing and Urban Development Department and the Treasury for a conference April 30 when both the bond and the pass-through type of mortgage-backed securities will be discussed.

FIGURE 2.3 An announcement of the first MBS issued by Ginnie Mae in 1970. Republished with permission of Dow Jones & Co. from the *Wall Street Journal*, April 24, 1970, p. 22.

in quite different products and markets, and were making money with their current business models. Because mortgage securities were a brand-new idea, investors were wary of them. Insurance companies and pension funds were very conservative investors that were highly regulated, and no one knew what an MBS was and whether the MBSs were as safe as people claimed.

Indeed, the obstacles to making a market in such securities were gigantic. Creating a new product from scratch is always a difficult business proposition. Figuring out how to make the product, how to find customers, and how to meet the needs of customers is part and parcel of market creation. Convincing investors that a new financial product had great risk-adjusted returns required the sellers of those products to be able to convince the buyers of their merit. The MBS market had the great advantage of large and well-funded quasi-government agencies to begin the market. But the theory of MBSs required a great many practical problems to be solved. Many of the problems would require creating additional legislation that would allow MBSs to be treated like other fixed-income investments.

To make a market, sellers need to find buyers. In this case, the investors were a diffuse group that included institutional investors such as pension funds, insurance companies, and mutual funds, as well as commercial banks and, over time, overseas banks. Many of these investors were quite conservative and preferred government bonds, which were nearly riskless. Investors were wary of the new product and the claim that MBSs were as safe as government bonds. They worried that if they bought the bonds, they would not get the returns they were being promised. There were three big problems. First, the tax situation surrounding MBSs was murky, and this made MBSs a product that could not be sold to institutional investors such as insurance companies and pension funds. Second, for private issuers of MBSs, state laws made it illegal to sell such securities. To solve these problems, in the end, would require federal legislation.

Third, and most importantly, investors were worried about prepayment risk. Mortgagors could pay back their mortgages at any time, and therefore bondholders might have their money returned before they could show a sufficient profit. This made MBSs very uncertain as investments and undermined the argument that they were as safe an investment as government or even corporate bonds. Since mortgagors were the most likely to do this when interest rates were low and they could refinance their loans, investors would find themselves with money they could only invest at lower rates of return.

Finally, I reiterate that from the perspective of 1968 and throughout the 1980s, no one thought that the MBS market was intended to replace the savings and loan model. This doesn't mean that the savings and loan banks and the GSEs were not in competition. The mortgages that the GSEs were going to originate and fund were not mortgages that were "in addition to" those funded by the savings and loan banks. The GSEs and the savings and loan banks were in competition for mortgages from the beginning. But because the savings and loan banks were still the dominant players in the mortgage market, any new way of funding mortgages was going to have to compete with their model. That meant that any attempt to create the MBS market would have to directly confront the savings and loan banks. Solving the problem of convincing investors that the MBS was a good product would be key to making the GSEs real players in the market.

Figure 2.2 shows how from 1970 to 1990 there was a steady growth in the GSE-related market share, mostly at the expense of the saving and loan industry. The graph shows a steady increase in the market share of the GSEs from 0 percent in 1970 to almost 30 percent in 1987 on the eve of the final collapse of the savings and loan banks. When that meltdown occurred, the GSEs and investment banks were able to complete a takeover of the mortgage market. Their model of making the business of mortgages shift from being about origination to being about securitization could take hold and dominate only with the utter collapse of the savings and loan buy-and-hold model of mortgages.

The share of total market originations for the GSEs increased. There was a steady increase in that percentage over the 1970s from 0 percent to about 15 percent in 1980. But the crisis of the 1980s saw the market share for the GSEs of new mortgage originations skyrocket from 15 percent a year to over 50 percent in 1982. As the savings and loan banks had a mild recovery from 1982 to 1984, that dropped back to around 30 percent. But with the shift away from mortgages engendered by the legislative reforms, the market share of the GSEs climbed to over 50 percent from 1984 to 1987. By 1987, one could say that the new model of mortgage securitization had become the dominant model by which American households were now obtaining mortgages.

Solving the problems of selling a new form of security required innovation on the part of both the GSEs and the investment banks. One of the most important people who helped bring the MBS market into existence was Lewis Ranieri, a trader for Salomon Brothers in the 1970s and 1980s (Ranieri, 1996; Lewis, 1990). Ranieri is often credited with coining the term *securitization*. He tells the following story:

> The term *securitization* has an interesting origin. It first appeared in a "Heard on the Street" column of the *Wall Street Journal* in 1977. Ann Monroe, the reporter responsible for writing the column, called me to discuss the underwriting by Salomon Brothers of the first conventional mortgage

pass-through security, the landmark Bank of America issue. She asked what I called the process and, for want of a better term, I said securitization. *Wall Street Journal* editors are sticklers for good English, and when the reporter's column reached her editor, he said there was no such word as securitization. He complained that Ms. Monroe was using improper English and needed to find a better term. Late one night, I received another call from Ann Monroe asking for a real word. I said, "But I don't know any other word to describe what we are doing. You'll have to use it." The *Wall Street Journal* did so in protest, noting that securitization was a term concocted by Wall Street and was not a real word. So, we have come a long way. (1996: 31)

Ranieri (1996) gives an insider's account of solving the problems that were plaguing the development of the MBS market. He recounts how in the world of the late 1970s, forty-seven states had laws that made it illegal for private issuers to sell MBSs. This was because it was difficult to assess whether these securities were safe. Ranieri describes his role in pushing for Congress to change the law, which they did in the Secondary Mortgage Market Enhancement Act of 1984. Other accounts of the events support Ranieri's role. This act gave private MBSs the same investment status as GSE-backed MBSs (Bleckner, 1984; Lewis, 1990; Jaffee and Rosen, 1990).

The tax situation for MBSs was also in question. Basically, MBSs were being taxed twice, once when they were issued and a second time when they paid interest to bondholders. As part of the Tax Reform Act of 1986, a new tax vehicle called Real Estate Mortgage Investment Conduits (REMIC) was created. These vehicles allowed investments to be treated like partnerships. Thus, they would be taxed only when they earned income.

A different problem was the problem of prepayment risk. As I described above, mortgagors had the right to prepay their mortgages without penalty any time they wanted. From the point of view of investors, this uncertainty made MBSs less attractive. If an investor did not know how much they were going to get on their investment, they would not be interested in buying bonds that were unpredictable. Investors who were highly risk averse such as pension funds and insurance companies bought US Treasury bills, which had a fixed end date and a fixed rate of interest. Why would they buy MBSs for a little higher yield if they could not know what their ultimate return was?

The first solution to this problem was to develop rules of thumb about how long the average mortgage would last before being prepaid. The rule of thumb that developed was twelve years. This allowed bond salesmen to price their product to potential buyers. But this solution was not enough to overcome the objections of customers. In order to give certainty to customers, the next innovation in securitization was the creation of the collateralized mortgage obligation, now called the CMO. The CMO takes a different angle on the pool of mortgages in an MBS. Instead of seeing the mortgages as a single group of thirty-year mortgages, the CMO approaches the pool as a series of unique annual cash flows each year for the next thirty years. It recognizes that cash flows can be carved up into separate tranches of maturities from one to thirty years. It also recognizes that cash flows will be heavier early on and lighter later. Each tranche can then carry a separate price at a spread off of Treasuries with the same maturity. This allows investors to choose their level of riskiness of prepayment as well as the level of interest they will be paid.

Ranieri suggests that by solving these three problems, the securitization industry was ready to take off: "We were now in a position to deploy all of the brilliant technology we had developed. The multitranche CMO, bifurcating mortgage cash flows into IOs, POs, inverse floaters, and devices yet to be invented were now all possible market investments. We won total flexibility" (1996: 37).

Ironically, the crisis of the savings and loan banks inadvertently helped grow the market for MBSs and hasten the demise of the savings and loan banks. Savings and loan banks were failing circa 1980 because they had lots of home loans on their books that paid very low interest. At the same time, the cost of raising new capital to make new loans was prohibitively high. As the savings and loan banks began to fail, they needed to raise capital in order to make new, more profitable investments. But how were they going to do that? One tactic was to use the newly raised limits on depository insurance to attract new accounts. Another was to try to shed their assets (i.e., existing mortgages) that were producing low returns on invested capital. There was also a large incentive to do this. As part of the legislation that was crafted to allow them to reorganize their firms, they were allowed to sell their mortgages without paying taxes in order to raise capital (Sellon and VanNahmen, 1988).

Lewis (1990) describes how Ranieri and his colleagues came to take advantage of the savings and loan banks in the early and mid-1980s. Essentially, Ranieri bought up mortgages at a deeply discounted rate. He then repackaged those mortgages into MBSs that were CMO and sold them to investors. This meant that the returns on these mortgages were now much higher given that the price paid for the cash flows left on the mortgages were so low. The investors who frequently bought these MBSs were the savings and loan banks. They would take the money they had just received for the loans and turn around and invest it in higher-yielding but smaller amounts of new MBSs.

This ploy was, for a few years, a business that was the monopoly of Salomon Brothers. The savings and loans were shedding their mortgages so fast that Ranieri and his group found themselves growing their business at an exponential rate. In 1983, Salomon Brothers issued about $4 billion worth of CMO. By 1987, this had ballooned to over $55 billion. Lewis reports that in 1984, the mortgage securities department at Salomon Brothers made more money than the rest of Wall Street combined (1990: 164). The massive success of Salomon Brothers brought the other Wall Street investment banks to realize that they needed to join the market in order to reap the large benefits. They began to hire people who had worked at Salomon Brothers and set up their own mortgage departments. By the late 1980s, Wall Street investment firms had all entered the mortgage securitization business. The shift of investment banks to the securitization industry was being driven by the opportunity to make billions of dollars from creating MBSs from the mortgages being sold at steeply discounted prices by collapsing savings and loan banks.

The chaos engendered by the savings and loan debacle led to a new set of opportunities for other kinds of financial firms as well. Between 1985 and 1993, a set of new niche markets emerged to work with the GSEs in the provision of mortgages and their being made into MBSs and sold to investors. One of the biggest beneficiaries of the collapse were commercial banks. Commercial banks had been undergoing a thirty-year decline in their main market of loaning money to businesses (Davis and Mizruchi, 1999). Large and medium-sized businesses stopped going to commercial banks for loans and instead entered into the public debt markets and issued bonds (Boyd and Gertler, 1994). This left commercial banks looking for new markets to survive (Gorton and Rosen, 1995). In the late 1980s and early 1990s, commercial banks increased their activity in the mortgage sector to pick up the slack for the collapse of the savings and loan banks. They increased their share of mortgage originations from 20 percent in 1982 to almost 35 percent by 1989 (P. Rose and Haney, 1992). They would then sell those mortgages to the GSEs and often purchase the MBSs for their own accounts.

Banks that specialized in originating mortgages grew their market share dramatically as well. They originated about 13 percent of mortgages in 1982, and this rose to over 19 percent by 1989 (Follain and Zorn, 1990). They would originate a mortgage and then sell it off to the GSEs. It also opened up the possibility for mortgage brokers whose sole job was to fund loans and sell them off to Fannie Mae and Freddie Mac for packaging into MBSs. Mortgage wholesalers arose who would act as middlemen to buy from small-scale originators and sell in packages to Fannie Mae and Freddie Mac.

Jacobides (2005) described what happened as a form of vertical disintegration. He argues that there were three phases of this process in the mortgage industry. In the first phase, 1978–1983, the GSEs substituted for the savings and loan banks in the securitization of loans. This also led to the development of a separate class of banks that either only originated loans or gathered loans together with the express purpose of selling them to the GSEs. From 1983 to 1988, the second phase of the disintegration involved the separation of the mortgage brokers from the mortgage wholesalers. Here, loan originators could be very small firms, sometimes only individuals. These firms would sell their loans to wholesalers, who would then sell the loans on to the GSEs. In the final phase, 1989–1993, the rights to service the loans also fell to a new group of firms. By 1993, the mortgage securitization industry had assumed a new, disintegrated form. The distinct parts of the mortgage securitization process were being played by very different firms of very different size classes.

This model of the market would later also be called the "originate to distribute model" (Ashcraft and Schuermann, 2008). The idea behind this term is that the mortgage moved from its origination across firms' exchanges to end up in the portfolio of an investor mostly as part of a security. This chain of firms had no intention to hold on to the mortgage; instead, they passed it on to the next firm in the line to prepare it for its ultimate placement with investors. The value added at each stage would be captured by a fee charged to the customer. A mortgage might go through the hands of an originator, a mortgage wholesaler, one of the GSEs, and an investment bank who would act as an underwriter for the MBS, ending up with an investor who got their monthly distribution of the cash flow from the mortgage payments from a firm that was involved only in servicing the loans. By 1993, the simple saving and loan model of "originate and hold" was now on the decline. The GSEs were now at the center of the new mortgage securitization industry. American households were getting their mortgages in an entirely different fashion, and they did not even know it.

Conclusions

While it is fashionable to argue that the regulation of the mortgage market that existed before 1980 was inefficient (see, for example, Sellon, 1990), it is the case that the Depression of the 1930s nearly destroyed the country by the complete failure of the financial system. The New Deal legislation put into place a series of regulations that stabilized savings and loan, commercial, and investment banking. In the case of the mortgage industry, it promoted the business model of the savings and loan banks. This mortgage system worked spectacularly well at helping raise the rate of homeownership.

But this business model was undermined by changing economic circumstances in the 1960s and 1970s. The changes in financial regulation that began at the end of the 1970s eventually dismantled all of the New Deal reforms, not just in mortgage finance but across the banking system. While these changes in mortgage finance have mainly been called deregulation, my discussion shows that the government was always responding to the current crisis in the mortgage market. The banks who controlled those markets were the main agents of convincing the government to create the new rules to support their activities. Deregulation was an ideologically loaded word that justified doing what the particular banks wanted to preserve their profits. From the 1980s until 2008, Congress and the executive branch always gave the banks what they wanted. For example, the crisis of the savings and loan banks in the 1970s and early 1980s involved creating a whole new set of rules that allowed those banks to pay whatever interest rates they wanted for deposits, make whatever investments they chose, and be guaranteed that the deposits they managed to secure would be paid back by the government if they failed to produce a profit.

When the savings and loan model met its ultimate demise in the late 1980s, it was replaced by the GSEs, which had been created during the 1960s and early 1970s to provide a backup for the savings and loan model. The GSEs were government-owned private corporations that relied on the implicit promise of the federal government to raise money, create securities, and fund the housing market. But the creation of the mortgage securitization market required a marriage of Wall Street and Main Street around MBSs. This meant that the GSEs had to enlist the support of the investment banks and the other players who remained in the mortgage business. The creation of that market required several additional pieces of legislation and some private-sector innovation to create a product that eventually attracted investor interest. By the late 1980s, the GSEs and the investment banks had formed a business model around MBSs that attracted a huge amount of investment. It was hugely successful in making money through the 1990s until 2008.

The rhetoric that surrounded these financial innovations during the 1990s assumed that the financial innovations set off by the mortgage securitization industry were both efficient and productive. But in the end, the effect of all this financial innovation was to barely raise the homeownership rate from 65 percent in 1980 to 69 percent in 2007. That rate has now dropped in the wake of the financial crisis to 64 percent. While regulation of the New Deal variety has gotten a bad name, it is clear that the financial revolution that innovated new forms of financial products based on mortgage securitization has done worse.

When the GSEs stepped into the breach left by the savings and loan banks, they created the possibility for an entire new group of financial firms to emerge. The disintegration of the mortgage business resulted in the creation of a new set of firms in very fragmented markets. By 1993, a mortgage might pass through four sets of hands before it ended up with its ultimate investor. Many observers and regulators thought that this model dominated the industry on the eve of the crisis in 2008 (Ashcraft and Schuerman, 2008; Purnanandam, 2011). But they were wrong.

From the perspective of 1993, what happened to the mortgage securitization industry next was totally unexpected. The large size of the mortgage market and the possibility to make money off of all phases of the mortgage securitization process played a major role in the reorganization of the entire American financial sector. This reorganization was just beginning in 1993 and would require the next eight years to come to fruition. Instead of remaining fragmented, the industry became vertically integrated. By 2001, almost all of the largest American commercial, investment, and savings and loan banks were involved in some or all of the phases of the mortgage markets. In the world of 1993, one could still tell the difference between savings and loan banks, commercial banks, and investment banks in terms of their main markets. By 2001, for many of the largest banks, they had all become the same bank. This new model of the banks was the structure that was in place post-2001 and the one that led the boom from 2001—until the crash of 2008.

3

THE RISE OF THE VERTICALLY INTEGRATED
PRIVATE BANKS, 1993–2001

The mortgage industry in the United States is one of the largest single industries in the economy. Figure 3.1 shows that during the 1990s, the total amount of mortgages originated fluctuated from $500 billion to $1.5 trillion. Between four and twelve million mortgages were originated each year as the total market rose and fell. But during the early 1990s, the firms that sold Americans' mortgages were of very different size, had quite different market strategies, and operated in many different segments of the industry. As late as 1995, for example, the GSEs securitized a little more than 40 percent of all the mortgages. There was still a substantial presence of savings and loan banks with the originate-to-hold model. While the savings and loan banks were in clear decline, they still accounted for about 25 percent of the market. In the early 1990s, the origination market, the wholesale market for mortgages, the private issuance market, the private underwriting market, and the servicing markets were all fragmented. No player in any of these markets held a large market share. Few of the firms were leaders in more than one of these markets.

The largest players who organized the mortgage industry were the GSEs, who helped create the market for mortgage securities. Figure 3.2 shows how dominant the GSEs were as the issuers of MBSs from 1990 to 2001. They issued between 86 and 97 percent of the mortgage securities during this period. Figure 3.1 also shows the distribution of the types of mortgages originated over the decade. Throughout the period, conventional mortgages made up most of the mortgages originated. We see the beginnings of an expansion in nonconventional mortgages from the middle of the decade onward. The largest category was "jumbo" mortgages, which were mortgages of a very large size; these became popular as house prices

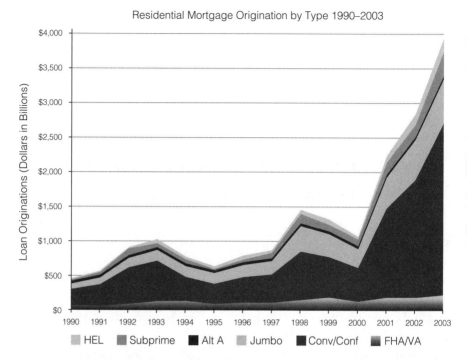

FIGURE 3.1 Residential mortgage origination by type, 1990–2003. Extracted and reformatted from Neil Fligstein and Adam Goldstein, "The Anatomy of the Mortgage Securitization Crisis," in *Markets on Trial: The Economic Sociology of the U.S. Financial Crisis*, edited by M. Lounsbury and P. Hirsch, p. 41, figure 5.

increased over the later part of the decade in many places. The subprime, Alt-A (a form of subprime), and home equity loan markets were relatively small parts of the business. It was these mortgages that were most frequently securitized by private banks (i.e., not the GSEs), which explains why the GSEs led in securitizations. This part of the market remained relatively small until after 2001.

From the perspective of 1993, the mortgage market still consisted of two market models: the residual savings and loan part of the market, where those banks would originate and hold mortgages for their own loan portfolios, and the mortgage securitization market, which was mostly occupied by a bunch of small specialist firms, minnows who swam around the GSE whales. The securitization market was fragmented in a number of ways. At the retail end were real estate agents who dealt with local mortgage brokers. These brokers would frequently arrange to sell the mortgage to a wholesaler. If their businesses were big enough, they might sell directly to the GSEs. The wholesalers would sell packages of mortgages to the GSEs to create MBSs. Savings and loan banks and commercial banks who originated mortgages would frequently sell those mortgages to the GSEs as well. At the other end of the process, investment banks would act

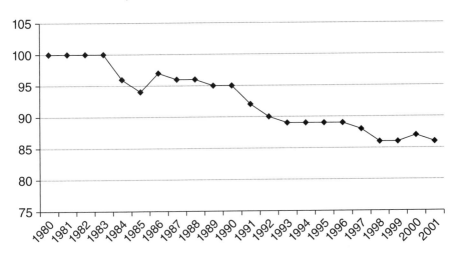

FIGURE 3.2 Percentage of securitizations done by GSE, 1980–2001. Data source: Inside Mortgage Finance (2009).

as underwriters for the GSEs, who would be the issuers of the MBSs. Investment banks would package the bonds, produce tranches, and sell them. Their customers included savings and loans, commercial banks, insurance companies, pension funds, and other institutional investors. To keep track of the mortgage payments and disburse payouts to holders of MBSs, a company would be hired to act as a loan servicer. This disintegration of the market was viewed by some as "efficient" (Jacobides, 2005).

One might wonder why the savings and loan, commercial, and investment banks sold their mortgages to the GSEs and then turned around to buy them back as MBSs. MBSs based on conventional mortgages were AAA-rated securities that many people felt were backed by the government. This meant they were thought to be as safe as government bonds. As a result, banks needed to hold less capital to own the MBSs than they did to own the individual mortgages. The MBSs also had a 2–3 percent higher return than government bonds. These two features of the MBSs made them safe and profitable investments.

The GSEs were among their own best customers. They would borrow money at low interest rates and purchase highly rated MBSs to hold on their own accounts. Even investment banks held onto some MBSs as investments. This model was later characterized as the originate-to-distribute model (Bord and Santos, 2012; Ashcraft and Schuermann, 2008). This term refers to the fact that those who originated the mortgages intended not to hold them as investments but instead to sell them to someone else. The issuers and underwriters who packaged the mortgages into securities also ended up selling most of those securities

Concentration in Mortgage Lending: Top 25 Market Share

FIGURE 3.3 Concentration in mortgage lending: top twenty-five market share. Reformatted from Neil Fligstein and Adam Goldstein, "The Anatomy of the Mortgage Securitization Crisis," in *Markets on Trial: The Economic Sociology of the U.S. Financial Crisis*, edited by M. Lounsbury and P. Hirsch, p. 45, figure 6.

to investors. Thus, the riskiness of the mortgage was passed on to the ultimate investor in the MBSs. During 1985–1993, the GSEs went from challengers in the mortgage field to the incumbents as the market model for securitization organized around them gained dominance.

But in the 1990s, the structure of the industry's markets began to change dramatically. A set of commercial banks, investment banks, and a few mortgage and savings and loan banks grew large and dominant by taking market share in each segment of the mortgage industry and engaging in mergers to eliminate their competitors. These banks became larger but also more vertically integrated. By this I mean that banks decided to invest in mortgage origination in order to secure the fees from that business and assure themselves of a supply of mortgages to package into securities. They then would build investment banking capacity to create securities and sell them to customers. Finally, they invested in those securities, mostly with borrowed money.

Figure 3.3 documents the increase in concentration within the origination markets. In 1990, the top twenty-five mortgage originators did only 30 percent

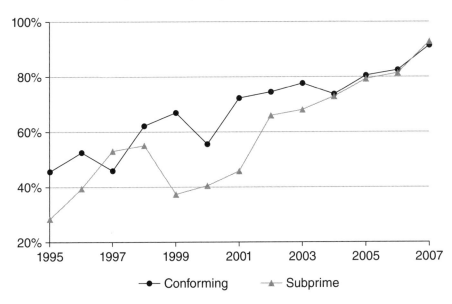

FIGURE 3.4 Percentage of all loans that were securitized. Data source: Inside Mortgage Finance (2009).

of the business. But by 2001, this number grew to over 70 percent and by 2007 to over 90 percent. A similar pattern can be observed in the subprime market. In 1996, the top twenty-five producers of subprime mortgages had less than a 50 percent market share. By 2007, this increased to over 90 percent. Similar patterns emerged in the issuing, underwriting, and servicing markets. The market had gone from being fragmented along product lines and market share to being concentrated within product lines.

By 2001, the savings and loan banks' originate-to-hold model had almost disappeared. Figure 3.4 shows the dramatic increase in the percentage of all loans that were securitized over the decade. In the mid-1990s, the rate of conventional mortgages that were made into securities was around 40–50 percent of the total. During the 1990s, this total steadily increased, and it reached 75 percent in 2001. By 2007, about 95 percent of mortgages originated were turned into securities. Subprime mortgages (which were a very small fraction of all mortgages in 1995) were securitized at an even lower rate. But as these mortgages became more standard products and as the size of the market grew, their rate of securitization rose as well. After 2001, the rate of securitization of these mortgages rose from about 40 percent to over 95 percent.

This shift in the percentage of mortgages being securitized reflected two forces. One was the increasing dominance of securitization in the mortgage business. But it also reflected the increasing integration of private banks. Once a bank had decided to be both an originator and a securitizer, the mortgages they originated were seen as raw materials for the securities they were going to create. Using these mortgages efficiently meant turning all of them into securities at high rates. Countrywide Financial, which started out as a mortgage bank that mainly wholesaled mortgages for the GSEs, became the poster child for the new model for the market. Countrywide participated in all of the segments of the industry by 2001 and was frequently the number-one or number-two producer in each segment. The spectacular success of Countrywide Financial provided a model for other banks that began to pursue the tactic of being an originator and securitizer in conventional and unconventional mortgage segments.

Despite this challenge, throughout the decade, the GSEs remained at the center of the market for securitizing conventional mortgages. Banks, even those that became integrated, continued to originate mortgages, acted as wholesalers by buying them from mortgage brokers and smaller banks, and then sold them to the GSEs for packaging into MBSs. Some of these banks became underwriters of MBSs and worked for the GSEs creating MBSs. These same banks might also be acting as issuers of MBSs themselves for the nonconventional loan market. At the other end of the securities production process, all of the banks bought GSE-issued MBSs to hold as investments. They often did so with money they borrowed in the commercial paper markets. MBSs were a good investment. They had high ratings, were thought to be safe investments, and paid interest above Treasury bonds.

The GSEs were able to dominate the conventional mortgage market mostly because their costs of borrowing money were so low. Since they borrowed at the lowest possible rates due to their implicit government guarantee, it was difficult for banks to compete with them to securitize conventional mortgages. But the GSEs were not allowed to enter the nonconventional mortgage market until 2005. This created an opportunity for banks that were willing to fund mortgagors who were unable to qualify for conventional funding or who wanted to take equity out of their homes without refinancing. Banks experimented with mortgages that allowed very low down payments, sometimes as low as 3 percent and eventually zero down payments. Banks also began to provide loans for people whose credit was impaired. These included Alt-A or B and C (these were officially what was meant by subprime) loans. These mortgages would charge higher interest rates and fees to reflect the riskiness of these loans. Whenever interest rates rose, banks would push mortgages that had adjustable rates. This would allow people to buy homes at a lower "teaser" rate and thereby have lower payments. This rate would be adjusted over time. These products proliferated as well and became more complex in how they worked. Finally, home equity loans began to appear. These allowed mortgagors to borrow money based on the equity in their homes. The banks that originated these loans then moved to turning them into securities. Figure 3.1 presents data showing that these markets increased steadily from a very small base over the 1990s. This market grew from almost 0 percent in 1990 to nearly 20 percent of the market by 2001.

By the time of the recession that began in 2001, the mortgage securitization market was the dominant way in which American mortgages were funded. There now were a plethora of products that were created to serve groups of customers who could not qualify for conventional mortgages. These new products produced higher fees and higher profits for the sale of MBSs. They offered investors higher rates of returns. They were being increasingly produced by a smaller and smaller number of banks who took part in many different markets, markets where they acted as originators, issuers, underwriters, servicers, and investors.

One important question is, why did smaller and specialist banks feel compelled to move outside of their comfort zones to produce new products in a vertically integrated structure? My basic argument is that in the wake of the collapse of the savings and loan model, a great number of banks found entering the mortgage market to be attractive. The national mortgage market was fragmented along both geographic and product lines. The collective acts of deregulation of banking meant that the barriers to interstate and multibranch banking had been removed. It also meant that the boundaries between product categories were weakened. Commercial banks, such as Citibank, continuously challenged the prohibition of commercial banks entering investment banking. By the early 1990s, they were able to gain substantial revenues from investment banking activities. The large size of the housing market meant that there were huge opportunities to build larger banks by expanding geographically and into new products. One of the main strategies of expansion was through mergers. Financial deregulation during the 1980s and 1990s meant that banks could buy banks in other states and expand across a range of products.

Moreover, the mortgage business was very lucrative because it was based on fees that could be charged for every service. Fees became the basis of the business. They quickly added up. For example, if one's goal was to sell the mortgages to the GSEs, then the start-up costs to run such a business focused on being able to borrow money to fund mortgage origination. Originators could use their own capital or borrow capital, fund new mortgages, and collect their fees. They would then turn around and resell the mortgage to a wholesaler or one of the GSEs, thereby getting back their capital. If they had borrowed the capital, they could return it to the lender. Many established lines of credit for this kind of fee-generating business. They could then reloan the money and begin the pro-

cess again. Entry into this phase of the market, particularly origination, brokering, and wholesaling, could require very little capital upfront. Since none of these
firms were going to hold on to the mortgages they originated, it was possible to
use the mortgage as collateral for a loan that would be repaid once the mortgage
was sold to a wholesaler or the GSEs.

This meant that there was a great deal of competition. This competition
pushed firms to get bigger by buying up their competitors. With competition
being so brutal, small firms' cost structures just did not allow them to compete
with bigger firms. Moreover, by shrinking the number of competitors, eventually
more oligopolistic conditions became the norm in these markets, thus lowering
competitive pressures as well. Competition also pushed banks into businesses
where there was less competition, such as nonconventional mortgages and servicing the mortgages that underlay the MBSs. The mortgage market experienced
large swings when interest rates rose or fell. The shift into multiple products also
produced a more diversified product base that could help stabilize the bank as
the housing market went through its ups and downs.

The pioneer in this tactic of finding new markets to enter was Countrywide
Financial. The top managers at Countrywide were both pragmatic and opportunistic. They took what opportunities the market appeared to offer and were not
concerned about getting into new businesses that they might not know. They
pioneered home equity loans and subprime mortgages and played a large role
in creating the jumbo market. They experimented with products with low down
payments. They also offered adjustable-rate mortgages when interest rates rose.
By creating new products, they helped start new markets, markets where profits
might be higher (at least at first) and competition less. They also were early en-
trants into mortgage securitization, particularly for nonconventional mortgages.
During the 1990s, Countrywide became one of the leaders in servicing existing loans. This meant that even if their mortgage business declined, they could
make money servicing existing mortgages and offering financial products to
those customers. Their business model, which had them participating in many
markets, was so successful that it became emulated by other firms. The lesson
Countrywide Financial and others took away was that they too could grow and
take market share if they entered many parts of the business and integrated from
mortgage origination through servicing.

The competition in mortgage origination produced pressures in two other
important directions. First, since the basic raw material of the MBS was the
mortgage, banks realized that they needed to secure a supply of mortgages to be
players in the securitization market. Investment banks such as Bear Stearns and
Lehman Brothers began to backwardly integrate and buy originators in the mid-

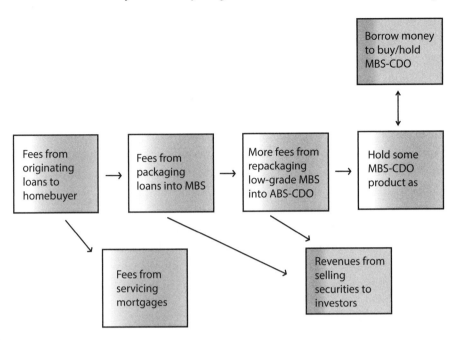

FIGURE 3.5   The vertically integrated bank, circa 2001.

1990s to insure the supply of mortgages. Second, commercial banks saw that investment banks were making money packaging nonconventional mortgages. They also saw Countrywide servicing the GSEs as an issuer and creating nonconventional MBSs during the early 1990s. Commercial banks such as Citibank, Bank of America, Wells Fargo, and Chase, all of which were originating large numbers of conventional mortgages, began to open investment banking facilities to capture the profits of becoming an issuer and an underwriter.

The entry into nonconventional mortgages was partially driven by competition for conventional mortgages. By finding new mortgagors, banks increased the supply of potentially securitizable mortgages without cannibalizing the existing base market. Over time, they realized that such mortgages earned higher fees and when packaged into MBSs could yield higher interest rates. These higher interest rates made them extremely attractive to investors, who saw them as relatively safe investments that paid much higher rates of return.

Figure 3.5 sums up how many of the largest banks made money off all of the parts of the MBS process. Vertical integration meant that banks got fees for originating the mortgages sold to individuals. By being issuers and underwriters, banks could absorb the fees for those activities. They would then make profits by selling MBSs to investors. Next, they would act as loan servicers for the securities they sold. Finally, they would buy some of the securities for their own investments. Instead of a fragmented set of markets with specialist firms, the integration of the largest banks across each part of the MBS process meant that all of the gains from engaging in securitization could be captured by a single firm. In practice, most banks were never totally integrated. They still bought and sold mortgages in the wholesale market. They still participated in GSE pools, sometimes as sellers of mortgages, sometimes as issuers. They would hire investment banks sometimes, and they would outsource servicing. But at the core of the mortgage securitization industry, the banks that came to dominate the mortgage industry did so by moving from being small-scale role players to being the largest players by playing every part.

In this chapter, I explore this process by showing how a small number of banks came to enter multiple markets in the industry in order to illustrate how leading banks began to morph toward a single type of bank. We consider Countrywide Financial (mortgage bank), Bear Stearns (investment bank), Washington Mutual (savings and loan), and Citibank (commercial bank). These banks were among the pioneers of the form that eventually would characterize most of the largest banks in the US economy. All moved into the individual markets that made up the mortgage securitization industry.

Citibank, Countrywide Financial, and Washington Mutual aspired to become universal banks or financial conglomerates, one-stop financial centers that would sell all kinds of financial products. Their aspirations caused them to expand into markets that were growing or seemed lucrative. While many of these banks saw this diversification as entry into insurance, mutual funds, or standard investment banking, it turned out that the products that grew the fastest and produced the most opportunities for profits were mortgages and mortgage-backed securities (Elsas et al., 2010; Stiroh and Rumble, 2006). There is a certain irony that while the goal of these banks was to become highly diversified financial conglomerates, they instead made most of their money becoming vertically integrated banks centered on producing mortgages and mortgage securities. Similarly, the great growth of investment banks in the 1990s and 2000s was mostly propelled by their participation in the mortgage markets. Of the five largest investment banks, only Goldman Sachs stayed away from becoming a vertically integrated mortgage securities producer. Bear Stearns, Lehman Brothers, Merrill Lynch, and Morgan Stanley all eventually bought mortgage originators to ensure themselves a supply of mortgages for securitization.

By 2001, the GSEs continued to dominate the conventional mortgage market by acting as the brokers in the process of producing MBSs based on those mortgages. But the number of banks who participated in this process shrank as they became larger and more integrated. They began to produce their own MBSs by issuing and underwriting nonconventional MBSs. This market grew up alongside the conventional market. In 2001, the nonconventional part of the market comprised only about 15–20 percent of the entire market for mortgage securitization. The private banks loved these new products because of their ability to issue and underwrite, thus taking on more of the fees and profits associated with securitization. The industry structure circa 2001 was the structure that was in place from 2001 until the crash in 2008. By 2001, at the core of the American financial system, there were no longer savings and loan, mortgage, commercial, or investment banks per se. There was instead an integrated financial services bank that was focused on all of the activities in the mortgage industry. While there were still smaller financial institutions that specialized, the core of these markets was dominated by a small number of gigantic banks. It was the GSEs and the largest financial services banks that were in place when the opportunity to grow was made possible by the huge wave of refinancing in 2001–2004 and the subsequent massive expansion of nonconventional mortgages.

The Rise of Countrywide Financial

Countrywide Financial collapsed in the fall of 2008. Many media observers came to see Countrywide as a central actor in causing the financial crisis (see, for example, *Huffington Post,* 2014; *Fortune,* 2010; *Time,* 2010; McLean and Nocera, 2010). They blamed the firm for having gotten rich by enticing unsuspecting mortgagors into taking mortgages they would never be able to pay off and then packaging those mortgages into securities that would inevitably default. Angelo Mozilo, CEO of Countrywide Financial, defended the actions of the company throughout the financial crisis and argued that the company had done nothing wrong. Most of these same observers came to view Mozilo's defense of his company as evidence that he was a crook and his company got rich by being corrupt.

The bitter and abrupt demise of Countrywide Financial makes it hard to remember that Countrywide Financial was the financial firm that pioneered a successful strategy in the brave new world of mortgage securitization that emerged in the 1980s when the savings and loan banks collapsed. Countrywide Financial, which was founded by David Loeb and Angelo Mozilo as a two-person operation in 1969, had by 2001 come to be the dominant firm in the US mortgage market. Their company had a top five market share in almost every market segment including origination, securitization, and servicing and in both the conventional and unconventional markets. Circa 2001, Loeb and Mozilo were viewed as pathbreaking entrepreneurs from within the industry, and their company was a case study for business schools (see, for example, Kurland and Flamholtz, 2005). Countrywide Financial, by being a presence in all of the main market segments of the mortgage securitization industry, presented a model of the vertically integrated financial corporation. My purpose here is to try to understand how Loeb and Mozilo conceived of their business strategy and how this eventually revolutionized the mortgage industry.

Their firm was consistently one of the most entrepreneurial of all the firms in the industry. Their analysis of market conditions in the mortgage industry and their position within that industry brought them to create new products and seek out new opportunities. While not all of these innovations turned out to be successful, they took risks and entered new businesses in a fearless fashion. They did so because they saw opportunity where others did not. Frequently, they were right. They, of course, also made mistakes. They understood how the existence of the GSEs could help them build a bigger firm, and they carved out market space for themselves. One of the most important things they recognized were market spaces where customers were potentially underserved. Their constant search for new opportunities brought them to diversify their customer base and, as a result, their product base.

Loeb and Mozilo never intended to build a vertically integrated mortgage bank involved in both conventional and unconventional mortgages. But they ended up doing so, because the opportunities to grow and stabilize the bank were pushed by entering into multiple market segments during the 1980s and 1990s. Instead, Mozilo's goal very early on for the firm was to create a full-service provider of financial services. For example, in November 1993, Countrywide began to try to sell insurance, mutual funds, and home equity lines to its mortgage customers (*National Mortgage News*, 1993a: 5). In 2002, they changed the name of the company to Countrywide Financial from Countrywide Credit to signify this strategic decision. But even with this aspiration, the core of the firm's business was the market for mortgage origination and securitization until its demise.

In the world of 1969, the savings and loan model of mortgage origination was still dominant. Loeb and Mozilo called their company Countrywide Credit because they wanted to build a national mortgage bank. It is useful to understand the business model they employed. Countrywide was not a savings and loan or commercial bank, and therefore they did not take deposits from individual or corporate clients. Instead, they depended for capital on being able to borrow money from commercial banks or the commercial paper market (*National Mortgage News*, 1996a: 18). Their goal was to originate mortgages using other people's money and then sell the mortgages off to an ultimate investor. They would retain the servicing rights to the mortgages in order to continue to collect fees for that function. They could then return the capital they had borrowed and begin the process anew. They also operated as wholesalers who would use borrowed money to buy mortgages from savings and loan banks, commercial banks, mortgage banks, and mortgage brokers. They would then sell these mortgages to investors to recover their capital. Their basic business model was to collect fees for all of these activities. They hoped to build a large firm by expanding the number of mortgages they originated, bought and sold in the wholesale market, and serviced.

The emergence of the GSEs in the 1970s and early 1980s provided a large and stable customer for newly originated conventional mortgages. Loeb and Mozilo recognized the opportunity that the existence of the GSEs presented early on. They built their business over this period as both an originator and an aggregator of conventional mortgages destined to be made into MBSs for the GSEs. To do this, Countrywide needed to obey the rules that the GSEs had laid down about obtaining the loans. That meant that they could only purchase conventional mortgages that met the GSEs' criteria. These rules worked to Countrywide's favor as they quickly gained a reputation as a company that originated only "good" mortgages. Countrywide's rise was facilitated by hitching themselves to the rising GSEs.

Loeb and Mozilo understood that to attract customers, they needed to offer loans that had attractive interest rates, lower fees, and quick approval and closing dates. Countrywide pioneered a set of organizational and technological tactics that made them low-cost originators who were then able to pass on savings to their customers. The conventional approach to mortgage banking had emphasized using highly compensated salespeople to find and close mortgages. Countrywide decided not to pay salespeople to find and close mortgages but instead to offer a standard product at low cost that would guarantee quick approval and very short closing dates for loans. They did this partially to save money. But they also believed that by paying salespeople, you gave them an incentive to try to fund loans to people who might not pay them back (*National Mortgage News*, 1991b: 24). In order to achieve this goal, branch offices operated as loan processors, not sales offices, with the central office taking care of sales by mailing out notices to realtors. In 1996, they began to advertise directly to consumers (*National Mortgage News*, 1996b: 13).

From the 1970s through the 1990s, Countrywide pioneered the use of computer technology to speed the process of application and approval along. By the mid-1980s, Countrywide would guarantee an interest rate and a closing date within thirty to ninety days of an application. In 1990, the company introduced its own origination service, which significantly reduced origination and process-

ing costs while accelerating funding time to less than thirty days on conventional loans. They were able to do this because of computerization that recorded a
potential mortgagor's information once and was then able to copy the information to other files automatically. In 1991, Countrywide made another advance by
creating a new system that expedited loan processing by using an algorithm to
decide whether a mortgage was approved automatically. The system was able to
approve a routine application in less than a minute. The 15 percent of mortgages
that were more complex were then sent to underwriters, who considered them
more closely. This reduced both the costs of mortgage approval and the time to
approval.

Loeb and Mozilo displayed an uncanny sense of where interest rates were
headed. For example, during the high-interest-rate period of the late 1970s and
early 1980s, Countrywide sold off its rights to service mortgages in order to raise
capital. They helped promote the adjustable-rate mortgage as way to make home
buying more affordable. By the mid-1980s, it was already becoming apparent
that interest rates were going to fall. As the market for refinancing mortgages
took off, Countrywide was in a good position to take advantage. By the end of
the 1980s, Countrywide could see that interest rates were going up, suggesting
that the boom in refinancing was going to end. To deal with this downturn in
their origination business, they decided to invest heavily in mortgage servicing,
going so far as to set up a division to purchase servicing rights, and they helped
to create a market in those rights. They increased their mortgages serviced from
about $1 billion in 1987 to $100 billion by 1994. Mozilo described this tactic as
a "hedge" for when times went bad. He argued that when interest rates were
low, the origination business was great. But when interest rates rose, that market dried up (*National Mortgage News,* 1994b). By taking on servicing in such a
large-scale fashion, Countrywide diversified its business and entered a business
that would be stable no matter what was going on in the housing market.

The explosive growth period for the company came during the collapse of the
savings and loan industry. This was the opportunity that took Countrywide from
a medium-sized mortgage bank to a national leader in the industry. From 1989
to 1993, the total number of loans increased from 39,634 to 234,407. The number
of conventional mortgages that the company originated increased from 19,304 in
1989 to 192,385 in 1993, a tenfold increase in four years (Countrywide Financial,
1993). Countrywide was among the largest mortgage originators in the country.

By 1993, Countrywide was engaged in a wide variety of activities and could be
already described as vertically integrated. The firm originated mortgages, turned
them into MBSs, sold them, held some on their own accounts, and serviced
loans. Every year, publicly held corporations have to submit a document to the

Securities and Exchange Commission that is called a 10-K. These documents outline how the company conceives of its products, challenges, and prospects. They make an excellent source of information about the firm. The 1993 10-K described the company in the following terms:

> Countrywide Credit Industries, Inc. (the "Company") is a holding company which through its principal subsidiary Countrywide Funding Corporation ("CFC") is engaged in primarily the mortgage banking business and as such originates, purchases, sells and services mortgage loans. The Company, through its other wholly owned subsidiaries offers products and services complementary to its mortgage banking business. A subsidiary makes and sells mortgage backed securities. In addition, another subsidiary acts as agent for homeowner's insurance in connection with CFC's mortgage banking operations. Another subsidiary receives fee income for managing the investments and operations of Countrywide Mortgage Investments including a real estate investment trust and the investment in individual mortgages and mortgage backed securities. The Company also acts to broker servicing of mortgages and runs an operation to service its own mortgages. (1993: 2)

The 10-K from 1993 describes the company's business model is the following way:

> The principal sources of revenue from the Company's mortgage banking business are (i) loan origination fees; (ii) gains from the sale of loans; (iii) interest earned on mortgage loans during the period they are held by the Company pending sale; and (iv) loan servicing fees. . . . The Company, similar to other mortgage bankers, customarily sells all loans it originates or purchases as part of its mortgage banking operations. The Company packages substantially all of its FHA-insured and VA-guaranteed first mortgage loans into pools of loans. It sells these pools in the form of modified mortgage-backed securities guaranteed by the Government National Mortgage Association to national or regional brokers. Conforming conventional loans may be pooled by the Company and exchanged for securities guaranteed by FNMA or FHLMC, which securities are then sold to national or regional broker dealers. (1993: 3–4).

The product divisions of Countrywide acted relatively autonomously of one another. This reflects the fact that they had come into existence at different historical moments to be participants in particular markets. For example, the re-tail division ran the storefronts the company had around the country, while the wholesale division purchased loans from other originators. Countrywide also ran a consumer division that serviced mortgages. This division tried to sell refi-nancing to already existing mortgagors and other services such as homeowner's insurance. When Countrywide decided to enter a new market or produce a new product, it would do so by setting up a new product division.

During the 1990s, Countrywide worked to create several new markets for mortgages, what we would now call nonconventional mortgages. I have already noted that Countrywide began to make what came to be called jumbo loans. The FHA has a limit on how much money mortgagors can borrow that is adjusted over time for inflation. Because prices in California and parts of the East Coast had risen so fast, many potential home buyers fund that while they could sup-port a larger mortgage, they lacked a large enough down payment. This caused mortgage originators to create jumbo mortgages, which frequently came with additional fees and higher interest rates. Countrywide also pioneered home eq-uity loans. These are loans that allow mortgagors to borrow money against the equity in their homes.

In 1993, Countrywide opened a special facility to originate and securitize nonconventional mortgages (*National Mortgage News,* 1993b: 1). This facility is called a "conduit" in the jargon of the industry. They introduced several new mortgage loan products. They created a loan with a 95 percent financing and another with a 100 percent financing, which they began to package into MBSs. In that same year, they also began to originate and securitize jumbo mortgages (*National Mortgage News,* 1993b: 1). Countrywide, which was one of the firms that pioneered home equity loans, began securitizing those loans in 1994 (*Asset Securitization Report,* 1994: 1).

Countrywide continued to invest in computer technology and to gain more control over the loan process. In March 1994, they began to offer loan applica-tions online (*National Mortgage News,* 1994d: 8). They also created a comput-er system called CLUES that allowed people to enter their information into a form once and have it applied to multiple parts of an application. This system was marketed to other companies and brokers more generally (*National Mort-gage News,* 1994c: 18). They also bought a title company that spring to lower the costs of closing a mortgage (*National Mortgage News,* 1994b: 1). In 1990–1998, the company invested heavily in mortgage servicing. By 1994, they had a $100 billion portfolio, and this grew to over $150 billion in 1998.

Countrywide began to buy subprime mortgages in the wholesale market in 1993. In 1996, they began to originate subprime mortgages themselves (*Nation-*

al Mortgage News, 1996a: 7). Subprime mortgagors are people who have a less-than-stellar credit history. During the mid-1990s, companies began to realize that this market could be offered mortgages by charging higher rates of interest and additional fees. Since the GSEs were not inclined to be involved in this market, private banks were able to get into the issuance of MBSs. Countrywide was a pioneer in these markets. Countrywide and other MBS producers began to create exotic securities by 1998 (*Asset Securitization Report,* 1998b: 1). These markets soared in the mid-1990s, albeit from a small base.

Countrywide's mortgage production and sales unit increased dramatically in size in the late 1990s as well. In 1999, they hired Ranjit Kripalani to head their MBS department. Mr. Kripalani had previously headed the MBS unit at Chase Securities. Countrywide also opened a New York office and, by the end of 1999, employed fifty people in that office to trade and sell securities (*Asset Securitization Report,* 1998a: 1). It hired a number of Wall Street veterans to create a more powerful group of sellers and traders (*Asset Securitization Report,* 1998a: 5).

By 2001, Countrywide Financial was a large and diversified corporation that participated in many market segments. Conventional mortgages grew from about 192,000 in 1993 to 327,000 in 2001 (Countrywide Financial, 2002: 2). FHA / VA mortgages increased from around 42,000 in 1993 to 143,000 in 1997 only to decline to 118,000 in 2001. Home equity loans increased dramatically from 2,000 in 1993 to 20,000 in 1997 and over 119,000 in 2001. Subprime mortgages totaled 2,000 in 1996 and grew to 52,000 in 2001. Alternative loan products increased their share of Countrywide's business dramatically over the eight-year period from 0 percent in 1993 to 16.8 percent in 2001 (Countrywide Financial, 2002: 2).

Countrywide entered the 2000s as a highly diversified mortgage originator, mortgage security issuer, and mortgage servicer. It was one of the main participants in the conventional market for mortgages and securities organized by the GSEs. But it also was a pioneer in the nonconventional mortgage market. The firm entered the 2000s poised to lead the industry into the largest refinancing boom in American history and the incredible expansion of the nonconventional mortgage market. Its tactics epitomized the industry and served as a role model for all of the large financial firms that were engaged in the mortgage market.

Bear Stearns: From Investment Bank to Vertically Integrated Mortgage Bank

Another of the villains of the financial crisis was Bear Stearns. The popular media came to view the investment bank as the poster child for all that had gone wrong in the financial markets (for example, see *Wall Street Journal,* 2009; At-

lantic, 2010; *Fortune*, 2008). Bear Stearns had the unfortunate honor of being the first of the big banks to stumble and fail because of its participation in the MBS market. In 2006 and 2007, it suffered large losses on its MBS-related business. In March 2008, the Federal Reserve Bank of New York provided an emergency loan to try to avert a sudden collapse of the company. The company could not be saved, however, and was sold to JPMorgan Chase. The collapse of the company proved to be a dress rehearsal for the problems of the entire banking sector in the United States and elsewhere that culminated in the global financial crisis of 2008–2009.

In the usual telling of the story, the demise of Bear Stearns is seen as a result of the risk-taking behavior of the firm, particularly its high level of debt used to fund its MBS and CDO business (Cohan, 2010). What is less well understood is how Bear Stearns transformed itself from a conventional investment bank in the 1980s to a vertically integrated bank whose main business was the production of mortgage-related financial instruments. Bear Stearns was a pioneer in the MBS market and one of the most innovative firms in the creation of new financial instruments throughout the 1980s and 1990s and into the 2000s. As a result of this creativity and the growth and profits it produced, the firm was viewed as one of the most innovative of the investment banks. For example, from 2005 to 2007, Bear Stearns was recognized as the "Most Admired" securities firm in *Fortune* magazine's annual "America's Most Admired Companies" survey (*Fortune*, 2007). This honor seems hard to square with what happened subsequently to the firm. Most observers have suggested that the firm was not really an innovator but was hiding its true nature as a firm taking outsized risks that resulted in its demise (Lowenstein, 2010; Cohan, 2010).

The truth about Bear Stearns involves understanding it as both an innovator and a risk taker. The opportunity presented by the MBS markets from the 1980s onward and its role as an innovator of products in those markets earned Bear Stearns its reputation as a most admired firm. One of the innovations that Bear Stearns decided to undertake was to secure itself a supply of mortgages by becoming a mortgage originator and wholesaler in the early 1990s. They pioneered the origination of nonconventional mortgages, including the extensive use of adjustable-rate mortgages, and used these mortgages to fuel their MBS business. By 2001, financial instruments based on mortgages had become the dominant source of profits for their business.

Another of their innovations was to massively borrow money to fund the origination of mortgages and their securities operation. It has been estimated that they had debt that was thirty-three times the amount of capital they owned when they collapsed in 2008 (Brunnermeier, 2009). Even as house prices stopped rising and home sales began to stall in 2005, Bear Stearns was under continued pressure to continue to originate mortgages to keep their securitization machine going. These pressures caused the firm to commit illegal acts of both predatory lending and securities fraud (Fligstein and Roehrkasse, 2016). When the MBS market came under scrutiny, Bear Stearns was so heavily exposed by having borrowed money to keep its vertically integrated securities pipeline going that it collapsed under its own weight.

Like Countrywide Financial, the executives at Bear Stearns did not start out to create a vertically integrated MBS business but ended up doing so because of the opportunities to earn outsize profits. Indeed, the company spent most of its existence as a more conventional investment bank. But the opportunity to participate in the MBS market after the collapse of the savings and loan industry was heavily exploited by Bear Stearns. They pioneered not just mortgage-backed securities but also other asset-backed securities. They also created a wide variety of credit debt obligation instruments and other forms of derivatives including credit default swaps. They sold these securities at home and abroad. The sheer size of the mortgage market meant that the supply of such instruments was quite large. Securitization meant that investors could buy yield and risk that fit their needs.

Bear Stearns was primarily an investment bank. This meant that its main business was in the creation, buying, and selling of financial instruments, both stocks and bonds. It came at the business of mortgages from the perspective of creating fixed-income securities and selling them to investors. Bear Stearns also traded on its own account and was thus a large investor in MBSs. During the 1990s, it saw nonconventional mortgages as an opportunity to make more money by providing bonds with higher yields. In order to guarantee itself a share of that market, it became the first investment bank to buy a mortgage originator, EMC, which originated nonconventional mortgages and participated in the wholesale market. EMC was a leader in the provision of subprime mortgages. By relying on EMC to provide it with the raw materials for securities, Bear Stearns ensured that it could supply its investors with high-yield bonds.

The paths that Countrywide Financial and Bear Stearns took to become vertically integrated are strikingly different. Countrywide Financial started as an originator and later took on the investment banking functions of issuing, underwriting, and trading securities. Bear Stearns started out as a trading firm that underwrote and issued stocks and bonds for corporations and government. But beginning in the 1980s, the growing opportunities associated with the housing market and more generally asset securitization brought the firm to change the course of its business. To make sure they had enough mortgages to package for sale into the securities markets, they eventually became an originator and wholesaler of mortgages. What observers of Bear Stearns have missed is just how complete the transformation of the company was. By 2001, Bear Stearns no longer was a conventional investment bank, but like Countrywide Financial it had become a vertically integrated producer of MBSs. Its traders sold mostly MBSs and related products. The production of those products was directed by those traders, who told the investment banking arm of the firm and the origination side what they could sell most profitably. The bank also was one of its own best customers, holding lots of MBSs, particularly for nonconventional mortgages, on its own account. It did all of this with borrowed money. As long as house values went up and mortgages were paid off, the company made large amounts of profit. But when the value of its MBS portfolio that featured so many nonconventional mortgages came under pressure, it was so highly leveraged that it was unable to borrow any more. What looked like a low risk in 2005 became a death event in 2007.

Bear Stearns was founded by Joseph Bear, Robert Stearns, and Harold Mayer on May 1, 1923 (Ryback, 2010). The firm was viewed as an outsider to Wall Street for almost all of its existence. As such, it tended to act aggressively in markets where there were new opportunities. It did not have access to vast pools of capital, so it learned to use its own capital and to mobilize other people's money. Its main business was the buying and selling of stocks, and it bought and sold on its own account as much as it did serving customers. When the Depression hit, the company shifted its main market away from the stock market and toward the trading of government debt. They were able to survive and even prosper throughout the 1930s.

In 1933, the firm hired Salim Lewis (known in the firm as "Cy") to start to build a business packaging and selling corporate bonds. At the time, there was very little business in corporate bonds because of the Depression. But Bear Stearns took one of its first gambles and invested in trying to build such a division. Lewis was a former football player from a modest background whose main business experience had been selling shoes. Lewis used the company's money to buy and sell corporate debt. During World War II, he bought a large quantity of railroad bonds whose price had fallen dramatically during the war. He borrowed money to buy these bonds and aggressively sold government war bonds to pay the interest on the money he borrowed. After the war, the value of the bonds rose dramatically, and the company profited enormously. Lewis rose in the firm because of his bet and was the managing partner of the company from 1949 to 1978. He oversaw the dramatic rise in the size and fortunes of the company.

During the 1950s, Bear Stearns pioneered several new businesses. First, Lewis began to trade large blocks of stock for large investors. A second new business was arbitrage, the tactic of buying the stock of a firm that was thought to be a merger candidate in order to profit from the rise in the share price that would occur when a bid was made. In 1949, Alan Greenberg, known as "Ace," entered the firm. He was born in Oklahoma, and his father was an entrepreneur who founded a chain of women's clothing stores in that state. Greenberg never completed college. But he wanted a chance to work on Wall Street because he liked the idea of risk taking, and he, of course, wanted to get rich. He began working on the arbitrage desk. During the 1950s and in particular during the 1960s, the mergers and acquisitions market heated up. Greenberg was a natural trader who made huge sums of money by using the firm's money to place bets on future mergers. Greenberg eventually succeeded Lewis as managing partner in 1978, and he remained in that position until 1993.

In the late 1960s, Greenberg wanted to expand the firm's retail brokerage business. Greenberg reasoned that baby boomers would start moving into their peak earning years and would have money to invest. Greenberg hired James Cayne to help start this new line of business. Cayne came from a middle-class Chicago family, where his father was a lawyer. He too never finished college, and he worked for a while in his father-in-law's scrap metal business as a salesman. Cayne was a world-class bridge player, and he began to play bridge professionally. This brought him to New York City. After realizing that earning a living playing bridge was impossible, he became a successful bond salesman at Lebenthal and Company. He then moved on to Bear Stearns. Cayne was a natural salesman who specialized in taking risks. He was extremely successful at finding and keeping individuals who had lots of money to invest. Cayne eventually became managing partner from 1993 until the firm's demise in 2008.

During the 1970s, the firm prospered by trading on its own accounts as well as those of its customers. It entered the business of "clearing trades" (i.e., settling stock trades at the end of each day). This business proved quite lucrative. Cayne made his name in the firm by buying and selling New York City municipal bonds in the 1970s. New York City was in dire financial straits in this era and almost went bankrupt. But Cayne figured out how to make a market buying such bonds at a low price and then selling them to others at a slightly higher price. Bear Stearns kept a large inventory of such bonds. When New York City's debt was refinanced, the bond bounced back in price. In essence, Cayne made money in a very similar way to how Lewis had done so during the 1940s on railroad bonds.

Not surprisingly, Bear Stearns's reputation entering the 1980s reflected the swashbuckling bet-the-firm tactics of an outsider organization that used its own money to aggressively make trades. It entered and helped create new markets. Moreover, its corporate culture emphasized results. The organization took pride in hiring people not for their academic credentials but for their willingness to work. If they failed to succeed, they left the firm. Bear Stearns was also run as a very opportunistic investment bank. They would use their own capital to enter and cultivate markets where there might be growth and the opportunity to make profits. They never had a strategy that caused them to focus on a particular set of businesses. Over time, they had developed the clearing, brokerage, and fixed-income businesses. They did so because they saw opportunity and were successful. It was this strategic openness (some might call it pragmatism) that succeeded for the firm through good and bad times. I note that this aggressive take-what-the-system-gives attitude toward one's business was akin to the way that Loeb and Mozilo ran Countrywide Financial. It was this openness that eventually led them to make the investments that led them to vertically integrate their fixed-income MBS and CDO businesses.

During the 1980s, there were several important changes in the firm. First, the firm was a leader in helping orchestrate the merger wave from 1978 to 1987. They helped many companies pursue mergers and acquisitions and were one of the leading investment banks involved in these deals. Second, in 1985, the firm moved from a partnership to a publicly held corporation. This made the partners in the firm instant millionaires. It also had the subtle effect over time of making the traders in the firm even more aggressive and likely to take on risks. Since their pay was tied to the profits from their trades and not their stakes in the investment funds of the firm, traders were more likely to engage in activities to make money quickly. The firm was no longer playing with the partners' capital when it made trades on its own account. It was playing with shareholders' money.

From my perspective, the most important change was the entry of the firm into the mortgage-related securities business. Bear Stearns created a mortgage-related securities department in 1981 with John Sites as head. They began act as underwriters for the securities produced by the GSEs. They also sold and traded those securities. Early on, they even acted as wholesalers who bought and sold pools of mortgages that had not been securitized, acting as a broker between originators and wholesalers and eventually investors. They were not at this time point involved in the origination of mortgages.

This business started small. But as with many of the firm's other businesses, Bear Stearns saw the market opportunity presented by the emergence of mortgage-backed securities and the GSEs. They observed that Salomon Brothers was making money buying mortgages from savings and loan banks on a deeply discounted basis and then turning around, creating MBSs, and selling those to investors. As the savings and loan banks unloaded their existing mortgages at low cost, Bear Stearns entered that market. When the savings and loans began to collapse and the mortgage market shifted to become the mortgage securities market dominated by the GSEs, Bear Stearns was there to act as an issuer, underwriter, and trader of GSE-backed securities. Bear Stearns also began to hold GSE bonds on their own account as an investment.

Bear Stearns helped pioneer the use of REMICs—real estate mortgage investment conduits. REMICs were the legal vehicle by which mortgages could be made into securities in the mid-1980s (*National Mortgage News*, 1986c). In 1986, they began to use REMICs to issue securities based on jumbo mortgages, mortgages that were too large for FHA standard loans (*National Mortgage News*, 1986a). They also helped pioneer securities based on other nonconventional mortgages. The securities created from mortgages began to morph into more varied products. For example, securities were produced that allowed investors to invest in the part of mortgages that paid for interest and the part paid for principal (*National Mortgage News*, 1987b). They pioneered creating securities that blended various income streams in complex ways that fit the desires of investors.

But the real growth came in the late 1980s when Bear Stearns hired Howard Rubin. Rubin had worked at Salomon Brothers for Lewis Ranieri. In 1986, the year before Rubin was hired, Bear Stearns was already the fifth-largest underwriter of MBSs (*National Mortgage News*, 1986b). Upon Rubin's arrival, the firm became the largest underwriter in the market in 1989. By the early 1990s, the mortgage market had become the single largest business at Bear Stearns (Ryback, 2010).

Bear Stearns was not the only investment bank to enter the MBS market, particularly the market to be underwriters for the GSEs. All of the other investment banks expanded into this business as part of their production of fixed-income securities. The expertise that banks like Goldman Sachs, Lehman Brothers, Salomon Brothers, Morgan Stanley, and Merrill Lynch had in issuing and underwriting corporate bonds was applied to MBSs and related products from the mid-1980s onward. The investment banks helped the GSEs make and market MBSs as the GSEs rose and the savings and loan industry collapsed. This market grew dramatically, and the investment banks helped expand the production of MBSs radically. This entry of the investment banks to underwrite mortgage securities issued by the GSEs opened the link between Wall Street and Main Street.

The financial innovation that was centered on securitization was creating a plethora of new products, and no investment bank ignored this vast and expanding market. By 1988, all of the main investment banks were competing to create and sell MBSs for the GSEs (*National Mortgage News*, 1988). But Bear Stearns was one of the clear leaders in this. By the mid-1990s, their fixed-income securities business focusing on mortgages dominated the firm in a way that few of the others, except Lehman Brothers, followed. In an earlier era, Bear Stearns had "bet the bank" on other financial products. By the mid-1990s, MBSs were their new bet. The other banks eventually followed Bear Stearns into expanding these businesses quite rapidly, particularly after 2001.

Bear Stearns was an innovator and a participant in every kind of product. They were one of the largest underwriters, and they participated in introducing a wide variety of derivatives based on MBSs. They sold these not just to institutional investors but also beginning in 1990 to retail investors (*National Mortgage News,* 1990a). It should also be noted that Bear Stearns participated in not just securitizing mortgages but all other asset classes as well. They led the way in creating securities in auto loans, credit card debt, student loans, and corporate receivables.

While most of the mortgage underwriting was done for the GSEs, Bear Stearns was also a pioneer in private label issuance. This was the business of creating securities for loans that did not meet the standards required by the GSEs for inclusion into their bonds. They were one of the two or three largest players in that market beginning in 1988 (*National Mortgage News,* 1990b). In the wake of the collapse of the savings and loan industry, the Resolution Trust Corporation was formed to liquidate the assets of the defunct banks. Many of these assets were securitized, and Bear Stearns commanded a substantial portion of the underwriting of these securities. This helped propel them in the early 1990s to a leading position in the industry.

It was this leadership in becoming an issuer that eventually pushed Bear Stearns to vertically integrate. Most of the mortgages that they were packaging into MBSs were nonconventional mortgages. It followed that in order to expand this business, they needed to have access to these mortgages. Bear Stearns established EMC in 1990 as its mortgage arm to facilitate the purchasing and servicing of mortgage loans. EMC was both an originator and a wholesaler of such mortgages. They contributed greatly to Bear Stearns's rise to the very top of the mortgage-finance industry by purchasing over $200 billion in residential whole loans and servicing rights over the next decade. EMC was able to do this by funding the purchase of mortgages by borrowing money from the repo or asset-backed commercial paper markets through the Bear Stearns parent company. This funding was typically very short term, less than ninety days, and mortgages were typically securitized within a forty-five- to ninety-day window. This created an incentive to try to create and sell the securities as quickly as possible to pay off these loans and minimize costs. It was possible to roll over the loans, but of course, that cost money.

Bear Stearns also bought a large number of these securities on its own account. Because it was an investment bank, it did not have depositors to provide it with capital. Instead, it had to borrow capital. It pioneered the tactic of borrowing money to purchase these securities for its own account. In the firm, the traders had direct authority over the securitization division and the mortgage origination and mortgage conduits. They instructed those up the pipeline what kinds of mortgages to buy and securitize. By the end of the decade, Bear Stearns, through its operating entities, was a mortgage originator, mortgage wholesaler, creator of mortgage securities, and mortgage securities trader. When it was taken over in 2007, it had about $30 billion of MBSs on its own account.

Washington Mutual's Evolution from Savings and Loan to Integrated Mortgage Bank

The path of Washington Mutual (hereafter WaMu) to becoming a vertically integrated bank was perhaps the most straightforward of our four case studies. The bank started out in the savings and loan business by taking deposits from customers and loaning many of those same customers the money to buy a house. It was very successful at doing this until the bottom fell out of the savings and loan business model in the 1970s and 1980s. In the early 1980s, the bank had good leadership that worked to raise money to help the bank find new businesses to enter. While many savings and loan banks engaged in risky businesses about which they knew very little, WaMu stuck to a relatively conservative set of investments. It stayed mostly focused on consumer lending and stayed away from commercial real estate. During the 1980s and 1990s, its main strategy of expansion was to buy other savings and loan banks who had failed in their attempts to find more lucrative investments.

WaMu aimed to become a full-service retail bank that would offer all kinds of financial services to its customers. Its vision was to become like Walmart or Costco as a supplier of insurance, retirement plans, consumer loans, credit cards, and, of course, home mortgages. But like Countrywide and Bear Stearns, the businesses it eventually found to be most lucrative were centered on mortgage financing and securitization. As it built itself out, WaMu entered the nonconventional mortgage market, bought and sold MBSs based on the mortgages it originated in that market, and held many on its own account. Eventually, it entered the investment banking business and began to issue and underwrite its own securities. It too relied on borrowed money to do much of this. While it retained its extensive retail business focused on savings accounts, credit cards, and personal loans, by 2002, it looked remarkably like both Countrywide and Bear Stearns.

Like those banks, it discovered that the market for mortgages and mortgage securitization was so large that it easily became the biggest and most profitable set of opportunities available. It had expanded across the country and was involved in the origination and securitization business everywhere.

WaMu had a long history in the city of Seattle. On June 6, 1889, the city experienced a large fire that destroyed much of the downtown area. The Washington National Building Loan and Investment Association came into existence on September 25, 1889, and began to take deposits to offer homeowners the opportunity to rebuild their homes. The company was organized as a mutual company, which means that its depositors were its owners, much like in a credit union. It made more than two thousand loans in the first twenty years of its existence. On June 25, 1908, the company changed its name to Washington Savings and Loan Association. The company stayed a mutual savings bank. It retained this structure until 1983. Before the Depression, it was the leading savings institution in Washington State. Its main activities were providing small savers with bank accounts and providing homeowners with mortgages. The depositors were the owners, and the bank worked to act in their interests.

By all accounts, it was a pretty conventional savings and loan bank during the postwar era. It was subject to Regulation Q, which set interest rates on deposits and loans. It was also restricted in the types of products it could sell and its ability to expand geographically. Its success was tied to a strong local economy. If the demand for mortgages was high and if interest rates remained relatively low, the bank prospered. It grew in the postwar era with the city of Seattle. But the same forces that began to destroy savings and loan banks all over the country in the 1970s began to impact WaMu. The high interest rates of the 1970s meant that the bank was increasingly unable to attract deposits as long as its ability to pay interest on deposits was fixed at a low rate. Similarly, it had massive numbers of mortgages as assets that had very low fixed interest rates and therefore paid small profits. Finally, because interest rates were so high during the 1970s, it mortgage business was suffering.

In 1981, Lou Pepper, a man who had been a career lawyer most of his adult life, was called on to lead the bank. While the bank had all of the problems of other savings and loans, it did have a few advantages. First, it had a good reputation in the Pacific Northwest as a bank that treated its customers fairly and gave good service. Second, it had more than $1 billion in assets, which made it one of the largest savings and loan banks in the country. Pepper worked diligently to cut costs and managed to keep the bank stable in the early 1980s. One of his most important moves was to reorganize the bank as a savings and loan bank that was a publicly held corporation (*American Banker*, 1983). This change allowed the bank to raise money in the public markets in order to keep it afloat. It also gave the bank a new set of opportunities that were just opening up for the savings and loan industry.

As a result of its crisis, the industry had persuaded Congress to pass deregulatory legislation that encouraged savings and loan banks to act more aggressively and take on more risk in order to insure their futures. Regulation Q had been abolished, and depository insurance had risen to $100,000 per account. Savings and loan banks were free to invest in any kind of financial investment including junk bonds, derivatives, and commercial real estate. Most of the banks that entered these riskier businesses failed. WaMu was an exception to this rule (*American Banker*, 1983). Instead, the bank pursued a more prudent course to cut its costs, realign its assets to reflect the high-interest-rate environment, and begin to offer its customers more financial products such as mutual funds and consumer loans along with its traditional home loan business.

Pepper turned out to be an excellent manager. By reorganizing the bank, he got himself access to more credit and the ability to expand his lines of business. But because he lacked any expertise in banking, he felt it was important to hire people who had relevant expertise to help him decide how to organize the activities of the bank and which opportunities to try to enter. He began to hire a team of executives who would lead the bank into its future. His two most important hires were William Longbrake and Kerry Killinger. Longbrake had been working at the Office of the Comptroller in Washington, DC. He became the head of finance at WaMu and was long considered a possible CEO successor to Pepper (*American Banker*, 1982a). Killinger was working for a securities brokerage called Murphey Favre, which was located in Spokane, Washington. The firm, as old as WaMu, had assets across the state. It sold a wide variety of securities including mutual funds and bonds. Killinger proposed to Pepper that the firms merge. The merger was announced in 1982 (*American Banker*, 1982b). Pepper agreed, but only on the condition that Killinger come to work at WaMu.

By 1987, WaMu was in the business of not only taking deposits from customers and selling mortgages but also selling other financial services to retail customers. They offered stocks and mutual funds; life, health, and property/casualty insurance; travel services; pension and actuarial service; and traditional banking services such as savings and checking accounts. Nonbanking business accounted for 14 percent of the bank's profits (*National Mortgage News*, 1987a). The company's profits grew dramatically, and its assets reached $5.6 billion.

Because WaMu was focused on the individual customer, it realized that in order to succeed, it needed to provide services in such a way that people would trust the bank. As financial products grew more complex, establishing and keeping this trust was part of the WaMu brand. For example, WaMu joined many banks in the 1970s and 1980s by introducing adjustable-rate mortgages. When interest rates were high, these products allowed banks to offer lower mortgage rates that would adjust over time with national interest rates. WaMu offered a customer-friendly version of this product. They fixed the adjustment of the loan at not more than 2 percent over its lifetime. They also gave customers the unusual option of changing to a fixed-rate loan without going through refinancing.

Pepper worked hard to create a corporate culture that reflected his view of how customers needed to be treated. He created a committee to come up with corporate goals and values. The committee agreed that the firm should serve customers, workers, community, and shareholders equally. It also proposed that the firm would value ethics, respect, teamwork, innovation, and excellence. While this seems like so much corporate hype, Pepper got buy-in from many employees who saw that the firm was a good place to work and one where nice guys did not finish last. In 1986, Pepper began to consider his retirement. He considered selling the bank to another bank. But he eventually decided to stay on as CEO and president. Killinger and Longbrake ran the bank in tandem for over a year. But in 1988, Pepper decided to retire, and Killinger was named president and, a year later, CEO and chairman of the board.

By the mid-1980s, the financial crisis of the savings and loan industry was in full swing. Savings and loan banks were failing all over the country. With deregulation, many of them had made risky investments, and many of those investments had failed. WaMu was one of the few of the large savings and loan banks to be in good financial condition. During this period, WaMu was profitable but not hugely so. Killinger announced a set of goals for the firm that implied making profitability the most important goal. He promised a 1 percent return on assets and a 15 percent return on equity in the nonfinancial services part of the business within two years. He also promised to cut back on unprofitable diversification and to focus on the consumer markets (*National Mortgage News*, 1989b).

To do this, Killinger did two things. First, he decided to cut back on some of the businesses that they had entered, such as insurance. Instead, he wanted to focus on three areas: residential lending, a full range of deposit offerings for retail customers, and sales of mutual funds, and tax-deferred annuities. Second, he intended to roll this out on a national scale (*National Mortgage News*, 1989a). In the next fifteen years, he did both of these things. Killinger oversaw the growth of WaMu to being one of the largest savings and loan banks in the country. He did this mostly by buying banks, many of which were failing.

In his first two years, Killinger bought eight small banks, adding close to $1 billion in assets. He doubled the size of the company and expanded its operations from Washington State to Oregon (*National Mortgage News,* 1991a). This rapid growth was reflected in the huge increase in the stock price. The *National Mortgage News* reported that the stock price of the bank had increased by 178 percent in 1991 (*National Mortgage News,* 1992). That same article reported that Killinger had attained his 1 percent return on assets and had a 13.7 percent return on nonfinancial equity close to his goals. The article concluded that this occurred because "the bank has de-emphasized commercial real estate lending, decreased the wholesale investment portfolio, and sold off businesses which did not meet corporate objectives of high returns, short lead time, and minimal corporate resources."

During the 1990s, WaMu engaged in several forms of product diversification. On the retail side, they expanded into offering checking accounts for customers and developed a large consumer credit business. In 1996, they bought two commercial banks in order to make loans to businesses. The bank was also expanding in servicing existing home and consumer loans. By 1996, they were servicing almost three hundred thousand loans with a value of $19.2 billion (*National Mortgage News,* 1997a). But their core business remained home loan origination. In 1996, they were the leading mortgage originator in Washington and Oregon (*National Mortgage News,* 1997b).

Killinger continued to absorb larger and larger banks. The big moment for the company came in 1997 when it entered into the bidding against Ahmanson (the largest savings and loan in the country, which operated under the name of Home Savings in California) for Great Western, then the second-largest savings and loan bank in the country. After a long campaign, they were able to buy the company. This purchase produced a foothold in California. It also made WaMu the biggest savings and loan bank in the country.

Even as WaMu was absorbing Great Western into its system, the CEO of Ahmanson, Charles Rhinehart, decided to offer WaMu the opportunity to buy his bank. Rhinehart believed that size was going to be the key to success in the banking business. Since WaMu had taken over the obvious target for Ahmanson, it made sense to join forces with WaMu. Rhinehart reasoned that getting bigger was the key to a successful bank. The merger with Ahmanson not only solidified WaMu's position as the largest savings and loan bank in the country, it made it the seventh-largest financial institution in the United States. It had more than two thousand branches and thirty thousand employees. When Pepper stepped down in 1988, the company had $7 billion in assets. After the merger with Ahmanson in 1998, WaMu had $150 billion.

The bank continued its pattern of buying banks across the country. It bought assets in Boston, Salt Lake City, Miami, and Texas and continued to purchase banks in California. It also continued to diversify its product lines. The bank began to purchase subprime lenders. It bought Long Beach Financial, one of the largest subprime lenders, in 1999 (*National Mortgage News*, 1999). This introduced it to the securitization business. In 2001, WaMu bought the assets of Fleet Bank. This acquisition allowed it to be number one in mortgage originations in the country and number two in servicing (*American Banker*, 2001). Later in the year, it bought Dime Bank, an NYC-based bank that gave WaMu access to that market for home loans and consumer checking accounts. The lowering of interest rates propelled the wave of refinancing of mortgages. WaMu was well positioned to take advantage and produced high growth and large profits. WaMu bought an investment bank in 2002 and began to underwrite its own securities. Like the other banks, WaMu used credit to buy some of these securities for its own account. By 2002, the bank had a more or less integrated pipeline that originated both prime and subprime mortgages, packaged them into securities, sold those securities to investors, and invested in some of those securities on its own account.

Killinger wanted to continue the growth of the bank. During the refinancing boom of 2001–2003, the bank worked hard to grow its market share and fully participate. It also continued to expand its nonconventional mortgage business. WaMu continuously ran an ad campaign focused on the theme of "The Power of Yes." Their basic message was that their goal was to work hard to approve anyone who wanted some kind of loan. The product that proved particularly attractive in this regard was called the option adjustable-rate mortgage, otherwise known as the option ARM. This product allowed borrowers to choose their payments every month. They could pay the full amount due, they could pay just the interest in a given month and not the principal, or they could choose to pay some fraction of the interest due. This last option meant that the interest not paid would be added to the mortgage total, resulting in a person owing more money than they did in the past month. This was called negative amortization. After five years, the loan would readjust, and the borrower would have to pay a fixed payment. This product sold well, but it became a ticking time bomb that eventually helped bring the company down (a story to be told later).

Between 1989 and 1999, WaMu became the largest producer of mortgages in the country. It did so mainly through an aggressive program of acquisitions of other banks. In the failing savings and loan industry and in the context of bank deregulation, WaMu gobbled up competitors across the country. It was able to do so because of its diversified product base and, ironically, its prudent lending practices. Its CEO, Kerry Killinger, and his executive team were adept at buying and integrating banks of all sizes. They successfully cut costs at banks they bought and added their assets to the company. They were able to meet their profit goals, which were ambitious. This, in turn, raised the stock price, which allowed further acquisitions.

Underneath this spectacular growth was an increasing reliance on mortgage lending as the core business. Although WaMu had a substantial consumer business centered on savings, checking, personal loans, and financial products, the mortgage business was so large that it generally provided the largest growth prospects and the largest profits. WaMu was aggressive in entering the nonconventional loan markets, particularly subprime but also home equity loans. They used adjustable-rate mortgages strategically and provided option ARMs to buyers who were less able to afford house payments. They also were active producers of securities based on these mortgages and held large numbers on their books. Finally, WaMu actively worked to be the largest loan servicer in the country as well.

As a result, by 2002, their business model for success had produced rapid growth for the bank. That growth reflected the rapidly reorganized mortgage business that emphasized mortgage securitization and nonconventional mortgages. The rapid growth of the company made it one of the industry leaders along with Countrywide Financial.

The Strange Transformation of Citibank

The case of Citibank is perhaps the most interesting transformation of the four banks. Indeed, its transformation was so subtle that two of the most popular trade books written about the company barely mention the mortgage business and how it had become core to the firm (Zweig, 1995; Stone and Brewster, 2002). Citibank was one of the oldest and largest banks in the United States. Its main business for much of its existence was being a commercial bank. This meant that historically it was a lender and banker for all kinds of businesses. In the 1960s and 1970s, it began an aggressive expansion overseas. This was partly to help its multinational corporation customer base manage their far-flung operations, but it also was oriented toward lending money to governments in the developing world. It was only in the late 1970s and early 1980s that the bank built a substantial consumer business. At the core of that business was a rapid expansion of credit cards. Its CEO at the time, Walter Wriston, was one of the earliest proponents of the idea that Citibank would become a globalized conglomerate bank (Johnston and Madura, 2005). He wanted to enter the investment banking business and the insurance business and expand its consumer business, and he wanted to own and operate these businesses across the developed and developing world.

Wriston championed financial deregulation and pushed constantly to have the government allow banks to expand geographically and diversify their products. Indeed, Citibank was one of the main drivers behind the removal of regulatory barriers. One of the reasons that it was so aggressive in its overseas expansion is that there were fewer rules governing its products. In the 1990s, Citibank was one of the leading banks that worked to have the Glass-Steagall Act repealed. That act, passed during the Great Depression, made it illegal for banks to be both investment banks and commercial banks. The separation had been eroding for almost fifteen years by the time it was repealed. The Federal Reserve formally allowed commercial banks to enter investment banking as long as it consisted of only 25 percent of their business. Citibank gambled that in the late 1990s, Congress would willingly remove the act formally. They engaged in a merger between Traveler's Insurance and Citibank, which was an illegal merger from the point of view of Glass-Steagall. Citibank, with the help of the top officials of the Clinton administration and a willing Congress, got their wish. The Gramm-Leach-Bliley Act was passed in 1999, removing the final barrier between investment and commercial banks (Lown et al., 2000; Barth et al., 2000).

Citibank was also a relative latecomer to the mortgage business. That business was not viewed as important to the growth of the firm, although it first entered the business in the 1980s. But beginning in the 1990s, Citibank began to rapidly expand its mortgage lending. It also became a central player in mortgage securitization and mortgage servicing. By the late 1990s, it had entered the unconventional loan markets. It held a large portfolio of MBSs funded by borrowed money. Like the other banks we have discussed, Citibank built a vertically integrated silo to house its housing activities. That part of the bank was eventually made into a division of the bank called CitiFinancial and a wholly owned subsidiary, CitiMortgage. The activities associated with mortgage securitization were so fundamental to the financial well-being of the bank that when the financial crisis hit, Citibank was one of the major banks at the center of the meltdown. Without the bailout by the government, Citibank would have gone bankrupt.

The curious thing is that if you read Citibank's 10-Ks or annual reports from this era, you would never realize how deeply the bank was dependent on the mortgage industry. The bank's self-presentation was as a global, conglomerate bank that considered all parts of the banking business relevant to its mission. But this self-presentation hid the fact that the largest and most lucrative business during the 1990s and the 2000s for the bank was in the origination, securitization, buying, and selling of MBSs. The purpose of this section is to unwrap how and why that was.

Citibank's massive involvement with the mortgage securitization industry reflected both a set of crises and an opportunity. The commercial banking business was in decline from the mid-1960s onward. Large corporations, the bread and butter of Citibank's business, increasingly moved away from borrowing at commercial banks and instead moved toward using the commercial paper markets for their borrowing needs. This decline accelerated during the 1970s and 1980s, and Citibank responded by looking for other businesses. It was this crisis that pushed them toward massive international expansion and entry into consumer lending. In the 1980s and early 1990s, the international economic situation made Citibank's position even more tenuous. By the early 1990s, Citibank's core businesses, except consumer lending and credit cards, were floundering.

The opportunity that presented itself to the company was the mortgage market. The collapse of the savings and loan banks and the emergence of the mortgage securitization market provided Citibank an opportunity to enter into a lucrative business based on fees. This was the growth opportunity par excellence in this historic period, and Citibank embraced it despite its seeming indifference to the idea. Moreover, mortgage securitization became Citibank's entrance to investment banking. It also discovered, like other banks, that mortgage securities were excellent investments that paid high returns and could be held using borrowed money. Citibank was not the only commercial bank to discover mortgage securitization. Other large commercial banks such as Bank of America, Chase, and J.P. Morgan entered the industry as well. Unpacking how this happened requires delving into how Citibank altered its banking strategy over time.

The original Citibank was the de facto successor to the Bank of the United States that was chartered in 1812. Throughout the nineteenth century, the bank, then called City Bank, had a series of ups and downs that followed closely the constant financial bubbles and panics. It operated mostly as a private merchant bank. This meant that it combined the activities of stock ownership and loans to command control over not just the financial sector but also the industrial sector. In 1895, City Bank was chartered as a national bank following the passage of the National Currency Act of 1863 and the National Bank Act of 1864. This legislation helped unify the US currency around the dollar and paved the way for the growth of banks. The bank, renamed National City Bank, became one of the most successful banks in New York and the entire country.

In 1881, James Stillman became president of the bank. Stillman was good friends of the Rockefellers, and with their support, he helped make the bank the most important one in New York City. The deposits of Standard Oil provided the bank with the liquidity it needed to pick and choose to whom it made investments. It took on the best customers (i.e., those with deep pockets and growing businesses) and took equity positions and made loans to help grow businesses.

In 1893, there was a financial panic, which ushered in the depression of the 1890s. This downturn had a profoundly negative effect on the railroads in the United States, at the time the largest industry in the country. Essentially, all of the railroads went bankrupt. National City Bank was at the center of a group of men (Stillman, William Rockefeller, Edward Harriman, and Jacob Schiff) who eventually took over the Union Pacific Railroad. They also took over the Chicago, Burlington, and Quincy Railroad and ended up controlling half of the US railroad system. At the same time, there grew up a competitor to challenge them. J.P. Morgan threw in with James Hill and George Baker, head of the First National Bank, to buy the Great Northern Railroad and Northern Pacific. These two groups were part and parcel of the politics of the early twentieth century, which focused on their roles in the creation of large corporate interests called "trusts" that came to dominate the American economy. Large parts of the American economy were controlled either directly or indirectly through the large New York banks.

But National City Bank was not just involved in the business of owning and lending to corporations. Stillman worked hard to establish National City Bank as a worldwide institution. They played an important role in overseas banking, financing exports, and importing, buying, and selling foreign exchange. In 1897, the bank consolidated all of its foreign business into a single business unit. It claimed to be able to move money anywhere in the world within twenty-four hours. The bank also became central in operating as a depository and trader for US Treasury bonds. In 1906, the company moved into foreign lending to corporations but mainly to governments. They started their long association with Latin American companies and governments. In 1908, Frank Vanderlip took over as president of the bank.

During the panic of 1907, National City Bank threw in with J.P. Morgan to save the financial system. This led to two important outcomes. First, populist forces called for an investigation of the so-called money trusts. The Pujo hearings documented the concentration of ownership and control of the Morgan interests and the group centered on National City. While these hearings never produced a legislative outcome, they did promote a national political discussion about stabilizing the financial system by creating a federal organization. In 1913, President Woodrow Wilson signed into law the Federal Reserve Act to establish such an organization.

In the next ten years, National City Bank increased its presence in foreign markets. In particular, it began to lend a lot of money in Cuba. During the Depression, these loans went bad, and the bank almost went under. More telling was National City's involvement in the stock market run-up that eventually led to the crash of 1929. National City's role in being both an investment and a commercial bank was a major part of the impetus toward the Glass-Steagall Act. The 1930s produced extensive regulation of all parts of the banking system. The Federal Reserve gained oversight over commercial banks with the Banking Act of 1933. By the end of the Depression, National City Bank was forced to find less risky businesses. However, the Second World War forced it to close almost of its branches in Asia and Europe (except London). By the end of the war, of its $5.6 billion in assets, $2.9 billion was in government bonds and $1.25 billion in government loans.

The postwar era was dominated by highly regulated banks. Savings and loan banks, commercial banks, and investment banks each had their own rules, regulators, and statewide or regional footprints. No commercial bank was involved in investment banking or even much retail banking. But in general, these regulations produced a stable banking system. The constant systemic financial meltdowns of the previous one hundred years ended. While particular banks still had crises, the whole system was stable from the mid-1930s until the late 1970s. The real opportunity right after the war for commercial banks was to resume lending to corporations. National City Bank led the way by going from having 70 percent of its loans to the government in 1946 to almost 65 percent loaned to businesses by 1956. The economic recovery brought National City to underwrite expansion in the shipping, airline, and automobile industries. National City was a leading lender to the rejuvenated multinational corporations. By the end of the war, the bank's presence overseas had dropped dramatically. But beginning in the mid-1950s, the bank began to restore its international businesses.

Citibank was organized into two main divisions at this point, the commercial credit division and the international division. The commercial credit division was also organized around industries, reflecting the need for bankers to have some expertise in what their customers were doing. The international division was organized on a geographic basis. In the mid-1950s, the bank almost closed down its international division. The war had devastated the bank's branches everywhere. The overseas expansion was undertaken by George Moore and his protégé Walter Wriston. Their strategy was to go anywhere in the world and offer whatever banking service they could. Their idea was that in the postwar era, world trade would expand dramatically, and that would require a rapid expansion of banking services. They decided to try to enter every major commercial center in the world.

They did so by engaging in several new organizational strategies. First, they decided to give bankers on the ground wide latitude in terms of the kinds of things they could approve for loans. Second, they worked to hire the best and brightest people to run these new banking centers. This was a radical departure for the bank in that previously its overseas posts had been under little pressure to produce profits. They were often staffed by second-tier employees. Moore and Wriston wanted smart people who would be opportunistic and take advantage of whatever investments would come their way. Many of these investments never worked out. One can argue that National City's aggressive overseas moves were important to the organization mostly because they reflected a shift in the organizational culture from one that was highly risk averse to one that embraced innovation and risk. By 1965, the overseas division had 177 offices in 58 countries. Both Moore and Wriston would ride the expansion of National City's international banking to the top of National City's executive ranks. Moore would become CEO in 1967.

By the mid-1960s, the bank had a sprawling, disorganized structure. They lacked enough financial controls to tell where and if they made profit. They had barely entered the modern age of computers. Then, Wriston hired John Reed. Reed eventually modernized the computing and accounting system of the bank. In doing so, he laid the foundations for the bank to be able to not only monitor its far-flung activities but engage in massive numbers of commercial and consumer transactions. He created a management information system that allowed the bank to decide how every one of its offices were producing returns on capital.

Wriston became CEO in 1970, and he served until 1984. In 1976, he changed the name of the bank to Citibank. One of Wriston's important goals was to increase the size and profitability of the bank by entering new businesses. He was one of the first bankers to push for the deregulation of banks. He lobbied against Regulation Q, regulations that prohibited interstate banking, and regulations that kept commercial banks from entering other kinds of financial services including mutual funds, investment banking, and insurance. Wriston also pushed the limits of what the law and regulators saw as the boundaries between businesses. His fights with Congress and regulators went on for his entire term. In essence, Wriston wanted there to be conglomerate banking. He wanted Citibank to be the pioneer in this.

During the 1970s, Citibank began to take the consumer market more seriously. The bank had for decades sold loans to individuals and offered checking and savings accounts. But this was never a large part of their business. Most of this business was in New York. What pushed them toward this expansion of services was their realization that the commercial market for loans to corporations had declined. During the 1960s and 1970s, corporations began to go to the financial markets directly to raise capital. This meant that banks were losing some of their biggest customers. The international business was subject to the ups and downs of both the world economy and, in many cases, the political vagaries of particular countries. Wriston and Reed began to see the consumer market as very large and possibly a source of good growth.

Reed proposed that the way to enter that market was through the rapid expansion of credit cards. His ambition was to expand Citibank's presence in national banking by rolling the card out across the country. This process took many years and had many dead ends. The high inflation and slow economic growth of the 1970s and early 1980s made it hard to make money on consumer loans and credit cards. With interest rates above 10 percent, there were few consumers who could afford to borrow. Moreover, given the cost of capital, giving consumers any kind of loan, secured or unsecured, was an unprofitable decision. The only way the business could grow was if interest rate ceilings were removed. Regulation Q had limited how much interest could be charge on these types of loans. When it was abolished, state laws on usury still made it unprofitable to issue credit cards.

Reed tried to get New York State to get rid of their usury laws. The State balked, and Reed was approached by South Dakota. That state was willing to suspend its usury laws in exchange for Citibank to move its credit card business there. In the end, Reed tried to play the two states against one another. New York State refused to change its law. So, Citibank moved its credit card center to South Dakota. The 1980s also witnessed a relaxation of rules of interstate bank ownership. Citibank expanded its consumer business across the country through mergers and through starting branches in states that would allow it. As the decade went on, Citibank began to explore other markets. It entered the mortgage market in a serious way beginning in 1981. It also began to enter the market for other financial products such as mutual funds and stocks. It toyed with the idea of selling insurance through its branches.

Reed became CEO in 1984. The bank was already in many ways a protoconglomerate. Its activities were far flung and produced many financial products for many markets. However, the late 1980s and early 1990s saw a continued deterioration in the commercial banking business. It was also a time when the international business underwent a series of scandals whereby the bank lost a great deal of money. But Reed managed to turn the bank around by ridding it of unprofitable businesses, investing in technology, and expanding the consumer market, particularly by rapidly expanding the mortgage business. In 1991, Citibank lost $457 million; in 1997, it had turned things around to earn $3.5 billion.

The company merged with Traveler's Insurance in 1998. Traveler's was led by Sandy Weill. Weill had been very active in building many financial firms. He, too, had the vision to create a financial conglomerate. The bringing together of Traveler's and Citibank meant the creation of a financial services firm that covered most of the main markets for banks. The firm had added a large capacity for investment banking in the merger as well as an insurance company. In 1999, the Congress passed the Gramm-Leach-Bliley bill to repeal Glass-Steagall. Citibank, which had promoted the financial conglomerate model since the 1970s, had finally attained that goal and become the world's largest and most complex bank. Weill and Reed shared the CEO job for two years, but eventually Weill took over. His main strategy was to engage in a series of mergers and acquisitions in order to complete Citibank's transformation and to make it even more profitable.

It is useful to understand how Citibank became so centrally involved in the mortgage industry. Most of our accounts of the rise of the bank focus on its efforts to be international and to be diversified. Yet by the early 2000s, in spite of becoming a financial conglomerate, the bank was growing most rapidly in the business of mortgages and mortgage securitization. Like the other banks we have discussed, the mortgage business proved to be quite large, generated massive fees, and was an industry that utilized investment banking services. The opportunities it presented fit well with a bank that had spent its entire history aggressively investing in whatever seemed to be the brand-new thing.

The selling of mortgages was always part of Citibank's consumer business. During the 1980s, the bank also began to participate in the mortgage securitization business. One of its main forays into investment banking was in the production of MBSs (*American Banker,* 1988). The bank underwent a financial crisis in the late 1980s. As a result, it cut back dramatically on its participation in all aspects of the mortgage market. But beginning in 1994, Citibank began to rebuild its mortgage presence (*National Mortgage News,* 1994a). By the mid-1990s, the bank had resumed mortgage lending to its customers and began to rebuild its MBS business. It also sold MBSs and held large amounts on its balance sheets as investments.

Because Citibank was so diversified in terms of the market segments it had entered, it was already a participant in originating, securitizing, trading, buying, and servicing mortgages. From the perspective of the 1990s, these businesses were spread across the divisions of the company. For example, in its annual report for 1996, Citibank reported making $9.8 billion in mortgage loans in its consumer division (Citibank *Annual Report,* 1996: 41). They securitized $2.6 billion in mortgage loans in their mortgage division. At the end of the year, they had a little over $1 billion in inventory of MBSs to sell (1996: 59). They also report having $23.4 billion in mortgages as investments in their investment division, of which $4 billion were GSE MBSs and $3.2 billion were private-label MBSs (1996: 58). They collected $2.2 billion in servicing fees for mortgages in their mortgage division (1996: 45).

When Citibank was merged with Traveler's Insurance, the mortgage business became subsumed in a new financial institution now called Citigroup that had a large insurance company and a huge brokerage business alongside its large international commercial banking business and all of its consumer businesses (checking accounts, credit cards, and personal and mortgage loans). In a book about Sandy Weill and the merger, Stone and Brewster conclude, "The truth is that Citigroup, under Weill, is so well diversified that there seems to be little chance of it running into crippling financial problems. Few companies in the world can boast such geographic diversification, coupled with strengths across disparate businesses. Crises that have buffeted the bank in the past—bad real estate loans, poor bets on technology, emerging market difficulties—would hardly put a dent in today's Citigroup" (2002: 218).

Obviously, these authors were wrong. The bank became more dependent on the mortgage business for so much of its activity, that without government help it was close to collapse in 2008. How can we square the idea that Citibank was so diversified with the reality of the vulnerability of the bank when the collapse happened? Citibank had already built businesses around all of the segments of the mortgage securitization industry by 1996. Like the other firms that followed the opportunities presented by the huge expansion of the industry from the late 1990s until its collapse in 2008, Citibank's various divisions came to focus their attention on the mortgage market. It recognized this when it created a division called CitiFinancial and its wholly owned subsidiary, CitiMortgage, to deal with the origination and securitization of mortgages in 1999. In the 1990s, that market was between $500 billion and $1.5 trillion. But from 2000 to 2003, the market rose to almost $4 trillion and stayed at over $2.5 trillion until the collapse began in 2008. This meant that the opportunities for growth and profits for Citibank's investment banking, consumer banking, and even international banking business became focused on the production and sale of MBSs.

It is useful to see how important Citibank was in those businesses by using tables generated by Inside Mortgage Finance (2009). In 1996, Citibank was only the twenty-first largest mortgage originator in the country. In 2007, it was the fourth largest and produced almost $200 billion in mortgages, which was almost an 8.7 percent market share. Not surprisingly, Citibank was the fourth-largest producer of MBSs in 2007. In 1996, Citibank was seventeenth in mortgage servicing. In 2007, it had risen to third in the ranks with $899 billion under management and an 8.1 percent market share. Citibank was only the twenty-first largest holder of all forms of MBS in 1996. It was fourth in 2007. Citibank owned $58.8 billion of GSE MBSs and $40.8 billion of nonconventional MBSs, making it the fourth-largest holder of these securities in 2007. This explosive growth in the mortgage securitization industry was the impetus to lead the bank to expand its activities in that direction dramatically. The collapse of that industry made the bank vulnerable when that market turned down.

Conclusion

The case studies of Countrywide Financial, Bear Stearns, Washington Mutual, and Citibank show clearly the convergence of mortgage, investment, savings and loan, and commercial banks on the model of vertically integrating their production of mortgages and securities. These firms represent ideal types in their categories in the sense that they were leaders for other banks and provided examples of how money could be made at all parts of the process. They benefited from the financial deregulation that removed interest rate ceilings, made national banking possible, and broke down the barriers between banking businesses. Arguably, all of these banks, except Bear Stearns, tried to represent universal or conglomerate banks. They used that rationale in their interactions with regulators and supported changing rules to make it easier for financial institutions to enter into one another's business.

The collapse of the savings and loan model of providing mortgages and its replacement with the mortgage securitization industry provided the opportunity to make massive amounts of money off of all phases of the mortgage securitization process. The managers of all of these firms saw these opportunities and grabbed them. They saw the fee-generating capacity of the business as quite lucrative. They found the production and sale of MBSs to be profitable precisely because investors become convinced that the products were relatively safe and paid high returns. Indeed, these financial institutions came to see that not only were these products great for customers, but they were great to hold as investments. By 2001, all of these banks were committed to being in all of these businesses because they could make money at every phase of the process.

4

FINANCIAL INNOVATION AND THE
ALPHABET SOUP OF FINANCIAL PRODUCTS

Most people think of innovation in the economy as being fundamentally about the production of new products. But innovation requires not just products but also new kinds of organizations and new processes that allow new products to be produced, marketed, and regulated (Engelen et al., 2010). Government is frequently there in a number of roles at the birth of a new set of markets or as a contributor and regulator in existing markets. There are two kinds of market innovations: piecemeal and revolutionary (Christensen, 1997). In established markets, firms can produce new products related to those that exist in order to maintain competitive advantage and secure their position. These kinds of innovations may entail new production processes and the emergence of new organizations. But generally, they are additions to what is going on and not a source of major disruption to incumbents. In entirely new markets, the process of creating products, processes, and organization all need to occur. This massive process of innovation attracts the most attention because of its sweeping character. It is these seemingly earth-shattering market innovations that rivet us to the dynamics of capitalism.

In the case of mortgage finance, we have seen both sorts of innovations. The collapse of the banking system during the Depression of the 1930s created the opportunity for an entirely different kind of mortgage market with the assistance of the government. The crisis of the 1970s brought about changes in the rules in the market and a new set of products. These changes were favored by the incumbent savings and loan banks and agreed to by the government. When these changes did not work out and the entire industry cratered, it was swept away by a whole new way of doing mortgages, mortgage securitization. This innovation required a couple of waves of change beginning with the emergence of the GSEs in the late 1980s and later the vertically integrated private banks in the 1990s.

The innovations to create mortgage securitization were breathtaking. They required whole new kinds of organizations (the GSEs and later the vertically integrated banks), whole new sets of regulations and regulators, the linking of disparate markets that came to supply inputs in the process of producing mortgage securities, the creation of a huge number of new processes to originate mortgages and turn them into securities, and a plethora of new financial products, both new kinds of mortgages and new kinds of securities and other financial instruments, the output of all of this innovation. All of this was part and parcel of what financial economists saw as a massive wave of financial innovation in the 1980s. At the core of this wave was the process of securitization. Not all financial innovation was restricted to the mortgage securitization industry, but a huge amount of it was.

In the world of 1975, there was only a single kind of mortgage product, the thirty-year fixed-rate mortgage with a 20 percent down payment, which is called the conventional or prime mortgage. This product was embedded in a set of organizations and processes that had been financial innovations when they were set up in the Great Depression of the 1930s in order to resuscitate the mortgage market. The conventional mortgage was invented by the Federal Housing Administration. The savings and loan industry was built up around this product.

But the production of conventional mortgages required a set of supporting institutions and processes. The business model of the savings and loan industry relied on local funding to support their granting of conventional mortgages. The banks were able to take deposits at a fixed interest rate from local savers, loan them long term in the local community at a higher fixed interest rate, and make money by holding on to the mortgages they issued. The FDIC and the FSLIC acted to insure the stability of individual banks and prevent cutthroat competition by not allowing banks to compete over deposits or loans. This set of financial innovations served the public well for over thirty years.

But the bad economic times that began in the late 1960s and accelerated in the 1970s undermined all of the Depression-era market innovations. By 1980, the government became convinced by the financial services industry that its survival depended on changing the models inherited from the Great Depression. Through a set of regulatory changes, the 1980s was the most sustained period of financial innovation since the 1930s, and much of that innovation centered on the emergence of the mortgage securitization industry (Frame and White, 2012; Greenwood and Scharfstein, 2013). These opportunities created an avalanche of new products, which themselves required new processes to produce, and the rise of new forms of organization. I have already described the rise of the GSE and the emergence of the vertically integrated financial institution focused on the origination of mortgages and the production of mortgage securities. In this chapter, I take up in more detail the nature of these new products and the myriad processes necessary to produce them. Many of these innovations were entirely new. Some built on what already existed but was repurposed to new uses to support the mortgage securitization model.

The shift to the mortgage securitization model reconfigured who was a player in the mortgage industry and also retooled the government's role in the market. The GSEs took up the role of coordinating the market and finding private capital to fund mortgages. The banks that participated in this reorganized market were drawn from all parts of what had previously been a segregated banking market. Investment banks, commercial banks, and new forms of mortgage banks all were attracted to the market built around mortgage-backed securities because it was so large, presented many opportunities to earn lucrative fees, produced massive numbers of financial instruments that produced excellent returns for the riskiness of the bonds, and thereby had the potential of large profits.

This massive shift in the organization of the mortgage market was accompanied by a more general deregulation of the financial system. The barriers between the types of banks eroded both across states and across functional types. Politicians and regulators bought into the idea that banks should be bigger and more diversified in order to be more efficient. The largest banks, such as Citibank, led a political campaign to push this process along. To preserve their privileges, politicians who had previously been under the sway of local and statewide banks, particularly savings and loan banks, ultimately bought into the logic of bank deregulation when the savings and loan industry began to tank.

This era of financial deregulation ushered in all sorts of financial product innovation. Deregulation allowed banks of all kinds to search out new products and processes and create new forms of organizations in order to deal with the 1970s crisis of high inflation and high interest rates. The crisis affected not just the savings and loans but the business models of commercial and investment banks as well. For the savings and loan banks, the issue was, how would they find capital to make house loans if interest rates on savings accounts were low and fixed? Equally important, how would households afford mortgages if interest rates produced very high monthly payments? With high interest rates, businesses turned from using their local commercial banks for capital to either generating their funds internally or going to the broader credit markets for cheaper rates and less meddling. This created an existential crisis for commercial banks, whose main line of business was threatened (Davis and Mizruchi, 1999). Who would commercial banks loan to, and how would they make money? With the stock market in the doldrums in the 1970s, investment banks too were experiencing some chaotic times. They were on the lookout for new products and markets that would rely on their ability to create and sell debt instruments.

The crisis in banking produced three sorts of innovations. First, new products would be needed to attract both investors and borrowers. In the case of mortgages, borrowers were offered a plethora of new types of mortgages, including adjustable-rate mortgages (ARM), mortgages with smaller down payments, jumbo loans, mortgages with both shorter and longer terms, home equity loans, and mortgages for households with less-than-stellar credit (what became subprime mortgages).

But the most important product innovation was securitization (Carruthers and Stinchombe, 1999; Carruthers, 2010). By taking loans and turning them into bonds, banks could break up and spread different kinds of financial risk and return tailored to the needs of particular customers. These bonds were then rated by the ratings firms to provide information about their relative riskiness. Given the size of the market, ratings firms innovated models to provide these rankings and their rapid use to do the ratings. For those who needed safety more than return, AAA-rated securities were paramount. Lower-rated securities provided assets for those who could afford to hold riskier assets and get higher rates of returns. Banks used securitization to spread risk and found new classes of buyers for their securities.

Second, new industrial processes needed to be developed to deal with these new products. By industrial, I mean that in order to scale up to service the potential size and complexity of the mortgage market, there needed to be large-scale methods of processing mortgages, first in origination, then into securities, and finally into portfolios of those who would hold them. The industrial production of mortgages required creating new software systems to aid the processing of mortgage applications and the creation of securities by the tranching of bonds. It also required a new set of legal devices to house financial products and systems to create them and keep track of them. The mortgage servicing industry grew large and depended on computer power.

The provider of capital for these mortgages changed as well. Instead of small savers who had passbook accounts, banks began to go to capital markets directly to raise money to fund mortgages. Structuring these relationships to process mass amounts of securities created a whole new set of processes. Because of securitization, these funds were usually borrowed for a short term, less than a year, and therefore had reasonable rates of interest. This created two sorts of new sources of funds, those who willingly lent banks money to fund mortgages and turn them into securities and those willing to hold on to those securities for a longer period.

Finally, these new processes and products required innovation in the nature of banks' organizational structures and the creation of new markets. By the early 1990s, financial institutions of all kinds realized that their future lay not in having long-term relationships with customers but instead in increasing the number and scope of transactions. This led many financial institutions to want to get bigger to find more customers, speed along, and expand the number and kinds of transactions. Financial innovation that created the possibility of larger throughput of transactions was utilized to build bigger and bigger banks. Banks lobbied to go national in their ability to draw on customers and borrowers. As the rules governing ownership of banks changed across the country, banks set out to either buy banks in other states or set up new branches of existing banks. These larger banks also desired the ability to enter new kinds of product markets as opportunities arose. Larger banks pushed for the ability to diversify products, and the idea of the conglomerate or full-service bank became the mantra of the industry. In the case of the mortgage industry in the 1990s, as I have shown, banks became vertically integrated by incorporating the origination, securitization, loan servicing, and trading functions internally in their organizations.

The mortgage securitization industry was built from the ashes of the savings and loan model. The government had provided much of the infrastructure for securitization and had created the GSEs, without whom the mortgage securitization industry never would have formed. But private banks played an important part by first playing roles generated by the huge opportunities that mortgage securitization presented and later innovating new products and processes to expand the industry and its product mix. The creation of the mortgage securitization industry is a marvel of capitalist innovation. With the help of the government, banks took pragmatic action to solve difficult problems to produce a new industry with profits like no one had ever seen.

What Is Financial Innovation?

Robert Merton, the Nobel Prize–winning financial economist, suggests that "the primary function of a financial system is to facilitate the allocation and deployment of economic resources, both spatially and across time, in an uncertain environment. This function encompasses a payments system with a medium of exchange; the transfer of resources from savers to borrowers; the gathering of savings for pure time transformation (i.e., consumption smoothing); and the reduction of risk through insurance and diversification" (1992: 12). Frame and

White, also financial economists, define a financial innovation as "something new that reduces costs, reduces risks, or provides an improved product / service / instrument that better satisfies financial system participants' demands" (2010: 4).

There are two perspectives in the economic literature on the overall contribution of financial innovation to modern economies (Frame and White, 2010; Silber, 1983). One emphasizes the centrality of finance in an economy and its importance for economic growth (R. Levine, 1997). Since finance is a facilitator of virtually all production activity and much consumption activity, improvements in the financial sector are thought to have direct positive effects throughout an economy. In the case of the innovations surrounding mortgage securitization, scholars have noted that connecting capital markets to mortgage markets made the allocation of capital across the economy more efficient. This works two ways. First, instead of depending on just savers for money to loan homeowners, access to the national capital market means that more investment can flow into housing. Second, it also means that the overall efficiency of the capital markets is enhanced, as the relative returns to mortgage investment versus all other forms of investment should now reflect real rates of returns across all kinds of assets on a risk-adjusted basis. This positive view of financial innovation and particularly the innovations that have linked the capital markets to the mortgage market has been discussed widely (Van Horne, 1985; Gerardi et al., 2010; Miller, 1986, 1992; Merton, 1992; Tufano, 2003; Frame and White, 2004, 2010).

But the financial crisis of 2008 has also caused some economists to search for evidence that financial innovation might produce instability in the overall functioning of financial markets (Lerner, 2006). Because financial innovations, like any innovation, can have negative as well as positive consequences on the economy and society more generally, at the very least one has to look at their overall net effects (Frame and White, 2010). From a sociological perspective, the critics of financial innovation are operating at a different level of analysis than those who look only at individual financial innovations. Their arguments focus not on whether a given product or process is useful for participants in an exchange but instead on how such innovations might have unintended consequences when aggregated across transactions or sets of actors.

For example, Lerner and Tufano (2011) show that failure can be especially costly for widely diffused innovations such as mortgage securities where the perception of the underlying value of those assets can change quickly with new information. Thakor (2012) and Gennaioli et al. (2010) have produced theoretical models that show that the diffusion of new kinds of loans or securities can be the source of bank runs or financial panics. This is because there is little structure in place to prevent the rapid spread of new information about the stability of such innovations and its sudden effects on asset prices. Beck et al. (2014) show empirically how financial innovation is associated with higher but more volatile economic growth and with greater bank fragility in a dataset indexing the experiences with financial innovation across many countries.

Herman Minsky (2008), a heterodox economist, proposed that financial innovation almost always leads to financial instability through an endogenous process centered on how financial institutions behave. Minsky's argument is that financial innovation begins as a way to create a stable financial regime by engaging in producing products that allow market actors to hedge risk. But during a long period of stability, those who use the products increasingly take on more risk. They do this by seeking out financial leverage (i.e., borrowing more money) in order to speculate on financial assets. This ends badly, often at the hands of monetary authorities who try to rein in speculation by raising interest rates, thereby making it more difficult for financial institutions to continue to have such high leverage. When that leverage is made problematic, a massive financial crisis can ensue.

While there are aspects of what happened in 2008 that fit these theories, they do not entirely explain what happened here. Minsky's argument centers on how the internal dynamics of finance drive financial innovation more than exogenous shocks. But Minsky's argument does not explain all financial crises. For example, it does a poor job of explaining the collapse of the savings and loan industry. As I have already shown, it was the exogenous financial shock of persistently high interest rates that destabilized the business model of the savings and loan banks, not an era of speculation in mortgages. While deregulation did subsequently produce an era of speculation for the savings and loan banks, it ended not because monetary authorities pulled the plug on easy credit but because banks had taken on many risky projects that simply failed or, in many cases, because the owners and managers engaged in the looting of the assets of their firms.

In the case of the 2008 meltdown, while financial institutions were certainly more vulnerable because of having high leverage, there were market conditions that pushed financial institutions to find new sources of mortgages and keep selling mortgage-based securities. In Chapter 5, I will show how the dynamics of the mortgage securitization industry pushed them to search for new sources of mortgages in order to keep their securitization machines going because they were seeking to continue make money off of originating, securitizing, and buying and selling asset-backed security collateralized debt obligations (ABS-CDOs). Minsky and the others provide good arguments about why financial innovation does not always produce good results. But in this context, the processes they describe are not sufficient without being embedded in the larger logic of the mortgage securitization industry. While financial innovation initially helped stabilize the housing market by producing the conditions under which many Americans could get mortgages, it eventually ran out of mortgages that made sense to fund. Without an alternative model of how to make money, the vertically integrated financial institutions of 2008 proved as vulnerable as the savings and loan banks of the 1980s.

Even as the savings and loan banks and smaller commercial banks failed in the 1980s, the financial sector grew dramatically, and capital markets expanded and benefited from the transformation of mortgage finance. The provision of financial products to consumers expanded dramatically in the 1980s and 1990s. This transformation caused a tighter linkage between the national (and international) capital markets and all of the biggest and most important banks in the US economy. Investment banks, commercial banks, the remaining large savings and loan banks, and newly emergent mortgage banks all used financial innovation to take advantage of the huge market for mortgages as a pipeline to create new products at all stages in that pipeline and earn massive profits. This larger, more diversified financial sector absorbed more and more capital and drove a massive housing price bubble from 2003 to 2006. Because of its large size and involvement in so much of the American economy, its downturn produced dramatic effects not just in finance but across the economy.

Financial Product Innovation

There are two main sorts of product innovations for the mortgage industry from the mid-1970s on. First was the proliferation of products for households that wanted to get mortgages but faced financial challenges in doing so. Financial innovation over time provided mortgages that relaxed all of the requirements for the conventional mortgage. Second, as the savings and loan model of holding mortgages began to erode and was replaced by mortgage securitization, it was necessary to find new sources of capital to fund mortgage origination. In essence, as the savings and loan model fell apart under the pressure of inflation and high interest rates, its replacements had to reinvent the mortgage and the methods used to fund them. The proliferation of financial instruments that created various kinds of mortgage securities proved to supply the innovative products that brought financial institutions into the market for these securities.

Innovation was not straightforward. Financial institutions began to experiment with different kinds of new products. Some failed, and some succeeded. To be successful, financial institutions needed to make products to please two sorts of audiences. New financial products were built to attract buyers. Households that could not afford conventional mortgages were the main candidates for financial innovation in mortgages. The period of high inflation and slow economic growth in the 1970s and early 1980s was particularly challenging for households wanting to buy homes. The breakdown of the savings and loan model of taking individual deposits in passbook accounts and using them to fund mortgages meant that new sources of capital needed to be found. Financial institutions moved from tapping individual savers to trying to raise capital from the capital markets. This entailed creating products to sell to short-term and long-term investors. Short-term investment was frequently provided by the commercial paper market. But long-term buyers of mortgages did so through buying mortgage securities. From its origins in 1970, it took almost fifteen years for the MBS to evolve sufficiently to make it attractive to a wide group of investors. The main problem was the need to create products that made sense to buyers given their need to satisfy their fiduciary responsibilities to justify holding different levels of risk in different kinds of investments.

Innovations in Mortgages

Many of the products required rewriting the rules that governed financial products. Financial institutions who were interested in selling these new products had to get the government to agree to change the rules governing mortgages in order to build markets for these new products. Congress and the regulatory authorities consistently acted to promote changes in the rules governing financial institutions to allow them to create new products. Here, I describe these products and briefly discuss the process by which they were brought to market.

The adjustable-rate mortgage (ARM) has a long history (Green and Wachter, 2005). Before 1930, at least half of American mortgages had interest rates that adjusted over time. But after the establishment of the conventional mortgage, it disappeared. During the high-inflation, high-interest-rate 1970s, state-chartered banks began to experiment with mortgages that had adjustable interest rates. Attempts in 1971 and 1974 by the Federal Home Loan Bank Board (FHLBB) to authorize residential ARMs met with stiff resistance by Congress (Cassidy, 1984). Opposition was widespread among consumer groups and labor unions that feared borrowers would be subjected to unmanageable increases in their mortgage payments.

By the end of the 1970s, however, as the condition of the thrift industry rapidly deteriorated, the political climate began to change (Barth, 2004). In December 1978, the FHLBB allowed federal savings and loan institutions in California to originate variable-rate loans in competition with state-chartered institutions.

This authority was expanded nationwide in 1979, but still with severe interest rate limitations. These limitations were eased slightly in 1980, and in April 1981 the FHLBB substantially relaxed its restrictions on ARMs originated by thrifts. In March 1981, the comptroller of the currency authorized national banks to originate ARMs for owner-occupied one- to four-family homes (Peek, 1990). The legislation that allowed adjustable-rate mortgages was the Garn-St. Germain Depository Institutions Act of 1982.

The ARM solved several problems. For banks that wanted to hold on to mortgages, it meant that mortgagors would assume the risk of rapidly changing interest rates. If rates went up, banks were able to cover their cost of capital. The buyers of ARMs during the late 1970s and 1980s were able to get mortgages that otherwise would have been unavailable. In many cases, the ARM came at lower rates than fixed-rate mortgages precisely because they could move with interest rates. Many of these mortgages came with initially low rates (called "teaser rates") whereby the loan would start out very low and adjust more rapidly. From 1980 on, the use of ARMs was very much related to overall interest rates (Moench et al., 2010). When rates fell, households would buy fixed-rate mortgages. Many who had ARMs would refinance when interest rates fell as well. As interest rates rose in the early 1980s, the share of total mortgages that were adjustable went from 29 percent in 1981 to 70.1 percent in 1985 (Peek, 1990). The use of ARM products has risen and fallen subsequently in response to interest rate changes (Green and Wachter, 2005).

Several features of ARMs are negotiated between financial institutions and mortgagors. Of course, one of the most important is the beginning interest rate. Equally significant is the length of time that the ARM is scheduled to remain unchanged and how much it can be reset. The reset rate is usually linked to some kind of market index such as the one- or three-year Treasury bill or what used to be the London Interbank Offer Rate (LIBOR) index. Often, there are caps on how high the interest rate can go over the life of the loan. There are frequently agreements that allow buyers to convert the ARM to a fixed-rate mortgage. But sometimes, there may also be special fees added if the ARM is paid off early. In the 2000s, a new product appeared called the option ARM. This gave the mortgagor the right to pay less than their payment in any given month. The amount of interest that was not paid would then be added to the loan, making what is called negative amortization. This product was popular during the subprime boom from 2003 to 2006.

The 1980s and 1990s produced other innovations that further expanded the range of mortgage choices in order to expand the number of households that could afford to buy houses. Financial institutions changed the level of down payment necessary, the credit requirements for loans, and the amount of money that households could borrow. These changes reflected the relatively high interest rates in place over this period as well as the increasing prices of houses and the desire of financial institutions, particularly commercial banks, to expand the size of the market for mortgages. While consumers benefited in having more choices and opportunities to get a mortgage, financial institutions found this type of expansion of the market quite lucrative. Anyone who took out one of the nonconventional mortgages could expect to pay a higher interest rate that was justified by arguing that such loans were riskier for financial institutions. Mortgagors also had to pay additional fees to get the loan and, in some cases, take out mortgage insurance to guarantee the loan. Financial institutions eventually discovered that giving credit to people who had had some impaired credit history or special financial circumstances turned into a lucrative business.

I will use the term *nonconventional* to describe all these types of loans that relax the terms of the conventional mortgage. Alt-A mortgages refer to mortgages where a household has some impaired credit history or lack of verifiable income. An impaired credit history would include less than two late payments on a mortgage; installment, or revolving credit debt in the past twenty-four months; no bankruptcy for the past five years; a credit score in the 620–660 range; and a down payment that is less than 20 percent and as little as 3 percent (Fligstein and Goldstein, 2010). I will reserve the term *subprime* for a particular type of nonconventional mortgage (which are also called B / C, where this letter refers to the credit rating given by a credit rating organization). A subprime or B / C mortgagor would have had an even more impaired credit history. This could include more than two late payments in the last twenty-four months; a judgment, foreclosure, or repossession in the prior twenty-four months; bankruptcy in the past five years; a FICO score of less than 620; and a down payment less than 10 percent and as low as 3 percent (Fligstein and Goldstein, 2010). I will discuss the origins and spread of these kinds of nonconventional mortgages in Chapter 5.

Two other forms of nonconventional mortgages were also pioneered in the 1980s and 1990s that catered to households with special circumstances. Jumbo mortgages are loans for households that have high credit quality but need a loan amount above what is called the "conventional conforming loan limits." These are standards set by the two government-sponsored enterprises, Fannie Mae and Freddie Mac, that refer to the maximum value of any individual mortgage they will purchase from a lender. Jumbo mortgages were initially marketed to high-income households who wanted to buy luxury homes. Such households could afford higher monthly payments but may not have had sufficient down payments to bring down the loan amount to a conventional level. As high prices inflated in the 1990s and 2000s, particularly in urban areas on the coasts, many middle-class households found themselves priced out of conventional mortgages. To get a loan, they needed to have a jumbo mortgage. The interest rates on jumbo mortgages are traditionally higher than for conforming mortgages. This is because it is thought that higher-priced houses are harder to sell if the owner defaults on the mortgage.

Home equity loans (HELs) are loans that borrow against the equity value of one's home. Before the 1980s, if a household had financial problems, they might have taken out a second mortgage. The companies that pioneered these loans usually marketed them to lower-income households who were in a more precarious financial situation. This would allow them to stay in their homes while waiting for their financial circumstances to improve. But during the early 1980s, financial institutions realized that households had accumulated equity in their homes. By offering people loans to extract that equity, financial institutions could create a financial instrument that was backed by collateral—that is, the value of the house. Several marketing campaigns used the term *home equity loan* instead of *second mortgage,* and it stuck. These loans also tended to have higher interest rates attached to them even though they were backed by the value of the home.

Rising home values in the 1980s increased the amount of homeowner equity in the United States. This asset became an attractive source of financing after the passage of the Tax Reform Act of 1986 (TRA). TRA prohibited taxpayers from deducting interest on consumer loans, such as credit cards and auto loans, while it allowed them to deduct interest paid on mortgage loans secured by their principal residence and one additional home. This change provided an incentive for homeowners to take home equity loans and use the proceeds to pay off consumer debt, finance the purchase of cars, or pay for their children's education. Another bonus was that all of these other forms of borrowing typically come with higher interest rates than home equity debt.

All of these qualifications to the conventional mortgage were possible only in a more deregulated financial services market. Two laws enacted in the early 1980s, the Depository Institutions Deregulation and Monetary Control Act (DIDMCA) and the Alternative Mortgage Transaction Parity Act (AMTPA), made it possible for lenders to originate mortgages with prices and features previously prohibited by individual states (Temkin et al., 2002). In particular, they made it possible for lenders to originate loans with higher interest rates and a broader range of terms than previously allowed under the various state lending laws.

DIDMCA, adopted in 1980, helped set the stage for the growth of subprime lending. The law produced sweeping changes in the way that banks operated across the country. It forced all banks to abide by the federal government's rules. It also allowed for cross-border mergers of all kinds. It also removed any ceilings or floors on interest rates that banks could charge or offer to customers. It increased deposit insurance for all banks and credit unions from $40,000 per account to $100,000. By deregulating loan rates through the preemption of state interest rate caps for first lien loans on a borrower's house, the law allowed banks to create whatever mortgage products they wished. DIDMCA was an important element in the subprime market's growth because it allowed lenders that originate de facto second mortgages and consumer loans to make more expensive first lien loans, the most common type of subprime loans.

AMTPA was adopted in 1982 and was part of the Garn-St. Germain Act. It preempted state laws that restrict a number of alternative mortgage features that are important subprime lending elements. Its intent was to increase the volume of loan products that reduced the up-front costs to borrowers in order to make homeownership more affordable. Specifically, the legislation allows lenders to originate mortgages with features such as variable interest rates, balloon payments, and interest-only mortgages in any "loan or credit sale secured by an interest in residential real property made, purchased or enforced by covered lenders" (*National Mortgage News,* 1982).

The wave of innovation in the production of types of mortgages was driven first and most importantly by the difficult economic times of the 1970s and early 1980s. High inflation and high interest rates made it imperative for the savings and loan industry to find new ways to fund mortgage origination and new strategies to charge more for mortgages but still be able to do originations. They were facilitated by a series of pieces of legislation that were friendly toward the industry but also more broadly toward commercial banks and mortgage brokers and banks who were interested in growing their share of mortgage originations.

While this new legislation did not save the savings and loan business model in the end, it did provide the legal underpinnings for whole new kinds of mortgages focused on segmenting the housing market. The 1980s and 1990s were an era for experimentation in mortgage finance for originations. As one market peaked or dried up, innovators looked for new markets to whom they could sell mortgage products. For example, jumbo mortgages were originally marketed to high-income households. But as the price of housing increased during the 1990s and early 2000s, financial institutions began to market this product, which earned higher interest, to more middle-class households, thus expanding their markets. The innovators in all of this were not the savings and loan banks by and large but a new group of mortgage banks such as Countrywide Financial and commercial banks such as Bank of America and Citibank.

Innovation in Financing Mortgages

The second problem presented to the savings and loan industry during the 1970s was the crisis of obtaining funds to originate mortgages. Their model of taking deposits from retail customers failed during the 1970s to provide savings and loans with enough funds to engage in creating mortgages and holding the mortgages. Regulation Q was being undermined by financial innovators who created money market funds, certificates of deposits, bond mutual funds, and other forms of investment so that ordinary people could make investments to take advantage of high interest rates. The savings and loan industry lobbied and got Regulation Q repealed in the Garn-St. Germain Act of 1982. They also managed to have depository insurance raised. This allowed them to access capital at whatever level of interest they needed in order to attract funds. This, of course, turned out to be a disaster, as in order to pay out higher interest rates, they had to engage in riskier ventures (Barth, 2004).

The savings and loan banks were not the only financial institutions to benefit from financial deregulation. The GSE model of using the capital markets to raise funds for mortgages by creating MBSs took over a decade to come into being. Many of the problems of creating MBSs ultimately required the government to create new rules to allow both sellers and buyers of MBSs to participate in the new market. In the wake of the collapse of the savings and loan banks, the GSEs took over the central role of organizing the mortgage market. This takeover meant that from the 1980s on, money for mortgage origination was increasingly being raised in the capital markets. It was not just the GSEs who went to these markets but also many financial institutions that were also originating and securitizing mortgages. During the 1980s, many financial institutions who originated mortgages turned around and sold them either to wholesalers or directly to the GSEs to have them packaged into MBSs. Many of these financial institutions had lines of credit from the capital markets that they would use to do origination.

While some of this capital came from borrowing from banks or relying on the firm's own capital, some of it also came from the commercial paper market where money could be borrowed short term (Post, 1992; Anderson and Gascon, 2009). The commercial paper market grew from $125 billion in 1980 to almost $500 billion in 1990 and a bit over $1.5 trillion in 2000. Most of this increase came with the introduction of the asset-backed commercial paper market in 1983. Before that, most of the activity in the market was for nonfinancial corporations to borrow money short term to fund inventories and meet payrolls. But banks increasingly used the market to borrow money short term to fund their financial activities.

The main products that came out of mortgage originations were mortgage-backed securities (MBSs), collateralized debt obligations (CDOs), and credit default swaps (CDSs). Each of these products was created to interest investors in owning bonds based on mortgages. MBSs and CDOs are distinct but overlapping categories. Mortgage-backed securities are any kind of asset-backed security where the underlying assets are mortgages. They may have one class (tranche), as in the case of pass-through securities, or many classes (tranches). CDOs can have underlying assets of any kind of debt (bonds, mortgages, even other securities). They always have multiple tranches with different priorities of payments. An MBS with a CDO-like structure is called a CMO (collateralized mortgage obligation) or sometimes an MBS-CDO. When a CDO contained a myriad of assets, it was frequently referred to as an ABS-CDO, where *ABS* was an abbreviation for asset-backed security.

The word *tranche* is French for slice, section, series, or portion and is a cognate to the English word *trench* (Fender and Mitchell, 2005). Bonds are divided into tranches in order to separate out how risky various parts of the underlying assets might be. The tranches are identified as those that are the most senior to most subordinate. The more senior-rated tranches have higher bond credit ratings than the lower-rated tranches and are thus considered safer than those below them. For example, senior tranches may be rated AAA, AA, or A, while mezzanine tranches might be rated BBB or below. Tranches with a first lien on the assets of the asset pool are referred to as senior tranches and are generally safer investments. Typical investors of these types of securities tend to be the GSEs, insurance companies, pension funds, and other risk-averse investors (Fender and Mitchell, 2005).

One of the most perplexing aspects of these distinctions is that CDOs could contain a mix of assets. CDOs originated to securitize assets from a variety of asset groups (Tett, 2009; MacKenzie, 2011). A particular CDO might include mortgages, credit card debt, and funding for planes rented by leasing companies. Since ABS-CDOs could contain any kind of financial asset, financial institutions began to package together tranches of other CDOs that they could not otherwise sell, either because the tranches were too risky or because they were too safe and paid too low a return, what were called "super senior tranches" (MacKenzie, 2011). When CDOs were exclusively made up of other CDO tranches, they were referred to as CDO-CDOs or CDO-squared. They could also sometimes, confusingly, be called ABS-CDOs.

In the case of MBS-CDOs, after 2001 financial institutions found that bondholders preferred more highly rated tranches over lower-rated tranches. This left them with lower-rated tranches that they could not sell. The CDO process allowed financial institutions to rebundle these unsalable BBB-rated mezzanine MBS-CDOs into highly rated securities. They did so by producing new tranches that allowed purchasers to buy whatever level of risk they chose (MacKenzie, 2011). How could riskier tranches end up being rated AAA? Given that not all of the mortgages from MBS-CDOs that were rated BBB or below in a CDO-CDO would fail (indeed, only a minority ever did), buyers could pay to buy a level of risk. This process could leave some tranches unsold. These could then be repackaged again into CDOs (sometimes referred to as CDO-cubed). While pricing a CDO-CDO can be difficult due to the disparate income streams from which it is constituted, for those based on mortgages, at root it is a claim on MBS-CDO payments, which in turn are claims on income from mortgage payments.

A credit default swap (CDS) is an agreement that the seller of the CDS will compensate the buyer of some asset in the event of a loan default (by the debtor). In essence, the seller of the CDS insures the buyer against a loan defaulting. The buyer of the CDS makes a series of payments to the seller and, in exchange, receives a payoff if the loan defaults. Early trades of the CDS were pioneered by Bankers Trust in 1991. The modern standard form of the CDS was created by Blythe Masters, who worked at J.P. Morgan in 1994 (Tett, 2009). It has been extensively used by financial institutions and corporations to modify all kinds of risks. One of the interesting features of a CDS is that one does not have to own a particular asset in order to create a CDS with some other party. For example, one could take out a CDS agreement about a particular CDO even if one did not own it.

In the case of MBS-CDOs, buyers of CDSs in the beginning used CDSs to protect themselves from potential downturns in the housing markets. By buying CDSs, holders of MBS-CDOs not only lowered their risks, but regulators would then allow them to hold less capital for holding those MBS-CDOs. If a financial entity bought AAA-rated CDOs that they then took out a CDS against the risk it would default, they had to hold little or no capital for that purchase. This allowed financial institutions to increase their purchases of CDOs and have a higher level of leverage. CDSs were also used in 2006–2008 by certain investors at hedge funds to bet against the CDO market. By buying CDSs for CDOs that investors thought were likely to fail, investors could profit if and when they did (Lewis, 2010).

The history of the creation of MBS-CDOs goes back to the 1960s (Quinn, 2019). The modern securitization market was a direct invention of the federal government. Their goal was to increase homeownership by increasing the pool of money available for investment in mortgages (Sellon and VanNahmen, 1988). In particular, the Johnson administration was concerned about whether the savings and loan model of mortgages would be able to provide enough money to fund mortgages for the baby boom generation that was coming of age in the 1960s. One solution that was discussed was to expand the FHA and allow the government to be the lender to millions of Americans. The problem was that the government did not want to get into the business of being the lender of last resort. It would mean that the government would absorb billions of dollars of debt into a budget already strained by the Vietnam War (Ranieri, 1996).

To deal with this, the Interagency Committee on Housing Finance was convened in 1966, and it was followed by the Mortgage Finance Task Force in 1967. The latter, led by Federal Reserve governor Sherman Maisel and James Dusenberry of the Council of Economic Advisers, decided that the preferred solution would be to bolster the secondary market for mortgages. This would allow the federal government to sell off the mortgages on its own books and help other lenders do the same (Sellon and VanNahmen, 1988; Green and Wachter, 2005). The goal was to free up capital held in reserves by private companies, generate new capital from sales to increasingly important investors such as mutual and pension funds, and thereby create efficiencies, savings, and new sources of capital that could be passed on to home buyers (Sellon and VanNahmen, 1988).

The federal government undertook sweeping housing regulation reform from 1968 to 1970, which began with the privatization of Fannie Mae and two years later resulted in the creation of the first modern securitization instruments. Fannie Mae had long been in the business of providing stability for the housing market by promoting the secondary market. Specifically, it purchased mortgages during market downturns in order to encourage renewed lending. However, going forward, it would do so as a private entity.

To make sure that the newly private agency was successful, Ginnie Mae was created in 1968 as a new governmental agency that would officially support the market on behalf of the federal government, mostly by providing guarantees for governmental debt held by and sold through Fannie Mae. Even as the government took steps away from direct ownership of mortgages, it found it needed to maintain a directive presence in order to secure investor confidence, and the step toward privatization of this governmental agency was offset by a complex set of governmental protections. Two years later (in 1970), Freddie Mac was created as a private entity modeled after Fannie Mae. Given a similar charter and privileges, it was to compete with Fannie Mae and help create a secondary market for mortgages originated by thrifts.

As government-sponsored enterprises (GSEs), Fannie Mae and Freddie Mac follow a congressional charter that requires them to support the secondary market for housing by promoting liquidity and stability. Their debt and obligations are not backed by the US government, but they have special privileges and tax exemptions and "conditional access" to a $2.5 billion line of credit from the government, and they are directly regulated by a special office in HUD. In 2003, the Securities and Exchange Commission (SEC) received authority over them after a set of scandals. Moreover, that their debt commonly trades at the level of government bonds suggests that investors believe that they are simply too big and important for the US government to ever let fail. In this way they carry an implicit, though not legal, guarantee by the US government. The hybrid public-private nature of the GSEs is best thought of as the place where the US government most directly intervened into structuring the housing market.

It was within this configuration of public and semiprivate agencies that the securitization market was born. They started with the idea of auctioning off Fannie Mae's mortgages and spent a good year figuring out how to make such a plan work. They decided in the process that some sort of government guarantee was crucial in order to secure investor confidence. Their efforts came to fruition when the first mortgage-backed security was issued in 1970. A group of mortgages backed by the FHA and VA were given a government guarantee of timely payment by Ginnie Mae and then sold off as bonds on the capital markets (Sellon and VanNahmen, 1988).

These deals were called *pass-throughs*, as the ownership of the mortgages was literally transferred to the investors along with their payments. Investors were mainly the thrifts, private banks, and insurance companies. They had been enticed with a chance to take a position in the housing market without taking any credit risk. There were, however, significant limitations to the use of pass-throughs. Throughout the 1970s, officials at Ginnie Mae and executives at Fannie Mae and Freddie Mac worked closely with investment bankers to develop new financial instruments that solved these problems.

The private sector was a partner in these efforts. Salomon Brothers was the leading investment bank interested in promoting MBSs. Robert Dall, a trader at Salomon Brothers, helped create the first private MBS with Bank of America in 1977. The deal was for $100 million. It was the first MBS that experimented with something like tranching. In 1983, people from both industry and government created the first securitization structures with tranches as they are now used, creating the collateralized mortgage obligations (CMO).[1] These multiclass issues were incredibly flexible and incredibly successful. Michael Lewis writes, "The CMO burst the damn between several billion investable dollars looking for a home and nearly two trillion dollars of home mortgages looking for an investor" (1990: 136).

Over the following decades, deals would be parsed in increasingly complicated ways; many would have over forty different classes of debt, and at least one contained more than ninety tranches (Kendall, 1996; Kochen, 1996: 109). Soon, new kinds of investors were entering the market (Sellon and VanNahmen, 1988), reportedly attracted by instruments designed with their preferences in mind (Ranieri, 1996; Fink, 1996). Within twenty-five years, the financial structures proposed by the government officials in the Mortgage Finance Task Force, and initially bolstered with government guarantees through Ginnie Mae, grew into a multitrillion-dollar trade of sometimes staggeringly complex instruments.

Innovations in Processing

During the 1980s, the most important innovations in processing were facilitated by advances in computer technology (Frame and White, 2010; LaCour-Little, 2000). The rapid expansion of financial markets was possible only with the growing speed, size, and data storage capacity of computers. Without computers, it would have been impossible for banks to get larger, ATMs to spread, and credit card operations to expand. All of the important process innovations in the 1980s and 1990s in the mortgage industry were based on the ability to use computers to collect and process massive amounts of information about consumers, mortgagors, and mortgages.

But this is not a story of technological determinism. The real story is that process innovations that were necessary to produce new financial products could work only with the ability to transact more rapidly. Indeed, financial institutions had pushed innovation in the gathering, processing, and storage of large amounts of data beginning in the early twentieth century (Yates, 2005). They were among the first customers of modern computers, and the large mainframe computer is still at the core of data processing for financial institutions.

But computers need to be told what to do. To make sense of all of these transactions, financial institutions had to produce a set of tools or devices that allowed them to process information in a meaningful fashion. Indeed, without processes to structure what the computers were doing, nothing interesting would have happened. A useful way of thinking about a process innovation is what might be called a market device (Callon et al., 2007). Callon et al. (2007: 2) define market devices as "material and discursive assemblages that intervene in the construction of markets. From analytic techniques to pricing models, from purchase settings to merchandising tools, from trading protocols to aggregate indicators, the topic of market devices includes a wide array of objects." The innovation of these devices wove together computer technology, computer programming, and the use of quantitative data to produce processes that transformed the mortgage industry.

In the case of mortgage finance, I focus on a small set of such innovations: computer programs to enter data and approve mortgages, credit scores, and securitization.[2] The most important of these innovations was securitization, which was the technique used to create securities out of financial instruments that were generating some kind of cash flow. There are three aspects to securitization that are necessary to explore: the creation of legal vehicles called special-purpose vehicles (SPVs) and relatedly the real estate mortgage investment conduit (REMIC) that "owned" the security being produced, the use of tranching to divide the security into pieces that could be sold to buyers, and the use of ratings to evaluate the riskiness of the tranches. My goal here is to explore how the process of making securities out of mortgages evolved and pushed the innovations forward. By the late 1990s, these market devices were well known and had widely diffused across the mortgage securitization industry.

Innovation in Loan Processing

Beginning in the 1980s, it became possible to automate the process of loan origination (Frame and White, 2010). But the relative fragmentation of the industry and the presence of the savings and loan model of origination meant that the industry did not see the need to computerize (Lipman, 1984). In order to see what was eventually computerized and who did it, it is useful to consider the steps in the loan origination process. In the first step, a home buyer would choose a lender and a loan type. Then, they would apply for a loan and await a decision, the loan would be underwritten, and then papers would be signed where borrowers took possession of the house.

By submitting an application, the potential mortgagor provides the mortgagee with information about the property in question and his or her present financial situation, including income, current housing costs, job, assets, and debts. During underwriting, the lender verifies the claims made on the application and determines if the applicant and the property meet the firm's approval criteria for the loan in question. Closing a home mortgage involves the actual transfer of the funds in question and signing of various loan documents. After a loan is closed, the chief task remaining for lenders or their agents is servicing the loan, which entails processing the periodic loan payments. Before 1980, this process would have taken at least ninety days and up to six months.

Savings and loan associations and savings banks traditionally provided the largest portion of mortgage financing. Their taking of applications and deciding whom to give the loan to were carried out entirely by hand. By the 1980s, there were also specialized mortgage bankers who would use their own funds or capital from other sources (such as banks and pension funds) to originate home mortgages. They often acted as middlemen, seeking out borrowers who met the desired risk profiles of the investors who provided loan capital. In these cases, it was not uncommon for the mortgage banker to retain the servicing of the loan for a fee paid by the investor (Barrett, 1992). Decisions about whether to lend the money in both cases were entirely up to the discretion of loan officers or mortgage brokers.

On the other side of the market, there was a growing national market for loan origination (Van Order, 2000). The secondary market has three major parts: mortgage originators who hold loans in portfolio, originators who sell loans directly to investors who hold loans in portfolio, and originators who sell loans to a conduit who packages and securitize the loans and sells interests in the securities to investors (Cummings and DiPasquale, 1997). Most frequently, the conduits to the secondary market for residential mortgages are the GSEs, Fannie Mae and Freddie Mac. By 2003, about 50 percent of the $6.3 trillion in outstanding US mortgage debt for single-family residences was either held in portfolio by the GSEs or held by investors in the form of mortgage-backed securities guaranteed by the GSEs (Cummings and DiPasquale, 1997).

Hess and Kemerer (1994) show that banks began to experiment with computerized application processes in the 1980s. These early efforts took two forms. Some companies tried to create systems where real estate agents or mortgage brokers could enter an application into a computer system and multiple financial institutions would decide whether they were interested in funding the mortgage. This approach helped create an electronic marketplace.

A second approach created more proprietary systems. Countrywide Financial and Citibank began to set up electronic mortgage systems where applicants would enter their information and get an answer to whether or not they qualified for a mortgage, often in under an hour (Hess and Kemerer, 1994: 266). These systems were proprietary, and the decision to fund was considered only by the financial institution that had accepted the loan. Malone et al. (1987) coined the term *electronic hierarchy* to describe the situation where buyers are linked by computers and telecommunications technology to a predetermined source for the product or service in question. In general, the hierarchical systems have won out (Markus et al., 2005).

Not surprisingly, both approaches produced idiosyncratic computer programs that were not comparable or compatible. Moreover, these innovations did not become industry-wide until the 1990s (Markus et al., 2005). The main agents to produce a standardized form for mortgage originations were the GSEs, who spurred the adoption of information technology standards in the industry (Kersnar, 2001). They were assisted in these efforts by the Mortgage Bankers Association (MBA), the main trade association for companies in the real estate finance business. The MBA operated a clearinghouse for information and was an organizer of diverse firm interests.

In the late 1980s, the GSEs and the MBA launched an electronic data initiative, designed to support the automation of interagency mortgage lending processes (Opelka, 1994). At the core of these efforts was the effort to increase the ability to predict defaults and to make automated underwriting decisions based on their predictions. Empirical research in the late 1980s and the early 1990s suggested that borrowers who defaulted did so when they owed more for a property than the property was worth. The condition that most often produced this outcome was a local downturn in the real estate market.

But the role of a borrower's credit history in defaulting was less well understood (Markus et al., 2005). Part of the problem lay in the lack of availability of sufficient credit data, which was distributed across many sources and reported in nonstandard ways. In the early 1990s, "virtually no institution was storing credit records on mortgage loans in an easily accessible medium" (Straka, 2000: 213). Motivated by the success of credit scoring techniques in predicting default in other financial services (particularly credit cards), the GSEs began exploring the applicability of that technique in mortgage lending. In 1992, Freddie Mac completed a study using credit scores (FICO scores, after Fair, Isaac and Company) and concluded that they were a significant predictor of mortgage default and thus should be a component of computer-based mortgage scoring models.

In 1994, Freddie Mac announced a successful pilot of its automated underwriting system, Loan Prospector. Shortly thereafter, Fannie Mae introduced its system, called Desktop Underwriter. These automated underwriting systems were not just computer programs. Using them involved credit data collected by and from a variety of organizations, credit scores, data on properties and loan terms, information about local market conditions, and help with managing these systems. The basic models used to decide whether to give a person a mortgage involved two stages. First, a general model of prepayment was created given historical data from mortgages. This model might be fit on hundreds of thousand cases and was updated each year as new information became available. The model gave a set of parameters that could be applied to a particular application. Then, a probability could be generated about the likelihood of a particular mortgage being prepaid. The factors in these models that had the biggest predictive effects were the recent history of home prices in the zip code and a person's credit score. These models were constantly being tinkered with as more data became available.

While the use of these systems started slowly, by the end of the 1990s, it had spread widely. In 2002, a freelance writer quipped, "If there is a [lender] left on the planet not using Internet technology to lock loans or an automated underwriting system to deliver decisions in minutes, we didn't find it" (*Mortgage Banking,* 2002). Fannie's Desktop Underwriter was referred to as an industry "standard" (*Mortgage Banking*, 2002). In early 2001, the results of an industry survey were reported as showing that more than 90 percent of lenders had implemented an automated underwriting system and 75 percent of new loans were underwritten with these systems (Markus et al., 2005).

The Innovation of Credit Scores

The second important innovation was the use of credit scores in the loan approval process. Credit scoring is a statistical method used to predict the probability that a loan applicant or existing borrower will default or become delinquent. The method, introduced in the 1950s, is now widely used for all forms of consumer lending (Poon, 2009). There are two parts of the credit rating industry: Fair, Isaac and Company, which invented the widely used FICO score, and the three credit bureaus, TransUnion, Equifax, and Experian (Poon, 2007).

Modern credit bureaus began to develop rapidly across the country in the 1950s and 1960s. They were community based, focused on tracking the behaviors of consumers in a specific county or town, and primarily focused on serving one kind of creditor, a bank, finance company, or retailer (Furletti, 2002). These early credit reporting companies typically limited their credit-related reporting to negative or "derogatory" information (e.g., delinquencies or defaults). For example, a group of retailers in a small town might have agreed to form a cooperative that kept track of customers who were considered delinquent by any member of the group. The individual merchants would then use this information in managing their own credit relationships with prospective and current customers.

In addition to capturing name, address, and some loan information, these early agencies would scour local newspapers for notices of arrests, promotions, marriages, and deaths. These notices would then be clipped and attached to a consumer's paper credit report. Requests or "inquiries" from creditors to see a particular consumer's information would also be noted in the report. These inquiries would indicate that a consumer was requesting credit. As such, "bureaus" sponsored by banks, retailers, or finance companies did not share loan or inquiry information with each other. This kept banks from knowing about loans or inquiries made by finance companies or retailers and vice versa. The situation limited any creditor's ability to understand a potential customer's entire debt situation.

Political, technological, and market pressures transformed the industry from the 1970s on. The decade began with passage of the Fair Credit Reporting Act (FCRA) (Furletti, 2002). The FCRA protected consumers by setting standards for accuracy of and access to their credit information. Subsequent to the FCRA's passage, the industry stopped reporting things like marriages, promotions, and arrests and focused on reporting verifiable credit-related information. This included both positive information, such as a consumer's ability to consistently pay their bills on time, and negative information, such as defaults and delinquencies. This act was subsequently modified in 1986 to increase consumer access to information about what information credit bureaus held on individual consumers (Poon, 2009).

As computers and databases grew larger and more able to process large volumes of data, the amount of information gathered increased dramatically. It became more organized and standardized. Those agencies that adopted computer technology were able to get larger. This, along with the costs associated with migrating to computer-based systems, compelled smaller operations that were not yet automated to sell their files and exit the industry. As a result of this consolidation and in order to meet the demands of an exploding unsecured lending market, credit reporting companies started including lending activity from banks, finance companies, and retailers from wider geographic areas.

By the end of the 1970s, a handful of companies emerged as leaders. TransUnion, Equifax, and TRW (now Experian) became the dominant players. By the start of the 1980s, the content, storage, and processing of credit reports had changed dramatically. More accurate information (e.g., names, addresses, and Social Security numbers) was electronically stored and accompanied by loan, inquiry, and public record information (e.g., bankruptcies, judgments, and liens). Histories that were once read over the phone to an inquiring business were now transmitted electronically.

While the consumer reporting agencies built up the industry for reporting on consumer credit worthiness, the creation of a score that would sum up the creditworthiness of a borrower was developed by a different company. Martha Poon has produced several articles that document the emergence of Fair, Isaac and Company, which pioneered the creation of a single score that would be used to evaluate whether or not to lend to a particular borrower (2007, 2009). The problem with what the credit reporting agencies were doing was that their information was verbal and did not result in a simple metric that would allow someone to decide to make a loan or not. Moreover, it contained a morass of nonstandardized information. The process by which a credit score evolved, spread, and became the standard in the models of whether to originate a mortgage was neither straightforward nor obvious. Indeed, Fair, Isaac and Company did not set out to create such a score. When they did, it ran counter to their historical business model.

William Fair and Earl Isaac founded Fair, Isaac and Company in 1956 in an apartment building in San Rafael, California, with an estimated $2,400 in capital (Poon, 2007). Their backgrounds were in operations research. They founded their firm to produce custom solutions to the problems of any interested business. They would help firms create material processes, embedded in both paper and hardware, and later, with mass computerization, in software. Their goal was to provide a business with ongoing information that might reduce the guesswork involved in making everyday decisions. Their orientation was to produce unique solutions to particular firms' problems.

In the early 1960s, they started working with firms such as department stores and car dealers who were trying to decide to whom they would extend credit. They invented an application scorecard. This was literally a printed card that served as a calculating tool for quantitatively evaluating and selecting applicants for credit above whatever risk threshold was fixed by the management of a particular firm. Assuming that what had happened in the past was indicative of what would occur in the future, scorecards gave lenders an easy-to-use procedure for numerically summarizing the recorded behavior of previous borrowers to help to decide if they should receive credit.

The scoring model they used was based on historical data and statistical theory. These models would be based on a particular company's data of their history with customers. Since the data at each company that was collected was not standardized, Fair, Isaac would create a scorecard unique for that firm. The method produced a "score" that a firm could use to rank its loan applicants or borrowers in terms of risk. To build a scoring model, or "scorecard," developers analyzed the historical data on the performance of previously made loans at a particular firm to determine which borrower characteristics were useful in predicting whether the loan performed well. The original system was carefully designed so that the answers provided by the credit applicant to a set of questions in person or on an application form could be classified in the table printed on the card and the associated point values added up to produce the credit score. This score represented a calculation of the empirically assessed odds that a person with a particular combination of characteristics, compared against the known outcomes of a lender's population of clients, would default on a loan. Then that model could be used for calculating how likely a new customer was to default after considering their personal characteristics. They confirmed the model by empirically testing the predicated score against whether a person subsequently failed to pay (Poon, 2007).

The first Fair, Isaac credit scoring systems were to be deployed in small towns in rural America at the point of sale. They had to be simple enough to be understood by people with no knowledge of statistics and no access to calculators. The person doing the evaluating literally checked boxes and summed up a number. One third-generation Fair, Isaac analyst (who joined the company in the early

1980s) recounted the history as it was handed down to him as follows: "The form of the model had to be simple enough that somebody could just ask a question, look up something, write down a single number, write down the question, look up something, write down another number, at the end of which, draw a line and add it up" (Poon, 2007: 289).

In the late 1970s, the company became interested in using credit bureau data to create more general credit scores. The main impetus to the creation of the modern credit score was the invention of credit cards (Furletti, 2002). Banks were interested in sending out mass mailings to consumers in order to get them to buy credit cards and use them. The main hitch was that banks did not want to get stuck with lots of bad debt owed by people who had unsecured credit cards. Moreover, since these were in most cases new customers, banks did not have long-standing relationships to judge the customers' creditworthiness. To deal with this, banks bought credit reports from the consumer reporting agencies to make their decisions about issuing credit cards. The problem was that this information was relatively raw and not necessarily consistently collected across individuals or firms. It made the task of processing thousands and thousands of applications time consuming and costly.

Fair, Isaac began by using these credit reports to create a database for some banks. Then, they were able to create a model based on past payment experience that would allow them to produce a single score for any applicant. But they soon ran into the problem that each of the consumer reporting agencies gathered data differently. They next approached the agencies for a representative sample of data, which they received already digitized and stored on magnetic tapes. They used these samples to create weights for various factors by creating statistical models based on actual experience. These weights could then be used by software at the banks to create a score for the lists of prospective customers.

Banks began to request that the consumer reporting agencies directly calculate the FICO scores instead of sending over written credit reports. At first, the agencies tried to create their own scores, but banks had grown to trust the FICO methods (Poon, 2007). Fair, Isaac would provide the algorithm, the consumer reporting agencies would run the models, and individuals would be assigned scores that could be bought by any customer who wanted to evaluate the creditworthiness of an individual. The genius of the product was that it turned the more descriptive credit reports into a single number that any user could plug into their decision-making. Now it was the use of a single number that generically provided lenders with information about potential customers.[3]

At the same time, the credit bureaus gathered more data and standardized their collection processes. This allowed them to calculate credit scores for everyone whom they had a file on. The technology that produces these scores now relies on a complex system of data collection, the ability to standardize the data, and a model that is constantly being updated and refined to generate a single score. By the early 1990s, these credit scores became widely available for any potential user. By the time the mortgage industry was evolving toward using computers to evaluate mortgage origination, they found the already existing FICO score. Thus, Fair, Isaac and Company turned from creating unique solutions for firms' problems to creating a generic product to be used by the consumer reporting agencies for all kinds of loan purposes.

The Innovation of Securitization

Houses, by their very nature, are objects that are hard to compare. They vary greatly in terms of size, amenities, location, and upkeep. The households that bought them had varied financial histories and different intentions. Some were wealthy and able to make a large down payment and monthly payment, others less so. Some households only intended to own the house for a short period, and others thought they would never move. A fair number of housing transactions, particularly after 2001, involved investment and speculation. The genius of the creation of mortgages securities is that it provided a set of market devices to take these "lumpy" mortgages and households with very different resources and goals and turn them into securities that appeared to be the same. In essence, the outcome of the securitization process was to take what was inherently a set of heterogeneous objects and turn them into a product with a homogeneous rate of return for a particular tranche with a particular bond rating. Theoretically, any AAA-rated tranche made up of mortgages of all kinds of houses was the same as any other AAA-rated tranche. How was this possible?

Securitization is the financial practice of pooling various types of contractual debt such as residential mortgages, commercial mortgages, auto loans, student loans, corporate debt, or credit card debt obligations and selling their related cash flows to third-party investors as securities (Leyshon and Thrift, 2007; Loutskina, 2011). These securities may be described as bonds, pass-through securities (in the case of mortgages), real estate mortgage investment conduits (REMICs), or collateralized debt obligations (CDOs). Investors are repaid from the principal and interest cash flows collected from the underlying debt and redistributed to the investors in the securities created from these loans. As discussed earlier, securities backed by mortgage receivables are called mortgage-backed securities (MBSs), while those backed by other types of receivables are asset-backed securities (ABSs). There are three process innovations necessary to produce these securities: the creation of SPVs and relatedly the REMIC that "owned" the security being produced, the use of tranching to divide the security into pieces that could be sold to buyers, and the use of ratings by the credit rating agencies to evaluate the riskiness of the tranches. These innovations took about fifteen years to put into place. Together they revamped the way that mortgages were funded (He et al., 2012).

It is useful to begin with a description of the process of securitization. An originator gathers a set of assets that are loans being paid on by borrowers. They place these assets into a legal entity called a special-purpose vehicle (SPV) or special-purpose entity (SPE). A SPV acts as a depository for a specific group of assets, and in turn, it issues securities to be purchased by investors. SPVs operate as a wholly separate entity from their creators. They are legally isolated, and their assets are no longer available to the seller or its creditors. The deposited assets can be used only to make payments on the securities issued to investors and may not be claimed by the seller (Klee and Butler, 2002).

The SPV can take a variety of legal forms, such as a corporation, trust, or limited liability company. By selling the assets to the SPV, the financial institution involved could take the loans they had made off of their books. Typically, these off-balance-sheet SPVs have the following characteristics: (1) they are thinly capitalized, (2) they have no independent management or employees, (3) their administrative functions are performed by a trustee who follows prespecified rules with regard to the receipt and distribution of cash, and (4) there are no other financial decisions made by the trustees (Gorton and Souleles, 2016). In short, SPVs are essentially firms that have no employees, make no substantive economic decisions, have no physical location, and if they go bankrupt, the financial liability is restricted to the assets of the SPV.

By being organized this way, the SPV has a set of advantages both for the sellers of the security and for the buyers. From the perspective of the sellers, creating the SPV and issuing asset-backed securities based on loans they have made allows them to obtain financing for those loans and cuts down their costs of doing so. Because the securities they sell are rated, it enables them to raise money more cheaply by having the level of risk associated with the security rated by the credit rating agencies (Klee and Butler, 2002). Because the assets are frequently "sold" to the SPV, it also protects the firm from the bankruptcy of the SPV. This means the assets in the SPV are "off books" and do not count against the amount of capital a financial institution needs to hold in order to control the SPV.

The hands-off nature of the SPV works in investors' favor as well. It protects the investors in those securities from the SPV going bankrupt by limiting their liability to what they own. It also protects the securitized assets from the originator's creditors if the originator develops problems. By separating the payouts on the bonds from the underlying assets, buyers do not need to know a great deal about those assets except for the rating by the credit rating agencies. The securities themselves are advantageous for a number of reasons. Because ABS-CDOs issued by the SPV are by nature diversified, investors diversify their risk. This is similar to investing in a mutual fund made up of many stocks. There is a secondary market for these securities, and this makes the investment more liquid in case the investor needs to sell it. Finally, many investors have regulators that force them to hold only AAA-rated bonds. By buying tranches that fit their needs, investors can fit their own preferences and comply with regulatory authorities.

In the 1980s and 1990s, the GSEs faced some challenges in creating MBSs that concerned the ability of investors to hold such securities and state laws that made it difficult to do so (Kendall, 1996). One problem of the SPV was that there were still legal barriers to investors holding MBSs. SPVs had to be managed completely passively, which meant that they could only contain a three-tranche structure. There were also state laws that made it difficult for investors to buy MBSs as investments because they were not truly equivalent to Treasury bonds. Lewis Ranieri helped develop a piece of legislation that became the Secondary Mortgage Market Enhancement Act of 1984 (SMMEA) (Ranieri, 1996). The law provided that if nationally recognized statistical rating organizations (NRSRO) rated MBSs AA or higher, these securities were legal investments equivalent to Treasury securities and other federal government bonds for federally chartered banks, state chartered financial institutions, and Department of Labor–regulated pension funds.

The Tax Reform Act of 1986 helped solve another problem of SPVs. The creation of an SPV meant there was double taxation of assets, first by taxing the income earned at the corporate level by an issuer and second by dividends paid to securities holders. The act created a new kind of SPV called a real estate mortgage investment conduit (REMIC). REMICs operate to effectively remove the loans from the originating lender's balance sheet by treating their inclusion in the vehicle as a sale instead of a debt financing in which the loans remain as balance sheet assets. Thus, the issuer was not responsible for taxes on the proceeds from the SPV. Investors, of course, do pay taxes on their investments. The act made it easier for savings institutions and real estate investment trusts to hold mortgage securities as qualified portfolio investments as well. A savings institution, for instance, can include REMIC-issued mortgage-backed securities as qualifying assets in meeting federal requirements for treatment as a savings and loan for tax purposes.

Among the major issuers of REMICs are Freddie Mac and Fannie Mae, the two leading secondary market buyers of conventional mortgage loans. Many

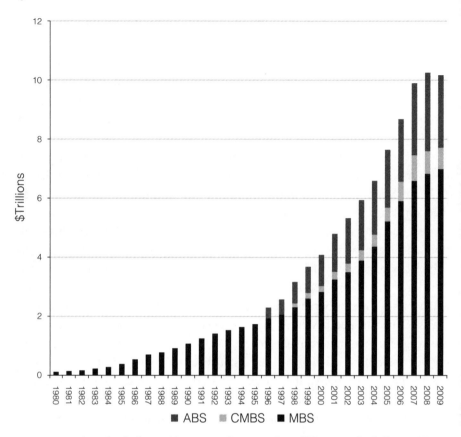

FIGURE 4.1 Asset-backed securities outstanding over time. ABS = asset-backed securities, CMBS = commercial mortgage-backed securities, MBS = mortgage-backed securities. Data source: Inside Mortgage Finance (2009).

privately operated mortgage conduits owned by mortgage bankers, mortgage insurance companies, and savings institutions have also found them advantageous. Figure 4.1 presents data on the increasing use of SPVs in the creation of asset-backed securities of all kinds. From 1980 to 2009, the total amount of all types of ABS issued goes from almost $0 to over $10 trillion. Obviously, the SPV as an organizing vehicle for ABSs was spectacularly successful.

The second process innovation that helped securitization was the division of ABSs into different financial instruments based on different kinds of claims on the cash flow generated by the underlying loans. The process by which these claims are divided up is called tranching. One of the main issues in getting investors to buy MBSs was prepayment risk (Becketti, 1989; Ranieri, 1996). In the 1970s and early 1980s, the basic sales pitch in trying to sell MBSs that were guaranteed by one of the GSEs was to argue that an investor was getting a bond that was as safe as a Treasury bond. Because the GSEs were thought to be ultimately creatures of the government, it was assumed that the securities they issued had the full faith and force of the US government. This meant that they were as safe as Treasury bonds but with a higher return. Investors understood that there was one important difference between MBSs and Treasury bonds. Because the mortgages in an MBS could be paid off at any time, the bondholder might not be able to recoup their initial investment in an MBS. There were a number of reasons that houses might be sold. Households might not be able to afford their homes and find themselves in foreclosure. Households might experience life-changing events such as children coming or going or retirement. New job opportunities could cause people to move. Finally, homeowners could decide to refinance their loans. This would be particularly attractive if interest rates fell. This last concern would mean that investors would be trying to reinvest their money at a time when interest rates had dropped.

In order to overcome this objection. Lewis Ranieri and his colleagues at Salomon Brothers began to develop MBSs that were tranched (Ranieri, 1996). The basic idea of tranching begin with mortgages for various properties that are pooled together in the SPV. Tranching involves dividing the cash flow from the mortgages into different claims with different rates of return and different risk profiles. Typically, bonds contain what are called "senior," "mezzanine," and "junior" tranches. The bond rating of each tranche is an indicator of the likelihood of nonpayment due to either prepayment of the loan or foreclosure. The junior tranches, typically rated BBB or below, are the first to experience prepayment risk. The senior tranches, rated AAA, are the last to be defaulted on. Investors who are willing to take on a higher risk of prepayment or foreclosure receive a higher yield, while those who take on a lower risk get a lower yield. Tranching solves the problem of investors worrying about prepayment risk by letting them choose how much risk they are willing to bear. For many investors, such as insurance companies and pension funds, it was essential to have AAA because of regulatory requirements. For others, such as mutual funds and hedge funds, more risks could be hedged by buying other bonds or investing in CDSs.

Because MBSs are bonds, they are regulated by the SEC. The SEC has the legal authority to establish financial accounting and reporting standards for issuers of securities sold to the public, including SPVs and their sponsors. When a financial institution wants to issue an MBS, it has to file a prospectus with the SEC. The credit rating agencies' evaluations of the tranches of the security are at the core of the prospectus.

It is useful to examine one MBS filing in order to get a feeling for what was in a typical MBS. All of the information contained here was taken from the prospec-

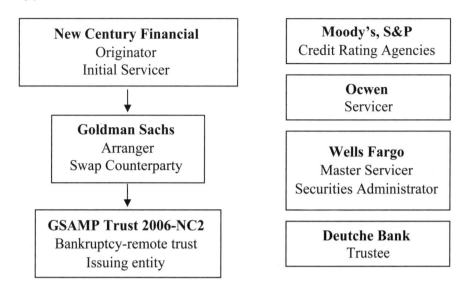

FIGURE 4.2 Key institutions surrounding GSAMP Trust 2006-NC2. Source: Securities and Exchange Commission.

tus describing the security that was filed with the SEC. Figure 4.2 illustrates the various players around the issuance of GSAMP Trust 2006-NC2 (Fligstein and Goldstein, 2010). The MBS contained mortgages originated by New Century Financial, one of the largest subprime originators. The SVP was set up by Goldman Sachs, an investment bank who produced the securities and marketed them. The bond was rated by Moody's and Standard and Poor's. The mortgage owners sent their payments every month to Ocwen, one of the largest servicers of MBSs. The activities of the trust were overseen by Deutsche Bank, who acted as the trustee of the SVP, and Wells Fargo, who acted to oversee the activities of Ocwen.

GSAMP Trust 2006-NC2 represents a typical structure for a subprime MBS. The SVP contained 3,949 subprime mortgages, which had a total value of $881 million. The prospectus provided some detailed information about the mortgagors: 43.4 percent of the mortgages were used to buy new homes, whereas 56.6 percent were refinancing existing mortgages; 90.7 percent of the mortgagors were going to live in the house; 73.4 percent were single-family houses, and the rest were condominiums; and 38 percent of the homes were in California, and 10.5 percent were in Florida. The average borrowers had a FICO score of 626; 30.4 percent had a score below 600, 51.9 percent between 600 and 660, and only 16.7 percent had FICO scores over 660. The ratio of monthly payments to monthly income was 42 percent in the whole set of mortgages.[4] Figure 4.3 presents the tranche description of the MBS. About 79 percent of the bonds were

Tranche description			Credit Ratings		Coupon Rate	
Class	Notional	Width	Subordination	S&P	Moody's	(1)	(2)
A-1	$239,618,000	27.18%	72.82%	AAA	Aaa	0.15%	0.30%
A-2A	$214,090,000	24.29%	48.53%	AAA	Aaa	0.07%	0.14%
A-2B	$102,864,000	11.67%	36.86%	AAA	Aaa	0.09%	0.18%
A-2C	$99,900,000	11.33%	25.53%	AAA	Aaa	0.15%	0.30%
A-2D	$42,998,000	4.88%	20.65%	AAA	Aaa	0.24%	0.48%
M-1	$35,700,000	4.05%	16.60%	AA+	Aa1	0.30%	0.45%
M-2	$28,649,000	3.25%	13.35%	AA	Aa2	0.31%	0.47%
M-3	$16,748,000	1.90%	11.45%	AA-	Aa3	0.32%	0.48%
M-4	$14,986,000	1.70%	9.75%	A+	A1	0.35%	0.53%
M-5	$14,545,000	1.65%	8.10%	A	A2	0.37%	0.56%
M-6	$13,663,000	1.55%	6.55%	A-	A3	0.46%	0.69%
M-7	$12,341,000	1.40%	5.15%	BBB+	Baa1	0.90%	1.35%
M-8	$11,019,000	1.25%	3.90%	BBB	Baa2	1.00%	1.50%
M-9	$7,052,000	0.80%	3.10%	BBB-	Baa3	2.05%	3.08%
B-1	$6,170,000	0.70%	2.40%	BB+	Ba1	2.50%	3.75%
B-2	$8,815,000	1.00%	1.40%	BB	Ba2	2.50%	3.75%
X	$12,340,995	1.40%	0.00%	NR	NR	N/A	N/A

FIGURE 4.3   Capital structure of GSAMP Trust 2006-NC2. Source: Securities and Exchange Commission.

rated AAA, the highest ratings. Less than 5 percent were rated B. One can see from the figure that the coupon rate (i.e., the payout) goes up as the riskiness of the tranche goes up.

The final process innovation involved the role of the credit rating agencies in the process. Credit rating agencies have a long history in the financial community. The precursors of today's rating agencies were established in the middle of the nineteenth century. The first such agency was established in 1841 by Lewis Tappan in New York City. It was subsequently acquired by Robert Dun, who published its first ratings guide in 1859. Another early agency was founded by John Bradstreet in 1849 and published a ratings guide in 1857. In 1933, the firms merged to form Dun and Bradstreet.

Credit rating agencies expanded their activities significantly in the late nineteenth and early twentieth centuries, mostly to rate railroad bonds (Carruthers, 2013). Henry Poor's publishing company produced a publication compiling financial data about the railroad and canal industries in 1901. In 1909, financial analyst John Moody issued a publication focused solely on railroad bonds. His ratings became the first to be published widely in an accessible format, and his company was the first to charge subscription fees to investors. In 1913, the ratings publication by Moody's underwent two significant changes: it expanded its focus to include industrial firms and utilities, and it began to use a letter-rating system. For the first time, public securities were rated using a system borrowed from the mercantile credit rating agencies, using letters to indicate their creditworthiness. In the next few years, antecedents of the "Big Three" credit rating agencies were established. Poor's Publishing Company began issuing ratings in 1916, Standard Statistics Company in 1922, and the Fitch Publishing Company in 1924.

The rating industry grew rapidly following the passage of the Glass-Steagall Act of 1933, which separated the securities business from the commercial banking business. This opened a market for more information about stocks and bonds. The creation of the SEC promoted more transparency in stock and bond offerings to the public. In 1936, a regulation was introduced to prohibit banks from investing in bonds determined by "recognized rating manuals" to be "speculative investment securities" (Carruthers, 2013). Banks were permitted to hold only "investment grade" bonds, and it was the ratings of Fitch, Moody's, Poor's, and Standard that legally determined which bonds were which. State insurance regulators approved similar requirements in the following decades.

In 1975, the SEC recognized the largest agencies as nationally recognized statistical rating organizations and relied on such agencies exclusively for distinguishing between grades of creditworthiness in various regulations under federal securities laws. This allowed the SEC to decide who was going to be able to be in the business of rating debt. The Credit Rating Agency Reform Act of 2006 created a voluntary registration system for credit rating agencies that met certain minimum criteria, and it provided the SEC with broader oversight authority. The practice of using credit rating agency ratings for regulatory purposes has since expanded globally. Rating agencies have grown in size and profitability as the number of issuers accessing the debt markets grew exponentially, both in the United States and abroad. By 2009 the worldwide bond market reached an estimated $82.2 trillion, in 2009 dollars. Today, financial market regulations in many countries contain extensive references to ratings. For example, the Basel III accord, a global bank capital standardization effort, relies on credit ratings to calculate minimum capital standards and minimum liquidity ratios.

Credit rating is a highly concentrated industry, with the Big Three credit rating agencies controlling approximately 95 percent of the ratings business in the United States. Moody's Investors Service and Standard and Poor's (S&P) together control 80 percent of the global market, and Fitch Ratings another 15 percent. As of December 2012, S&P is the largest of the three, with 1.2 million outstanding ratings and 1,416 analysts and supervisors. Moody's has 1 million outstanding ratings and 1,252 analysts and supervisors; and Fitch is the smallest, with approximately 350,000 outstanding ratings.

Credit rating agencies generate revenue from a variety of activities related to the production and distribution of credit ratings. Before the 1970s, the credit rating agencies were mostly paid by investors, who had to have a subscription to the service. But it proved difficult to control the dissemination of the ratings because that information could be shared across investors or between the sellers of securities and the buyers. So, beginning in the 1970s, the source of their revenue shifted to the issuer of the securities or the investor. While this set up a potential conflict of interest, this was thought to be ameliorated by having to have two agencies rate any bond. In the MBS era, the issuer of the securities paid the credit rating agencies for their ratings. Many observers have blamed these agencies for overrating bonds and thus contributing to the crisis (Financial Crisis Inquiry Commission, 2011; White, 2009). While there was pressure put on the credit rating agencies to turn out favorable ratings very quickly, it is also the case that the models used to create tranches of MBSs were overly optimistic (Benmelech and Dlugosz, 2010; White, 2010; Rona-Tas and Hiss, 2010).

It is useful to turn to a discussion of the process technology that allowed the credit rating agencies to help assign mortgages to tranches of MBSs. In the beginning, issuers would submit their assignment to tranches to the credit rating agencies, and the agencies would decide if they approved of the division. But over time, as the volume of ABSs increased, issuers would be given the models used by the credit rating agencies.

The models that the credit rating agencies used contained a variety of information, mostly based on the data gathered when the mortgager applied for the loan. There were two issues involved in the assignment to a tranche. First was the probability that a particular mortgagor would prepay the mortgage either by defaulting or selling the house in a few years. Second was data on where the house was located. Since one of the main predictors of prepayment risk was local market conditions (i.e., whether house prices were rising or falling), the credit rating agencies were worried about having too many houses in a tranche being in the same area.

The idea was that if all of the houses were in a small set of nearby zip codes, then if that market began to have falling house prices, all of the mortgages in that area would be in greater danger of prepayment. In statistical language, one wanted the probability that any mortgage would be prepaid to be independent of the probability of any other mortgage to be prepaid. This was measured by the correlation coefficient, a measure of the degree of association that is standardized from -1 (totally negatively correlated) to $+1$ (totally positively correlated). If the cases were independent of each other, the correlation would be 0. To deal with this, the credit rating agencies wanted tranches to be diversified geographically so that the correlation between local market conditions of the mortgagors in the tranche would generally be low. It turns out that one of the reasons that the tranches of CDOs began to fail is that the correlation between mortgages was much higher than built into the models (Benmelech and Dlugosz, 2010; White, 2010).

The process innovations of computer programs to enter data and approve mortgages, credit scores, and securitization allowed new forms of financial products to proliferate. They provided financial institutions with the ability to process massive numbers of mortgages and aided in creating a national market for both mortgage origination and mortgage securitization. They were at the core of financial innovation in the mortgage industry because they were the foundation of the shift from the mortgage market to the mortgage securitization market. They operated as the how-to of mortgage securitization by creating the possibility of faster mortgage creation and the industrial creation of mortgage securities.

Market and Organizational Innovations

The innovations in products and processes were accompanied by a set of changes to the markets and firms that populated the MBS industry. In Chapter 3, I discussed how the field of the mortgage industry was transformed into the field of mortgage securitization with the collapse of the savings and loan model of products, process, and organization. Here, I want to discuss three kinds of organizational innovation and briefly mention the growth of markets related to banks participating in an increasing number of markets with an increasing scope. The world of banking that had formed in the era of the Great Depression had separated the investment, commercial, and savings and loan banks into separate markets with different regulations and regulators. Banking was also fragmented across the country as states produced laws to favor their small, home-grown banks.

The business models for all branches of banking were in crisis in the 1980s and early 1990s, as I have already discussed. The largest banks lobbied Congress to break down state banking laws in order to allow cross-border mergers and market takeover. During the 1980s and 1990s, the mantra of the industry became the idea of the conglomerate or full-service bank. In a series of reforms, banking regulators gradually allowed banks to enter into new industries. In 1999, the Gramm-Leach-Bliley Act formally removed the last barrier between investment and commercial banking. As we have already documented, by the time this happened, the law was more or less not being enforced. One outcome that was less noticed was that the removal of this barrier did not bring most banks to engage in the traditional investment banking activities of selling government bonds or helping corporations engage in mergers and initial public offerings. Ironically, instead of producing conglomerate banks as the new business model, the breakdown of the barrier between investment and commercial banking mostly led to vertical integration of banks by incorporating the origination, securitization, loan servicing, and trading functions of MBS internally in their organizations.

These organization changes produced growth in a set of markets. Of course, the mortgage origination market became national. The MBS-CDO market became focused on Wall Street, and the products produced generated a large international market, particularly after 2003. Finally, the repo, money market, and asset-backed commercial paper (ABCP) markets expanded dramatically to provide capital for banks to borrow short term to fund mortgage origination (Stighum, 1989). This eventually also allowed them to borrow money to fund their investments in the securities they produced based on these mortgages.

Conclusion

The upshot of this chapter is that financial product innovation was deeply rooted in the transformation of banking and finance more generally. The impetus to all of this change was the high inflation and slow economic growth of the 1970s. This condition, called stagflation, undermined the business models of savings and loan, commercial, and investment banks. Savings and loan banks could no longer make money by borrowing at low interest rates and lending for thirty years. Commercial banks found their corporate customers going directly to the financial markets to protect themselves from high inflation, high interest rates, and potential bank control. Investment banks found that the stock market was not growing, so new businesses needed to be found in order to rekindle growth.

It is not surprising that in order to save their firms, executives lobbied to have the regulations that had governed banking and finance changed. Those barriers, mostly erected during the Great Depression of the 1930s, had provided stable profits for forty years. But as financial institutions found that the protection afforded to their markets was no longer guaranteeing profits, they needed to change their business models. Thus, they were willing to make trade-offs to potentially open their protected markets to others in order to create new products and processes. In the face of a crisis in one's main line of business, these trade-offs were not hard to make.

Banking and finance circa 1975 consisted of highly regulated markets that were segregated by products, geography, and types of banking organizations. Both state governments and the federal government responded to these lobbying efforts by allowing banks to get bigger, enter into new product lines, and engage in activities across state borders. These changes were sometimes resisted by local banks or parts of the financial services industry. But, over time, the resistance was worn down, and by 1999 banks and financial institutions were free to enter any business they wanted.

The financial challenges of the 1970s also brought banks to create new products in order to find customers in a slow-growth and high-inflation era. In particular, the evolution of mortgages sold to home buyers and mortgage-backed securities sold to investors was propelled by creating products to overcome the objections of potential buyers. In the 1970s, interest rates were so high that mortgagors could not afford to buy houses. In the next twenty years, new kinds of mortgages were created to allow more and more people to buy homes even as the cost of doing so rose. Selling MBSs and CDOs required creating products that overcame the objections of investors. Having high-rated securities that paid relatively high interest rates and appeared to have the tacit backing of the government eventually brought legions of new buyers into the market. The complexity of these instruments was the outcome of trying to please buyers who had to be convinced the product met their needs.

But the creation of these products also required new financial processes. Without high-speed computers, credit scores, and credit ratings, financial instruments could not be created or sold. Computer programs that allowed the rapid entry of mortgagor information and a quick turnaround in mortgage approval processes revolutionized the industry. They drastically lowered the costs associated with the origination of mortgages and drove a dramatic increase in the number of such mortgages that could be originated. On the other side of the market, the innovations associated with securitization became technologies that allowed the production of massive numbers of bonds out of mortgages and other financial assets that seemed too different for such treatment. This in turn stimulated the growth of the largest financial firms, who used these new processes to create new markets for their products.

By 2000, all of the product, process, and market innovations that structured the mortgage securitization industry were in place. The largest financial institutions in the country were operating in many product markets, across many states, and with a great deal of volume. As was documented in Chapter 3, the great surprise in all of this was that the main product that could be counted on to attain the scale necessary to keep financial institutions growing was the mortgage securitization industry. And the main organizational vehicle for all of this was vertical integration, whereby banks controlled or owned mortgage originators, ran investment banking units that produced mortgage-backed securities, sold these securities to investors, and bought these securities for their own accounts. All of this was done using borrowed money.

This business model and the system that had been built to support it proved to be one of the most profitable of all time. The first eight years of the twenty-first century witnessed a dramatic rise in the use of this new structure as the housing refinance boom of 2001–2004 increased the origination market from about $1.5 trillion to almost $4 trillion. This opportunity brought the mortgage securitization industry to dominate not just the financial sector but the whole economy. Banks from around the world came to participate in this feeding frenzy. The financial sectors of many of the largest, most developed countries in the world, including Great Britain, France, the Netherlands, Germany, Ireland, Iceland, and Switzerland came to share in the profits generated by the mortgage securitization industry.

5

THE SUBPRIME MOMENT, 2001–2008

During the 1990s, the market for mortgage origination fluctuated between $500 billion and $1.5 trillion and provided the raw material for MBSs. The banks that entered multiple parts of these markets profited greatly. Banks that had experienced difficulties in producing growth in their other businesses found explosive growth opportunities in the mortgage securitization industry. While the mortgage origination and securitization businesses were large in 2000, the industry was about to hit a growth spurt that can be described as nothing less than breathtaking. Beginning in 2000, the volume of residential mortgage origination climbed dramatically and reached almost $4 trillion at its peak in 2003, an increase of 400 percent from its base. This kind of growth is unheard of and historically unprecedented. Even after reaching this peak, the market for mortgage origination still was $3 trillion from 2004 to 2006 and $2.5 trillion in 2007. It was only in the year of the crisis, 2008, that it dropped back down to $1.5 trillion, still at the high end of what it had been throughout the 1990s.

Obviously, the roots of the financial crisis have to be traced to this rapid expansion and eventual contraction of mortgage origination. The low interest rates after 2000 provided fuel for a large surge in house purchases, house refinancing, and house price appreciation. But interest rates began to rise in 2003, and the level of origination stayed high anyway. This is because when this rocket fuel was spent, banks were hungry to keep the party going. The banks were driven by the need to originate mortgages in order to secure fees to feed the demand for MBSs which remained high in an investment environment where lots of investors who now had experience buying MBSs were looking for safe, fixed-interest bonds. The basic problem was to find new originations in order to keep the securitization business going. That meant finding households to give mortgages to who had not participated in the first wave of refinancing or purchasing new homes.

Households who had been historically excluded from home purchases (such as racial and ethnic minorities) and people with more impaired credit became the target of originators and securitizers.

It was not just the desire on the part of home loan originators to keep their loan machines going that drove the process. Without the huge demand for securities produced with those mortgages, the origination boom might have collapsed earlier. Instead, the demand for securities based on mortgages that had high bond ratings and paid relatively high rates of return meant that mortgages were not just necessary to keep originators going; they also provided the raw material for securities that were greatly in demand. For vertically integrated banks that were making money off both of these markets, it was imperative to continue to secure mortgages and to turn them into securities. There were two indicators of this. Over time, the demand for MBSs pushed securitizers to also use the mortgages they had more effectively. After 2000, the percentage of mortgages that were eventually turned into securities rose from about half to almost 90 percent. From 2005 to 2007, the demand for securities remained high, and this brought banks to repackage their hard-to-sell lower tranches into CDO-CDOs, where they could claim that the top tranches were AAA rated.

Not surprisingly, Countrywide Financial led the way to pivot toward the nonconventional mortgage market as a source for new mortgages when the market for refinancing existing homes and purchasing new homes was saturated. From 2003 to 2007, the entire industry increasingly became involved in providing credit for the subprime, adjustable-rate, interest-only, home equity, and Alt-A markets. The fees associated with these loans were larger. The MBSs based on them paid higher rates of return because the mortgages they were based on charged higher interest rates for nonconventional mortgages. This pushed banks to increase their integration by buying up providers of those loans and increasing their output of MBSs. By 2007, this process had reached its peak.

But eventually, even this market began to dry up. Banks pursued mortgagors who had less and less ability to pay back their loans. Nearly everyone who could have refinanced their loans had done so, and most households who wanted home equity lines had purchased them. By 2006, the quality of loans being made deteriorated. When house prices began to drop beginning in the summer of 2006, it made it more difficult for borrowers in distress to sell their homes. This process cascaded in places where prices had risen the fastest. As loans began to be foreclosed, the entire structure came under duress.

The banks didn't change their tactics when this happened, because their business model depended not just on originating mortgages but in turning those mortgages into securities that would be sold or held on their own accounts.

When the raw material for that throughput began to fail, the only real option was to double down and hope that they would be the last bank standing. Most banks had little choice but to keep going. Moreover, there was a huge worldwide demand for their end products: MBSs. The low interest rates of the early 2000s meant that investors were looking for higher rates of return on safer investments. Since most MBSs had AAA ratings and paid attractive returns, integrated banks could not get enough mortgages to produce securities to take advantage of the booming market for those securities. In the face of all of this, vertically integrated banks could do only one thing: try to buy and process more mortgages (*Mortgage Banking*, 2005; *American Banker*, 2007).

While it is difficult to prove, it is certainly plausible that part of what kept the housing price bubble going was the demand for MBSs. After the demand for refinancing lessened in 2004 and the Federal Reserve began to raise interest rates, originations should have dropped off much more. But because financial institutions needed mortgages for their MBS products, instead of following the cycle down (which is what has happened historically), they were pushed to find new mortgages to originate. The move toward giving credit to less-qualified buyers makes sense only in a world where those mortgages were valuable instruments as inputs into MBSs (Nadauld and Sherlund, 2013).

It is no surprise, then, that as the mortgages became harder to find, desperate financial institutions began to repackage tranches of MBSs with lower ratings into CDO-CDOs that could then be rated as AAA bonds. The proliferation of these products shows how large the demand for MBSs was. But the overall quality of loans deteriorated as borrowers with worse and worse credit were given loans. The lower tranches of existing MBSs and CDOs were already based on loans with higher risk. Not surprisingly, it was the MBSs and CDO-CDOs that were created in 2006–2008 that had the worst financial performance. In essence, the vertically integrated model whereby banks needed to keep making securities in order to keep their vertically integrated businesses going pushed the banks to continue to scrape the bottom of the origination barrel. When that failed, they took to cannibalizing MBS tranches that they could not sell and turned them into CDO-CDOs that they could. The result was bonds that might be rated AAA but contained lots of mortgages that were guaranteed to fail, particularly as prices for houses stopped rising.

The final aspect of these markets was that all of the banks were running their integrated structures on borrowed money. This started out somewhat innocuously. Banks would borrow money to purchase mortgages in either the repo or asset-backed commercial paper (ABCP) markets. These markets are what we now call "shadow banking" (Pozsar et al., 2011). The main players in these markets were other banks who would loan money at low interest rates for short periods of time. The original idea was that once the loans were processed into securities and sold, the lines of credit would be paid back, and the process would start again. But over time, banks used these markets to not only fund their short-term needs for capital but also borrow money to buy securities on their own accounts. They would use the bonds that they bought as collateral for the loans.

The problem here was that these loans were supposed to be short term, ninety days to a year. But banks thought that they could either roll the loans over or go back to the markets to borrow to continue to hold the bonds and, if necessary, sell them. Gorton (2010) has termed this tactic "borrowing short to go long." This tactic proved quite lucrative. One made profit on the borrowed money without having to use one's own capital to fund the investment. This pushed banks to increase their indebtedness and explains why, on the eve of the crisis, banks were unable to come up with capital to cover their borrowings for mortgages and securities whose value was difficult to assess.

The vertically integrated structure of the largest banks meant that their business models were highly profitable when the origination market was deep and the demand for MBSs high. They lived off of borrowed money and used it to buy securities for their own accounts. But as the market for originations got more difficult and as the demand for MBSs began to dry up when mortgage defaults and foreclosures rose, these same banks found themselves having to come up with cash to either pay back the money they owed or increase the collateral on the money they had borrowed.

Beginning with Bear Stearns in the spring of 2007 and ending with Lehman Brothers in the fall of 2008, the vertically integrated model of mortgage securitization began to collapse. When banks had to cover what they had borrowed, their main assets were MBSs whose value was difficult to determine because of the defaults and foreclosures of the underlying mortgages. This created what was widely viewed as a liquidity crisis. Banks had assets, but they could not sell them fast enough to cover their short-term debts. But once banks started to teeter in the summer of 2008, it became difficult to price MBSs, and there was little market for them. This meant that many banks were unable to sell what they held at any price, and their liquidity crisis quickly meant they were insolvent. They did not have enough capital to pay back their loans. In the fall of 2008, all of the major players in these markets were bankrupt, were forced into mergers, or ended up taking government money to keep them solvent.

In this chapter, I will document how this process unfolded. I begin with basic data on what happened from 2000 to 2008. Then, I consider how the industry operated to take advantage of low interest rates from 2000 to 2003. Next, I turn to how the banks shifted from conventional mortgages to unconventional mortgages as their main source of MBSs after 2003. While this worked for a couple of years, it eventually broke down as the supply of these mortgages was limited. Banks were desperate to keep their securitization machines going, and, in essence, they kept going by trying harder to find such loans. I show that banks proliferated CDO-CDOs in order to meet the demands of their securities customers.

The Basic Facts

During the 1990s, all of the stock indices, particularly the NASDAQ index, increased dramatically. The market was driven by interest in the initial public offerings of a wave of internet companies coming to market. Beginning in 2000, that market peaked and began to fall dramatically. The NASDAQ index was at about 1,000 in 1995, and it peaked at 5,048 in 2000, an increase of 500 percent. By the end of 2001, it had fallen to 1,500. The Federal Reserve Bank was worried about the effect of the stock market crash on the economy and began to dramatically lower interest rates.[1] During the 1990s, the rate was around 5 percent, and it peaked in 2000 at 6 percent. Within twenty-four months, the rate dropped to 1 percent. It began to rise in 2003 but remained under 3 percent until 2005.

The most important impact of this dramatic lowering of the federal funds rate was that credit throughout the economy grew dramatically cheaper. This created an amazing opportunity for banks that were originators and securitizers (Westhoff and Kramer, 2001; *Asset Securitization Report,* 2001). For originators, low interest rates meant ramping up their financing and refinancing activities. Many homeowners had mortgages purchased in the 1990s that had 7–8 percent interest rates. As interest rates for mortgages dropped to 4–5 percent, originators aggressively sought out customers. The low interest rates had a huge effect on the demand for MBSs as well. Treasury bonds, the safest investments, now had very low yields (1–2 percent). For investors who needed safe investments but wanted higher returns, MBSs that paid 4–5 percent interest and were AAA rated seemed like a godsend. This perfect storm of low interest rates produced record profits for banks, particularly those who were making fees off both origination and securitization. Often these same banks held MBSs for investment.

Figure 5.1 shows that in 2000, before the rates were lowered, the mortgage origination market was about $1 trillion. But as rates dropped, the market dramatically increased. It is no surprise that in the three years (2001–2003) when interest rates were below 3 percent, mortgage originations increased almost 400 percent. Figure 5.1 also shows that the bulk of the mortgage activity was for con-

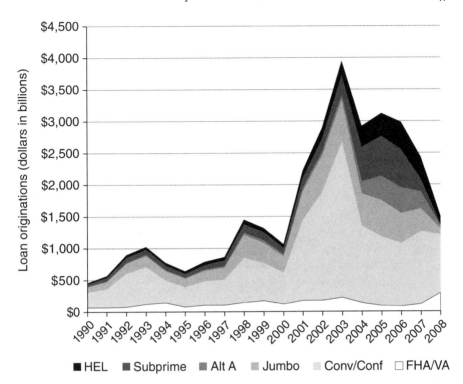

HEL ■ Subprime ■ Alt A ■ Jumbo   Conv/Conf □ FHA/VA

FIGURE 5.1 Residential mortgage origination by type, 1990–2008. Reformatted from Neil
Fligstein and Adam Goldstein, "The Anatomy of the Mortgage Securitization Crisis," in
Markets on Trial: The Economic Sociology of the U.S. Financial Crisis, edited by M. Lounsbury
and P. Hirsch, p. 41, figure 5.

ventional mortgages, which increased from $500 billion to $2.5 trillion, about
500 percent. There were increases in jumbo loans and subprime loans as well,
from about $500 billion to $1.25 trillion, but most of the action was for conventional mortgages.

Figure 5.2 presents data on the degree to which the mortgages were for either
newly bought houses or refinancing for existing homeowners. I note that all of
the conventional and unconventional forms of mortgages except home equity
loans could be for either new homes or refinancing. During the 1990s, the percentage of all mortgages that were refinanced fluctuated with interest rates. Most
of the time, refinancing was a smaller part of the total package than new mortgages. But beginning in 2000, one can observe that refinancing took off. During
2003, the peak year for mortgage originations, refinancing comprised almost 75
percent of all new mortgages. Taken together, these figures show the effects of
the huge drop in interest rates on the housing origination market. Given that
mortgage interest rates during the 1990s had been relatively high, the low-interest-rate environment of 2000–2003 opened a floodgate of refinancing.

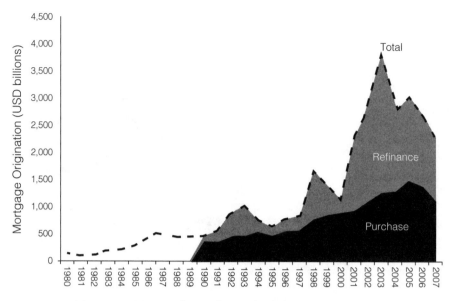

FIGURE 5.2 Mortgage originations by purchase and refinance. Data sources: Mortgage Bankers Association and US Department of Housing and Urban Development.

As the refinancing boom took off, house price appreciation also increased dramatically. Low interest rates meant that households could afford to buy more expensive houses, and they did. Indeed, prices increased dramatically. The Case-Shiller index shows that house prices were on an upward slope for much of the 1990s (Federal Reserve, 2018). But beginning in 2000, prices spiked dramatically. Between 2000 and 2005, house prices doubled. One impact of these rapidly escalating house prices was a spike in jumbo loans. Recall that jumbo loans were invented for people who bought very expensive houses without a 20 percent down payment. As prices increased by double digits, particularly in a few states such as California, New York, and Massachusetts, more and more households found themselves having to purchase a jumbo loan in order to get into the housing market. From Figure 5.1, one can see the growth of jumbo loans throughout the period.

The low-interest-rate environment stimulated investors to seek out higher returns on their investments. MBSs were AAA rated and paid anywhere from 2 to 3 percent more in interest than did government bonds (Vanguard, 2013). In the suddenly low-interest-rate world of the early 2000s, the demand for MBSs went through the roof. Figure 5.3 presents data on the increases in holdings of MBSs by various kinds of investor types. At the top of the graph, one can see that the GSEs held \$1–1.2 trillion throughout the period. The largest increases come from

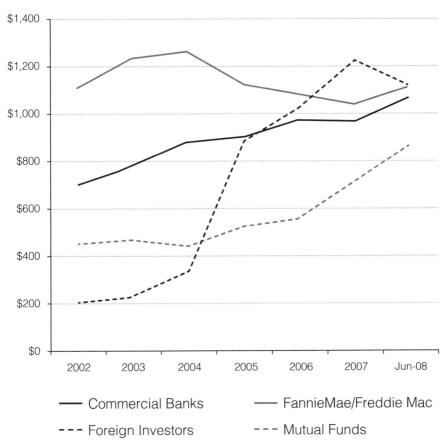

FIGURE 5.3 Mortgage-related security holdings of four largest investor types, 2002–2008. Reformatted from Neil Fligstein and Adam Goldstein, "The Anatomy of the Mortgage Securitization Crisis," in *Markets on Trial: The Economic Sociology of the U.S. Financial Crisis*, edited by M. Lounsbury and P. Hirsch, p. 47, figure 7.

financial institutions in the private sector. Commercial banks went from owning $700 billion in MBSs in 2002 to owning $1.1 trillion by June 2008. Mutual funds increased their share of MBSs from $400 billion to $850 billion. Finally, foreign investors were the largest purchasers of MBSs in this period, increasing their holdings from a little over $200 billion to a peak of $1.2 trillion. This figure shows quite clearly that the demand for MBSs continued to be dramatic even after the initial wave of refinancing ended in 2003 and interest rates rose. The pivot toward nonconventional mortgages was thus not just about keeping mortgage origination going. Finding more mortgages to package into MBSs was imperative to meet the demand for MBSs. Figure 5.3 confirms that the banks were among their own best customers for MBSs. Simply put, they held on to many MBSs because they were high-earning and safe investments.

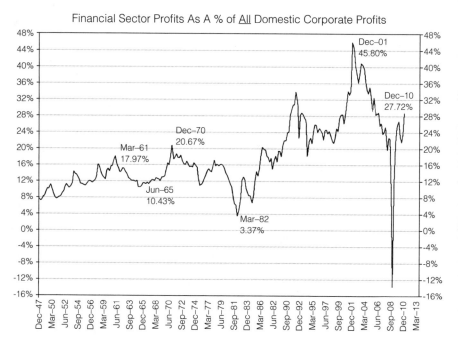

Financial Sector Profits

Consists of credit intermediation and related activities; securities, commodity contracts, and other financial investments and related activities; insurance carriers and related activities; funds, trusts, and other financial vehicles; and bank and other holding companies.

FIGURE 5.4 Financial profits as a share of all profits. Source: Bureau of Economic Analysis, Department of Congress, National Income and Product Reports, 2012.

Finally, it is useful to see how this huge spike in mortgages, refinancing, house prices, and the purchase of MBSs affected the fortunes of the financial sector. The financial sector of the economy employed about 6 percent of the labor force during this period and had accounted for about 8 percent of GDP (Greenwood and Scharfstein, 2013). Figure 5.4 shows the massive overrepresentation of finance as a percentage of corporate profits in the United States since the 1990s. From 1949 until about 1990, the share of profits in finance was anywhere from 5 to 15 percent of the total in the economy, roughly in line with their weight in the economy. But beginning in the 1990s, it began to increase. From 2000, it went from about 25 percent to a peak of 40 percent in 2003. It remained above 30 percent until 2008. Greenwood and Scharfstein (2013) decompose the parts of finance that are generating these profits. They conclude that in 1990, only 20 percent of the activity in finance was involved in mortgages. In 2007, 80 percent of the activity in finance was involved in mortgages or mortgage securitization.

The vertical integration strategy of the largest banks proved to be robustly profitable in the face of declining interest rates. Both of their main products, mortgages and securities, benefited from the low-interest-rate environment. Not only was the business of originating mortgages and packaging and selling securities lucrative, but financial institutions led the way in accumulating MBSs as investments (Scharfstein and Sunderam, 2013). What is breathtaking about this expansion was the sheer size of the markets for mortgages and MBSs. At its peak in 2003, almost $4 trillion of mortgages were originated. It goes without saying that this huge expansion was one of the core industries driving the American economy in this period. This tactic of originating, securitizing, and buying MBSs was so profitable that by 2003, with 6 percent of the labor force and 8 percent of GDP, financial institutions were sucking up 40 percent of all corporate profits in the US economy.

But, as with every market that exuberantly expands, eventually the demand for products is saturated. Here, the conventional market for originations and refinancing mortgages started to decline in 2004, partially because of interest rate increases but also because the number of households left to refinance their mortgages began to dwindle. But the demand for MBSs remained high. In order to keep their vertically integrated businesses going, the industry was confronted by a need to find new mortgages to securitize. From 2004 to 2008, financial institutions shifted from conventional mortgage products to unconventional mortgage products in order to keep their securitization machines moving. For four years, it worked.

From Conventional Mortgages to Nonconventional Mortgages

It is important to dig down to understand how the financial institutions behaved strategically to face these opportunities and challenges. But while vertically integrated financial institutions were on the rise in the 1990s, it was really only with the opportunities presented by the huge expansion of the mortgage origination and securitization markets after 2000 that those opportunities were fully realized.[2] The 1990s and 2000s witnessed two important forms of consolidation: first, a growing concentration of mortgage originators, and second, the growing use of mortgages in securitization. These changes are consistent with the view that vertical integration strengthened in this period.

In 1992, the twenty-five largest financial institutions controlled only 30 percent of the mortgage origination market. The collapse of the saving and loan banks and the fragmentation of the market for both origination and securitization meant that the markets were populated by specialists, not generalists (Jacobides, 2005). This led to the rise of the originate-to-distribute model of the market where originators would sell off loans to brokers and wholesalers, who might then sell them to banks, or directly to the GSEs. Then, investment banks would be hired to underwrite and sell MBSs. Finally, the MBSs would end up in the portfolios of a wide variety of financial institutions. This disintegration is accurately reflected in the fact that originators were widely dispersed and did not control much market share.

But during the 1990s and continuing throughout the 2000s, concentration of origination steadily proceeded. By 2000, the twenty-five largest financial institutions controlled 70 percent of the market for both prime and subprime lenders. By 2008, this had increased to 90 percent (Inside Mortgage Finance, 2009). This did not make mortgage origination a particularly concentrated market by conventional measures (such as the Herfindahl index). But the goal of consolidation was not to create an oligopoly or monopoly in order to raise prices to consumers for originating mortgages. The goal instead was to guarantee integrated banks a supply of mortgages to securitize. By buying up market share in origination, financial institutions could secure a supply of mortgages to turn into securities and create a pipeline where they could reap fees at all stages of production.

A similar process was occurring in the growth of securitization of mortgages. In 1995, a little under 50 percent of conventional mortgages were being turned into securities. Mortgages from the subprime market, which was quite small at this early date, were being securitized at a rate of only 28 percent. These figures suggest that at least half of all mortgages were still being held in portfolios as investments. Throughout the late 1990s, the rate of securitization of mortgages of both types rose, and by 2000, about 60 percent of all mortgages were being securitized. Again, these low levels of securitization reflected the fragmentation of the mortgage origination market in the early 1990s and, even more so, the fragmentation of investors. Many mortgages throughout the 1990s were not part of the originate-to-distribute system, and about half ended up being held by investors who owned individual mortgages. But beginning in 2000, the rate of securitization rose dramatically. By 2007, 90 percent of all mortgages eventually ended up in securities (Inside Mortgage Finance, 2009).

What caused this to happen? This reflected two forces. First, as I have already suggested, the demand for MBSs after 2000 rose dramatically, as they became safe and high-yielding investments for many financial institutions. This meant that mortgages as the raw materials for securitization became more valuable as inputs into a production process. Financial institutions that were in the securitization business had to buy more mortgages in order to feed the demand for MBSs. Given this demand, this meant buying up originated mortgages at higher and higher rates in order to create those securities. Second, vertically integrated production was a good tactic to guarantee that there were enough mortgages for throughput to make MBSs. By owning originators or buying them up, vertically integrated securities producers were able to ensure themselves a supply of mortgages to drive their securitization businesses. As the demand for securities increased even in the face of a lower level of origination activity after 2003, getting mortgages became even more paramount in order to keep securitization machines going. This was all compounded by the fact that as more and more financial institutions entered both the origination and securitization businesses, mortgages became scarcer and thus more likely to end up in securities.

The one part of the story that I have not yet documented is how a few large financial institutions came to dominate both origination and securitization. Table 5.1 shows how this worked over time by examining the identities of the nine largest originators and the nine largest issuers of securities in both the conventional and subprime markets. In the world of 1996, one can observe the relatively low level of concentration in origination of both prime and subprime originators. There are several large banks on the list, such as Countrywide, WaMu, and Bank of America, but there are also relatively small and regional banks, such as Norwest, Nations-Bank, and FT Mortgage. The subprime originators were even smaller financial

Table 5.1 : Dominant firms in selected mortgage finance segments, 1996 and 2007

Top overall mortgage originators and market share (%)				Top subprime originators and market share (%)			
1996		**2007**		**1996**		**2007**	
Norwest	6.6	Countrywide Financial	16.8	Associates Capital	7.0	Citibank	10.2
Countrywide	4.9	Wells Fargo	11.2	Money Store	4.3	Household Finance (HSBC)	9.3
Chase	4.3	Chase	8.6	ContiMortgage	3.5	Countrywide	8.8
Fleet Financial	2.3	Citibank	8.1	Beneficial Mortgage	2.8	Wells Fargo	8.0
Bank America	2.0	Bank of America	7.8	Household Finance	2.6	1st Franklin (Merrill Lynch)	7.0
NationsBank	1.5	Washington Mutual	5.7	United Co.	2.3	Chase	6.0
WaMu	1.4	EMC (Bear Stearns)	4.0	Long Beach Mortgage	2.2	Washington Mutual	5.8
Standard Federal	1.3	1st Franklin (Lehman)	3.9	Equicredit	2.1	EMC (Bear Stearns)	4.1
FT Mortgage	1.3	Residential Capital (GMAC)	3.2	Aames Capital	2.0	Ameriquest (Lehman Brothers)	3.3

Table 5.1 : (continued)

Top nonagency MBS issuers and market share (%)				Top subprime MBS issuers and market share (%)			
1996		2007		1996		2007	
GE Capital	8.4	Countrywide	13.6	Money Store	10.3	Merrill Lynch	10.1
Independent National	5.0	Wells Fargo	7.8	United Co.	6.4	Countrywide	7.9
NW Assets	4.5	Lehman Brothers	7.1	ContiMortgage	5.3	Morgan Stanley	7.8
Merit	3.6	Bear Stearns	6.8	Beneficial	5.0	Lehman Brothers	5.5
Prudential	3.3	Washington Mutual	5.7	AMRESO	4.5	Bear Stearns	4.3
Salomon Bros.	3.3	Citibank	5.7	Aames	4.3	Barclays	3.4
Merrill Lynch	3.1	Merrill Lynch	5.6	Household Finance	4.2	Citibank	3.3
Donaldson, et. al.	2.0	Morgan Stanley	4.8	Residential Finance	4.2	Wells Fargo	3.2
Structural Assets	2.0	Bank of America	4.4	Associates Mutual	4.1	Washington Mutual	2.7

Source: *Inside Mortgage Finance* (2009).

institutions, and many of them were household lenders, not banks. These included such lenders as the Money Store, Associates Capital, and Household Finance.

In 1996, 90 percent of all the MBSs issued were from the GSEs (see Chapter 3). Thus, the data on market shares of nonagency issuers are all for very small producers. While there are a few investment banks on this list (such as Salomon Brothers, Merrill Lynch, and Donaldson, et. al.), most of the firms listed are smaller investors or insurance companies. The issuers of subprime MBSs at this point were many of the firms that specialized in subprime loans. None of the larger investment banks were in this line of business. This is because the business was still small. But it was also because it was viewed as inherently risky. The GSEs were not involved in subprime because their mandate was to issue securities from only conventional mortgages in this era. This made a market segmentation whereby GSEs dominated issuance in the prime market, while securitization of nonconventional loans was conducted almost solely by private firms. Before 2000, given the small size of the nonconventional market, most of the securitization was being done by small financial institutions.

By 2007, the picture for all four markets changed dramatically. The mortgage origination business was dominated by a large number of very large banks. This included Countrywide, Wells Fargo, Citibank, Bank of America, and Washington Mutual. The top issuers included all of these banks plus several of the investment banks such as Bear Stearns, Merrill Lynch, and Lehman Brothers, all of which also owned a mortgage originator. Seven of the top nine originators also appeared on the list of the top nine issuers. This clearly reflects the vertical integration of the largest banks.

The lack of competition from the GSEs for nonconventional mortgages meant that as they increased in volume after 2003, an opportunity to increase production of MBSs based on nonconventional mortgages opened up for private financial institutions. By 2007, seven of the top nine subprime originators appear on the list of the top issuers. Vertical integration clearly had spread not just to the overall origination market but importantly to the subprime part of the market. I note that six financial institutions appear on all four lists: Countrywide Financial, Bear Stearns, Lehman Brothers, Citibank, Bank of America, and Merrill Lynch. Washington Mutual (WaMu) appears on three of the four lists. This suggests that the banks with the largest market shares were involved in the origination and issuance of securities for both the conventional and subprime markets. By the time the crisis hit, the largest integrated banks dominated the origination and securitization businesses.

It is useful to see how big the expansion of the nonconventional MBS was after 2000. Figure 5.5 shows that before 2000, the level of private (i.e., non-GSE) MBS production was between $30 billion and $200 billion a year. Most of the MBSs being produced were subprime or Alt-A because the GSEs were not participants in that market. The GSEs obviously had cornered the MBS market for conventional MBSs throughout the 1990s and played the largest role in issuance. Beginning in 2000, with the great increase in securitization, opportunities opened up for non-GSE financial institutions. There was a significant increase in the production of prime MBSs. But the largest increases occurred in the production of subprime, Alt-A, and home equity loans. The overall level of MBS issuance increased from about $150 billion in 2000 to a peak of $1.15 trillion in 2005. The vertically integrated financial institutions named in Table 5.1 grew large and profitable after 2003 by the origination and securitization in the rising market for nonconventional loans. This is important because this expansion is part of why the industry was so susceptible to a crash. At the end, it was their MBS businesses that were producing the most toxic products, and when the bottom fell out, they were the ones whose business models collapsed.

Taken together, there is substantial evidence that the integration of origination and securitization in the largest banks moved from the periphery of the industry to the center from 1990 until 2008. By the late 1990s, there was already integration. Throughout the 1990s, financial institutions increased their origination activities and increasingly securitized the mortgages that were originated. Once the refinancing and new house markets took off in the wake of the dramatic lowering of interest rates, the largest financial institutions increased both their origination and issuance. This integration was most strongly reflected in the

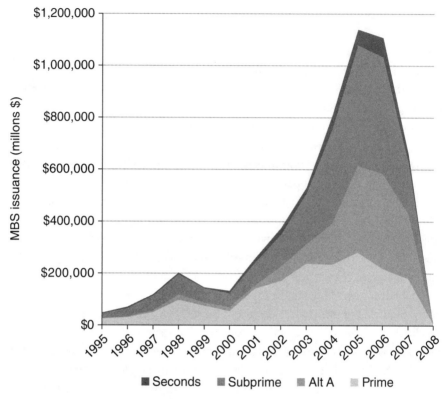

FIGURE 5.5 Amounts of MBS issuance by type for nonagency firms. Reformatted from Neil Fligstein and Adam Goldstein, "The Anatomy of the Mortgage Securitization Crisis," in *Markets on Trial: The Economic Sociology of the U.S. Financial Crisis*, edited by M. Lounsbury and P. Hirsch, p. 50, figure 8.

nonconventional mortgage market, where the GSEs did not directly complete until quite late. It is useful to consider more closely how this process worked at the firm level. I now turn to the rise of the nonconventional mortgage market in general and the move toward subprime mortgages in particular after 2003.

The Subprime Moment

After a record year in 2003, the mortgage securitization industry experienced a supply crisis in 2004. Figure 5.1 shows that the 2004 drop-off in new mortgages was severe, with monthly origination volumes declining over 70 percent from $200 billion in August 2003 to under $60 billion a year later. Several factors were at play, including a slight uptick in interest rates from their historic lows. But the foremost cause was that the 2003 refinancing boom had run its course. Of the $3.8 trillion of new mortgages written in 2003, $2.53 trillion, about two-thirds, was attributable to refinancing as borrowers took advantage of low rates.

The precipitous drop in mortgage originations posed a major source of concern for industry actors given that the dominant business model was based on high throughput. Interest rates were still relatively low, and there still existed a large demand for MBSs from investors. Moreover, originators had grown their operations and needed new markets for their suddenly excess capacity. As an editorialist in the Mortgage Bankers Association trade newsletter wrote, "Mortgage originators who geared up their operations to capitalize on the boom now face a dilemma. Given a saturated conforming market that is highly sensitive to interest rates, where can retail originators turn for the new business, they need to support the organizations they have built?" (*Mortgage Banking,* 2004).

Concerns about raw mortgage supply reverberated up the value chain. Barclays Capital researcher Jeff Salmon noted in May 2004 that "the recent dearth of supply has caught the [secondary] market off guard. If the financial industry is to keep the mortgage securitization machine churning, firms need to find a new source of mortgages" (*Asset Securitization Report,* 2004b).

Reporting on discussions at the June 2004 American Securitization Forum, the trade journal *Asset Securitization Report* noted that mortgage supply remained the "hot topic" but also noted the generally "harmonious agreement" among analysts from the major banks that the largely untapped nonprime markets could offer a solution to the supply crunch (*Asset Securitization Report,* 2004a). An editorial in *National Mortgage News* from March 2005 also highlighted the compensatory logic driving the growth of the nonprime markets: "The nonconventional market is booming this year. Taking up the slack (as it did last year) for the big drop off in prime lending and keeping record numbers of people employed in the mortgage industry."

Countrywide Financial was one of the first to take advantage of this shift, and they became a model that other firms emulated in order to profit from nonconventional lending. Their annual report boasted, "Countrywide's well balanced business model continues to produce strong operational results amidst a transitional environment. Compared to a year ago, the total mortgage origination market is smaller as a result of lower refinance volume. This impact has been mitigated by Countrywide's dramatic growth in purchase and funding of record volumes of adjustable rate, home equity, and nonconventional loans" (2005).

The rapidity with which the main players reoriented toward nonconventional lending and securitization after 2003 is evident in Figure 5.2. By 2005, the formerly niche nonconventional lending and securitization sectors had been rapidly transformed into a core business for the largest financial institutions in the country. Nonconventional origination and securitization turned out to be enormously profitable. Mortgagors with worse credit ended up paying higher fees for their loans and higher interest rates reflecting the riskier nature of the loans. Securities based on nonconventional loans paid higher rates of return and were rated AAA just like securities based on conventional loans. Over time, investors came to prefer the MBSs based on riskier mortgages because they liked the higher returns.

Not surprisingly, according to a study by the consulting firm Mercer Oliver Wyman, nonconventional lending accounted for approximately half of originations in 2005 but over 85 percent of profits (*Mortgage Servicing News,* 2005). Commercial banks, mortgage banks, and investment banks learned to profit from nonconventional MBSs in multiple ways simultaneously, earning money both from fees on MBS production and from investment income on retained MBS assets. As they were able to continue to fund both the production and the investment of securities with capital borrowed in the repo and ABCP markets, profit margins on nonconventional mortgages grew dramatically.

In sum, the shift toward nonconventional markets was caused by both a crisis and an opportunity. The crisis was the decline of the conventional market for mortgages that began in 2004. The opportunity was the realization that originating, packaging, and holding on to nonconventional MBSs was likely to result in higher returns than conventional mortgages. The absence of the GSEs allowed integrated firms to capture all the fees at every step. The riskier nature of the mortgages allowed the issuing and underwriting firms to charge a higher percentage fee for the more elaborate financial engineering that these non-agency-backed MBSs required. The resulting MBSs also paid out higher returns, as riskier loans had higher interest rates attached to them. After 2003, the large banks invaded nonconventional segments aggressively, wrested control from small subprime specialists, and, along with a few of the larger new mortgage firms such as Countrywide, applied the vertically integrated business model and grew these formerly marginal niche segments into a multitrillion-dollar-a-year business.

Vertical Integration Explored

The expansion of the nonconventional market promoted the final integration of the industrial model. The investment banks that had not already purchased originators began acquiring nonconventional originators aggressively after 2003 in a bid to feed their securitization machines (McGarity, 2006; J. Levine, 2007). Investment banks were also the leaders in the new nonconventional mortgage securities, and their buying of subprime originators assured them of material for their financial products. By 2005, Lehman Brothers was self-originating almost two-thirds of the mortgages contained in its $133 billion of MBS issues (Currie, 2007: 24). It was also common for commercial and investment banks to enter into formal agreements with independent originators in order to guarantee themselves additional supply of mortgages. So, much of the integration was not through formal ownership of originators.

The vertical integration of mortgage finance was spurred on by the desire of banking entities to control the mortgages from the point of origination to their ultimate sale. Jonathan Levine (2007: 59) concludes, "Why have the Wall Street firms so aggressively embraced this vertical integration strategy? The answer is to protect and leverage their returns from their mortgage underwriting and securitization desks. In fact, revenues from the fixed income divisions currently represent the largest components of the revenue mix for commercial and investment banks."

This analysis comports with the contemporaneous rationales voiced by executives of the leading players. Anthony Tufariello, head of the Morgan Stanley's Securitized Products Group, suggested in a press release distributed when Morgan Stanley bought mortgage originator Saxon Capital that "the addition of Saxon to Morgan Stanley's global mortgage franchise will help us to capture the full economic value inherent in this business. This acquisition facilitates our goal of achieving vertical integration in the residential mortgage business, with ownership and control of the entire value chain, from origination to capital markets execution to active risk management" (Morgan Stanley, 2006).

Dow Kim, president of Merrill Lynch's Global Markets Investment Banking group, made the very same point in announcing the acquisition of First Franklin, one of the largest nonconventional originators in 2006: "[Franklin's] leading mortgage origination and servicing franchises will add scale to our platform. . . . This transaction accelerates our vertical integration in mortgages, complementing the other three acquisitions we have made in this area and enhancing our ability to drive growth and returns" (Merrill Lynch, 2006). According to Jeff Verschleiser, then cohead of mortgage trading at Bear Stearns, "The key point to remember is that it's not just the buying that counts. It's the integration. Simply buying a mortgage originator and having it operate in a stand-alone capacity without leveraging the infrastructure of your institution is not something I would consider vertical integration." In short, executives at the core of the industry expressed a commonality in espousing an explicit orientation toward vertically integrated production of MBSs. Backward integration allowed them to secure raw product and scale up throughput to the lucrative securitization desks.

What was driving this process was the increased demand for low-risk, relatively high-return financial instruments—that is, MBSs and CDOs. There was simply an almost unlimited market for AAA-rated securities that yielded 2–3 percent more interest than government bonds in an era of low interest rates and low returns on government bonds. Nonconventional mortgages provided an important bonus for both originators and securitizers: they generated more fees for origination and allowed lenders to charge higher rates of interest. This meant that MBSs and CDOs could be AAA rated with higher returns, which of course made them even more attractive to investors. This drove integrated financial institutions to direct their originators to find nonconventional mortgages. At the hearings of the Financial Crisis Inquiry Commission (2011: 89), Kurt Eggert, a law professor, testified,

> I think we've had a presentation of the secondary market as mere passive, you know, purchasers of loans, that it's really the originators who decide the loan. But if you talk to people on the origination side, they'll tell you the complete opposite. They'll say, you know, our underwriting criteria are set by the secondary market. They tell us what kind of loans they want to buy. They tell us what underwriting criteria to use. And that's ahat we do because we are selling to them.

William Dallas, CEO of bankrupt mortgage seller Ownit, which was partially owned by Merrill Lynch, told the New York Times, "Merrill Lynch told me we should offer more low documentation loans in which the borrower's income is not verified. They wanted these loans because they could make more money off of them. They told me that if we did not provide these loans, we would forego profits" (New York Times, 2007a).

It is useful to see how the opportunity presented by the growth of the nonconventional market was taken up by the twenty-five largest financial institutions in the country. In 1998, only four of the twenty-five largest financial firms in the country were in the top twenty-five of any of the segments of the nonconventional MBS market. By 2006, fourteen of the twenty-five (56 percent) were involved in the nonconventional MBS market. The opportunities to make money in the nonconventional food chain were so large that a massive number of the largest financial firms could not resist. Fligstein and Goldstein (2010) also show that these same firms became vertically integrated into the nonconventional mortgage market segments by buying originators and extending their activities to the production and servicing of these loans. In 2002, only 25 percent of these firms had these large commitments to nonconventional mortgages and participated in three or four segments in that market. But by 2006, this had risen to 45 percent. In 2002, nearly 40 percent of these firms participated in only one segment of the market, and by 2006, this had fallen to less than 20 percent.

In the face of the expanding nonconventional mortgage market, the largest financial firms—major investment, mortgage, savings and loan, and commercial banks—dramatically increased their operations in those markets and came to participate in multiple segments of those markets. Those markets proved so lucrative that financial firms of all kinds would originate mortgages, act as underwriters for bonds based on those mortgages, find customers for those bonds at home and around the world, and use the low interest rates available in the ABCP market to profit from holding a portion of those bonds themselves on their trading books.

The Demand for MBSs and ABS-CDOs

The evidence I have presented shows that from 2003 to 2007, the largest financial institutions dramatically increased their participation in the origination and securitization of nonconventional mortgages, and most financial institutions were also large-scale investors in the securities they produced. The evidence also shows that the largest of these institutions that were not integrated into the nonconventional origination market by 2003 did so by 2007. There are two remaining pieces of the puzzle. First, I want to return to the question of the role of the demand for MBSs and CDOs in this process. Second, I want to consider how investors were funding these purchases by borrowing money from the asset-backed commercial paper (ABCP) market.

I have presented some statements from the business press and executives at some of the financial institutions that it was the high level of demand for MBSs and CDOs that caused them to double down to find new mortgages even as the supply of mortgages was drying up after 2004. The large expansion of the mortgage market from 2000 to 2003 created the opportunity for investors to buy low-risk, relatively high-reward financial products based on conventional American mortgages. As I have shown, many of them were the same financial institutions who were originating and securitizing mortgages. The demand for these investments continued to rise from 2003 to 2008, as evidenced in Figure 5.3.

Most observers of the crisis accurately document the role of nonconventional mortgages, MBSs based on those mortgages, and the rapid expansion of ABS-CDOs, CDO-CDOs, and CDO-cubed as being responsible for most of the losses that banks suffered in the financial crisis. What has been missing in many of the accounts of the crisis is why the market moved so swiftly to nonconventional originations and MBSs based on them from 2004 to 2006 and then expanded even more rapidly into ABS-CDOs beginning in 2006–2007 (Jarrow, 2011; MacKenzie, 2011; Mian and Sufi, 2015). ABS-CDOs are securities that include

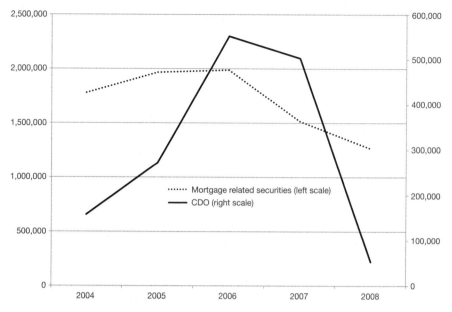

FIGURE 5.6 Total of collateralized debt obligations and mortgage-related securities issuance, 2004–2008 ($ millions). Source: Efraim Benmelech and Jennifer Dlugosz, "The Credit Rating Crisis," NBER Working Paper, 2010.

not just mortgages but also tranches of other MBSs and other forms of debt. It turns out that even the large and expanding nonconventional mortgage market did not provide enough mortgages to satisfy the demand for MBSs. In essence, the demand for highly rated securities that paid above the price for government bonds was enormous and expanded over time to fill the demand for such securities when the supply of mortgages began to falter. This was particularly true as the supply of MBSs based on conventional mortgages stopped growing in 2003 and began an eventual contraction beginning in 2005.

It is useful to examine evidence on this point. Figure 5.6 shows data on the issuance of MBSs and CDOs from 2004 to 2008. MBSs predominated security issuance in every year. But Benmelech and Dlugosz (2010) show that beginning in 2006, the level of MBSs declined. The production of CDOs spiked beginning in 2004 and peaked in 2006–2007, taking up the slack for the drop-off in MBSs. Barnett-Hart (2009) analyzed a sample of 735 ABS-CDO deals from 1999 until 2007. She shows that the number of CDOs issued rose dramatically after 2003 and peaked in 2007, consistent with the overall pattern of CDO issuance presented by Benmelech and Dlugosz (2010).

I note that early in the period, before 2003, nonmortgage assets predominated in ABS-CDO packages. But beginning in 2003, the number and composition of ABS-CDOs changed, and mortgage-based products came to predominate. The largest parts of these ABS-CDOs were made up of home equity loans, with smaller parts consisting of residential and commercial MBS tranches and other CDO tranches. Taken together, this evidence shows that the market for securities based on real estate products remained big throughout 2001–2008. As mortgages became harder to find, banks found themselves packaging whatever assets they could in order to satisfy the demand for these securities.

This evidence on the continued demand for highly rated, relatively high-yield securities shows why banks were so anxious to be vertically integrated if they were not already. Simply put, they needed to secure as many mortgages as they could in order to keep their securities businesses going. This pushed them to buy originators even as the overall market for origination was slowing down. The demand for securities based on mortgages was, in the end, what kept pushing banks to originate mortgages to customers with worse and worse credit. Even as defaults and foreclosures increased in 2006 and 2007, banks worked hard to get mortgages. When that faltered, they replaced nonconventional mortgages in their securities issues with anything else they had to keep their securitization machines going. The demand was so high that hard-to-sell, lower-rated tranches of MBSs could be packaged into CDOs profitably.

The Role of the Asset-Backed Commercial Paper Market in Funding Mortgages

Many observers agree that the proximate causes of the financial crisis were the inability of banks to pay back their loans from the ABCP market and the "repo" market (Gorton, 2010; Brunnermeier, 2009; Covitz et al., 2013). Historically, the main purpose of these markets was for banks and other firms to be able to borrow on assets for very short periods, usually from one day to one year. Banks are constantly borrowing and lending into these markets, and the same bank may actually be doing both, as one part of the bank has money to lend for a very short term and another a need for funds. Firms use these markets to borrow against accounts receivables for short-term cash and often to meet payrolls while waiting for payment for goods and services. In the case of mortgage securitization, these markets had been used since the 1980s to borrow money to purchase mortgages and pay it back when the securities that were being made from the mortgages were sold.

But over time, banks came to use these short-term loans not to just to hold mortgages until their eventual sale as securities but as a source of capital to buy those securities on their own accounts. It was this business practice that put banks most at risk. By borrowing money short term to hold securities that had long maturities, banks were taking the risk that they could keep rolling over those loans or, if a problem arose, that they could not sell those securities. The meltdown in finance began in earnest when Lehman Brothers collapsed in September 2008. This collapse was caused by their inability to pay back loans to creditors in several of these markets (Swedberg, 2010). The unexpected effect of the Lehman Brothers collapse was to cause the lenders in these markets to suddenly worry about all of the loans they had made to banks holding MBSs and CDOs. This effect cascaded and became a panic that eventually brought down many of the largest banks (Covitz et al., 2013). It is useful to describe the two most important of these markets, the repo market and the ABCP market.

In the business model of the repo market, one party sells an asset (usually fixed-income securities such as Treasury bonds but also corporate bonds, MBSs, and CDOs) to another party at one price at the start of the transaction and commits to repurchase the assets from the second party at a different price at a future date (Adrian et al., 2011). If the seller defaults during the life of the repo, the buyer as the new owner can sell the asset to a third party to offset their loss. The asset therefore acts as collateral and mitigates the credit risk that the buyer has on the seller. Although assets are sold outright at the start of a repo, the commitment of the seller to buy back the assets in the future means that the buyer has only temporary use of those assets, while the seller has only temporary use of the cash proceeds of the sale. Thus, although repo is structured legally as a sale and repurchase of securities (hence the term *repo*), it is more like a collateralized loan or secured deposit for a loan.

The ABCP market is more complex, both in the way that assets are packaged into legal vehicles called special investment vehicles (SIVs) and in the roles of banks and other financial institutions in packaging, selling, and servicing such vehicles. The SIV is a kind of special-purpose vehicle used in the ABCP market. ABCP is typically a short-term instrument that matures between 1 and 270 days (with an average of 30 days) from issuance and is issued through the use of a legal entity called a SIV. The purpose of these vehicles is to purchase and hold financial assets from a variety of asset sellers. The purchase of the assets in the vehicle is made possible by selling asset-backed commercial paper to outside investors. The assets act as collateral for the loan. The assets, as is the case with mortgages, may also have cash flows attached to them, which accrue to the purchaser of the bonds.

The financial assets that serve as collateral for ABCP can be a mix of many different assets, mostly asset-backed securities (which could include car loans, student loans, or credit card debt), residential mortgages, commercial loans, and

CDOs. Most of the assets are AAA rated, and the mixtures are jointly judged to have a low risk of bankruptcy by a rating agency. These high ratings are justified because the different assets in the SIV are diversified, and thus the risk that any one asset class will default is theoretically uncorrelated to others failing, making such packages attractive investments. Many large institutions heavily invested in these assets because they represented a very attractive investment opportunity. They benefited from high ratings from agencies and gave institutions the ability to invest cash assets safely for short periods.

As mentioned above, historically, banks used the ABCP market to help fund their purchase of mortgages that would then be made into securities. By creating a SIV, a bank could borrow money short term and then repay it when the mortgage-based securities were sold. This form of organization allowed banks to take the purchase of the mortgages off their books by creating walled-off investments (Gorton and Souleles, 2005). Thus, they did not count against the amount of capital banks had to hold. This meant that banks could borrow more to buy more mortgages and produce more securities without fear of running into limits on their ability to borrow. This made the ABCP market ideal for banks who wanted to be aggressive in taking on debt in order to take advantage of a large and expanding market for mortgages and securities based on mortgages. It also made it cheap to fund mortgage securitization.

Over time, banks began to create SIVs to obtain funds for longer-term investments, mostly made up of MBSs and CDOs. They would use the MBSs and CDOs they bought and create investment vehicles that still had the advantage of being off books. SIVs set up by some commercial banks came to finance their longer-term, higher-yield investing through sales of ABCP. This had been very profitable when ABCP was considered safe, as ABCP buyers accepted a low interest rate. For example, one might borrow for a year in the ABCP market for 2 percent and earn 5 percent return on the MBSs and CDOs during that period. At the end of the year, one would seek to roll over the loan for another year or find a different funder.

This worked only if buyers in the ABCP market continued to see the MBSs and CDOs in the SIVs as safe investments. As mortgagors began to default in 2006 and house foreclosures began to increase, the value of the MBSs and CDOs in the SIVs came into question. Moreover, since many of the SIVs contained a wide variety of assets, the buyers of assets did not really know what was in the package they were buying. Eventually, this made participants in this market become unwilling to purchase ABCP. This caused trouble for financial institutions that had relied on sales of ABCP to obtain funds for use in longer-term investments. When Lehman collapsed in September 2008, this created a panic in the

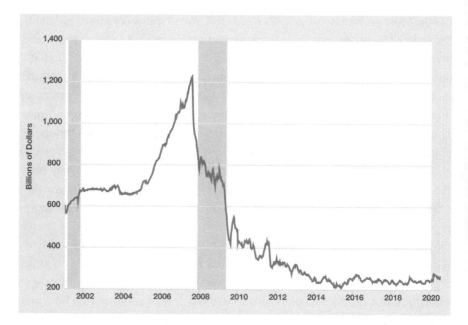

FIGURE 5.7   Rise and fall of the ABCP market. Source: Board of Governors of the Federal
Reserve System (US), "Asset-Backed Commercial Paper Outstanding [ABCOMP]," retrieved
from FRED, Federal Reserve Bank of St. Louis.

ABCP market (Covitz et al., 2013). At this point, no one knew what asset prices
should be, and investors were less willing to buy or roll over ABCP. As these
doubts spread, a financial panic ensued.

It is useful to present some data on the size of these markets and the identities of the market participants. Figure 5.7 presents data on the size of the ABCP
market. Before 2004, the ABCP market was relatively stable at about $600–700
billion in transactions per year. But in the next three years, it increased to over
$1.2 trillion. Almost all of this was used to fund the purchase of MBSs and CDOs.
One can observe that beginning in late 2006, the ABCP market began to shrink
dramatically. By the end of 2008, it returned to around $700 billion. Essentially,
all of the MBSs and CDOs that were being funded by ABCP were no longer being funded short term.

We now know that this lack of funding meant that banks that held large
amounts of ABCP were going to find themselves in a serious liquidity crisis, and
for most, this turned into insolvency. This single figure dramatically shows why
the financial crisis happened so swiftly and with such devastating consequences.
Banks who were funding their MBS and CDO activities by borrowing in the
ABCP market had no more than a year to figure out how to sell those assets,
because continuing to borrow to hold them had become impossible. This cre-

ated a perfect storm. Since many of the Mbss and CDOs had nonconventional mortgages in them and these mortgages were starting to fail, no one knew how to value the underlying assets. As banks tried to sell these assets, they ended up quickly having to take such large losses that they went from being illiquid to being insolvent.

Acharya et al. (2013) explore the identities of firms that were involved as conduits in the ABCP market over this period.[3] They show that the largest US banks who were participants included Citigroup, Bank of America, Morgan Stanley, Bear Stearns, GMAC, State Street Corporation, Lehman Brothers, and Countrywide Financial. I note that six of these eight financial entities (Citibank, Bank of America, Morgan Stanley, Bear Stearns, Lehman Brothers, and Countrywide Financial) appear in the top ten of conventional and nonconventional mortgage originators and issuers of conventional and nonconventional MBSs in Table 5.1. Not only were the largest vertically integrated originators and issuers of mortgage products large and integrated, but they inordinately relied on the ABCP market for their funding.

This last finding should not be a surprise. If a bank was going to be vertically integrated, they were going to need capital to purchase mortgages, make securities, and borrow to hold those securities on their own accounts. When Lehman Brothers collapsed, it makes sense that those banks who were deepest into the vertical integration strategy were the ones who had borrowed the most money to fund their efforts and found themselves at greatest risk. While the vertical integration strategy worked dramatically to produce record profits from 2001 to 2006, it left the banks most deeply involved with large amount of debt that was effectively hidden off books in SIVs funded by the ABCP market. This borrowing short to go long worked spectacularly well while it worked, but once the confidence in the banks that employed it most successfully was in question the bottom fell out quickly (Swedberg, 2010).

Why Did Integrated Financial Firms Not Exit when Prices of Housing Started to Fall?

The crisis that eventually exploded in the fall of 2008 was several years in the making. The second half of 2005 augured trouble in the real estate market as housing prices started to decline, delinquency rates rose steeply, foreclosures experienced an uptick, and several home builders went out of business. Nonetheless, Wall Street continued to expand aggressively in nonconventional mortgages through early 2007. During late 2006 and early 2007, Bear Stearns, Merrill Lynch, and Morgan Stanley all acquired additional nonconventional originators even as house prices peaked and started to fall. The degree to which the tactics of vertical integration shaped these seemingly irrational expansionary strategies is suggested by an excerpt from a brief published in early 2007 by the trade group the American Securitization Forum (2007: 2):

> In the past, predicting what investment banks would do at this stage of the housing cycle used to be simple. Having ramped up the business while the going was good, they would then shutter it at the first sign of trouble. That's what happened with the mortgage conduit business in the 1980s, and again in the early 1990s. This time, it's different. Wall Street seems to have thrown out its old and trusty playbook. Instead of pulling back in 2006, several major firms went on a spending spree. That might sound strange to some. Buying at the start of downturn surely risks overpaying for an asset whose business is in decline. So why do it? Well, despite the gloomy outlook, competition is not letting up. First, clients [of investment banks] have been setting up capital-markets desks to securitize their own loans in their own version of vertical integration. Countrywide is the most renowned for doing this, but others from SunTrust to IndyMac have taken the plunge, and still others are following. Second, more players are trying to buy loans that are still for sale. That's especially true of the mortgage market, where vertical integration has been most rampant. "In 2000 we'd have maybe five or six groups bidding on a loan sale," says Commaroto. "Now there are 20 or more. . . . The more bidders, the higher prices can go, and that, of course, can undermine the economics of a securitization. It also means a desk has more chance of not getting enough loans in a timely manner."

The broad implication of this is that the vertical integration of MBS and CDO production that financial firms built to maximize their nonconventional business locked them into the business and rendered executives less responsive to signs of impending trouble. Even at JPMorgan Chase, which adopted a relatively cautious MBS strategy and was a laggard in terms of vertical integration, Gillian Tett documents reluctance among top executives to "'shut the spigots' of the nascent mortgage pipeline they had worked so hard to build once subprime defaults began to rise" (2009: 123–124). Failure to continue acquiring even highly risky mortgages would mean choking off tightly coupled revenue streams, which for many integrated firms had become the largest chunk of their business. Banks were making money off of origination, securitization, and borrowing money in the ABCP market to fund and hold on to high-yielding securities. Stopping any part of this process meant that profits, which had soared from 2001 to 2005, would be threatened. The natural human tendency to think that the worse could not happen took over. Everyone thought they would hunker down and be the last firm standing. It turns out that they were all wrong.

6

THE CRISIS AND ITS SPREAD WORLDWIDE

One way to think of what happened is to consider the system of mortgage finance as an ecological environment where organisms look for sources of nutrients to grow larger and more prosperous. Consider the supply of mortgages to be nutrients gushing out of the bottom of the ocean. For the largest banks, the refinancing boom and the takeoff of house prices brought about rapid growth in the size and success of the banks that were integrated producers (Mayer, 2011). Indeed, the quadrupling of the size of the market in four years set off a huge gold rush among firms that were already doing mortgage securitization and those that saw the promise of a large business with huge profits. In ecological terms, the environment turned magnificently munificent, and firms blossomed.

But when those gushing nutrients began to dry up in 2004, the banks, now more of them and many that were suddenly larger and more profitable, had to seek out a new source of nourishment in order to continue producing MBS-CDOs. They discovered a nearby pool of nutrients, nonconventional mortgages (Swan, 2009). By moving to this new stream, banks were able to continue to make record profits. But eventually this pool of nutrients dried up too. Simply put, there were no more households to whom it made sense to make loans in order to keep the business going. Just like creatures that fight over declining nutrients in an ecosystem, the banks continued to the very end to try to survive by being the ones who would find the very last mortgages to produce the very last securities. They took on borrowers with worse and worse credit. They worked hard to make sure more and more of the mortgages were securitized (Sanders, 2008). When eventually they reached the limits of that, they recycled lower-rated tranches of securities they could not sell into CDO-CDOs or added assets of any kind to their ABS-CDOs. And as all of this failed, they engaged in mortgage and securities fraud in order to keep their pipelines full and their profits up.

Moreover, all of this was based on borrowed money, money that had to be paid back in less than a year. As house prices turned down, foreclosures rose, and the market for MBS-CDOs tightened, this desperate struggle to survive ultimately resulted in the death or massive reorganization of most banks (Immergluck, 2010). Banks who had risen by taking advantage of the low interest rates, the rapid growth in mortgages, and the production of MBS-CDOs found that their business models that were profitable in 2001–2007 began to fall apart in 2008. While the proximate cause of their problems was the ABCP market, the real cause of their eventual demise was their dependence on profits based on the vertically integrated business model (Goldstein and Fligstein, 2017). Their need for high throughput of mortgages to produce securities that could be sold or borrowed against and held as investments created a catastrophe when the raw material for the whole process disappeared.

Anatomy of the Crisis

The financial crisis began in the most financially murky part of the financial world, the ABCP market, which has been termed "shadow banking" (Gorton, 2010; Lowenstein, 2010). That market had for many years been the place where banks and firms had gone to borrow money to fund their activities short term. But when the mortgage market shifted from conventional to nonconventional mortgages, the use of the ABCP exploded to provide the capital to produce and fund the purchase of MBSs and CDOs. Whereas previously this market provided funding for the production of securities, after 2004, financial institutions began to use the market to fund their holdings of these instruments (Acharya et al., 2013). They were thus not borrowing money long term but borrowing short term to fund their investments in MBS and CDO structured investment vehicles.

Many observers have sought to locate the cause of the financial crisis in one or another part of the chain that produced mortgages and ended up placing them with investors (see the papers in Lounsbury and Hirsch [2010] for different views of this process). But my analysis shows that this misunderstands the nature of the system that was built. By 2007, the largest players in all of these markets had become vertically integrated. Investment banks purchased originators, and savings and loans, commercial banks, and mortgage banks produced securities. All of them bought and sold those securities for their own accounts. By being vertically integrated, banks were able to maximize their profits by making sure that all of the gains in the process accrued to them (Wilmarth, 2009). Countrywide Financial pioneered this model in the 1990s, and every bank that followed them profited greatly. One of the reasons this business model was so successful was the extremely large size of the mortgage market. With originations over $2.5 trillion from 2002 until 2007, up from $1 trillion in 2001, the opportunities to make huge profits were available to all who participated.

But like many business models that are built for one set of market conditions, this business model failed miserably when the number of mortgages for origination decreased and the ability of mortgagors to keep paying those mortgages declined. Because banks were locked into the model of vertical integration, it proved impossible for them to shift their businesses when house prices declined, mortgagors began to be delinquent on their payments, and foreclosures spiked. But as the mortgages failed, the MBSs and CDOs that required people to pay their mortgages every month to produce cash flow started to fail as well. This forced ratings companies to begin to downgrade all tranches of all bonds. For most banks that were holding these instruments using borrowed money, this meant that they had to either increase their collateral by putting down more money or else seek out new funding. The market for MBSs and CDOs that were being produced eventually dried up as well. Banks who were producing and holding these instruments found themselves running short of funds (i.e., a liquidity crisis) and eventually becoming insolvent. Because many of these banks held their MBSs and CDOs in SIVs that were off books and therefore did not need to be protected by the holding of additional capital, they found that their capital quickly ran out.

It follows that the banks that were most at risk in this process were those who were involved in all phases of mortgage securitization (Goldstein and Fligstein, 2017). After all, if you were making profits off of originating mortgages, producing securities, and holding them using borrowed money off books, and all of these businesses went into decline, you were more at risk than if you were in only one of these businesses. Even more important, given that your entire organization depended on the throughput of mortgages, it became very difficult to shift your business activities as mortgages became harder to find and riskier.

It is useful to document the events as they unfolded from 2003 to 2008. Beginning in January 2003, the Federal Reserve began to raise interest rates. This meant that households that wanted to refinance their home or buy a new one had to borrow at higher interest rates to do so. By January 2007, these rates peaked at 6.25 percent. While the higher rates would eventually affect the availability of new mortgages, mortgage originations fell from their peak in 2003 of almost $4 trillion to $3 trillion from 2004 to 2006 and to $2.5 trillion in 2007. The big dropoff in 2003–2004 was caused not by interest rate changes but by the dropping off of refinancing. Even as interest rates were rising from 2003 until the end of 2007, the total size of the mortgage origination market remained large by historic standards. The biggest change in the composition of these mortgages after 2003 was

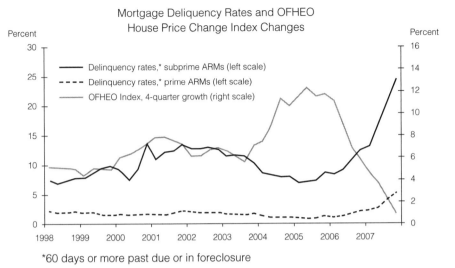

Mortgage Deliquency Rates and OFHEO
House Price Change Index Changes

*60 days or more past due or in foreclosure

FIGURE 6.1 Quarterly percentage change in national housing price index and share of prime and subprime mortgages ninety-plus days delinquent or in foreclosure. Data sources: Office of Federal Housing Enterprise Oversight; Bloomberg.

a shift from conventional mortgages to nonconventional mortgages, particularly home equity loans but also subprime, Alt-A, and jumbo mortgages.

Beginning in 2006, house prices stopped rising. This had the biggest effect on new mortgagors, many of whom had taken on nonconventional mortgages (Mayer et al., 2009). Figure 6.1 shows that as housing prices began to drop in 2006, the rate of mortgagors who were delinquent on their payments and the rates of foreclosure of rose on subprime mortgages. By the first quarter of 2009, 15 percent of subprime mortgages were in foreclosure, and another 15 percent were over ninety days delinquent. Thus, 30 percent of all the subprime mortgages were in trouble. To put this into some context, the ordinary rate of foreclosure and delinquency is more like 1–2 percent.

Prices increased the most between 2004 and 2006 in California, Nevada, Arizona, and Florida (Fligstein and Goldstein, 2012). While prices were increasing in much of the rest of the country during those years, it was at a much lower rate. But beginning in 2006, prices started to drop steeply in the four states just mentioned. By the first quarter of 2007, prices were going down, and by the first quarter of 2009, prices in these four states had dropped an astounding 25 percent. In two years, the market turned from being booming to crashing. Beginning in 2006, foreclosure rates began to rise in California, Nevada, Arizona, and Florida, where prices had been the highest and were taking the steepest plunge (Fligstein and Goldstein, 2012).

Why were price increases so high in these states, and why when they fell did households stop paying their mortgages and enter into foreclosure? The answers to these questions can be understood by returning to the shift to nonconventional mortgages (Mayer et al., 2009). Banks were looking to find customers for nonconventional mortgages after 2003. By examining zip code data, they discovered that the four states mentioned above had had the highest rates of home appreciation. They decided to focus their attention on those states by sending out salespeople to get potential customers interested in buying a house. They sold to people who had less good credit and not enough of a down payment the idea that the housing market was the source of wealth. They did so by pointing out how their local area had seen the most appreciation. They encouraged people to join in with their neighbors to buy into the housing market.

Many of these new mortgagors were sold nonconventional mortgages, particularly mortgages with adjustable rates or interest-only loans, or else given mortgages where they put down very little money (as low as 3 percent and in some cases 0 percent). If they had adjustable-rate mortgages, when the teaser rate adjusted, mortgagors could face a steep rise in their monthly payments. In the case of interest-only loans, mortgagors could quickly find themselves owing more than the mortgage they had bought as unpaid principal and interest were added to the loan amount. If mortgagors did not have much equity in their homes, then when house prices started to fall in their zip codes, their houses were suddenly worth less than they paid. When prices were rising, mortgagors who could not afford their payments would turn around and sell the house. But as prices dropped, this was not an option. If the house payment adjusted quite a bit higher, it made a lot of sense for mortgagors to just walk away from their homes. Once house prices started to drop and houses were abandoned, prices for existing homes would continue to spiral down. Such negative price spirals meant that more and more people walked away from their mortgages. In the end, prices dropped as much as 50 percent in some areas.

The massive growth of nonconventional mortgage securitization had spread at least $3.8 trillion of assets directly linked to these mortgages to financial institutions around the world by the beginning of 2007 (Fligstein and Habinek, 2014). Nonetheless, it is clear that the markets, the credit rating agencies, the regulators, and most of the large banks all registered comparatively little response when housing prices started to stall out and mortgage default rates began to rise in late 2006. As already has been documented, several large banks such as Merrill Lynch and Citibank continued expanding their nonprime businesses aggressively during the first two quarters of 2007. In March 2007, Federal Reserve chairman Ben Bernanke stated in congressional testimony that "at this juncture, the impact on the broader economy and financial markets of the problems in the subprime market seems likely to be contained" (*New York Times*, 2007a).

The credit rating agencies also continued to maintain an implausibly upbeat outlook through the first two quarters of 2007. Only after they faced widespread mocking on the financial blogosphere, congressional questioning, and an over-all crisis of legitimacy did the agencies take serious steps to adjust MBS bond ratings to reflect the deteriorating conditions in the mortgage market. Their reasons for reticence were clear. First, they had a vested interest in hoping the situation would improve, since their reputations and a significant portion of their revenues rested on a strong MBS market. Second, they knew what downgrades would mean. Moody's CEO Raymond McDaniel justified its cautious approach to downgrades, noting that "because we are an influential voice, we can create a self-fulfilling prophecy by saying that there are risks in the market ahead of those risks being revealed" (*New York Times*, 2007c).

By July 2007, the credit supply for nonconventional mortgages ground to a halt as the secondary market demand plummeted and banks became wary of the quickly weakening housing market. The volume of subprime originations declined by 90 percent between the first and second half of 2007 (Fligstein and Goldstein, 2010). The drying up of credit to fund nonconventional originations began hampering attempts by borrowers with adjustable-rate mortgages—even those whose houses had not yet declined in value—to refinance before their mortgage got reset to a higher rate. It also imperiled the business of large mortgage specialists such as Ameriquest and Countrywide and began eating into the revenue streams of the commercial and investment banks, which had come to rely on fee revenues from their vertically integrated mortgage finance franchises.

Bond defaults were initially concentrated among the lower-rated equity tranches that were the first in line to lose in the event of revenue losses. But the rising tide of subprime delinquencies and foreclosures soon put pressure on the supposedly safe "AAA" tranches as well. Figure 6.2 shows weekly counts of negative credit actions taken by one of the big three rating agencies against nonagency MBSs and mortgage-related CDOs. Aside from a few small blips of activity in April and July 2007, there were few downgrades on MBSs until they increased rapidly in September. Credit downgrades throughout 2008 averaged about three hundred a week. In September and October 2008, with the collapse of Lehman Brothers, credit downgrades spiked to nearly one thousand.

The downgrade plot's resemblance to a seismograph image is apt. Each round of mass downgrades sent tremors through the financial system. The significance of credit downgrades was that they forced leveraged banks that had taken loans to buy MBSs to either pay off those loans or post additional collateral with their

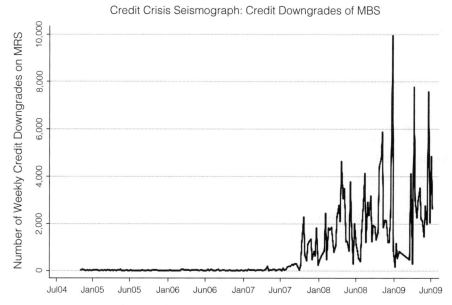

Credit Crisis Seismograph: Credit Downgrades of MBS

FIGURE 6.2 Timeline of MBS credit downgrades. Reformatted from Neil Fligstein and Adam Goldstein, "The Anatomy of the Mortgage Securitization Crisis," in *Markets on Trial: The Economic Sociology of the U.S. Financial Crisis*, edited by M. Lounsbury and P. Hirsch, p. 52, figure 10.

creditors. This was because most of their loans contained covenants that required them to increase their capital investment if bond prices fell or the credit rating on the MBS collateral was downgraded. The problem, however, was that most banks were already very highly leveraged and eventually found it impossible to raise enough capital to cover their loans. Banks found that their counterparties in the ABCP and repo markets were not inclined to roll over their loans and, without more collateral, demanded payment. This was the link between the implosion in the mortgage market and the freezing of the credit system.

While the financial meltdown emerged from a novel configuration of forces, it spread in the relatively straightforward mold of a classic banking panic (Gorton, 2010). Lenders made calls on collateral, and the entities that had become highly leveraged in order to buy MBSs suddenly found themselves in a liquidity crisis, unable to raise funds to cover debt backed by assets whose value was rapidly plummeting. This process first played out in the shadow banking system of special investment vehicles, which were usually linked to a larger institution but funded themselves through short-term debt. As the price of their MBS and CDO assets fell, they needed cash to post as collateral with creditors, but since the credit markets were weary of extending them emergency money, they generally

Average Magnitude of Subsequent Alt-A, B/C, and HEL Downgrades by Vintage

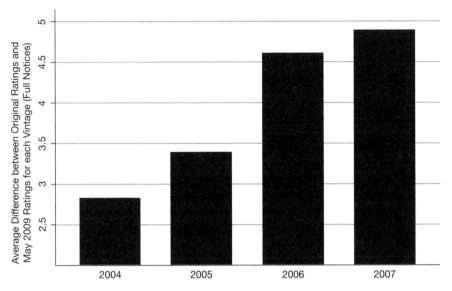

FIGURE 6.3 Average magnitude of subsequent Alt-A, B/C, and HEL downgrades by vintage. Reformatted from Neil Fligstein and Adam Goldstein, "The Anatomy of the Mortgage Securitization Crisis," in *Markets on Trial: The Economic Sociology of the U.S. Financial Crisis*, edited by M. Lounsbury and P. Hirsch, p. 53, figure 11.

had to be rescued by their parent firms and placed back on the parent's balance sheet.

Figure 6.3 shows how the year of issue of nonconventional MBSs and CDOs had a big effect on the quality of the underlying loans. If an MBS or CDO based on nonconventional mortgages was created in 2004, it had an average downgrade of 2.75 grades. That would make a AAA bond turn into a BBB bond. By 2007, MBSs and CDOs made up of nonconventional mortgages experienced almost five downgrades. This turned a AAA bond into a B bond, one step above being a junk bond. This is evidence that the last mortgages originated and securitized were the ones most likely to fail. These loans were the riskiest because the borrowers were the least qualified for the loans. It is estimated that around 25–30 percent of the loans issued in the last two years contained some element of mortgage fraud whereby the borrower's qualifications for the loan were overstated. These loans were also at risk because if the prices in their markets turned down, the borrowers had the least incentive to stay in their houses.

Two hedge funds affiliated with Bear Stearns were the first major banking institutions to fail in July 2007. A similar crisis soon afflicted Citigroup, which would take over $55 billion in write-downs on mortgage-related assets (*New York Times*, 2008b). The problem, as Gillian Tett (2009) and others have dramatically documented, was that the elaborate system of accounting vehicles that banks

Table 6.1 : What happened to the main players in the market

Lehman Brothers	Bankrupt (2008)
Bear Stearns	Bankrupt (2008)
Indy Mac	Bankrupt (2008)
Merrill Lynch	Sold to Bank of America (2008)
Salomon Brothers	Sold to Citibank
JPMorgan Chase	Government bailout
Bank of America	Government bailout
Countrywide	Sold to Bank of America (2007)
Citibank	Government bailout (2008)
Wachovia	Sold to Wells Fargo (2008)
Morgan Stanley	Reorganized as commercial bank (2008)
Goldman Sachs	Reorganized as commercial bank (2008)
New Century Financial	Bankrupt (2008)
Washington Mutual	Sold to JPMorgan Chase (2008)
Fannie Mae	Government takeover (2008)
Freddie Mac	Government takeover (2008)

built to hide their leverage from regulators and the elaborate network of credit default swaps they created to hedge their risks made it impossible for the market to discern which banks were exposed to the worst of the nonconventional mortgage securities, what came to be called "toxic assets." The financial crisis escalated throughout the summer of 2008 in spite of efforts by the Federal Reserve to make emergency capital available.

Table 6.1 looks at what happened to the top banks that were leaders in the mortgage securitization business circa 2005 by 2010. Seven of the ten largest subprime lenders in 2005 were either out of business or absorbed by merger. Eight of the ten top subprime-MBS-issuing firms in 2005 were either out of business or merged into other entities. The collapse of the subprime market essentially wiped out all of the firms that had grown large on that business. Fannie and Freddie were taken over by the government. The big investment banks at the core of the subprime MBS market no longer existed, except Morgan Stanley and Goldman Sachs. Citibank, Bank of America, JPMorgan Chase, and Wells Fargo emerged as large conglomerate banks, having absorbed many of the subprime losers, while both Goldman Sachs and Morgan Stanley reorganized themselves to become commercial banks in order to avail themselves of cheap loans from the Federal Reserve. Most of the institutions that survived only did so on account of the Troubled Asset Relief Program (TARP) bailout, and most took massive write-downs on MBS assets.

The Unraveling of Banks

In Chapter 3, I documented the rise of four of the most important banks that had become vertically integrated: Countrywide Financial, Bear Stearns, Washington Mutual, and Citigroup. Each bank took a different path to vertical integration, starting out respectively as a mortgage company, an investment bank, a savings and loan bank, and a commercial bank. When the crash hit in 2007–2009, all four were severely impacted, with three of the banks becoming insolvent and sold off to other banks. Only Citigroup survived, mostly because the government decided they were too big to fail and thereby worked to save the company. Each of their paths to insolvency started with the downturn in house prices and the rise of foreclosures in nonconventional mortgages. Their vertically integrated business models pushed them to continue originating and securitizing mortgages. All held substantial amounts of MBSs / CDOs on their own accounts, mostly bought with money borrowed from the ABCP market. But each of their paths was a little different, reflecting their origins as different kinds of banks, their internal organizations, and the differential timing of their ultimate demises. It is useful to give short accounts of how they approached the opportunities presented by the massive increase in originations in 2001 and their eventual unraveling.

Bear Stearns

In 2006, Bear Stearns produced $9 billion in revenue, earned $2 billion in profits, and employed over thirteen thousand employees worldwide with stock market capitalization of $20 billion. By March 2008, the company was nearly bankrupt and was sold off to JPMorgan Chase for $1.2 billion. Its demise, beginning in the spring of 2007, is thought to be the beginning of the financial crisis.

The cause of Bear Stearns's demise was based in its strategy to make, buy, and hold CDOs. It had totally embraced the vertical integration business model and had aggressively entered all parts of the nonconventional mortgage market. The unwinding of Bear Stearns followed the downward path I have outlined. Its need to originate and securitize mortgages to stay in business, all funded by borrowed money, eventually caused it to collapse. The firm was deeply into originating mortgages, particularly by buying and originating nonconventional mortgages through its EMC subsidiary, and creating CDOs, some of which it came to own. It bought these CDOs using borrowed money. The bank "insured" the CDOs by buying credit default swaps. They made money as long as the cost of the debt and the insurance was less than the return on the CDOs.

Unfortunately, as house prices decreased and the mortgages that underlay the CDOs experienced nonpayment and foreclosure, this caused sharp decreases in the market values of these types of bonds. In April 2007, bond dealers told the managers of two Bear Stearns hedge funds that they should write down the value of the assets in these funds. The funds, High-Grade Structured-Credit Strategies Fund and Enhanced Leverage Fund, owned $20 billion for the purchase of CDOs based on mortgage-backed securities (Burrough, 2008). The funds started losing value in September 2006 when housing prices began falling that year. In May 2007, the Enhanced Leverage Fund announced that its assets had lost 6.75 percent. Two weeks later it revised that to an 18 percent loss. Investors began pulling out their money. Then the fund's bankers called in their loans. Parent company Bear Stearns scrambled to provide cash for the hedge fund, selling $3.6 billion in its assets. One of its creditors, Merrill Lynch, wasn't reassured. It required the fund to give it the CDOs as collateral for its loan. In the end, Bear Stearns agreed to buy the securities from Merrill and other lenders for $3.2 billion. It bailed out the failed hedge fund to protect an even larger run on the bank.

As a result of continuing pressure on their CDO holdings, on December 20, 2007, Bear Stearns announced its first loss in eighty years. It lost $854 million for the fourth quarter. It announced a $1.9 billion write-down of its subprime mortgage holdings. In January 2008, Moody's downgraded Bear's mortgage-backed securities to B or below, junk bond status. Now Bear was having trouble raising enough capital from the ABCP to stay afloat. On March 11, 2008, the Federal Reserve announced its Terms Securities Lending Facility. It gave banks like Bear Stearns a credit guarantee. The same day, Moody's downgraded Bear Stearns's MBSs to B and C levels. The two events triggered an old-fashioned bank run on Bear Stearns. Its clients pulled out their deposits and investments.

By March 13, Bear Stearns was nearly out of cash to meet its borrowing obligations. Bear Stearns had relied on short-term loans from the repo and ABCP markets to fund its securities, just as other banks were doing. As the agreements in these markets ended, the banks who had lent the money wanted their funds back. Bear Stearns hemorrhaged cash when the other banks called in their loans and refused to lend more. No one wanted to get stuck with Bear's junk securities. Bear Stearns didn't have enough cash to open for business the next morning.

It asked its main bank, JPMorgan Chase, for a $25 billion overnight loan. Chase CEO Jamie Dimon told them he needed more time to research Bear Stearns's real value before making a commitment. He asked the New York Federal Reserve Bank to guarantee the loan so Bear Stearns could open on Friday. Yet Bear's stock price plummeted when the markets opened the next day. That weekend, JPMorgan Chase realized Bear Stearns was worth only $236 million.

That was just one-fifth the value of its headquarters building. To solve the problem, the Federal Reserve held its first emergency weekend meeting in thirty years.

On March 16, 2008, JPMorgan Chase announced that it would acquire Bear Stearns in a stock-for-stock exchange that valued the bank at $2 per share. The Federal Reserve Bank lent $30 billion to JPMorgan Chase to purchase Bear Stearns. They agreed that JPMorgan Chase could default on the loan if Bear Stearns did not have enough assets to pay it off. Without the Fed's intervention, the failure of Bear Stearns could have spread to other overleveraged investment banks. These included Merrill Lynch, Lehman Brothers, and Citigroup.

Countrywide Financial

Between 2000 and 2003, Countrywide Financial tripled its workforce to more than thirty-four thousand as its mortgage origination business exploded. In 2001, the company changed its name from Countrywide Credit Industries to Countrywide Financial Corporation, a proclamation that it was no longer a mere mortgage company. A full-fledged diversified financial-services company, it owned a bank, sold title insurance, created MBSs and CDOs, traded these securities, and held these securities on its own account. It, of course, used borrowed money to fund its activities. Like Bear Stearns, it was ultimately the combination of higher rates of delinquencies and foreclosures and their impact on MBSs and CDOs that brought Countrywide down. But while Bear Stearns's problems were centered on its borrowing to hold on to MBSs / CDOs, because Countrywide was more centered on the origination and holding of mortgages, its troubles were even more directly tied to the housing market.

In spite of its diversification and vertical integration, mortgage origination was the core of its business. In 2001, Countrywide Financial was the third-largest home loan provider in America, after Wells Fargo and Washington Mutual. Its CEO, Angelo Mozilo, wanted Countrywide Financial to be number one. It held that position briefly, in the early 1990s, before being overtaken by the competition. In 2001, Mozilo announced he wanted to achieve a huge market share in mortgage originations—30 to 40 percent—that was far greater than anyone in the financial services industry had ever attained.

During the housing boom from 2001 to 2003, Countrywide thrived. In 2004, the company edged out Wells Fargo to become the largest home-mortgage provider. In 2005, *Fortune* placed Countrywide on its list of "Most Admired Companies," and *Barron's* named Mozilo one of the "thirty best C.E.O.s in the world." The following year, *American Banker* presented him with a lifetime achievement award. By 2006 the company ranked 122 on the Fortune 500, with $18.5 billion in

2005 revenue, $2.4 billion in profits, and a mortgage-origination engine that had generated a staggering $490 billion in loans.

Countrywide Financial kept the riskiest piece of a securitization, the tranches it could not sell because they had the lowest ratings, on its own balance sheet. This was a common practice for originators who issued securities that made their financial positions more transparent. Starting in 2005, Countrywide began to keep both interest-only ARMs and a chunk of home equity loans, both the loans themselves and the lowest-rated tranches from home equity loan securitizations, on its balance sheet as well. By the end of 2006, Countrywide had $2.8 billion worth of low-rated tranches on its balance sheet, representing about 15 percent of its equity. The rationale was that while there would be some delinquencies on the mortgages in the securities, the income stream from these loans would provide stability during tougher times. By the end of 2006, Countrywide had $32.7 billion worth of interest-only ARMs on its balance sheet, up from just $4.7 billion at the end of 2004. Much of these holdings were being supported by money borrowed in the ABCP market.

In 2006 and early 2007, as house prices were starting to fall and originations were getting more difficult, Countrywide Financial ramped up its business of buying mortgage loans from banks that were faltering in order to stay at the top of the rankings for originations and provide raw materials for their securitization business. In the second quarter of 2007, the company announced that delinquency rates on Countrywide's subprime mortgages had more than doubled, to 23.7 percent from less than 10 percent at the end of March. Delinquencies for prime mortgages also spiked. The company revealed that it was taking several other hits, including $417 million worth of impairments, mostly due to declines in the value of home equity tranches, and another $293 million in losses in loans held on its balance sheet.

As 2007 progressed, subprime defaults continued to escalate, and Countrywide's creditors started to stop rolling over loans made in the ABCP market. By August, it was difficult for Countrywide Financial to obtain any short-term funding, a move that constricted its ability to operate. Within days, Countrywide drew down its entire $11.5 billion line of credit, an obvious sign of desperation. It tried to get the Federal Reserve to use its emergency lending authority to loan it money to stay solvent, but the Federal Reserve refused. On August 23, 2007, Countrywide Financial announced that Bank of America would invest $2 billion, giving the market the confidence that Countrywide had access to the deep pockets it needed to keep running.

But throughout the fall of 2007, Countrywide experienced continued pressure on its MBS-CDO portfolio and continued to have difficulty raising money in the ABCP market. As a result, its stock continued to fall. By the end of the year, Mozilo began to look for someone to buy the company. In July 2008, Bank of America acquired Countrywide for $4 billion. Less than a year earlier, its market capitalization had been more than six times that amount, at nearly $25 billion.

Washington Mutual

In the 1990s, Washington Mutual (WaMu) had been a conservative savings and loan bank. At the end of 2007, WaMu had more than forty-three thousand employees, twenty-two hundred branch offices in fifteen states, and $188.3 billion in deposits. In 2008, it became the largest failed bank in US history. This was the result of WaMu's aggressive entry into the nonconventional mortgage origination market throughout the 2001–2007 period. Chairman and CEO Kerry Killinger's goal in this period was to build WaMu into the "Wal-Mart of Banking" by catering to lower- and middle-class consumers to whom other banks deemed too risky to lend. They offered many forms of nonconventional mortgages that had terms that made it easy for the least creditworthy borrowers to get financing. They expanded into big cities, including Chicago, New York, and Los Angeles.

After 2004, when it became more difficult to find new mortgagors, WaMu aggressively entered the nonconventional loan market. It pressed sales agents to approve loans while placing less emphasis on borrowers' incomes and assets. WaMu set up a system that enabled real estate agents to collect fees of more than $10,000 for bringing in borrowers. Variable-rate loans, option adjustable-rate mortgages (option ARMs) in particular, were especially attractive, because they carried higher fees than other loans and allowed WaMu to book profits on interest payments that borrowers deferred.

Washington Mutual's ultimate failure was caused by its aggressive pursuit of nonconventional originations. But they were particularly vulnerable because of the way they went about doing this. For example, they did a lot of business in California. By December 2007, the national average home value was down 9.8 percent. In California, there was fifteen months' worth of unsold inventory, and prices had dropped more than the national average. By the end of 2007, because house prices in California had dropped so much, many of their outstanding loans were more than 100 percent of the home's value, making borrowers more likely to default on their loans.

Even as house prices were falling, WaMu continued to aggressively pursue nonconventional mortgages as the market for originations turned down. Because they were more focused on the nonconventional mortgage market to begin with, they were more vulnerable as the customers who bought those loans began to default. After originating these mortgages, WaMu found it difficult to either sell the mortgages to others to securitize or sell the securities it was producing itself. This was particularly true after August 2007 when the market for mortgage-backed securities dramatically declined. Like many other banks, WaMu could not resell these mortgages or the securities they had produced. As their problems became apparent, they also ran into the problem of finding it difficult to raise money in the ABCP market. In the fourth quarter of 2007, they were forced to write down $1.6 billion in defaulted mortgages. Bank regulators made them set aside cash to provide for future losses. As a result, WaMu reported a $2 billion net loss for the quarter. Its net loss for the year was $6.7 billion, which dwarfed its 2006 profit of $3.6 billion.

In December 2007, WaMu reorganized its home loan division, closing 160 of its 336 home loan offices and removing twenty-six hundred positions in its home loan staff (a 22 percent reduction). In April 2008, as a result of the ongoing foreclosures in subprime mortgages, the company announced that three thousand people companywide would lose their jobs, and the company stated its intent to close its 176 remaining standalone home loan offices, including 23 in Washington state and its loan-processing center in Bellevue, Washington. At the same time, as a result of the difficulty of selling MBS-CDOs, it stopped buying loans from outside mortgage brokers. To try to stem the outflow of its capital to support its portfolio of loans and MBS-CDOs, WaMu also announced a $7 billion infusion of new capital by new outside investors led by TPG Capital. TPG agreed to pump $2 billion into WaMu, while other investors agreed to buy an additional $5 billion in newly issued stock.

But WaMu was so deeply leveraged and so involved in nonconventional mortgages that ultimately all of these moves failed. Simply put, as delinquencies and foreclosures for nonconventional mortgages increased, WaMu could not raise enough capital to support what it had borrowed to obtain mortgages and buy securities. In June 2008, Kerry Killinger stepped down as the chairman, though remaining the chief executive officer. On September 8, 2008, under pressure from investors, the Washington Mutual holding company's board of directors dismissed Killinger as the CEO.

By late September 2008, WaMu's share price had closed as low as $2. It had been worth over $30 in September 2007 and had briefly traded as high as $45 in 2006. While WaMu publicly insisted it could stay independent, it had hired Goldman Sachs to identify potential bidders. However, several deadlines passed without anyone submitting a bid. When Lehman Brothers went bankrupt in September 2008, WaMu experienced a bank run on their deposits. Depositors withdrew $16.7 billion out of their savings and checking accounts in less than a month, representing 9 percent of WaMu's deposits.

By early October, the Federal Deposit Insurance Corporation (FDIC) said the bank had insufficient funds to conduct day-to-day business. This led the Federal Reserve and the Treasury Department to step up pressure for WaMu to find a buyer, as a takeover by the FDIC could have been a severe drain on the FDIC insurance fund. The FDIC ultimately held a secret auction of Washington Mutual Bank. On the morning of Thursday, September 25, regulators informed officials at JPMorgan Chase that they were the winners. They paid $1.9 billion and agreed to assume the bank's secured debts and liabilities to depositors.

Citigroup

Citigroup began the twenty-first century as a large, diversified conglomerate bank. It had operations in every major financial market including retail, commercial, insurance, and investment banking. It had extensive credit card operations and far-flung outposts around the world. It truly was a global bank. But, by all accounts, the company was large and poorly run. Its merger activities in the 1990s had created such a large collection of banks that its activities were never fully integrated. One of the main ways this became a problem was around the issue of taking on risks of various kinds.

For example, during the financial crisis, the Federal Reserve took the bank to task for poor oversight and risk controls in a report it sent to Citigroup. Lynn Turner, a former chief accountant with the Securities and Exchange Commission, said the bank's balkanized culture and management made problems inevitable: "If you're an entity of this size," he said, "if you don't have controls, if you don't have the right culture and you don't have people accountable for the risks that they are taking, you're Citigroup." (*New York Times*, 2008c)

Citigroup's lack of integration meant that as the company rapidly expanded its mortgage origination and securitization activities from 2001 to 2008, management was unaware of the riskiness of the ventures and the exposure of the bank (Wilmarth, 2013). The principal architects of Citigroup's great expansion into CDOs were Charles Prince, CEO, and Robert Rubin, an influential director and senior adviser. Rubin had been cochairman of Goldman Sachs and later Treasury secretary during the Clinton administration. There he helped push for the repeal of the Glass-Steagall Act. This repeal had helped the creation of Citigroup possible by allowing banks to expand far beyond their traditional role as lenders and permitting them to profit from a variety of financial activities. During the same period, he also helped beat back tighter regulations over mortgage securities products.

For some time after Sanford Weill, an architect of the merger that created Citigroup, the bank had been less focused on bond trading. But in late 2002,

Prince, who had been Weill's longtime legal counsel, was put in charge of Citigroup's corporate and investment bank. As the housing market around the United States took flight, the CDO market grew apace as more and more mortgages were pooled into securities. Prince and Rubin correctly saw that the expansion of the US mortgage market from 2000 to 2003 presented a huge opportunity for the bank. Prince saw that the production and creation of MBSs / CDOs would rapidly increase Citigroup's earnings and have a positive impact on its share price.

From 2003 to 2005, Citigroup more than tripled its issuing of CDOs, to more than $20 billion from $6.28 billion, and this transformed Citigroup into one of the industry's biggest players. Firms issuing the CDOs generated fees of 0.4 percent to 2.5 percent of the amount sold, meaning Citigroup made up to $500 million in fees from the business in 2005 alone. In 2005 as prices in the housing market peaked, Citigroup decided to double down on the MBS-CDO market. They moved even more aggressively, particularly into the nonconventional MBS-CDO market. They added to their trading operations and snagged crucial people from competitors. Bonuses doubled and tripled for CDO traders. In December 2005, with Citigroup diving into CDOs, Prince assured analysts that all was well at his bank: "Anything based on human endeavor and certainly any business that involves risk-taking, you're going to have problems from time to time," he said. "We will run our business in a way where our credibility and our reputation as an institution with the public and with our regulators will be an asset of the company and not a liability" (Wilmarth, 2013: 87).

But the bank never quite appreciated the riskiness of the MBS / CDO market. Starting in June 2006, Senior Vice President Richard M. Bowen III, the chief underwriter of Citigroup's Consumer Lending Group, began warning the board of directors about the extreme risks being taken on by the mortgage operation that could result in massive losses. The group bought and sold $90 billion of residential mortgages annually. Bowen's responsibility was essentially to serve as the quality control supervisor ensuring the unit's creditworthiness. When Bowen first became a whistleblower in 2006, foreclosures were rising, and Citigroup was deeply involved in origination and securitization of the riskiest mortgages and mortgage products (Terris, 2007).

On November 3, 2007, Bowen emailed Citigroup chairman Robert Rubin and the bank's chief financial officer, head auditor, and chief risk management officer to again expose the risk and potential losses, claiming that the group's internal controls had broken down and requesting an outside investigation of his business unit. But the board chose to ignore him. Citigroup eventually stripped Bowen of most of his responsibilities and informed him that his physical presence was no longer required at the bank (*New York Times*, 2008b).

As the crisis began to unfold, Citigroup announced on April 11, 2007, that it would eliminate seventeen thousand jobs, or about 5 percent of its workforce, in a broad restructuring designed to cut costs and bolster its long-underperforming stock. But top management at Citigroup continued to be in denial about the potential problems for the bank. After securities and brokerage firm Bear Stearns ran into serious trouble in summer 2007, Citigroup decided that the possibility of trouble with their CDOs was so tiny (less than 1 / 100 of 1 percent) that they excluded them from their risk analysis. But eventually, with the crisis worsening, Citigroup announced on January 7, 2008, that it was cutting another 5 percent to 10 percent of its 327,000-person workforce.

Heavy exposure to troubled mortgages in the form of CDOs, compounded by poor risk management, led Citigroup into trouble as the subprime mortgage crisis worsened in 2008. Citigroup not only had massive amounts of MBSs / CDOs on its books but also owed creditors money it had borrowed to produce and buy those securities. By November 2008, Citigroup was insolvent, despite its receipt of $25 billion in taxpayer-funded federal TARP funds. On November 17, 2008, Citigroup announced plans for about fifty-two thousand new job cuts, on top of twenty-three thousand cuts already made in 2008. The same day, its stock dropped, and the company's market capitalization fell to $6 billion, down from $300 billion two years prior. Eventually, staff cuts totaled over one hundred thousand employees, and shares of Citigroup common stock traded below $1.00 on the New York Stock Exchange.

As a result, on November 23, 2008, Citigroup and federal regulators approved a plan to stabilize the company and forestall a further deterioration in the company's value. The US government announced a massive bailout for Citigroup designed to rescue the company from bankruptcy while giving the government a major say in its operations. A joint statement by the US Treasury Department, the Federal Reserve, and the FDIC announced, "With these transactions, the U.S. government is taking the actions necessary to strengthen the financial system and protect U.S. taxpayers and the U.S. economy" (Federal Reserve, 2008).

The bailout called for the government to back about $306 billion in loans and securities and directly invest about $20 billion in the company. The Treasury provided $20 billion in TARP funds in addition to $25 billion given in October. The Treasury Department, the Federal Reserve, and the FDIC agreed to cover 90 percent of the losses on Citigroup's $335 billion portfolio after Citigroup absorbed the first $29 billion in losses. The Treasury would assume the first $5 billion in losses, the FDIC would absorb the next $10 billion, and the Federal Reserve would assume the rest of the risk.

In return, on February 27, 2009, Citigroup announced that the US government would take a 36 percent equity stake in the company by converting $25 billion in emergency aid into common stock with a United States Treasury credit line of $45 billion to prevent the bankruptcy of the company. The government guaranteed losses on more than $300 billion of troubled assets and injected $20 billion immediately into the company. The salary of the CEO was set at $1 per year, and the highest salary of employees was restricted to $500,000. The US government also gained control of half the seats in the board of directors, and the senior management was subject to removal by the US government if there were poor performance.

The bailout worked. By December 2009, the US government stake was reduced from a 36 percent stake to a 27 percent stake, after Citigroup sold $21 billion of common shares and equity in the largest single share sale in US history. By December 2010, Citigroup repaid the emergency aid in full, and the US government had made a $12 billion profit on its investment in the company. In 2010, Citigroup achieved its first profitable year since 2007. It reported $10.6 billion in net profit, compared with a $1.6 billion loss in 2009.

The Spread of the Crisis to Other Countries

The collapse of the vertically integrated banks took out the center of the American banking system. But it did not just affect American banks. It created a financial crisis around the world because many banks, mostly in Europe, proved susceptible to the same downturn as the American banks. Some of those banks were deeply involved in the origination and securitization of mortgages. But mostly, they too bought MBSs and CDOs on borrowed money, working to emulate their American counterparts (Lipuma and Lee, 2004; Park, 2009). In countries where the leading banks were investing in MBSs and CDOs, these crises struck swiftly and suddenly. It is to the rapid spread of the crisis around the world that I now turn. By the fall of 2008, banks in the United States and western Europe were announcing devastating losses, touching off a financial panic that culminated in a wave of bank failures in the United States and at least ten different European nations during September and October of that year. By one count, twenty-three countries experienced a systemic bank crisis by the end of 2009 (Laeven and Valencia, 2008; see Table 6.2). These crises were followed by deep and long-lasting recessions.

There are three unusual features of this global financial crisis (Longstaff, 2010). First, it started in the United States. While the United States has not been immune to financial crises in the postwar era (Kaufman, 2009), they have tended to be mostly contained and not spread to other countries. But rarely has the largest economy produced the panic that caused the world financial system to

Table 6.2 : Countries that experienced a banking crisis, 2008–2009

Systemic banking crisis (13 countries)	Borderline banking crisis (10 countries)
Austria (late 2009)*	France
Belgium	Greece
Denmark	Hungary
Germany	Kazakhstan
Iceland	Portugal
Ireland	Russia
Latvia	Slovenia
Luxembourg	Spain
Mongolia (late 2009)*	Sweden
Netherlands	Switzerland
Ukraine	
United Kingdom	
United States	

Data source: International Monetary Fund.

*We treat these cases as nonincidences of systemic banking crises in our models because they did not meet Laeven and Valencia's conditions for a systemic banking crisis before the end of 2008.

convulse. Second, the crisis was most severe in the advanced industrial societies and particularly in western Europe. Most of the cases of economic contagion in the postwar era have involved less developed countries, but this crisis did not spread to the less developed world (Forbes and Rigobon, 2001; Forbes, 2004). Finally, the crisis spread almost instantaneously in the fall of 2008 to these countries, and most of the developed countries found themselves in recession in 2009. This implies that whatever the American banks were doing, the vulnerable European and Japanese banks were doing it as well. What happened?

In international economics and political economy, economic contagion and the mechanisms by which financial crises spread are a central concern (Forbes and Rigobon, 2001; Reinhart and Rogoff, 2009a, 2009b; Claessens et al., 2001; Allen and Gale, 2007; Moser, 2003; Forbes, 2004; for a recent review, see Claessens and Forbes, 2004). This perspective has been applied to the financial crisis of 2007–2009 (A. Rose and Spiegel, 2010; Claessens et al., 2010). Here, scholars have drawn mostly negative conclusions that the typical processes that push financial contagion were in operation in 2008 and 2009. There is little evidence that countries that went into recession in 2008 and 2009 shared fundamental features such as an overblown housing market that may have left them more likely to have a recession or pushed financial investors toward a flight to safety. Fligstein and Habinek (2014) provide evidence on this point.

What explains what happened instead is that the European and Japanese banks were looking for products to increase their profits that appeared to have little risk. These foreign banks came to realize that the American banks had hit on a formula that produced record profits. MBSs and CDOs were highly rated products that paid relatively high interest with seemingly little chance of default. This meant that banks could borrow money to fund their purchases of these securities and hold them on their own accounts. Their national regulators who audited their books saw this happening. But they observed that their national banks were buying AAA-rated products with high returns and gave them their blessings.

The process by which this unfolded followed the lines of what had happened in the United States. After 2001, the largest banks in the United States and in other developed countries faced economic recession, low interest rates, and the need to find new sources of profit. Banks in Europe and Japan watched as their American counterparts made billions of dollars originating, securitizing, and buying and holding MBSs and CDOs from 2001 to 2003. Starting in 2004, foreign banks came to hold massive amounts of securities based on American mortgages. By 2007, the main source of profit for the largest banks became their investments in American MBSs and CDOs that were bought using short-term finance procured in the US ABCP market. In essence, banks from around the world came to be major players in the same market and pursued the same strategies as their American counterparts to make profits. When the housing market in the United States turned down, banks around the world suffered the same crisis that American banks did. They first had liquidity crises, and when it was difficult to price or sell their bond holdings, they quickly became insolvent. Like in the United States, they turned to their governments for bailouts. The banking crises then became the basis of economic downturn and caused recessions in many countries. Essentially, by realizing that many European and Japanese banks had the same strategies as their American counterparts, one can see why particular countries were vulnerable to the downturn and why it happened so quickly.

Which Banks Owned MBSs and CDOs, and Who Borrowed from the ABCP Market?

Between 2001 and 2007, investors increased their holdings of American MBSs dramatically (Inside Mortgage Finance, 2009). In this period, US commercial banks increased their holdings from about $700 billion to almost $1.1 trillion, an increase of over 50 percent. Mutual fund holding more than doubled from

Table 6.3 : Foreign countries with the highest amount of MBSs/GDP in 2006 and countries with the highest amount of ABCP/GDP

Highest MBSs/GDP (US Department of the Treasury, 2007)
Ireland
Belgium
France
Germany
Iceland
Netherlands
Norway
Switzerland
United Kingdom
Japan
Highest ABCP/GDP (Acharya et al., 2013)
Netherlands
Belgium
Germany
United Kingdom
France
Canada
Switzerland
Japan
Denmark
Spain

Source: Neil Fligstein and Jacob Habinek, "Sucker Punched by the Invisible Hand: The Spread of the Worldwide Financial Crisis, 2007–2010," Socio-Economic Review 12(4): 1–29, table 1. © The Authors. Published by Oxford University Press and the Society for the Advancement of Socio-Economics.

about \$425 billion to almost \$850 billion. But the category that showed the most dramatic increase was foreign holdings of MBSs. Holdings grew from about \$200 billion to over \$1.2 trillion at the peak. In the space of five years, foreigners increased their holdings of US MBSs by \$1 trillion, an increase of nearly 600 percent.

The Inside Mortgage Finance data does not allow one to decompose the holders of those bonds by country. The US Treasury, however, gathers this data on a yearly basis (2007, table 11, p. 15, table 24, pp. 51–55). Table 6.3 provides evidence on the ten largest holders of MBSs by country in 2006. The ten countries who were the largest holders of American MBSs in 2006 were the United Kingdom, Belgium, Ireland, Japan, Germany, Iceland, the Netherlands, Norway, Switzerland, and France. All of the largest holders of American MBSs were advanced industrial societies, and nine out of ten were in western Europe. I note that all of these countries were at the center of the ensuing financial crisis, and all had serious financial crises.

Unfortunately, neither Inside Mortgage Finance nor the US Treasury collects information about individual bank holdings of US MBSs and CDOs. But the Federal Reserve Bank bought $1.25 trillion of government-sponsored enterprise MBSs during the crisis from thirteen banks including eight foreign banks. Barclays (United Kingdom), BNP Paribas (France), Credit Suisse (Switzerland), Deutsche Bank (Germany), Mizoho (Japan), Normura (Japan), RBS (United Kingdom), and UBS (Switzerland) sold almost $625 billion of MBS-CDOs based on conventional mortgages to the Federal Reserve. These foreign banks all were in advanced industrial countries, and most were in Europe. Beginning in January 2008, the Federal Reserve expanded its short-term loan activities for banks to help them through a "liquidity crisis." In 2008–2009, the Federal Reserve lent money to 438 banks, of which 156 were branches of foreign-owned banks. Most of the banks (138) were branches of European banks.

A very similar pattern is apparent in the market for asset-backed commercial paper. Table 6.3 also contains information on the countries where the banks resided who were the largest purchasers of ABCP as of January 2007. These include the Netherlands, Belgium, Germany, the United Kingdom, France, Canada, Switzerland, Japan, Denmark, and Spain. We note that this list overlaps with the list on MBSs for seven of the ten countries, implying a link between a country's banks purchasing MBSs and CDOs and the ABCP market. This provides evidence that foreign banks that were buying MBSs and CDOs did so by borrowing capital in the ABCP market (Acharya and Schnabl, 2010).

There is some information on the identities of the largest banks in the ABCP market. Table 6.4 presents the twenty largest foreign banks in that market and the eight largest US players. The foreign list confirms that many of the world's largest banks were substantially involved in the ABCP market. All of these banks except Mitsubishi and the Royal Bank of Canada either were substantially reorganized or went bankrupt during the crisis. On the US list, all of the banks either were bailed out by the government or went bankrupt. We note that both Bear Stearns and Lehman Brothers are on the list. Lehman Brothers' failure was the proximate event that caused the crisis to spike (Swedberg, 2010). Data on the number of bank failures in various countries across Europe shows that many of the countries with the largest number of bank failures were large holders of MBSs and high levels of borrowings in ABCP (Alves, 2012). France, the United Kingdom, Germany, Ireland, Iceland, Switzerland, Belgium, and the Netherlands all appear among countries with high levels of MBSs and ABCP and had the largest number of per capita bank failures.

Table 6.4 : Largest banks with ABCP holdings with country of origin

Foreign

ABN Amro (Netherlands)

HBOS (United Kingdom)

HSBC (United Kingdom and Hong Kong)

Deutsche Bank (Germany)

Societe Generale (France)

Barclays (United Kingdom)

Mitsubishi (Japan)

Rabobank (Netherlands)

Westdeutsche Landesbank (Germany)

ING Groep (Netherlands)

Dresdner Bank (Germany)

Fortis (Belgium)

Bayerische Landesbank (Germany)

Credit Agriciole (France)

Lloyds Banking Group (United Kingdom)

Hypo Real Estate (Germany)

Royal Bank of Canada (Canada)

BNP Paribas (France)

KBC Group (Belgium)

Bayerische Hypo-und Vereinsbank (Germany)

US

Citigroup

Bank of America

JPMorgan Chase

Bear Stearns

GMAC

State Street Corporation

Lehman Brothers

Countrywide Financial

Source: Neil Fligstein and Jacob Habinek, "Sucker Punched by the Invisible Hand: The Spread of the Worldwide Financial Crisis, 2007–2010," Socio-Economic Review 12(4): 1–29, table 2. © The Authors. Published by Oxford University Press and the Society for the Advancement of Socio-Economics.

The largest banks in the world financial system became players in the American MBS market during the peak of the housing bubble from 2001 to 2007. They increased their holdings 600 percent in a six-year period and came to own almost $1.2 trillion in American MBSs. The bulk of these banks were located in Europe with a few in Japan. Many of these banks were funding their purchases of MBSs by using the ABCP market. US MBSs were huge investment vehicles for the largest banks and investors in the developed world, particularly in western Europe.

Many of the banks that had participated in these markets eventually failed, causing banking crises in their home countries (Beltratti and Stulz, 2012). Fligstein and Habinek (2014) provide multivariate models that confirm this result.

Conclusion

The Great Recession originated in the United States and spread to western Europe and other parts of the developed world. The main path to the crisis was through the American housing market. The housing price bubble in the United States fueled the production of MBSs and CDOs. These securities were extensively sold and marketed around the world to banks and investors in the richest countries, who funded much of these purchases with ABCP. Foreign investors increased their holdings of these securities by $1 trillion between 2002 and 2008. As those securities began to lose their value in 2007 and 2008, banks in the United States and in foreign countries began to fail. Hardly anyone saw that securities based on nonconventional American mortgages were the hottest commodity being traded across this system. These failures spurred systemic banking crises in many countries around the world. These crises forced governments in the rich world to intervene aggressively in their banking systems to stabilize them. But the damage was so extensive that a deep recession followed. It was the globalization of the American mortgage-backed security market, the sale of securities backed on American mortgages and financed by the American ABCP market, that set off a worldwide financial crisis and a deep recession in the richest countries of western Europe.

7

FRAUD AND THE FINANCIAL CRISIS

I made a mistake in presuming that the self-interests of organizations, specifically banks and others, were such as that they were best capable of protecting their own shareholders and their equity in the firms.

—ALAN GREENSPAN (*New York Times,* October 23, 2008).

One of the great public outcries in the wake of the financial crisis was the issue of why executives of banks did not go to jail for their roles in the financial crisis. This was coupled with the perception that banks had intentionally loaned money to mortgagors, who had received mortgages that they would never be able to pay back. Indeed, one of the founding moments of the Tea Party political movement came in response to outrage that the Obama administration was considering a program to help people whose mortgages were in danger of foreclosure in February 2009 (McGrath, 2010). The Tea Party was founded by people who were infuriated that the government was going to help people who they believed did not deserve to get mortgages in the first place.

The purpose of this chapter is to explore the link between the massive fraud that was committed and the eventual collapse of the mortgage securitization industry. The drying up of conventional mortgages and the great expansion of nonconventional mortgages after 2003 drove banks to originate worse and worse mortgages over time. Eventually, banks became so desperate for mortgages to securitize that they loosened lending standards and started down the slippery slope to commit mortgage fraud. They also engaged in predatory lending, particularly to minority communities, in order to secure mortgages that attracted higher fees and higher interest rates. Vertically integrated banks were particularly susceptible to these pressures and were the most likely to have paid fines for mortgage and securities fraud (Fligstein and Roehrkasse, 2016).

To begin, it is useful to consider the three kinds of fraud that were being committed and who instigated the fraud. Mortgage fraud is the "intentional misstatement, misrepresentation, or omission by an applicant or other interested parties, relied upon by an underwriter or lender to fund, purchase or insure a loan" (Federal Bureau of Investigation [FBI], 2007). There is good evidence that a huge amount of misreporting on loan documents occurred, including borrower income inflation on loan documents (Ben-David, 2011; Jiang et al., 2014; Mian and Sufi, 2017), the concealment of second liens (Piskorski et al., 2015; Griffin and Maturana, 2016), and suspected appraisal inflation and misstatements about occupancy status (Griffin and Maturana, 2016). Somewhere around 30 percent of all mortgage applications from 2003 to 2007 are thought to have had false information on them (for a review, see Mian and Sufi, 2017). While some individuals were intentionally committing mortgage fraud in order to get loans, the FBI estimated that 80 percent of the misrepresentation of loan applications was the result of collusion between borrowers and lenders (FBI, 2008, cited in Smith, 2009: 479). It turns out that the political outcry that put the blame for such mortgages at the feet of the banks was not misplaced.

Mortgage fraud in terms of misinformation in the application process was only one kind of fraud that was being committed. As loans became more important to the securitization process, originators engaged in predatory lending. Predatory lending is a kind of fraud in which loan originators engage in unfair and deceptive practices during the loan origination process (Forrester, 2005). While predatory lending has no consensus legal definition, the Federal Deposit Insurance Corporation characterizes the behavior as "imposing unfair and abusive loan terms on borrowers, often through aggressive sales tactics; taking advantage of borrowers' lack of understanding of complicated transactions; and outright deception" (Federal Deposit Insurance Corporation, 2006: 1). A variety of laws regulate predatory lending. At the federal level, deceptive lending practices are criminalized under the Truth in Lending Act, most particularly the subsidiary Home Ownership and Equity Protection Act. Discriminatory lending practices are covered under the Fair Housing Act and the Equal Credit Opportunity Act. Moreover, at least twenty-five states have some form of anti-predatory-lending laws.

Lenders stand to gain and borrowers lose from predatory lending practices in three ways. First, lenders may misrepresent or conceal information about eligibility criteria and may offer excessively costly loans to groups that have had difficulty obtaining a mortgage, such as racial or ethnic groups. In this way, lenders can channel borrowers into loans that are more expensive than those to which they are entitled. Second, lenders may misrepresent or conceal information about loan features such as add-ons or balloon payments or about the estimated likelihood that a borrower will default. This practice allows lenders to extract unexpected fees and penalties from borrowers.[1] There is extensive evidence that borrowers who lived in minority or low-income communities were more likely to be taken advantage of in both of these ways (Baumer et al., 2017; Rugh et al., 2015). Finally, such loans were often more attractive for securitizers because they paid higher interest rates that increased the value of mortgage security tranches.

A third kind of fraud is securities fraud. Securities fraud is the situation in which actors misrepresent, withhold, or otherwise misuse information used by investors to make decisions. Securities fraud is regulated by diverse federal and state laws and enforced by an array of federal and state agencies. In this case, however, it is pursued chiefly by the Securities and Exchange Commission, the Department of Justice, and the attorneys general of major states such as New York and California. In the mortgage securitization industry, securities fraud usually takes the form of misleading investors or shareholders about the quality or composition of the mortgage assets underlying MBSs.

Issuers and underwriters stand to gain at these actors' expense in at least two ways. On the one hand, they may inflate securities prices by willfully or negligently misrepresenting the characteristics of MBS products to investors. Indeed, Piskorski et al. (2015) show that at least one in ten mortgages originated between 2005 and 2007 and packaged into MBSs were misrepresented to buyers. Short of false statements of material fact, issuers or underwriters may market and sell investments that they but not their customers know to be poor ones.[2] On the other hand, issuers and underwriters, themselves among the largest purchasers of low-quality MBSs (Fligstein and Goldstein, 2010: 47), had incentives to misrepresent their MBS holdings, with traders deceiving managers in pursuit of commissions or executives deceiving shareholders in order to secure corporate performance-based compensation.

Why would banks want to give mortgages to people who could not pay them back, and why would they risk their reputations by committing mortgage and securities fraud? One explanation has been that the originators of these mortgages were not going to hold them and would instead sell them to banks, who would then package them into securities. Those banks would not care about the riskiness of the loans because they intended to sell them to someone else. This was one of the reasons why the originate-to-distribute model was thought to be the main source of the origination and securitization of bad mortgages (Ashcraft et al., 2010). While this was true for some originators and securitizers, there is strong evidence that vertically integrated banks were the most likely to have encouraged their loan originators to commit mortgage fraud and knowingly packaged these mortgages into securities, thereby committing securities fraud (Fligstein and Roehrkasse, 2016). Why was this the case?

The shift to nonconventional mortgages was necessitated by the need to keep finding mortgages to create securities beginning in 2004. The demand for those securities was so high that originators and securitizers had little choice but to obtain such mortgages if they wanted to continue to make high profits. But once that shift began, originators and securitizers realized that such mortgages generated larger fees and had higher interest rates, and thus the securities based on them would appeal to investors who wanted higher returns. In the case where investors were borrowing money from the ABCP market to fund their purchasers, securities that paid higher returns resulted in higher profits.

When the market for nonconventional mortgages began to dry up by 2005, finding even these mortgages to produce securities became harder and harder. It was at this moment that the pressure from securitizers on originators to continue to produce new mortgages caused many originators to relax their mortgage standards, and this encouraged them to falsify loan documentation (Dell'Ariccia et al., 2012). This competition over an increasingly shrinking pool of mortgages pushed banks to begin the chain of fraudulent behavior by faking information on loan applications in order to secure those mortgages to keep their securitization machines up and running (Barnett, 2011, 2013).

This process was particularly acute for vertically integrated banks. Because their business models were predicated on using mortgages as raw materials, they felt particular pressure to keep originating mortgages. Without the mortgages, their entire pipeline would collapse. While there was awareness that these mortgages were riskier and more likely to be foreclosed on, people in banks that were vertically integrated and who wanted to remain employed had little choice but to do their jobs and respond to the pressures to keep producing.

These pressures resulted in the vertically integrated banks taking on the riskiest of mortgages, which resulted in them eventually having the largest losses and made them more likely to face bankruptcy (Goldstein and Fligstein, 2017). As a result, they were also the ones who were the most likely to engage in mortgage fraud. Indeed, committing mortgage fraud goes hand in hand with originating and securitizing the riskiest mortgages. Vertically integrated banks had the most to lose if their business models collapsed. Banks that were only originators or who produced securities (i.e., pure investment banks) could enter other businesses or scale their MBS businesses down (which is what Goldman Sachs did) as mortgages dried up. Banks that were vertically integrated needed to keep their pipelines going no matter what (Wang and Holtfreter, 2012).

Vertical integration also increased the likelihood that within the bank, no one had any interest in doing due diligence in value chains. When performed by multiple firms, the mortgage securitization process entails several distinct transactions, each of which provides opportunities not only for malfeasance but also for monitoring the quality of loans. When securitization is integrated within firms, originators, issuers, and underwriters share rather than oppose one another's interest in misrepresenting the characteristics of mortgages and MBSs. Firms that engaged in fraudulent lending perpetrated securities fraud because they were forced to hide the low quality of the mortgages they had originated.

While fraud was not the cause of the financial crisis, it was a symptom of the increasingly problematic business models of banks. Loans given to people who could not afford to make mortgage payments proved to be risky, as these were the first mortgagors to face foreclosures. As house prices stopped rising, those who could not pay their mortgages and could not sell their homes were inclined to walk away from their homes. This put further pressure on house prices. That created a spiral that meant that the securities that were built last in the process were at the greatest risk of failure. The financial debacle that followed exposed the predatory tactics that were being used to keep the mortgage securitization boom going.

This chapter is organized in the following way. First, I present some of what we know about the extent of the three kinds of fraud. Then I tie together the strands of the argument more explicitly about who committed fraud and why, and I consider some evidence for that account. Next, I turn to considering the internal organizational dynamics for how Bear Stearns and Washington Mutual committed fraud from origination to the sale and purchase of securities. It has been very difficult for researchers to get information on what was going on inside banks through this process. These case studies are based on two sources: court documents including testimony by executives who were involved in cases and public documents, particularly evidence presented at the hearings of the Financial Crisis Investigation Committee (Financial Crisis Investigation Commission, 2010a, 2010b). They reveal evidence that the basic outlines of the story I am telling about vertically integrated banks rings true. Finally, I consider the generality of my explanation of the role played in the fraud by vertically integrated banks by examining what we know about the banks that have paid large fines to settle lawsuits regarding various kinds of fraud.

How Much Fraud Was There?

The issue of measuring how much fraud was perpetrated in 2001–2008 is fraught with difficulties. What is legal and illegal behavior is a difficult question. Our definitions of fraud and our legal standards for proving it reflect how financial businesses have influenced the laws and regulations that are supposed to govern their businesses (Calavita et al., 1997). Fraud as legally defined in the United States does cover some cases where deception was intentionally used to obtain mortgages. But not all opportunistic behavior is illegal (Passas, 2005). For example, it was not illegal for banks to seek customers who they knew might not be able to pay back their mortgages. It is also not illegal for them to package risky loans into securities packages even if the probability of that mortgage being foreclosed is high.

A second problem is detecting fraud. Detecting fraud in mortgage documents is not straightforward and requires objective sources of information in order to decide if someone has filled out their paperwork fraudulently. Detecting predatory lending is even more difficult. Determining whether a particular mortgagor was targeted for a worse loan than they qualified for is almost impossible. One must decide whether that targeting was excessive with the goal of predation or whether the mortgagor just could have gotten a better deal somewhere else. Whatever estimates can be generated around these activities require innovative techniques in the face of questionable data quality. Discovering predatory lending can require those who are its victims to recognize what happened and then go public by trying to sue their bankers. A large amount of predatory lending is simply not detected because its victims remain unaware or inactive.

Much of our data on mortgage fraud comes from official sources. That data tries to infer the motives of those committing the fraud. Since we rarely have direct data on the individuals or firms involved in the fraud, those sources certainly undercount the amount of fraud. So, the problem of figuring out how much of the market contained mortgages where some form of fraud was committed is not easy. Thus, the wide range of estimates (from 10 percent to 50 percent with an average between 25 and 30 percent) concerning the overall amount of mortgage fraud is imprecise.

With those caveats, in the housing bubble that preceded the financial crisis of 2007–2008, there is significant evidence that much financial crime existed in the form of mortgage fraud (Bitner, 2008; Nguyen and Pontell, 2010; Patterson and Koller, 2011; Barnett, 2011, 2013; Fligstein and Roehrkasse, 2016; Baumer et al., 2017; Financial Crimes Enforcement Network, 2008). The mortgage industry can be thought of as consisting of two distinct segments. In the primary mortgage market, mortgage originators, with the help of brokers, escrow agents, and appraisers, originate and provide loans to borrowers. In the secondary mortgage market, investment banks, government-sponsored enterprises, and credit rating agencies engage in the business enterprise of securitizing and managing loans originated in the primary mortgage market (Nguyen and Pontell, 2010: 597; Collins and Nigro, 2010: 634). Fraud was rampant in both segments of the mortgage industry. Vertically integrated banks, of course, committed both kinds of fraud.

Evidence overwhelmingly suggests that mortgage fraud and predatory lending became a systemic problem in the years before the mortgage meltdown (Koller, 2012; Patterson and Koller, 2011; Frieden, 2004). Under US federal law, mortgage fraud is prosecuted criminally as bank fraud, wire fraud, mail fraud, or money laundering. The rapid rise of mortgage fraud in the early twenty-first century has also led states to develop their own penalties for mortgage fraud. According to the FBI, 80 percent of all reported mortgage fraud losses involve collaboration or collusion by industry insiders (FBI, 2008, cited in Smith, 2009: 479; FBI, 2010). This includes mortgage brokers, real estate appraisers, escrow agents, title officers, builders, and land developers (Collins and Nigro, 2010; Nguyen and Pontell, 2010; Smith, 2009; Gans, 2011). Mortgage brokers, who assume a crucial position in the overall mortgage origination process, played a major role in mortgage origination fraud (Nguyen and Pontell, 2010; Gans, 2011).

Baumer et al. (2017) have used a unique data set to try to estimate the overall prevalence of mortgage fraud. That data set examines all US mortgages and uses an algorithm to locate suspicious applications. That algorithm is in current use by banks and mortgage companies. They suggest that 24.2 percent of all applications contained some fraudulent information. We have several other estimates of such fraud. At the low end, Piskorski et al. (2015) estimate that about 10 percent of all loans in a sample of MBSs created by the GSEs contained fraudulent information. Griffin and Maturana (2016), using different data and techniques, report that around 48.1 percent of all mortgages contained at least one element of fraud. Many of the differences are due to different samples, different data sets, and different methods to estimate fraud. For example, the Piskorski et al. (2015) data set contains only mortgages used by GSEs. These mortgages were likely to have contained less fraud because they were based on more conventional mortgages. Even if one takes the middle of the range of estimates (about 25 percent), one can conclude that mortgage fraud involved at least a quarter of mortgages and was a large problem.

Richard Bitner, a former president of the subprime mortgage lender Kellner Mortgage, reported that that he was well aware of the fraudulent nature of loan applications coming from mortgage brokers. He says, "At the end, 70 percent of submissions from brokers to the company were deceptive, half of the property values related to loans were over-edged by up to 10 percent, a quarter had property prices exaggerated by 11 to 20 percent, and the rest were so overvalued, they defied all logic" (Bitner, 2008: 97).

Predatory lending was widespread among mortgage originators (Willis, 2006). Predatory lenders often target potential and current homeowners who are generally not seeking loans (Renuart, 2004). In most cases, predatory lenders target subprime borrowers with little prior experience in the credit market (Engel and McCoy, 2001: 1261; Delgadillo et al., 2008). They capitalize on these borrowers' lack of financial literacy and lack of access to unbiased financial advice (Engel and McCoy, 2001). In the prime market, mortgages are extended to borrowers who are deemed to have a high level of creditworthiness and good credit histories. The predatory market has been conceived of as constituting a separate section of the subprime market and has been said to target "people who, because of historical credit rationing, discrimination, the exodus of banks from inner-city neighborhoods, and other social and economic forces, are disconnected from the credit market and hence are vulnerable to predatory lenders' hard-sell tactics" (Engel and McCoy, 2001: 1279).

Estimates of the prevalence of predatory lending, especially those forms that reach the level of illegality, are hard if not impossible to come by. The diversity of practices subsumed under predatory lending, the different credit markets involved, and the lack of a common definition of predatory lending make it difficult to quantify its prevalence and costs. Moreover, as already noted, victims of predatory lending rarely understand that they have been wronged, and if they do, they rarely bring lawsuits. Ryder (2014) concludes that "It is impossible to determine how many of the subprime loans issued before the start of the financial crisis fell within the definition of predatory lending" (75–76). There is, however, a shared understanding in the literature that, at least in the United States, predatory lending practices were widespread during the housing boom that preceded the financial crisis of 2007–2008 and that hundreds of thousands of homeowners have been victimized in the past decade (Willis, 2006; Fligstein and Roehrkasse, 2016; Ryder, 2014).

Fligstein and Roehrkasse (2016) report that each of the top ten mortgage originators, which in 2007 had a 71.7 percent market share, have been implicated in fraudulent or discriminatory lending practices. These lenders have settled lawsuits brought by regulators and borrowers alleging predation. In certain cases, banks such as Goldman Sachs and Morgan Stanley that underwrote but did not directly broker mortgages have been found liable for the predatory practices they helped finance.[3] Agarwal et al. (2013) estimate that predatory lending practices led to a one-third increase in the probability of subprime mortgagors defaulting on their loans.

Investment banks, acting as issuers and underwriters for securities, have been shown to have made false statements to investors and other market participants about the quality and character of those securities (Ferguson, 2012; Barnett, 2013; Fligstein and Roehrkasse, 2016; Ryder, 2014: 95–103; Piskorski et al., 2015). According to one observer, "almost all prospectuses and sales material on mortgage-backed bonds sold from 2005 through 2007 were a compound of falsehoods" in the United States (Ferguson, 2012: 191). Fligstein and Roehrkasse (2016) show that all of the top ten underwriting firms, which together represented 74.1 percent of the market, have all been implicated in securities fraud cases. All settled with regulators or investors over underwriting-related fraud allegations (Fligstein and Roehrkasse, 2016: 28).

In their study, Piskorski et al. (2015) found that about one out of every ten loans in their dataset involved some sort of misrepresentation. The authors of the study emphasize that these results are complicated by the fact that it is difficult to determine where exactly in the supply chain of credit, be it at the level of the borrower, the lender, or the underwriter, the misrepresentation took place (Piskorski et al., 2015: 32). They also found that the delinquency rate of misrepresented loans was 60 to 70 percent higher than the delinquency rate of otherwise similar loans, potentially impacting MBSs with a combined outstanding balance of up to $160 billion (Piskorski et al., 2015: 5).

Taken together, there is ample evidence that fraud was built into the mortgage business during 2001–2008. Fraud was being committed by literally everyone in the mortgage business. Mortgagors accepted loans under conditions where they knowingly lied on their applications (Jiang et al., 2014). Originators helped mortgagors obtain loans and frequently took advantage of unsophisticated borrowers by locking them into mortgages that paid high fees but were guaranteed to fail. Those who made the securities were knowingly packaging loans that were obtained fraudulently. How the industry became so corrupt is the question we turn to next.

Why Was There So Much Fraud?

Fraud was committed across the value chain that sold mortgages to households, took those mortgages and turned them into securities, and bought and sold those securities. Mortgage fraud, predatory lending, and securities fraud all increased as the conventional mortgage market peaked in 2003 and began its decline. Non-conventional loans on the rise after 2003, especially subprime mortgages, adjustable-rate mortgages, and interest-only mortgages, were particularly open to both kinds of fraud. As I have just documented, mortgagors with worse credit were frequently offered loans, and the conditions of those loans proved to be onerous. This entailed high fees and loan conditions that made these loans more expensive. Indeed, it was the move by all participants in the mortgage origination and securitization markets to these nonconventional mortgages that brought fraud from the edges of the mortgage market to its center.

In this section, I want to return to what was going on in the market for mortgages from 2001 to 2008. My purpose is to offer an account of why fraud moved from being peripheral to the mortgage market to occupying such a central place that by 2008, it could be described as systemic. I want to consider what brought all of the banks that had previously abided by the rules, more or less, to commit fraud in the origination of mortgages and their securitizations. While this fraud became ubiquitous across all parts of the production process, it was most concentrated in the largest players in the market, the vertically integrated banks (Fligstein and Roehrkasse, 2016). The vertically integrated banks were not passing on the risks of bad mortgages to other players but instead were taking on those risks in their origination, securitization, and investment businesses. The question of why they were more likely to push for fraudulent mortgages and predatory lending is what I seek to explain in the rest of this chapter.

The story I told in Chapters 5 and 6 helps us understand how the shifting character of mortgage originations pushed the vertically integrated banks at the core of the mortgage securitization industry to rapidly move into the nonconventional mortgage market in 2004–2008. The market for mortgage securities remained strong from 2003 to 2007. AAA-rated mortgage-backed securities that paid high yields were one of the most important investments for banks in the United States and western Europe throughout this period. During the growth of nonconventional mortgages from 2004 to 2008, banks of all kinds borrowed money and loaded up on securities made from these mortgages. Recall that foreign banks bought nearly $1 trillion worth of securities from 2003 to 2008. The securities based on nonconventional mortgages paid higher interest and produced more profit.

After the refinancing boom in conventional mortgages slowed down in 2004, finding a supply of mortgages to continue to feed the securitization market became paramount to keeping the highly profitable business of vertically integrated banks going. The downturn in conventional mortgages in 2004 pushed banks to shift their marketing strategy from households with excellent credit to households that had less-than-stellar credit. This pressure to continue to produce securities created incentives for all involved to keep originating mortgages even when the supply of mortgagors who could be reasonably expected to be able to pay off those mortgages declined.

As even those mortgages got harder and harder to find, originators began to loosen their standards for mortgage approval to fund almost anyone. This loosening was accompanied by their cutting corners on mortgage applications, which produced increased mortgage fraud. It also encouraged predatory lending because originators could roll the higher fees into the cost of the mortgage. It was this continuous need for mortgages to securitize that brought the increase in fraud and predatory lending. By 2005, almost all of the securities being produced contained mortgages that were fraudulently originated. Given the relatively poor income and credit situations of these mortgagors, they were more likely to default once they found they could not pay their mortgages.

The shift toward mortgagors with less good credit was originally viewed with some trepidation. But quite quickly, banks realized that such mortgages were more valuable than conventional mortgages. The additional fees to originate such mortgages and the higher interest rates that came with them meant that the securitization machines of the vertically integrated banks not only could continue to prosper but could actually make more money. The rise of the nonconventional market became a huge opportunity for investment banks such as Lehman Brothers, Merrill Lynch, Morgan Stanley, and Bear Stearns. They were able to ramp up their securitization businesses because the GSEs were unable to securitize nonconventional mortgages. Even after the housing market began to turn down in 2005, banks had to chase after mortgages. But because mortgages were becoming scarcer, as I showed in Chapter 5, investment banks began to buy originators to insure them with supply. Banks that were already integrated, such as Countrywide, Washington Mutual, and Citibank, were chasing after fewer and fewer loans, and they intensified their efforts to originate and buy more loans.

In Chapter 5, I showed that the opportunity to sell MBS-CDOs and hold on to them for investments caused banks to securitize a higher and higher percentage of the mortgages being originated. By 2007, almost 90 percent of subprime mortgages were being securitized. It also brought banks into the subprime industry and created more vertical integration as banks sought out more supply of mortgages. This lack of supply of mortgages got banks that were producing securities to put pressure on their origination department and other mortgage brokers to bring them more and more nonconventional mortgages.

The appetite for MBSs and CDOs based on these mortgages was insatiable. Indeed, the repacking of unsaleable tranches of MBSs into CDOs was stimulated by the size of the market for these products. When the supply of mortgages began to dry up in 2005, banks that were holding on to lower-ranked tranches of securities that had been rated BBB or lower ramped up their CDO production to offer new products to sell and hold as securities. This meant that riskier mortgages were being securitized at high rates. The need for new mortgages encouraged originators who were either free standing or employed by vertically integrated banks to offer mortgages to people with impaired credit and little ability to pay back loans.

At a meeting in May 2005 on CDOs and the market for those securities, the main topic of conversation was how the demand for CDOs was driving the mortgage market:

> In a panel on the effect of CDOs on the fixed-income market, Bear Stearns traders said mortgage issuers and CDO managers are playing off one another. While one group provides the fuel—borrowers induced by new mortgage products to buy a new home or refinance—the other supplies the structure as well as the investors, replenishing liquidity through securitization. All seemed to agree that as long as investors are willing to pay, there will be managers willing to do deals. (Pyburn, 2005: 8)

In particular, there was brisk demand for CDOs based on nonconventional mortgages:

> The innovation surge in the mortgage industry, such as subprime IO loans, the 40-year mortgage, and a slew of so-called option ARMs, is needed to create more and more structured finance CDOs. Product innovation will likely continue as the mortgage industry, sated after the refinance boom, prowls for untapped markets—such as borrowers without a social security number—to keep volume high amid rising interest rates. "As long as there are investors willing to purchase the product, the market will continue to grow more and more levered", said Jeff Zavattero, senior managing director in the CDO group at Bear. And demand right now is very high. One REIT executive recently said that CDOs are simply a machine that must be fed to keep going, noted Bear traders. (Pyburn, 2005: 9)

In this perverse situation, loans that had little or no documentation were actually more valuable because fees and interest rates were higher, making profits sustainable even at lower loan volumes. The line between aggressive and risky lending and fraudulent lending turned out to be a fine one. If investors who bought securities based on low documentation were informed of that, they expected higher rates of return. This was not illegal. But the low-documentation loans were more subject to risk of fraud. So-called "liars' loans" meant that mortgagors were literally lying about their circumstances. Banks also had huge incentives to engage in predatory lending to less sophisticated mortgagors. Banks began to court people with impaired credit, and they did so by intentionally misstating information on loan forms and loading those mortgagors up with fees and higher interest payments. They also put many mortgagors into mortgage products that were more lucrative for originators but potentially more problematic for mortgagors. It became not just something one or two rogue banks were doing but a systemic feature of how the mortgage market operated from 2004 to 2008.

Note that these pressures existed for all banks no matter where they resided on the value chain. Originators who knew they were going to sell loans to securitizers found themselves able to make more money on fees and selling riskier mortgages to securitizers. They also found that banks that were buying mortgages preferred these mortgages, and they came under pressure to produce these mortgages if they wanted to sell them in the secondary market. Some originators were certainly pirates, by which I mean that they enthusiastically took the opportunity to engage in mortgage fraud to profit. But all faced the same pressure to produce nonconventional mortgages that would yield higher profits for those producing securities.

Vertically integrated producers were more susceptible to committing mortgage fraud and predatory lending. This was because their entire business depended on mortgages as raw materials. Their success at finding mortgages by internalizing the origination function gave them an advantage over nonintegrated producers of securities. It also pushed investment banks who did own nonconventional originators to backwardly integrate into the origination business in order to continue to be able to securitize mortgages.

As the market for mortgages dried up, everyone else felt compelled to do whatever they needed to in order to ensure a supply of mortgages to secure. Those who were vertically integrated held on to lots of these securities even though they knew they were riskier. Since they paid out higher returns, having some of the riskier MBS-CDOs made a great deal of sense. All of this got worse as finding mortgages in the origination market got harder. This made banks that had taken on risky mortgages more desperate and more likely to commit mortgage fraud and predatory lending to ensure a supply of mortgages for securitization.

In 2005, when house prices stopped rising and foreclosures (particularly of recently lent subprime mortgages) increased, the pressure to continue to originate and securitize mortgages did not let up; if anything, it intensified. Instead of cutting back on their origination and securitization businesses, vertically integrated banks doubled down on doing whatever they had to do to keep going. After all, their businesses had risen on taking advantage of the ability to borrow money, originate millions of mortgages, and turn those mortgages into highly profitable securities. But as those securities came under pressure because they contained riskier and riskier mortgages, vertically integrated banks could do little but continue to originate and produce securities. In order to keep their business model going, they had originated many mortgages fraudulently and created securities based on those mortgages. When they fell, they experienced larger losses, and most of them went out of business, were forced to merge with other banks, or, for the lucky few, were bailed out (Goldstein and Fligstein, 2017). The push to keep going meant that committing fraud was baked into their products (Fligstein and Roehrkasse, 2016).

Vertical Integration and the Production of Fraud

It is useful to explore this process by examining how two banks, Bear Stearns and Washington Mutual, came to incorporate fraudulent practices into their business models. One of the most difficult aspects of understanding the financial crisis is to understand the internal processes of banks. While the story I just told is plausible and fits with the facts, it does not dig inside the banks to make sense of how they were organized and how they committed fraud on the ground to keep their vertically integrated businesses going. Understandably, most of the people involved in this have chosen not to speak publicly about their role in this process. All of our knowledge about how this worked comes from court documents or official investigations. It makes sense to review some cases in order to see how fraud became part of the process of securitization.

It is here that we can see how the incentives inside the bank operated. In both banks, the people at the top wanted to fund mortgages to participate in securitization. Their salaries and bonuses depended on the bank growing and getting more profitable. They encouraged those who worked for them to do whatever it took to make the most money. The bond traders who sold securities were the most in touch with customers who wanted to buy securities. They discovered that it was easier to sell securities that were AAA rated and had higher returns. They also, of course, earned more money if they sold more securities, and so they encouraged their originators to find mortgages to securitize that produced the most saleable securities.

The magic of securitization allowed banks to put securities together that, while containing some risky mortgages, were able to pass tests that made them look less risky. In order to comply with the wishes of the traders in the firm, the securitization facilities put pressure on originators to produce mortgages with higher yields. Originators' jobs depended on this. If they could not find such mortgages, they were out of work. They also had the incentive to originate mortgages with higher fees and higher interest rates, as their pay was tied to their performance. So the process of vertical integration linked everyone's incentives to produce more and more risky loans together.

Bear Stearns

According to the Financial Crisis Inquiry Commission (2011: 200), "in mortgage securitization, Bear followed a vertically integrated model that made money at every step, from loan origination through securitization and sale. It both acquired and created its own captive originators to generate mortgages that Bear bundled, turned into securities, and sold to investors."

At the top of Bear Stearns's organization were the traders who bought and sold securities and derivatives of all types. Tom Marano was the head of the Global Mortgage- and Asset-Backed Securities Department at Bear Stearns from 2003 to 2007.[4] Marano had been with the firm since it had started trading mortgage-backed securities in 1983. He was responsible for supervising the traders of mortgage- and asset-backed securities (MBSs and ABSs) and was involved in supervising securitization in the firm during the period when the market shifted from conventional to nonconventional mortgages.

Marano described how Bear Stearns found the loans to securitize in the following way: "We got loans from three sources. We would buy loans from third-party originators. But we also had the capacity to originate loans through firms we owned and controlled. Bear Residential Mortgage Corporation (Bear Res) originated Alt-A loans, while Encore Credit Corporation was acquired late in the game and did subprime. EMC Mortgage Corporation serviced and collected payments on subprime and Alt-A loans" (Financial Crisis Investigation Commission, 2010b: 6).

Bear Stearns's strategy of vertical integration had a long history back to 1990 when it first bought EMC. When the conventional market for originations began to dry up in 2003, Bear Stearns was positioned to rapidly expand its nonconventional origination business to take up the slack. But by 2005, that market began to dry up as well. In order to keep the mortgage pipeline flowing, Bear Stearns created a new firm, Bear Residential Mortgage Corporation (known as Bear Res), in 2005 to originate and buy mortgage loans for their pipeline. Bear Stearns was not the only investment bank involved in mortgages to purchase originators. Currie (2007: 23) explains why:

Wall Street seems to have thrown out its old and trusty playbook. Instead of pulling back in 2006, several major firms went on a spending spree. Well, despite the gloomy outlook, competition is not letting up. First, clients have been setting up capital-markets desks to securitize their own loans in their own version of vertical integration. Second, more players are trying to buy loans that are still for sale. That's especially true of the mortgage market, where vertical integration has been most rampant. "In 2000 we'd have maybe five or six groups bidding on a loan sale," says Commaroto. "Now there are 20 or more. And it's not just us banks bidding, but hedge funds and whole-loan trading boutiques." The more bidders, the higher prices can go, and that, of course, can undermine the economics of a securitization. It also means a desk has more chance of not getting enough loans in a timely manner.

Currie (2007: 23) continues,

> It would be unfair in the extreme to characterize vertical integration as little more than a headlong rush into lending as a way of staving off ABS underwriting desks' death spiral because of a lack of access to product. There are also significant advantages to owning a lender. For starters, having a captive lender eliminates the need to hunt for as many loans in the marketplace. Next, as owners, the investment banks earn all the fees from originating the loans to the gain on selling into a securitization. And they can even become loan sellers themselves should the product not fit their MBS vehicles—though it's more likely they would sell to a CDO fund or a whole-loan investor than to a rival player.

Encore Credit Corporations was acquired in February 2007, just a few months before Bear Stearns went bankrupt. Marano describes the motivation to buy the subprime mortgage originator as follows:

> Between 2005 and 2006, we experienced early payment defaults on subprime mortgages—loans defaulting in the first ninety days—at a fairly high rate. We set up a team to put the loans back to the originators. It would have been due to the poor origination standards by third parties. They were defaulting before they were securitized. We ended up walking away from New Century and First Long Beach in 2006 that had been providing us with loans. We decided to buy Encore in 2007 in order to secure a supply of mortgages for securitization. The mortgage markets had taken a few hits and the price of the company was trading very low. We thought we could implement our own standards in originating loans, and we could get better quality subprime loans in order to continue our business of producing MBS and CDO. (Financial Crisis Investigation Commission, 2010b: 9)

One crucial question in understanding how Bear Stearns operated is to consider the link between the trading desk that sold securities to customers and the originators who provided mortgages for sale to investment banks. Mary Haggerty was in charge of procuring loans for securitization at Bear Stearns. She was the person who linked the originators of the loans to the traders through her overseeing the procurement of loans for securitization.[5] In her testimony to the Financial Crisis Investigation Commission, Haggerty said that the traders would provide the originators with a sheet describing the types of securities they would be able to most readily sell. They would consult with the trading desk to set up rating sheets that would be used by Bear Res and EMC to price mortgages to originators and brokers. The traders would have direct input into the terms of mortgages by establishing the parameters of those terms. They would base those parameters on considerations of what they could currently sell to investors.

In her testimony, Haggerty described how this process worked:

> On a day to day basis, the decision to purchase mortgage loans comes from the trading desk and it comes in two ways: one is through a flow channel and one is through a bulk channel. The bulk channel is highly—can be highly controlled by the trading desk because, by its nature, the traders can choose to bid on the loans or not bid on the loans or bid on them to lose, frankly. The flow channel is a situation where the traders publish pricing daily and an approved seller can deliver loans that meet the criteria pursuant to those prices. So, in order to control volume, among other things, the traders control pricing where, in the case of bulk, decide whether or not to bid. So, the volume was really controlled by that pricing mechanism and what the traders wanted to buy. (Financial Crisis Investigation Commission, 2010a: 29).

Bear Stearns was one of the banks that began to aggressively enter nonconventional markets after 2003. It was among the largest and most important issuers / underwriters for mortgage securities from 2000 to 2007. It was the leading underwriter of nonagency MBSs in 2001, 2004, and 2005 and the second- or third-largest underwriter in the other years. In the same era, Bear Stearns was in the top ten in issuers, and in 2004–2006, it was in the top five (Inside Mortgage Finance, 2009: vol. 2, pp. 18–25).

In 2000, when it was the second-largest underwriter, Bear Stearns produced $9.4 billion worth of mortgage securities. At its peak in 2005, it underwrote $130.8 billion worth of mortgages. In order to keep its securitization business going, Bear Stearns needed to rapidly increase its role as a conduit for mortgages (i.e., as a wholesale buyer). It grew from wholesaling about $2 billion mortgages in 2000 to $57.2 billion in 2007. But it found that it needed to not just buy mortgages but also produce them itself. In 2000, Bear Stearns did not originate any mortgages. After its integration of EMC into its Mortgage Department in 2005, the total leaped to $72.4 billion in mortgages originated in 2006 (only to decline to $31.2 billion in 2007; Inside Mortgage Finance, 2009: vol. 1, pp. 43–54). Of that $72.4 billion, $53.4 billion was in option ARMs (again, there was a steep decline in 2007 to $19 billion; Inside Mortgage Finance, 2009: vol. 1, pp. 43–54).

While Bear Stearns was a player in underwriting and issuing many different kinds of nonconventional mortgages, it specialized in option ARMs. An option ARM is a fifteen- or thirty-year adjustable-rate mortgage that, after the expiration of a very short teaser rate period (typically one month to one year), offers the borrower four monthly payment options (only the lowest option is set forth in the loan contract): a specified minimum payment that is fully amortizing based on the teaser rate (which is no longer in effect) and that is the only payment amount set forth in the borrower's loan documents, an interest-only payment based on the sum of a margin and index that is substantially higher than the teaser rate, a fifteen-year fully amortizing payment, and a thirty-year fully amortizing payment.

When a borrower makes a monthly payment that is less than the accrued interest in that month, there is negative amortization, which means that the unpaid portion of the accruing interest is added to the outstanding principal balance. Many of these loans contained prepayment penalties that made it very costly for borrowers to refinance until twelve or sometimes thirty-six months had passed. This meant that borrowers could easily find themselves with mortgage loans that were experiencing substantial negative amortization while their ability to refinance was restricted (Kramer and Sinha, 2006).

It is useful to show the relative importance of different kinds of nonconventional mortgages fed into Bear Stearns's overall securitizations. In January 2007, the product breakdown for Bear Stearns was 48.8 percent option ARM; 12.2 percent Alt-A, second lien; 11.2 percent Alt-A, ARM; 6.9 percent Alt-A fixed; and 3.7 percent subprime. Bear Stearns committed itself to the option ARMs business in a significant way. The market for option ARMs exploded in 2005 and 2006 but fell from $775 billion in 2006 to $618 billion in 2007 (Inside Mortgage Finance, 2009: 140–141). Its expansion was part of the general expansion of nonconventional mortgages in this period:

> The reason the U.S. mortgage industry profits remain high in 2004 and 2005 is tied to the rise of the nonconventional sector. The reason mortgage companies take on riskier mortgages is because of the loan yield. If a conventional mortgage is offered at 5.5%, an A-loan would fetch 7%

allowing the lender to make more profit. But something new is afoot. Subprime lenders such as New Century, Option One, and First Franklin have expanded their menus to include exotic mortgages such as interest only adjustable rate mortgages and payment Option ARMs that allow consumers low monthly payments. (Muolo, 2005: 43)

In August 2006, Friedman Billings Ramsey issued a report stating that the market for option ARM securities was quite strong:

FBR said investors were paying prices of 103 to 104.5 for payment Option ARMs. The investment banking firm says these prices can result in gain on sale margins of 150 to 200 basis points. "As a result, we would be buyers of the Option ARM lenders into second quarter earnings," writes analyst Paul Miller. "It is one of the few products that can be put into a portfolio today and earn a respectable return. Despite fears in the equity markets over Option ARM credit quality, it appears the fixed income market is less concerned given their appetite for the product." (*Origination News*, 2006: 44)

Bear Stearns (2006: 7) argued that the great increase in the sale of option ARMs was attributed to the demand for such mortgages from people who might not otherwise be able to afford to buy the house that they wanted. In the same document, they elaborate by saying, "In recent years, adjustable rate lending has increased in prominence in the U.S. mortgage market. The steepness of the yield curve in 2004 was instrumental in raising the percentage of new originations that were ARMs" (Bear Stearns, 2006: 9).

The yield curve began to flatten in 2005 and 2006. The change in the yield curve, however, did not slow down the number of option ARM originations; in fact, in those two years, the sale of those products increased (as we have already documented). Bear Stearns (2006: 9) reports, "However, even as the curve started to flatten in 2004, innovation in affordability products kept ARM demand high. And with the flat or inverted curve since mid-2005, ARM market share has not dramatically declined in the non-agency sector. Thus, it appears that ARM lending has gained a leadership position in the non-agency, sector that may not appreciably change in response to possible future changes in the shape or level of the yield curve."

This raises the question of why the option ARM market did so well in the face of a flattening yield curve. *Businessweek* reported,

As home prices soared, banks pushed adjustable rate loans with lower initial payments. When those got too pricey, banks hawked loans that require only interest payments for the first couple of years. And then they flogged Option ARMS as affordability tools for the masses. Banks tapped an army of unregulated mortgage brokers to do what needed to be done to keep the money flowing, even if it meant putting dangerous loans in the hands of people who couldn't handle or did not understand the risks. Wall Street greased the skids by taking on much of the new risk banks were creating. (Der Hovanesian, 2006: 73)

So where was the fraud? Option ARMs were a tool that produced predatory lending and fraud. Many people who were offered option ARMs were sold the product as a low-cost way to buy or refinance a house. Often, they could have qualified for a more conventional mortgage. But the underlying conditions of option ARMs were often obscured to buyers in order to facilitate making more profits on the part of sellers. It is useful to consider one of the most important fraud cases decided against banks in the financial crisis: *Monaco v. Bear Stearns.*[6]

The case was filed as a violation of truth in lending laws in California. The plaintiffs in the case, two homeowners, claimed that Bear Stearns through Bear Res and EMC hid the basic facts of the loan from them. It is worth quoting their claim at some length in order to understand how the fraud took place:

> The two most important pieces of information in any mortgage loan are the interest rate and the amount of the monthly payments. For the Defendants' Option ARM loans, the disclosures of both pieces of information were misleading and omitted material facts. The loan documents disclosed a teaser rate, but they did not disclose that this rate would sharply increase after only one month. The loan documents disclosed a low monthly payment for the first 3–5 years of the loan, which was based on the teaser rate, but did not reflect the actual amount of interest being charged or the amount Plaintiffs actually owed each month.
>
> Plaintiffs were not informed of the sharp increase in the interest rate and the fact that their monthly payments were not enough to pay the interest accruing on the loan until they made multiple payments following the close of the loan. Had Defendants disclosed this material information, Plaintiffs would not have purchased the Option ARM loans. (*Monaco v. Bear Stearns*: 13)

In 2013, the case was settled in favor of the plaintiffs. They received a payment of $18.3 million. What this case proves is that Bear Stearns knowingly omitted information about loans to mortgagors. There is good evidence that Bear Stearns then turned around and made securities out of these mortgages. To sum up, Bear Stearns aggressively entered the option ARM market, worked hard to convince mortgagors to take the mortgages, and, in order to keep making these loans, mislead them about the actual terms of the mortgages.

The last issue to consider is the degree to which the loans that were given to people with less-than-stellar credit failed. The banks were certainly complicit in working to sell as many mortgages as they could. As the ability of potential mortgagors to repay their loans increased, banks became more desperate in finding new loans to make. The option ARM loan was designed to allow mortgagors to get into a house because of the low teaser rates at the beginning. But because these rates adjusted quickly, many of those who got these loans found themselves unable to pay. With loans that had negative amortization and with loan conditions that meant that owners could not easily refinance, many mortgagors ended up in foreclosure.

Table 7.1 shows how various vintages of mortgages issued from 2002 to 2006 performed as of 2010. There are two important patterns to note. First, over time, loans of both conventional and nonconventional mortgages increased their rates of delinquency. Mortgages that were originated in 2002–2003 were less likely to have problems than those issued in 2004–2007. This suggests that there was a clear deterioration in loan standards from 2004 to 2008 for all mortgages. This reflected the need of banks to originate mortgages in order to securitize. Overall, the loans that were the most likely to have trouble were those issued in 2006–2007.

Table 7.1 : Loan performance of nonconventional mortgages issued in 2002–2008

Product	Current LTV	Current combined LTV	60+ days past due	Foreclosure	REO	Total serious delinquency
Prime first lien FRM						
2008 vintage	93.7	97.0	5.49	2.48	0.59	8.56
2007 vintage	105.6	112.0	5.90	4.18	0.64	10.72
2006 vintage	106.7	111.1	5.65	3.82	0.54	10.01
2005 vintage	94.2	96.7	3.63	1.98	0.31	5.92
2004 vintage	69.3	70.4	1.59	0.82	0.08	2.49
2003 vintage	53.5	54.2	1.13	0.54	0.06	1.73
2002 vintage	50.4	50.4	2.24	1.34	0.18	3.76
Prime first lien non-option ARM						
2008 vintage	94.2	98.2	5.76	5.73	1.43	12.92
2007 vintage	110.6	116.8	7.36	7.18	1.09	15.63

Table 7.1 : (continued)

Product	Current LTV	Current combined LTV	60+ days past due	Foreclosure	REO	Total serious delinquency
2006 vintage	115.9	121.9	6.81	5.97	1.14	13.92
2005 vintage	102.8	107.4	4.36	3.46	0.56	8.38
2004 vintage	83.7	87.0	3.78	2.64	0.49	6.91
2003 vintage	65.3	66.5	2.42	1.47	0.36	4.25
Alt-A first lien FRM						
2007 vintage	106.2	113.0	11.33	11.57	2.83	25.73
2006 vintage	107.5	115.4	10.67	11.97	3.13	25.77
2005 vintage	95.7	100.8	5.79	5.46	1.19	12.44
2004 vintage	75.4	77.6	3.67	3.18	0.65	7.50
2003 vintage	60.8	61.4	2.48	1.88	0.36	4.72
2002 vintage	61.4	61.4	5.27	3.86	0.78	9.91
Alt-A nonoption ARM						
2007 vintage	124.9	136.9	15.11	18.43	5.04	38.58
2006 vintage	126.9	140.7	13.85	16.73	4.37	34.95
2005 vintage	115.6	125.8	8.76	11.14	2.90	22.80
2004 vintage	93.1	99.8	6.33	7.15	2.01	15.49
2003 vintage	72.8	74.6	5.79	3.84	1.10	10.73
Alt-A option ARM						
2007 vintage	138.7	145.3	17.35	17.76	4.70	39.81
2006 vintage	148.7	156.7	20.96	19.98	4.81	45.75
2005 vintage	137.7	142.3	18.00	16.35	3.27	37.62
2004 vintage	111.1	113.2	11.74	11.34	2.46	25.54

Source: J.P. Morgan (2010: 5)

Note: LTV = Loan to Value; FRM = Fixed Rate Mortgage; REO = Real Estate Owner, refers to properties that have been foreclosed on that have come into the possession of a mortgage lender.

The second important pattern is that the worse-performing loan categories were Alt-A loans. In this category, the option ARMs were the ones most likely to have problems: 46 percent of the Alt-A option ARMs issued in 2006, the peak year for that type of mortgage, were delinquent in some fashion. Almost 20 percent were ultimately foreclosed on. This compares with foreclosure rates of less than 4 percent for those who got conventional mortgages in 2006 (up from less than 1 percent in 2002). The leader in originating this category was Bear Stearns. Bear Stearns, by committing fraud through lying to people about how much they would have to pay for their mortgages, actually made the financial crisis worse. Many of the people who got those loans found the conditions so onerous that they felt it necessary to walk away. The Bear Stearns case shows how fraud and the ultimate disaster that was the financial crisis were intertwined. In their desire to continue to securitize mortgages, Bear Stearns found it necessary to originate any mortgage they could, including many that no one would be able to pay back. This made them cross the line in their dealings with mortgagors by engaging in predatory lending and fraudulent truth in lending. Those who were on the receiving end of these too-good-to-be-true mortgages found themselves going deeper into debt with little ability to refinance. Being unable to pay their mortgages, they lost their homes at high rates.

Washington Mutual

Washington Mutual Inc. (known as WaMu) called itself "the bank for everyday people" because it focused on consumers and small-to-medium-sized business-es. WaMu grew by the end of 2007 to be the nation's largest savings and loan in both assets ($328 billion) and revenues ($25.5 billion). The CEO at WaMu was Kerry Killinger, who joined the company in 1983 and became chief executive in 1990. He inherited a bank that was founded in 1889 and had survived the Depression and the savings and loan scandal of the 1980s. An investment ana-lyst by training, he was attuned to Wall Street's hunger for growth. Between late 1996 and early 2002, he transformed WaMu into the nation's sixth-largest bank through a series of acquisitions. A crucial deal came in 1999 with the purchase of Long Beach Financial, a California lender specializing in subprime mortgages. From 2000 to 2003, WaMu's retail branches grew 70 percent and reached twen-ty-two hundred across thirty-eight states.

As the conventional mortgage market dried up in 2003, WaMu found itself in the same position as the other vertically integrated banks. In order to turn around its lagging mortgage division, WaMu had to shift its mortgage origina-tion strategy. It did so by following Bear Stearns and pushed nonconventional mortgages, most notably ARMs but also subprime mortgages. In prepared re-marks for the 2004 third-quarter conference call, CEO Killinger said, "We are paying closer attention than ever to product mix to assess our profit by product and distribution channels, and exercise stronger controls than ever. The goal is to ensure that we are disciplined about originating higher margin product whenev-er we can. In this market our emphasis is ARM product origination, principally for our balance sheet. These ARMs helped the balance sheet to grow by $10.3 billion this past quarter" (Kennedy and Bowen, 2008: 2).

During the same third-quarter 2004 conference call, Killinger said, "The op-tion–ARM product is the key flagship product for our company" (Kennedy and Bowen, 2008: 2). Between April 2004 and the end of 2007, WaMu underwrote $184.8 billion in option ARMs. Most of these mortgages were securitized, and many remained on WaMu's balance sheet. WaMu's ARMs expanded from about 25 percent of new home loans in 2003 to 70 percent by 2006.

Although WaMu appeared to exit the subprime lending business in 2003 when it sold Washington Mutual Finance to Citigroup, it retained a significant presence in the subprime market through its 1999 purchase of Long Beach Mortgage. As of early 2008, Long Beach Mortgage was one of the country's largest lenders to people with damaged credit. While Long Beach operated in all fifty states except Mississippi, its largest market by far was California. In 2005, Long Beach Mortgage made more than one-quarter of all WaMu home-purchase loans.

As the conventional mortgage market turned down, Mr. Killinger expressed a desire to see that business grow faster than WaMu's traditional mortgage lending because it was more profitable: "We earn better margins in the subprime business because we're very efficient and have an advantage over some competitors" (Mayo and Allison, 2005). In late 2005, WaMu planned to expand subprime lending along the East Coast, taking subprime mortgages directly to consumers through its retail branches and home loan offices. In prepared remarks for a conference call discussing WaMu's 2004 results, Senior Vice President and CFO Tom Casey said, "First, we remain comfortable that we can achieve average asset growth in the 10 to 12% range. While we sell a significant portion of our ARM production into the secondary market, we still expect ARM retention to be a driver of asset growth. We also expect growth to come from planned increases in the home equity, multi-family, and nonprime lending" (Kennedy and Bowen, 2008: 5).

Pressures were brought on employees of WaMu to increase the sale of ARMs and subprime mortgages. This pressure pushed sales agents to pump out loans while disregarding borrowers' incomes and assets, according to former employees. The bank set up what insiders described as a system of dubious legality that enabled real estate agents to collect fees of more than $10,000 for bringing in borrowers, sometimes making the agents more beholden to WaMu than they were to their clients. WaMu gave mortgage brokers handsome commissions for selling the riskiest loans, which carried higher fees, bolstering profits and ultimately the compensation of the bank's executives. WaMu pressured appraisers to provide inflated property values that made loans appear less risky, enabling Wall Street to bundle them more easily for sale to investors. "It was the Wild West," said Steven M. Knobel, a founder of an appraisal company, Mitchell, Maxwell & Jackson, which did business with WaMu until 2007. "If you were alive, they would give you a loan. Actually, I think if you were dead, they would still give you a loan" (Goodman and Morgenson, 2008).

A *New York Times* article written by Peter Goodman and Gretchen Morgenson (2008) included interviews with a large number of people who worked for WaMu in its offices in California, Florida, Texas, and New Jersey. It is useful to tell a few of the stories, as they capture the flavor of how WaMu was aggressively pursuing loans:

> An employee at WaMu's San Diego processing office, Sherri Zaback's job was to take loan applications from branches in Southern California and make sure they passed muster. Most of the loans she said she handled merely required borrowers to provide an address and Social Security number, and to state their income and assets. She ran applications through WaMu's computer system for approval. If she needed more information, she had to consult with a loan officer—which she described as an unpleasant experience. "They would be furious," Ms. Zaback said. "They would put it on you that they weren't going to get paid if you stood in the way." (Goodman and Morgenson, 2008: 4)

The sheer workload at WaMu ensured that loan reviews were limited. Ms. Zaback's office had 108 people and several hundred new files a day. She was required to process at least ten files daily. "I'd typically spend a maximum of 35 minutes per file," she said. "It was just disheartening. Just spit it out and get it done. That's what they wanted us to do. Garbage in, and garbage out" (Goodman and Morgenson, 2008).

WaMu flourished in Southern California, where housing prices rose so rapidly during the bubble that creative financing was needed to attract buyers. To that end, WaMu embraced so-called option ARMs, adjustable-rate mortgages that enticed borrowers with a selection of low initial rates and allowed them to decide how much to pay each month. But people who opted for minimum payments were underpaying the interest due and adding to their principal, eventually causing loan payments to balloon. Customers were often left with the impression that low payments would continue long term, according to former WaMu sales agents. For WaMu, variable-rate loans, option ARMs in particular, were especially attractive because they carried higher fees than other loans and allowed WaMu to book profits on interest payments that borrowers deferred.

WaMu's retail mortgage office in Downey, California, specialized in selling option ARMs to Latino customers who spoke little English and depended on advice from real estate brokers, according to a former sales agent who requested anonymity because he was still in the mortgage business. According to that agent, WaMu turned real estate agents into a pipeline for loan applications by enabling them to collect "referral fees" for clients who became WaMu borrowers. Buyers were typically oblivious to agents' fees, the agent said, and agents rarely explained the loan terms (Goodman and Morgenson, 2008: 6).

As the boom faded in 2006 and 2007, nearly half of all option-ARM borrowers made minimum negative amortization payments. WaMu recorded a net loss for 2007 of $67 million, compared with a net income of $3.56 billion in 2006. The decline was primarily the result of significant deterioration in the company's residential mortgage loan portfolio and a sudden and severe contraction in secondary mortgage market liquidity for nonconforming residential loan products such as ARMs (Kennedy and Bowen, 2008: 4). By April 2008, WaMu had posted a first-quarter loss of $1.14 billion and increased its loan loss reserve to $3.5 billion. Its stock had lost more than half its value in the previous two months.

In September, CEO Killinger was forced to retire. Later that month, with WaMu buckling under roughly $180 billion in mortgage-related loans, the FDIC seized the bank and sold it to JPMorgan Chase for $1.9 billion, a fraction of the $40 billion valuation the stock market gave WaMu at its peak. Because the bank was taken over by the government and liquidated, it has been difficult for people who were harmed to sue. As a result, victims of the predatory lending and mortgage fraud the bank committed have not been compensated. It is clear that WaMu behaved very much like Bear Stearns. It promoted mortgages to people with little chance to pay them back. It made money off of fees and the securities it made using the mortgages. It ended up insolvent as those mortgages ended up in foreclosures. It continued to hold many of the securities based on those mortgages and as a result suffered huge losses.

Systemic Fraud in the Mortgage Securitization Industry

One way to see how this played out among the largest banks is to consider the settlements that the banks made with the government over mortgage fraud, predatory lending, and securities fraud. Figure 7.1 shows that between 2007 and 2017, $133.2 billion was paid out by banks in settlements for mortgage and securities fraud. These settlements peaked in 2014 when almost $45 billion were paid out to the government and various groups of private investors. Fifty-five percent of all settlements went to the federal government, while 26 percent went to class action suits, 7 percent to insurance companies who were being paid for securities fraud, and 12 percent to other litigants (Sabry et al., 2017). Fligstein and Roehrkasse (2016) show that vertically integrated banks were the most likely to have settled predatory lending and securities fraud cases. They show that thirty-two of the sixty largest banks in the conventional and nonconventional mortgage origination and securitization businesses settled some kind of lawsuit for mortgage or securities fraud. All nine firms involved in investment banking and nine of the eleven largest commercial banks settled such lawsuits. Banks involved in

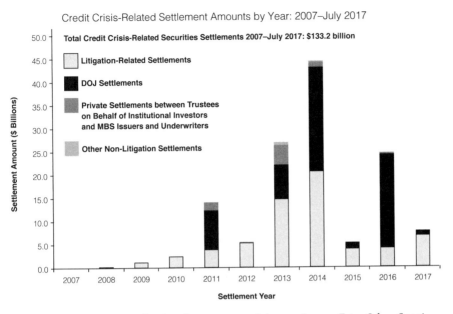

FIGURE 7.1 Credit-crisis-related settlements, 2007–July 2017. Source: Faten Sabry, Sungi Lee, and Linh Nguyen, "Trends in Credit Crisis Settlements," NERA Consulting, 2017, exhibit 1. Used by permission of Portfolio Media, Inc.

both origination and securitization were more likely to settle lawsuits than banks who were participants in only one or the other.

The cases of Bear Stearns and WaMu illustrate how the pressure to continue originating mortgages after 2003 in order to be able to create MBSs and CDOs worked. Both firms went aggressively into the nonconventional mortgage market and in particular dramatically increased their origination of option ARMs and subprime mortgages. The pressure to continue originating mortgages in order to have them as inputs into securities never decreased, even as the number of potential customers for new mortgages began to decline. In fact, as the supply of mortgages started to shrink, instead of pulling back from the market, both of these vertically integrated banks doubled down and chased after more and more customers who they knew had impaired credit and not enough income to support their mortgages. To keep their securitization machines running, they helped many of these customers commit mortgage fraud, and they engaged in predatory lending by offering terms that were too good to be true to other mortgagors. Both of these actions were to provide them with nonconventional mortgages that were more lucrative to turn into securities because they were able to generate higher fees and greater returns on MBSs and CDOs. Using these loans that they knew were likely to fail to make securities meant that they were committing securities fraud as well.

They sold those mortgage securities as AAA rated and held many of them on their own accounts. They borrowed money to originate and securitize mortgages. They also borrowed money in the ABCP and repo markets in order to support their own purchases of those securities. In the end, many people, particularly those who committed fraud or were the victims of predatory lending, were foreclosed on at a historically high rate. That put more pressure on other homeowners who saw the value of their homes decline and caused the housing market to crash. It also meant that many securities that were built on these mortgages, particularly those built in 2006–2007, were susceptible to default.

My analysis shows that the nature of the whole system was in fact at fault. The demand for MBSs and CDOs pushed banks to take on riskier and riskier mortgages. Their activities kept house prices rising for a while as they focused their attention on zip codes where there had already been a high level of house price appreciation. But eventually, to keep going, they had to cut corners and engage in mortgage fraud and predatory lending. The banks that were the most susceptible to these pressures were those who were involved in both origination and securitization. The massive fraud committed from 2004 to 2007 was driven by the need of banks to keep originating mortgages in order to meet the demand for securities based on those mortgages. As the supply of mortgages dried up, banks had to work harder and harder to find mortgages to keep their securitization machines going. This meant that they normalized mortgage and securities fraud as a necessity to keep the party going. In the end, the securities based on those mortgages began to fail. When they did, banks had to quickly pay back funds borrowed in the ABCP market. They quickly went from illiquid to insolvent.

The narrative that no one was punished for their role in creating the crisis is only half true. Banks did pay huge fines for their illegal activities. But those activities were not the main thing driving the banks over the cliff. Their reliance on procuring mortgages to create securities meant that as the conventional and then the nonconventional mortgage markets dried up, vertically integrated banks became desperate to keep their securitization machines going to keep their high profits intact. They realized the only way this could work was to cut corners by engaging in mortgage fraud and predatory lending. This worked for a short time, but eventually many of those bad mortgages faced foreclosure because the people who bought them simply could not afford the payments.

What the American public did not realize is that just because all of this ended badly, it did not have to be because someone committed a crime. The crimes of mortgage fraud, predatory lending, and securities fraud were oddly the collateral damage at the end of the whole mortgage cycle centered on the vertical integration of the banks and their focus on securitization. The market for MBSs and CDOs was kept going by the mortgages that were obtained fraudulently. But the bad end is inevitably what happens in capitalism when all of the easy profits get made and the market is saturated. It pushed banks to do whatever they could to keep their vertically integrated structures going. Without regulators watching to ensure that firms don't cross the line from aggressive to illegal, things tend to end badly. But of course, such regulators would have had to understand what was going on. I finally turn to how the regulators missed this whole thing.

8

WHY DID THE FEDERAL RESERVE MISS THE FINANCIAL CRISIS OF 2008?

Economic growth appears to have slowed recently, partly reflecting a softening of household spending. Tight credit conditions, the ongoing housing contraction, and some slowing in export growth are likely to weigh on economic growth over the next few quarters. Over time, the substantial easing of monetary policy, combined with ongoing measures to foster market liquidity, should help to promote moderate economic growth. Inflation has been high, spurred by the earlier increases in the prices of energy and some other commodities. The Committee expects inflation to moderate later this year and next year, but the inflation outlook remains highly uncertain. The downside risks to growth and the upside risks to inflation are both of significant concern to the Committee.

—FEDERAL OPEN MARKET Committee Statement,
September 16, 2008

The Federal Open Market Committee of the Federal Reserve is charged with making monetary policy for the United States. It is also one of the major economic forecasters for the US government. As such, its meetings (about every six weeks) are widely watched by participants in the financial markets for clues regarding the future trajectory of the economy (Holmes, 2014). The Federal Reserve and the Federal Open Market Committee (hereafter, FOMC) are among the leading players in formulating policy responses in when a financial crisis is brewing. On September 16, 2008, the day after the investment bank Lehman Brothers collapsed, precipitating the largest financial meltdown in postwar history (Swedberg, 2010), members of the FOMC met and issued the above statement.

Why was the FOMC so sanguine in its economic projections? Even though they recognized the distress being caused by the drop in home prices, the rise in foreclosures, and the increasing problems for financial institutions that held MBSs and CDOs, the FOMC consistently underestimated the risks to the economy during the months and years that preceded the financial crisis of 2007–2008. This was for two reasons. First, the shared framework of the members of the FOMC was macroeconomics. This framework consistently led them to underestimate the degree to which the entire economy depended on what was going on in the financial sector (for general discussions of how framing affects perception, see Diehl and McFarland, 2010; Goffman, 1974).

Second, we know that the dynamic of meetings often leads participants to downplay uncomfortable facts and try to find a positive spin to whatever challenge they face (Cerulo, 2006; Turner, 1976; Vaughan, 1996; Zerubavel, 2015). The FOMC's misperception of the financial crisis was a function of organizational and cultural tendencies to ignore and normalize discordant information (Cerulo, 2006; Turner, 1976: Vaughan, 1996; Zerubavel, 2015). This is particularly true in contexts where the information is incomplete and sometimes contradictory and the right thing to do is not obvious. Members of the FOMC operate in a highly opaque world. Indeed, their job is to examine fragmentary evidence and come to a prediction about the near future. As I will show in this chapter, this led members of the FOMC to use whatever data they had to generally offer positive stories in the face of data that seemed to suggest worst-case scenarios.

Any framework a group uses to understand the world operates as a filter through which a group understands its world (Diehl and McFarland, 2010; Goffman, 1974; Weick et al., 2005; Weick, 1988; Starbuck and Milliken, 1988). This filtering helps groups arrive at decisions by focusing arguments around constructing a coherent narrative. But by its very nature, any way of looking at things highlights certain facts while excluding others. This makes it difficult or impossible to see facts that are inconsistent with a group's prior beliefs and easy to downplay them, whatever those beliefs are. But group interaction is difficult or impossible without a shared framework and set of assumptions that can be used for discussion and settlement.

The actual cultural content of a framework helps explain the substance of what a source of risk is (Weick, 1988). The FOMC failed to see the depth of the problems in the housing and financial sectors because of its overreliance on macroeconomics as the frame it used for making sense of the economy. Participants adhered to a version of macroeconomic theory and modeling that had achieved high consensus among academics and central bankers alike by the early 2000s—the so-called "new neoclassical synthesis" (Goodfriend and King, 1997; for its use at the Federal Reserve, see Brayton et al., 1997; Goodfriend, 2007). Consistent with modern macroeconomic reasoning, FOMC participants believed that the large and complex American economy could be successfully understood in terms of a small number of aggregate-level indicators such as the inflation rate, the unemployment rate, productivity, and growth in GDP (for the privileging of parsimony in modern macroeconomics, see Solow, 2008).

The most important implication of this perspective is that macroeconomic theory views finance as just one sector of the economy, one that was unlikely to cause spillovers to other sectors that could affect economic growth in a dramatic way. Specifically, the FOMC failed to see the importance of housing-related financial instruments in fueling the economy. In fact, the financial industry was producing $4 trillion in mortgages and nearly 40 percent of the profits in the entire economy by 2003 (Fligstein and Goldstein, 2010). When mortgages began to fail, the financial instruments built on them began to lose value as well. Banks who had borrowed money to finance their holdings began to collapse. In the fall of 2008, this caused financial markets in the United States to freeze and made it difficult for anyone to borrow or lend. What made the downturn in housing so fundamentally destabilizing to the economy was the size of the market combined with the connection of that market to the largest investments that banks had. Because of its overreliance on macroeconomics, the FOMC was unable to see the size and extensiveness of these connections and understand why the economy was so vulnerable to this downturn, even as members of the FOMC were aware that the financial sector was experiencing great difficulties.

Most readers will not find it surprising that the FOMC focused on macroeconomic analysis as its main tool for framing and justifying its actions. But there are several reasons why this overreliance on macroeconomics is curious. One of the central missions of the Federal Reserve is to regulate the financial system. As such, the Federal Reserve is understandably concerned with financial stability. After all, any threat to that stability would spill over to the rest of the economy and produce a serious recession. Hence, it might be expected that a certain attention would be paid to the stability of the relationship between the providers of finance and its consumers. If the FOMC had been dominated by such a perspective, it might have been more cognizant of how the banking system, not just in the United States but in western Europe as well, had become overinvested in the housing market. This was made worse by using borrowed money from the ABCP market that needed to be paid back or rolled over in less than a year, making them vulnerable to a housing downturn.

Moreover, the FOMC's policymaking orientation is toward the financial markets, the providers of equity and debt for the economy, which the FOMC views as the primary audience for its pronouncements (Holmes, 2014). There is a great deal of discussion at the meetings of the FOMC about what is going on in the financial markets. Such an orientation could have directed the FOMC to orient its conceptual focus toward the important role the financial sector had come to play in the economy. But instead, the FOMC focused on the stock market and bond prices and did not pay much attention to the underlying investment strategies of the largest market players. In spite of this possibility, while the FOMC worried about banks and hedge funds, it never framed its concern in terms of the risks to the entire economy. It did not take seriously the financial sector's role as the principal intermediary between the suppliers and consumers of capital in the context of the enormous markets for securities based on home mortgages.

The main evidence used in this chapter is the presentation of representative opinions from the detailed transcripts of FOMC meetings that took place between 2002 and 2008.[1] In particular, I consider two periods in the FOMC deliberations in order to support my points about why the Federal Reserve did not see the severity of the crisis. First is the degree to which the FOMC saw that there was or was not a housing price bubble in the American economy from 2001 to 2005. In the summer of 2005, the FOMC held a meeting devoted specifically to considering whether there was a housing price bubble and, if so, what they might do about it. While some participants emphasized the link between finance and the broader economy and its attendant risks, they were in a very small minority. For the most part, the members of the FOMC downplayed the existence of a bubble and underestimated its effects on the rest of the economy, drawing explicitly on macroeconomic theory for support. They concluded that the macroeconomic effects of the bubble bursting (which many of them doubted existed) would not be that large. This case illustrates how the FOMC tended toward a positive viewpoint on possible troubles in the economy and how the frame of macroeconomics reinforced that bias.

Then, I consider how the FOMC interpreted the initial period of the financial crisis from 2006 that culminated in the bankruptcy of Lehman Brothers in September 2008 (captured in the quote at the beginning of this chapter). The FOMC was well aware of the crisis in home foreclosures and later of the problems of financial institutions. But I show that the macroeconomic framing led many members of the FOMC to underestimate the peril presented by the financial crisis. They never articulated the close link between the size of the housing market, its shift to nonconventional mortgages, the financial instruments that now were the largest investment of most of the big banks, and the high degree of credit that banks were using to fund those investments. Instead, as the quotation at the top of this chapter shows, their macroeconomic perspective had many of the members of the FOMC emphasizing their ongoing concern with inflation in September 2008, an issue at the heart of macroeconomic theory and central to the role of the Federal Reserve in the economy.

The Federal Reserve and the FOMC

The Federal Reserve is the central bank of the United States. It is charged with making monetary policy and with partially regulating the country's banking system (Blinder, 1998). In practice, this means three things. The Federal Reserve supervises and sets regulations for a variety of commercial banks, including capital reserve requirements. It sets the discount rate, the rate at which banks can borrow from the Federal Reserve. Finally, it engages in open market operations, the buying and selling of US Treasury securities and other assets, in order to control the federal funds rate and thereby influence economic activity and inflation. The Federal Reserve also uses this power to actively manage the links between the US economy and the world economy. The Federal Reserve has a congressional mandate to set monetary policy consistent with achieving maximum employment and price stability.

The FOMC is the primary policymaking body of the Federal Reserve. The FOMC consists of twelve members: the seven members of the Federal Reserve Board of Governors; the president of the Federal Reserve Bank of New York, who serves as vice chair; and four of the other eleven Reserve Bank presidents, who serve on an annually rotating basis. All other Reserve Bank presidents attend FOMC meetings, presenting reports and participating in discussion, but they cannot vote (Blinder, 1998).

The FOMC holds eight regularly scheduled meetings per year, about once every six weeks. The main purpose of these meetings is to discuss economic and financial conditions in the United States and to make monetary policy decisions. The meetings are highly structured (Abolafia, 2012; Baez and Abolafia, 2002). Every meeting begins with a round of oral reports on the current conditions and future direction of the economy. These reports fall into two categories, those presented by staff and those presented by each committee member and Reserve Bank president. Staff reports always include general data about GDP growth, employment, and inflation. But they can also be geared to a special topic that the FOMC wishes to explore. The reports by the governors and presidents concern their own analyses and forecasts of output and inflation based on their econometric modeling. The presidents' reports also cover current business conditions

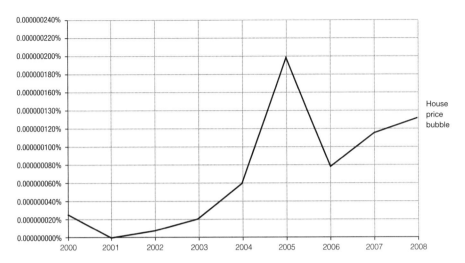

FIGURE 8.1 Ngram for "house price bubble". Source: Google Ngram.

in their respective districts. These can be more quantitative and based on surveys in the district, or more qualitative and based on discussions with district business contacts such as CEOs of important companies.

Even though the meetings are highly structured, when one reads the transcripts, one is impressed at how much give-and-take there is at each meeting. After speakers present, there is a question-and-answer period and an opportunity for people to take issue with the interpretations provided by the speakers. The meeting at this point resembles a university seminar where someone has given a presentation and then the audience discusses the presented materials. This makes total sense given that many of the members of the FOMC have PhDs and have taught in universities and participated in such seminars. The decision to raise or lower interest rates has a wide-ranging discussion where every person who gets a vote gets to speak and express their opinion. That opinion matters to the outcome.

Not surprisingly, the FOMC pays especially close attention to unique economic developments that might impact policymaking. If something was being reported in the press, the FOMC certainly took note of it and considered it. After 2001, meetings devoted time to the current state of the American economy including events such as 9 / 11, Hurricane Katrina, and the Gulf War (Fligstein et al., 2017). This connection to what is going on in the world shows up in the transcripts as well. Members of the FOMC often quote articles in the business press to make a point in their discussions about relevant issues of the day.

It is useful to examine one pertinent case to show how economic events in public media tracked discussions at the FOMC. Figure 8.1 presents an ngram

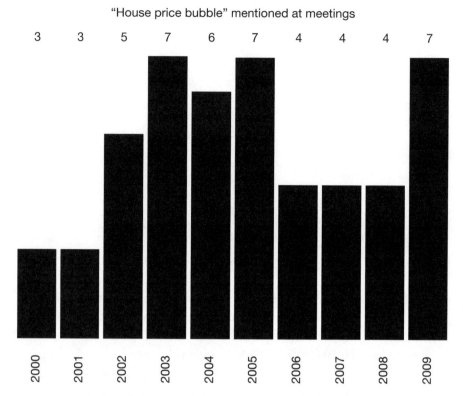

FIGURE 8.2 Number of FOMC meetings where "house price bubble" was a topic, 2000–2009. Source: Federal Open Market Committee.

generated in Google that illustrates the amount of media interest in the term *house price bubble.* One can see that mentions of the term increase dramatically from 2000 to 2005, the period of the greatest increase in housing prices. House prices peaked in 2005 and declined thereafter. One can observe that interest in the topic in the media dropped in 2006 as those prices stopped rising. It rose again in 2007 and 2008 in the wake of the financial crisis. Here, the term was mostly used to describe how the house price bubble had burst.

Figure 8.2 tracks the interest of the FOMC in the topic of the house price bubble. The figure examines how many meetings of the FOMC had mentions of the term. One can see that beginning in 2002, mentions of the house price bubble increased, peaking in 2005. In 2005, the FOMC had a meeting to discuss whether there was a bubble and, if so, whether the Federal Reserve should do something about it. Later in this chapter, I present evidence of what the members of the FOMC were saying at that meeting. From the figure, one can see that once house prices stopped rising, the issue becomes less salient in 2006–2007. But the issue reemerged in 2008 when the topic of house prices shifted from a bubble to a burst bubble. These two figures illustrate that the FOMC's interest in a particular economic topic tracked almost exactly the public's interest in the topic. Not all issues considered by the FOMC show up as clearly in the national media as the term *house price bubble*. But the FOMC was diligent in paying attention to how events in the real world might impact the economy enough that it could impact their decision-making about the direction of the economy and whether they should change the level of interest rates.

The second part of the meeting is devoted to the FOMC's main policy decision: setting the target for the federal funds rate. Committee members discuss whether to raise, lower, or hold constant the federal funds target rate. At the end of that discussion, committee members vote on the policy decision. The result is announced publicly in a press release immediately after the meeting, which states the balance of risks to growth and inflation and notes the reasons for the vote. The FOMC spends a great deal of time crafting the wording of the press release. They know that financial market analysts will read the document carefully in order to try to predict the direction of the economy. If the vote is split, the press release documents the difference of opinion. The FOMC's actions are widely watched by Wall Street and the financial community at large as a harbinger of the future direction of the real economy, inflation, and interest rates. These actions move financial markets in the United States and the world (Holmes, 2014).

Framing and Macroeconomics at the FOMC

It is useful to develop my arguments about why the FOMC failed to see the crisis in more detail. Obviously, the FOMC is a committee that has members, holds discussions, and arrives at conclusions. It is embedded in a large bureaucratic organization. As such, our general understanding of how such meetings work and how conclusions reflect group processes can be illuminating in making sense of why the FOMC never caught up to what was going on in the link between the financial industry and the housing sector and downplayed the worsening financial crisis.

Central to my discussion is the idea of a framework by which people interpret the world. The key explanatory tool here is the frame construct, defined by Goffman (1974: 11) as "principles of organization which govern subjective meanings we assign to social events." As Goffman (1974: 21) explains, framing gives order and meaning to our experience by enabling us "to locate, perceive, identify, and label a seemingly infinite number of concrete occurrences defined in terms of a given frame."

Frames are not just mental structures situated in individuals. They are inter-subjective constructs that must be maintained in ongoing interaction (Diehl and McFarland, 2010: 1717). Framing and the situation in which framing takes place form a coherent whole that helps make interaction possible (Goffman, 1974). Actors have a set of rules and roles, and it is within those that they use, share, and modify a common set of frames to produce meaning (Fligstein and McAdam, 2012). As Diehl and McFarland (2010) point out, this interactionist perspective implies that the content of frames is a product of history and setting.

While a particular frame in a particular setting is likely to be unique in time and space, the process of framing itself is ubiquitous. Since it is both a system of particular meanings and a general way to make sense of what is going on, any frame will be open to some interpretations of reality and closed to others. Thus, it is conceptually necessary to separate the general features of the framing process that limit thinking from the specific ones that create historically and situationally variable blind spots. In trying to understand how frames work, one must keep in mind that all frames have blinders that cause us to pay attention to some things and not others. But different frames will blind us to different things. Frame analysis implies that if we are to understand how a group interaction works, we need to decode its primary framework and observe it in action. Framing will lead actors to concentrate on a certain set of terms and facts and leave out others.

To apply frame analysis to the context of the FOMC, it is necessary to consider how such a frame would be formed at the FOMC. The FOMC is a case where professional economic knowledge is at the core of the framing problem (Hirschman and Popp Berman, 2014). Its legal mandate is to guide the economy by focusing on controlling inflation and promoting employment. It accomplishes those goals through the use of economic theory by its members. Such professional and expert work involves the creation, communication, and application of expert knowledge, knowledge used to solve concrete problems (Gorman and Sandefur, 2011: 282–283).

Part of the problem of using expert knowledge is to take abstract principles and apply them to solve a particular problem. Indeed, the meetings of the FOMC entail exactly this task: use abstract principles and current information and decide whether to change interest rates, which are the main policy tool that they use to control inflation and promote employment. Interpreting the current state of the economy and its potential for change is a difficult task. As new potential problems emerge, the FOMC must decide whether they are significant enough to justify changing the course of interest rates in the economy. In order to do this, framing around the meaning of "facts" and deciding what those facts are in the first place is the topic of discussion and argumentation.

There are three relevant aspects to the application of professional knowledge. First, the abstract knowledge of economics forms a set of styles of reasoning that can be used to inform policy ideas (Hirschman and Popp Berman, 2015). Second, that knowledge implies the use of policy devices that allow people to make sense of the world through the use of statistics, measurement, and models (Muniesa et al., 2007). Finally, the experiences of actors either in their training as economists or in the public or private sectors will shape how they see what is going on (Fourcade, 2009). I suggest that macroeconomics is a particular version of economics that contains a style of reasoning, relies on particular kinds of evidence to support its argument, and is the dominant training of the members of the FOMC.[2]

Macroeconomics as a form of abstract knowledge focuses on aggregate-level economic features such as output, growth, productivity, employment, inflation, and interest rates. Macroeconomists' models explain the relationships among indicators of these and related factors like savings, investment, and consumption (*Palgrave Dictionary of Economics*, 2008). The particular version of macroeconomic theory and modeling that dominated academic and policy circles during our period of interest is the new neoclassical synthesis, also sometimes called the "new Keynesian synthesis" (Goodfriend and King, 1997; Woodford, 2003, 2009). This approach seeks to develop dynamic general-equilibrium models of entire economies that synthesize neoclassical theories of the perfectly efficient business cycle with a neo-Keynesian understanding of so-called rigidities and frictions, especially regarding prices and wages.

There is good reason to believe that this way of approaching macroeconomic issues prevailed at the FOMC from 2000 to 2008. The primary model of the US economy employed by the Federal Reserve Board during this period, the FRB / US model, was explicitly founded on the principles of the new neoclassical synthesis (Brayton et al., 1997).[3] This model can be seen as a policy device by which participants analyzed the economy (Sbordone et al., 2010). Academics and Fed economists writing in the 2000s took for granted that such principles directly informed the FOMC's efforts to analyze the economy and make monetary policy (Chari and Kehoe, 2006: 3–5; Goodfriend, 2007: 65; Schorfheide et al., 2010). Indeed, these scholars saw the victory of the new neoclassical synthesis as marking an unprecedented level of consensus among academics and central bankers worldwide (Solow, 2008). As the macroeconomist Michael Woodford (2009: 274) put it, "there are not really alternative approaches to the resolution of macroeconomic issues any longer."

The FRB / US model is the basis for many predictions as to how shocks might impact the US economy. For example, at a meeting where the FOMC discussed whether there was a bubble in housing prices in the summer of 2005, one of the participants, John Williams of the San Francisco Federal Reserve, made a presentation to consider the macroeconomic effects of a bubble bursting. Mr. Williams's presentation was based on his use of the FRB / US model. His presentation consisted of constructing several scenarios about how a decrease in housing prices might affect the economy. He used the model to provide upper- and lower-bound estimates of the potential hit on GDP. He concluded, "In summary, assuming that the FRB / US model does a good job of capturing the macroeconomic implications of declining house prices, such an event does not pose a particularly difficult challenge for monetary policy" (FOMC, 2005b: 19). This use of the model worked to give a set of reasons why even if a financial bubble existed, its demise would not have a large impact on the American economy. This use of the model led the members of the FOMC to miss or underestimate the relationships between the housing market, financial instruments, the financial system, and the economy as a whole.

Quantitative macroeconomic models, like the Fed's FRB / US model, take as their core the "real business cycle" theory that formed a central element in the neoclassical revolution of the 1970s and 1980s (Brayton et al., 1997; Goodfriend, 2007).[4] Real business cycle theory reinterprets economic fluctuations, such as the business cycle, as an efficient response to exogenous shocks (Plosser, 1989: 52, 71). It locates such shocks in "purely real factors . . . such as productivity shocks, fiscal shocks, and international terms-of-trade shocks" (Goodfriend, 2007: 59). The new neoclassical synthesis (Goodfriend and King, 1997; Woodford, 2003), by contrast, is more attuned to nominal factors, incorporating a variety of neo-Keynesian rigidities and frictions—most important, sticky prices and wages. It does not reject real business cycle theory per se; rather, it regards the real business cycle as a special case (Woodford, 2009: 269). Indeed, it suggests that the goal of monetary policy, in particular, is to smooth wage-price rigidities to "make the economy conform to its *underlying real business cycle core*" (Goodfriend, 2007: 61; emphasis added). The implication of this, one could argue, is that the real business cycle really does exist in the world and *would* operate according to its theory absent certain obstacles, which it is the role of monetary policy to remove.

This had two important effects on the FOMC's ability to perceive the risks associated with a financial crisis. First, to the extent that participants leaned toward the neoclassical aspects of their framework, they would maintain a default position of optimism in the face of any economic disturbance, since they viewed fluctuations themselves as elements of a self-regulating economy. Second, even if participants leaned toward the neo-Keynesian aspects of their framework, they were unlikely to direct attention to the key place that could undermine optimism—the housing-finance nexus—precisely because the new neoclassical synthesis overwhelmingly brackets the real economy from the financial system. That is, because this framework incorporates "nominal" factors (such as money and financial intermediation) as rigidities and frictions atop a "real business cycle core," it retains the basic assumption that economic shocks have "real" (non-financial) sources (Borio, 2014: 182).[5]

Seen from this perspective, financial markets and the banking system may distort, extend, or amplify underlying economic fluctuations (Bernanke et al., 1999), but they do not generate such fluctuations (Borio, 2011, 2014). Instead, the underlying model of the economy is a set of sectors that have relationships to one another. The business cycle is a function of how events in one sector might affect other sectors and the overall economy. The tendency is to view the spillover effects of such shifts as relatively minor. As a result, events in the financial sector were no more or less likely to lead to spillovers than events in any other sector.

Finally, the professional composition of the FOMC leans toward macroeconomics as well. Table 8.1 contains a list of the members on the FOMC from 2000 to 2008. It includes information on their education and work background. The table shows that twenty-two out of thirty-six (61 percent) of those with permanent or rotating votes on the FOMC had received an economics PhD with an emphasis in macroeconomics. These figures do not imply complete dominance by macroeconomists, but they do suggest that their way of seeing was likely to constitute the majority position at the FOMC. By contrast, only five governors and Reserve Bank presidents (14 percent) had prior experience working in the financial sector.

Culture, Cognition, and Group Dynamics at the FOMC

Cognitive sociology alerts us to the notion that individuals cannot process huge amounts of information and that a model of human agency that assumes full knowledge and rational action is therefore improbable (Martin, 2010). People generally lack coherent worldviews and act typically—though not exclusively—out of habit (Cerulo, 2006; DiMaggio, 1997; Martin, 2010; Vaisey, 2009; Zerubavel, 2015). One potential solution to this problem, particularly in organizations, is the creation of a set of cognitive shortcuts that are embodied in standard operating procedures and inform decision-making.

Cerulo (2006) shows how such schemas are shaped by the nature of social groups. She argues that the structure and culture of most organizations lead actors to either downplay negative information or reinterpret it in a positive light. The latter is similar to another endemic feature of organizations, which Vaughan

Table 8.1 : Voting members of the Federal Open Market Committee, 2000–2008

Name	FOMC position	Year(s)	Previous sector	Career central banker?	Advanced degree(s)	Dissertation branch of economics
Bernanke, Ben	Governor, chairman	2002–2005, 2006–2008	Academic and public	No	Economics PhD	Macroeconomics
Bies, Susan	Governor	2001–2007	Academic, public, and private	No	Economics PhD	Macroeconomics
Broaddus, J. Alfred	Reserve Bank president	2000, 2003	Public	Yes	Economics PhD	Macroeconomics/ microeconomics
Duke, Elizabeth	Governor	2008	Private	No	MBA	—
Evans, Charles	Reserve Bank president	2007	Public	Yes	Economics PhD	Macroeconomics
Ferguson, Roger	Governor	2000–2006	Private	No	Economics PhD, JD	Industrial organization
Fisher, Richard	Reserve Bank president	2005, 2008	Public and private	No	MBA	—
Geithner, Timothy	Vice chairman	2003–2008	Public	No	Economics MA	—
Gramlich, Edward	Governor	2000–2005	Academic and public	No	Economics PhD	Macroeconomics
Greenspan, Alan	Chairman	2000–2006	Public and private	No	Economics PhD	Macroeconomics
Guynn, Jack	Reserve Bank president	2000, 2003, 2006	Public	Yes	MBA	—
Hoenig, Thomas	Reserve Bank president	2001, 2004, 2007	Public	Yes	Economics PhD	Macroeconomics
Jordan, Jerry	Reserve Bank president	2000, 2002	Public and private	No	Economics PhD	Financial economics
Kelley, Edward	Governor	2000–2001	Private	No	MBA	—
Kohn, Donald	Governor	2002–2008	Public	Yes	Economics PhD	Macroeconomics
Kroszner, Randall	Governor	2006–2008	Academic	No	Economics PhD	Macroeconomics
Lacker, Jeffrey	Reserve Bank president	2006	Academic and public	Yes	Economics PhD	Macroeconomics
Lockhart, Dennis	Reserve Bank president	2008	Private	No	Economics MA	—
McDonough, William	Vice chairman	2000–2003	Public and private	No	Economics MA	—
McTeer, Robert	Reserve Bank president	2002	Public	Yes	Economics PhD	Macroeconomics

Meyer, Laurence	Governor	2000–2001	Academic and private	No	Economics PhD	Macroeconomics
Minehan, Cathy	Reserve Bank president	2001, 2004, 2007	Public	Yes	MBA	—
Mishkin, Frederic	Governor	2006–2008	Academic	No	Economics PhD	Macroeconomics
Moskow, Michael	Reserve Bank president	2001, 2003, 2005, 2007	Academic, public, and private	No	Business/applied economics PhD	—
Olson, Mark	Governor	2001–2006	Public and private	No	None	—
Parry, Robert	Reserve Bank president	2000, 2003	Public and private	No	Economics PhD	Macroeconomics
Pianalto, Sandra	Reserve Bank president	2004, 2006, 2008	Public	Yes	Economics MA, MBA	—
Plosser, Charles	Reserve Bank president	2008	Academic	No	Economics PhD, MBA	Macroeconomics
Poole, William	Reserve Bank president	2001, 2004, 2007	Academic and public	Yes	Economics PhD, MBA	Macroeconomics
Rosengren, Eric	Reserve Bank president	2007	Public	Yes	Economics PhD	Macroeconomics
Santomero, Anthony	Reserve Bank president	2002, 2005	Academic	No	Economics PhD	Macroeconomics/financial economics
Stern, Gary	Reserve Bank president	2002, 2005, 2008	Public	Yes	Economics PhD	Macroeconomics
Warsh, Kevin	Governor	2006–2008	Public and private	No	JD	—
Yellen, Janet	Reserve Bank president	2006	Academic and public	No	Economics PhD	Macroeconomics

Data source: Federal Reserve for names and terms of service and Wikipedia for biographical information.

(1996) calls the "normalization of deviance" (see also Turner, 1976). The result is that organizations "often gravitate to data that supports the best case scenario" (Cerulo, 2006: 58). Cerulo (2006: 6) calls this "positive asymmetry," a tendency to see the best cases clearly and the worst cases only vaguely.

The structure of the FOMC embodies some of the organizational and situational features that Cerulo (2006: 216–231) associates with positive asymmetry. Committee meetings have a strongly hierarchical role structure. This consists, in descending order, of the chairman, vice chair, board of governors, presidents who vote (but exercise no decision-making autonomy), presidents who do not vote, and staff who present reports but rarely take positions of their own. While the Federal Reserve takes pride in its insulation from politics and its arcane expertise (Blinder, 1998; Holmes, 2014), the tendency for the group to be inward looking and self-referential is apparent.

Another way that looking for a positive outcome comes into play is that there is some pressure in the meeting to try to attain consensus as to whether to change interest rates. So, while people may disagree on how to add up the facts and details, at the end, they work to form a consensus opinion as to what the FOMC should do. A consensus generally follows a median path, not too radical in either direction. This means that if things might be looking bad, the tendency will be to not be alarmist and to go along with the majority until the evidence is so clear that no one can deny it. People with outlier positions will back off in the end and support median opinion. That consensus will most often be optimistic that whatever is going on, the FOMC has time to make informed decisions.

Prior research has demonstrated the presence of such tendencies at the FOMC. Abolafia's (2004, 2010) analyses of FOMC meetings from the 1980s and 1990s show that meeting participants construct a narrative account of the economy. Much of the give-and-take of the conversation is oriented toward making sure that small disagreements do not turn into large disagreements. He also shows that there is a kind of groupthink whereby discordant facts tend to be ignored. This observation suggests that the tendency toward thinking the same thing allied with a tendency toward positive bias means that the outcome leans toward optimism.

Framing and Cognition at the FOMC: The Role of Macroeconomics in Discussion of Housing Market "Fundamentals"

House prices nearly doubled from 1995 to 2005. Rising home values directly stimulated residential investment and indirectly boosted consumption as borrowers extracted equity when they refinanced. By the end of 2003, however, the market for conventional mortgages was saturated, and so mortgage originators began aggressively targeting borrowers unable to qualify for prime loans. As a result, subprime and other nonconforming mortgages proliferated over the course of 2004, exceeding conventional mortgage originations for the first time (Fligstein and Goldstein, 2010).

The meeting transcripts reveal that committee members were aware of the historic run-up in housing prices. Figure 8.2 shows that they discussed the possibility of a house price bubble more and more over time. But they generally made sense of that run-up by referring to the "fundamentals" of supply and demand in the physical stock of housing. At the August 13, 2002, meeting, for instance, Chairman Alan Greenspan raised but quickly rejected the possibility of a housing bubble:

> There is clearly concern at this stage about a housing value bubble that is going to burst. But I think that most of those who look at this in some detail question whether that's a valid notion . . . the impact of immigration superimposed upon the difficulty of finding viable land for homebuilding is keeping significant upside pressure on home prices over and above the construction productivity issue. So, the likelihood of any really important contraction in the housing area would in my view require a very major contraction in the economy overall. (FOMC, 2002: 74)

Federal Reserve governor Ned Gramlich concurred with Greenspan's assessment, adding, "I agree that there is no bubble. I agree that there is no productivity change in housing construction. So, the relative price of housing is rising compared with income and other prices *for what we'll call real reasons*" (FOMC, 2002: 82; emphasis added). The causal model of house-price appreciation employed by Greenspan and Gramlich thus assumed the following form: immigration—a "real," demographic factor—was increasing the demand for homes (relative to a fixed supply of land and static construction productivity), which in turn was raising the price of housing.

Committee members were attentive to the wave of mortgage refinancing that preceded the subprime expansion. Yet when the refinancing boom subsided in late 2003, the FOMC showed little recognition that subprime mortgages were replacing refinancing as the driving force behind mortgage and housing markets. Indeed, a simple search of the transcript corpus reveals that the word *subprime* appears a mere four times before mid-2005—and not at all in 2004, when the subprime market became the largest part of the mortgage market.[6] In fact, the first time that the committee made any reference to changes in the composition of the mortgage market was February 2005, after these changes had already occurred (FOMC, 2005a: 119).

A Bubble in the Housing Market?

At the June 29–30, 2005, meeting, the FOMC held a special discussion on the possibility of a housing price bubble and its implications for monetary policy. The general tone of the meeting was to first consider the evidence for there being a bubble. Many of the comments suggested that participants were not convinced that there was a bubble, and they sought out explanations that supported their perspectives. There is evidence of using macroeconomic thinking and the FRB / US model to consider what the effects might be of a rapid housing price decrease on the economy. But mostly, there was a tendency to either doubt the data or offer explanations why there was not really a housing price bubble if one considered the economic fundamentals. This showed a clear tendency to not embrace a worst-case scenario.

The opening presentation, by staff economist Josh Gallin, introduced the basic data and reported on a regression analysis using that data:

> The first point to note is that the measured price-rent ratio is currently higher than at any other time for which we have data. . . . Most notably, in the first quarter of 2002, the last observation for which we have a reading for the subsequent three-year change in house prices, the price-rent ratio stood at 22. Although the regression suggests that real prices should have been about flat since then, real prices actually increased more than 20 percent, and the price-rent ratio rose to about 27—literally off the chart. The regression analysis also suggests that prices are about 20 percent too high given rents and carrying costs. (FOMC, 2005b: 5–6)

The meeting continued with a series of reports that considered the data from a variety of perspectives. It is useful to present some of this discussion, as it shows how a possible house price bust was analyzed from a macroeconomic point of view. Glenn Rudebusch, of the San Francisco Federal Reserve, laid out the basic logic of how the Federal Reserve should think about what to do if there was a housing bubble by considering its potential impact on the economy from a macroeconomic perspective:

> I will review some general issues related to monetary policy and asset prices. Let me start by assuming that an asset price can, in theory at least, be separated into a component determined by underlying economic fundamentals and a non-fundamental or bubble component. Two types of monetary policy responses to movements in an asset price have been

proposed. I refer to the first type as "Standard Policy" because there is widespread agreement that it represents the minimum appropriate policy response. The Standard Policy responds to an asset price to the extent it conveys information to the central bank about the future path of output and inflation—the goal variables of monetary policy. For example, a booming stock market is usually followed by higher demand and increased inflationary pressures, so tighter monetary policy (i.e. higher interest rates) would be needed to offset these consequences.

The second type of response, the "Bubble Policy," follows the Standard Policy as a base case, but, in certain circumstances, it also takes steps to contain or reduce the asset price bubble. Proponents of a Bubble Policy argue that movements in the bubble component can have serious adverse consequences for macroeconomic performance that monetary policy cannot readily offset after the fact, so it is preferable to try to eliminate this source of macroeconomic fluctuations directly. Furthermore, because bubbles often seem to display a self-reinforcing behavior, a little preemption and prevention early on can avoid later excesses. (FOMC, 2005b: 14–15)

San Francisco Reserve Bank senior vice president John Williams was one of the few participants who unequivocally thought there was a house price bubble. He accepted Mr. Gallin's estimate that house prices were 20 percent above their true value. He then used the FRB / US model to estimate the effect of several scenarios about what would happen to the economy if there was a decrease in housing prices of 20 percent:

As Josh Gallin indicated, it would take up to a 20 percent decline in house prices to bring the price-to-rent ratio back in line with fundamentals. With housing wealth standing at around $18 trillion today, such a drop in house prices would extinguish $3.6 trillion of household wealth. That's equal to about 30 percent of GDP. Based on a marginal propensity to consume from housing wealth of 3½ cents on the dollar, this decline in wealth would entail a nearly 1½ percentage point increase in the personal saving rate. (FOMC, 2005b: 17)

But he went on to suggest that while this was substantial, its impact was not as grave as that of the stock market crash of 2000–2001:

It may be useful to put these figures into context by comparing them to those associated with the stock market overvaluation reached in early 2000. Stock prices at that time were arguably some 50 to 70 percent overvalued. Correction of prices to fundamentals at that time would have implied a reduction in household wealth of $6.7 trillion, equal to about 70 percent of contemporaneous GDP. In the event, stock market wealth fell by $4.6 trillion between March 2000 and March 2001, and at its lowest point was down $8.5 trillion. There is considerable uncertainty regarding the magnitude of the effects of changes in stock market and housing wealth on household spending; nonetheless, it seems clear the magnitude of the current potential problem is much smaller than, and perhaps only half as large as, that of the stock market bubble. (FOMC, 2005b: 18)

Other committee members sought ways to explain the house price run-up in terms of economic fundamentals. Alan Greenspan focused on the price of land, asking, "Is it credible that we can have a consistently more rapid rise in prices of existing homes unless the value of land is rising faster for those homes?" (FOMC, 2005b: 70). Other members adopted similar frames. Governor Mark Olson's assessment focused on land values and "the incidence of teardowns," while Dallas Reserve Bank president Richard Fisher stressed "land use restrictions" (FOMC, 2005b: 39–41).[7] Thus, committee members fit housing prices into a narrative of "hard," observable factors affecting supply and demand.

Not surprisingly, then, many participants questioned the very notion of a bubble. New York Reserve Bank vice president Dick Peach captured this sentiment:

Hardly a day goes by without another anecdote-laden article in the press claiming that the U.S. is experiencing a housing bubble that will soon burst, with disastrous consequences for the economy. Indeed, housing market activity has been quite robust for some time now. . . . But such activity could be the result of solid fundamentals underlying the housing market. After all, both nominal and real long-term interest rates have declined substantially over the last decade. Productivity growth has been surprisingly strong since the mid-1990s, producing rapid real income growth primarily for those in the upper half of the income distribution. And the large baby-boom generation has entered its peak earning years and appears to have strong preferences for large homes loaded with amenities. (FOMC, 2005b: 11)

Peach further suggested, "Home prices actually look somewhat low relative to median family income" (FOMC, 2005b: 13).

Similarly, St. Louis Reserve Bank president William Poole only half-jokingly argued, "Just for the hell of it, I'd like to offer the hypothesis that property values are too low rather than too high" (FOMC, 2005b: 57). House prices, in Poole's understanding, were a function of low real interest rates, which in turn reflected transformed fundamentals in the global economy. Poole concluded, "I offer those observations because, if we are in a world that is going to have much lower real rates of interest for some time to come, one would expect to see the price-to-rent ratio go up. Maybe this line in the chart has another 40 percent to go to get to equilibrium!" (FOMC, 2005b: 58).

Jeffrey Lacker, president of the Richmond Federal Reserve Bank, offered his own explanation for the rapid rise in house prices in some urban areas:

> I've been struck by the fact that a collection of large metropolitan areas increasingly dominates the national housing figures and that house-price appreciation seems different across various urban regions. It suggests to me that housing values may be affected significantly by—I don't know exactly how to phrase this—sort of the relative microeconomic value of agglomeration. By that I mean the value of the amenities in a city or the enhanced productivity associated with living in or near where one works. Now, in this age of telecommuting and the Internet, it's easy to deduce that the value of living in a city has declined. But it seems plausible to me that the value of a thick labor market might be increasingly important for certain skill specialties. And it also seems plausible that the strong demand for urban amenities is evident in the recent vitality of many older urban cores. (FOMC, 2005b: 62)

Mr. Lacker concluded by noting,

> It seems to me as if there are a lot of plausible stories one can tell about fundamentals that would explain or rationalize housing prices. Obviously, low interest rates have to top the list. Strong income growth among home owning populations would be on the list, as would land use restrictions, which were mentioned earlier, and the recent surge in spending on home improvement. . . . So, from that point of view, it's hard for me to see how it would be reasonable to place a great deal of certainty on the notion that housing is significantly overvalued, or that there's a bubble, or that it's going to collapse really soon. (FOMC, 2005b: 62–63)

Several participants did note the possibility that demand for securitized mortgage debt and the associated proliferation of novel mortgage products might have been driving a price bubble. While the FOMC was aware that this shift had occurred, they mostly argued that the housing market was being driven by consumers who wanted to buy houses. They remained skeptical of the idea. For instance, Janet Yellen, president of the San Francisco Reserve Bank, questioned the notion that "creative financing" was producing a bubble:

> One view that I think is very prevalent is that the use of credit in the form of piggyback loans, interest-only mortgages, option ARMs [adjustable-rate mortgages], and so forth, involves financial innovations that are feeding a kind of unsustainable bubble. But an alternative perspective on that is that high house prices, in fact, are curtailing effective demand for housing at this point and that house appreciation probably is poised to slow. So, the increasing use of creative financing could be a sign of the final gasps of house-price appreciation at the pace we've seen and an indication that a slowing is at hand. (FOMC, 2005b: 36)

Note that in her argument, the high prices for housing would eventually shut off the demand for housing. Implicit in this perspective is the notion that finance was not causing events in the real economy but was only responding to the underlying supply of housing and the demand for it.

In sum, given the real supply-and-demand factors thought to be driving the housing market, most of the FOMC judged that evidence of a bubble was at best inconclusive and perhaps even nonexistent. Even if one granted that house prices might be overvalued, the worst-case scenario provided by macroeconomic modeling did not appear to be very dramatic. As Chicago Reserve Bank president Michael Moskow concluded, "I come away somewhat less concerned about the size and consequences of a housing bubble than I was before" (FOMC, 2005b: 48).

Housing Price Correction

After this discussion of bubbles, housing markets stayed on the FOMC agenda. By early 2006, committee members were anticipating a "correction" in housing prices and an associated "cooling" in housing activity, but they remained broadly optimistic about its consequences.[8] The risks posed by housing to the real economy involved two principal channels, according to the narrative constructed by the FOMC. First were the direct effects on the residential construction and real estate industries. Second were the indirect effects on consumer spending through declining home equity and, even less directly, declining consumer confidence.

Neither of these channels constituted a major source of concern. First, from the FOMC's macroeconomic perspective, the contribution of the housing sector to GDP was not that large. As Federal Reserve chair Ben Bernanke noted in March 2006, "residential investment is, of course, only about 6 percent of GDP" (FOMC, 2006a: 97). Even when including the potential damage to associated manufacturing industries such as appliances and furniture, Bernanke reminded the committee in December 2006 that "this is about 15 percent of the economy compared with 85 percent of the economy" (FOMC, 2006c: 81). Second, committee members believed that consumption would be cushioned by strong employment, rising real wages, and supportive lending conditions. Gary Stern, president of the Minneapolis Reserve Bank, captured the general consensus: "As long as employment continues to go up, incomes continue to go up, and mortgage rates remain relatively moderate, then I would expect that we would avoid severe difficulties in housing except for a few markets that are particularly inflated at this point" (FOMC, 2006a: 55–56).

Over the course of 2006, as incoming housing data grew increasingly weak, members began talking of a "bimodal economy"—softening housing, manufacturing, and autos versus a robust service sector. Yet the committee maintained that as long as the housing correction failed to produce "spillovers" into other sectors—which, they agreed, was unlikely—it would actually be good for the long-run stability of the economy. As Federal Reserve governor Frederic Mishkin argued in September 2006, "We're actually moving resources from a sector that had too much going into it, into sectors that need to have more resources at the present time. So, in that sense, I'm actually quite positive" (FOMC, 2006b: 85). Mishkin stuck to this rebalancing narrative as late as June 2007, after the deterioration of the subprime market was underway:

> My view of what has been happening in the economy is that we have been basically going through a rebalancing. We had a sector that was clearly bubble-like with excessive spending, and now we are getting the retrenchment, which is taking a bit longer than we expected. But the good news is that we are going through a rebalancing in which we are just moving resources to other sectors and that is actually going much along the lines that we want to see. (FOMC, 2007b: 87)

In fact, while the FOMC saw housing as the major threat to growth during this period, the committee's predominant concern was not growth at all but inflation. Until September 2007, official FOMC statements continued to maintain—and most members agreed—that inflation remained the principal risk to the dual mandate.

This analysis reflected the macroeconomic framework that the FOMC employed to make sense of housing. Committee members visualized the economy in terms of sectors, each making an independent contribution to GDP. They betrayed a deep-seated bias toward primary markets (such as home sales and home loans) and the nonfinancial sectors of the real economy (such as construction and manufacturing) rather than secondary markets embedded in the financial economy (such as MBSs, CDOs, CDSs, and the financial institutions that held them on their books).

The structure of the Federal Reserve System reinforces this sectoral thinking and bias toward nonfinancial markets. A large part of every FOMC meeting is devoted to the oral presentations of Reserve Bank presidents regarding business conditions in their respective districts. Much of this discussion involves presidents' reports from CEOs and other business contacts in their districts. But, while there are twelve districts in the Federal Reserve System, the financial industry is overwhelmingly concentrated in a single physical location, lower and midtown Manhattan. Consequently, when presidents talked to their contacts about the housing market, they overwhelmingly talked to homebuilders, realtors, construction companies, and regional mortgage originators, actors attuned precisely to local real estate conditions rather than the financial economy. This made it difficult for members of the FOMC to see where the dangers from housing really resided—at the heart of the financial industry itself.

The Onset of the Financial Crisis

If the internal sense-making of the FOMC did not lead members to readily associate housing and financial markets, external events would eventually force that association on them. In February 2007, an unexpected jump in delinquencies and defaults on subprime adjustable-rate mortgages began to produce turmoil in the subprime and associated securities markets. In June, subprime turmoil increased in the wake of severe losses at two Bear Stearns hedge funds that were heavily invested in subprime. But beginning at the August 7 meeting, the issue of financial market turmoil ascended massively, remaining the FOMC's dominant issue-specific topic for the rest of 2007 and much of 2008 (Fligstein et al., 2017).

While the foreclosures in the subprime markets were a significant theme beginning in March, the modal way in which committee members made sense of subprime was through a narrative that minimized the risks involved. Jeff Lacker captured the continued optimism of most members:

> On the national level, risks seem to have risen lately, but my sense is that
> prospects are still reasonably sound. Subprime mortgages, obviously, have
> dominated the financial news in recent weeks. Concerns about the welfare

of families suffering foreclosures are quite natural, and anecdotes about outright fraud suggest some criminality. But my overall sense of what's going on is that an industry of originators and investors simply misjudged subprime mortgage default frequencies. Realization of that risk seems to be playing out in a fairly orderly way so far. (FOMC, 2007a: 41)

As already stated, committee members viewed the mortgage market as a collection of distinct sectors rather than an integrated network or system. This framework led them to further downplay the risks from subprime. Thus, in March 2007, Mishkin found it reassuring that the subprime market "is a fairly small part of the overall mortgage market," concluding, "the subprime market has really been overplayed in the media, and I do not see it as that big a downside risk" (FOMC, 2007a: 69–70).

This optimism was belied by incoming data. By August 2007, in the wake of renewed financial turmoil, the FOMC was forced to acknowledge that problems in the mortgage market had spread beyond subprime and that the CDO market was beginning to be impaired. On September 18, 2007, Chair Ben Bernanke referred to the presence of a "financial crisis" for the first time (FOMC, 2007c: 93).[9]

In their presentations to the FOMC, staff also began to acknowledge the limitations of macroeconomic models for grappling with unfolding financial events. As staff economist David Stockton explained, also on September 18, "The financial transmission mechanisms in most of the workhorse macro models that we use for forecasting are still rudimentary. As a result, much of what has occurred doesn't even directly feed into our models" (FOMC, 2007c: 20).

Despite these admissions, however, the FOMC adhered to its basic conceptual apparatus. For instance, participants continued to take heart from the "resiliency" of the underlying real economy. As Philadelphia Reserve Bank president Charles Plosser explained at the September 2007 meeting,

> The national economy looks more vulnerable to me than it did six weeks ago, but it would be a mistake—and I think Dave Stockton did an excellent job of reminding us—to count out the resiliency of the U.S. economy at this early stage. I think there can be a tendency in the midst of financial disruptions, uncertainty, and volatility to overestimate the amount of spillover that they will exert on the broader economy. (FOMC, 2007c: 47)

If their sectoral thinking led committee members to minimize the economic risks posed by financial markets, their regional thinking led them to view these risks as geographically dispersed. Plosser insisted on this fact as late as December 2007: "Based on such observations and the news that I hear from my District, I sense that the stresses in the economy vary significantly by region, and we must be mindful that the weaknesses on Wall Street are in those states that have exaggerated housing volatility and may not be representative of the rest of the economy" (FOMC, 2007d: 56).

Once again, this optimism was wrong. Conditions rapidly deteriorated in the winter of 2007–2008. By January 2008, Sandra Pianalto, president of the Cleveland Reserve Bank, was "detecting the first signals of a credit crunch" (FOMC, 2008a: 76). By March, Mishkin could claim, "The reality is that we are in the worst financial crisis that we've experienced in the post-World War II era" (FOMC, 2008b: 69). It was also in March 2008 that the staff's economic projections first forecasted a recession, albeit a mild one (FOMC, 2008b: 14–16).

The FOMC's chief source of concern during the winter was the development of an "adverse feedback loop" whereby tightening credit conditions restrained economic activity, which further weakened financial markets and thus further tightened credit conditions (FOMC, 2008b: 69). At the same time, participants also began to worry about the liquidity and ultimately the solvency of individual financial institutions.

At the January 29–30, 2008, meeting, William Dudley, chief economist at the Federal Reserve, connected the turmoil in the credit markets to the problem in home foreclosures:

> I'll start today by noting that U.S. and global equity and fixed-income markets have behaved in a way consistent with a dark economic outlook. Market price risk has increased. The problems of the financial guarantors have been an important part of the story. In recent years, the major financial guarantors have diversified into insuring structured-finance products, including collateralized debt obligations (CDOs). Currently, their exposure to all structured-finance products is about $780 billion.
>
> Because the structured-finance guarantees have typically been issued against the highest rated tranches at the very top of the capital structure, until recently the rating agencies did not think that these guarantees would result in meaningful losses. However, as the housing outlook has continued to deteriorate and the rating agencies have increased their loss estimates on subprime and other types of residential mortgage loan products, the risk of significant losses has increased sharply. This is particularly the case with respect to these firms' collateralized debt obligation exposures—a portion of their total structured-finance exposure. As I discussed in an earlier briefing, given the highly nonlinear payoffs built

into these products, modest changes in the loss assumptions on the underlying collateral can lead to a sharp rise in expected losses on super senior AAA-rated collateralized debt obligations. Unfortunately, the CDO exposures of several of these financial guarantors are quite large relative to their claims-paying resources. These exposures and the uncertainty about how these exposures will actually translate into losses are the proximate cause for the collapse in the financial guarantor share prices and the widening in their credit default swap spreads. This is why new sources of capital have been either prohibitively expensive or dilutive or both to existing shareholders. (FOMC, 2008b: 6)

It is clear from this meeting that there was widespread concern that the financial crisis was going to be much larger than they had originally anticipated. This concern rose precipitously in the wake of the Bear Stearns collapse of March 2008. The policy response to the Bear Stearns collapse was pretty much a dress rehearsal for what would happen in the fall of 2008 after Lehman Brothers collapsed. Mr. Dudley led off the meeting on March 18–19, 2008, by giving his account of Bear Stearns's demise and its implication for the credit markets:

In my view, an old-fashioned bank run is what really led to Bear Stearns's demise. But in this case it wasn't depositors lining up to make withdrawals; it was customers moving their business elsewhere and investors' unwillingness to roll over their collateralized loans to Bear. The rapidity of the Bear Stearns collapse has had significant contagion effects to the other major U.S. broker–dealers for two reasons. First, these firms also are dependent on the repo market to finance a significant portion of their balance sheet. Second, the $2 per share purchase price for Bear Stearns was a shock given the firm's $70 per share price a week earlier and its stated book value of $84 per share at the end of the last fiscal year. The disparity between book value and the purchase price caused investors to question the accuracy of investment banks' financial statements more generally. (FOMC, 2008b: 3)

The issue of the possible spillover from Bear Stearns's demise dominated the discussion at the meeting. Federal Reserve governor Kevin Warsh explained, "Over the past couple of weeks, not just in the episode with Bear Stearns, counterparty risk is becoming the dominant concern in markets. As has been pointed out around this table, it is increasingly difficult to separate liquidity issues from solvency issues" (FOMC, 2008b: 60). Warsh concluded, "Financial institutions, more broadly than financial markets, are having a hard time finding their way" (FOMC, 2008b: 61).

Fredric Rosengren, president of the Federal Reserve Bank of Boston, summed up the sentiment of the meeting:

> News of the problems at Bear Stearns and the very fragile situation in financial markets complicate our decision today. Federal funds futures indicate that the market is anticipating a reduction of at least 75 basis points and probably more than that. Normally the expectations of financial market participants would not factor heavily in my decision making. However, given the fragility in the market and my own expectation that, even with this move, further easing will be necessary, I strongly prefer lowering interest rates by .75%. (FOMC, 2008b: 68)

The meeting came up with a series of policy initiatives. First, the FOMC decided to expand its credit lines to banks. It also agreed to begin to buy some agency MBSs for either cash or Treasury bonds in order to bolster the balance sheets of banks. The most important move was to lower interest rates by 0.75 percent.

From Financial Markets to Inflation Fears

By spring 2008, then, the FOMC had managed to make the connection between housing and financial markets that they had missed at the start of the deterioration in the performance of nonconventional mortgages. But just as the external events forced these connections on them, external events would turn their attention elsewhere. In the late spring and summer of 2008, financial turmoil temporarily receded, at the same time as energy, food, and other commodity prices unexpectedly spiked. In consequence, beginning in April 2008 and continuing through the summer, many participants shifted focus away from financial markets to inflation.

Dallas Reserve Bank president Richard Fisher spelled out this shift in emphasis at the April 29–30 meeting: "While there are many who have voiced concern with the adverse feedback loop that runs from the economy to tighter credit conditions and back to the economy, I am very troubled by a different adverse feedback loop—namely the inflation dynamic whereby restrictions in the fed funds rate lead to a weaker dollar and upward pressures on global commodity prices, which feed through to higher U.S. inflation." Fisher concluded, "I believe the risk posed by inflation is more significant than the extension of further anemia in the economy" (FOMC, 2008c: 54).

Some participants even began to suggest parallels with the inflation environment of the 1970s. As Plosser warned in April 2008, "In the 1970s one of our mistakes was that we accommodated relative price shocks with very accommodative monetary policy, and in so doing helped convert a relative price shock into sustained inflation. I think we should be careful not to fall into that same trap" (FOMC, 2008c: 107–108).

To be sure, such claims were a source of conflict. Relative to the high levels of consensus that characterized the FOMC during much of our time frame, the spring and summer of 2008 represented a period of contestation. Mishkin, for instance, chastised his colleagues for making inappropriate comparisons: "It's very important to emphasize that this is not the 1970s, and I really get disturbed when people point to that as a problem" (FOMC, 2008c: 130).

Broadly speaking, the board of governors, along with the New York, Boston, and San Francisco Reserve Bank presidents, exhibited comparatively greater concern for financial markets and growth during this period, while most of the remaining presidents stressed commodity prices and inflation. Of course, the former group exercised decision-making power, although the latter was numerically stronger and thus dominated discussion if not policy. Even official FOMC statements, however, maintained from April 2008 onward that inflation had reemerged as a risk roughly equaling the risks to growth. At least one member of the board, Kevin Warsh, went further. Warsh insisted on August 5, 2008, "My view is that inflation risks are very real, and that these risks are higher than growth risks" (FOMC, 2008d: 84).

Thus, a mere forty days before the failure of Lehman Brothers and ensuing stock market free fall, many participants maintained that the risks of financial collapse were no longer the committee's major concern. Making standard reference to the economy's "resilience," Chicago Reserve Bank president Charles Evans summarized a widely held viewpoint as of early August: "One year on the economy has withstood the financial shock in a resilient fashion, especially given the add-on shock from oil. I don't know what more we could have hoped for from the vantage point of the fall of 2007" (FOMC, 2008d: 107).

Indeed, the FOMC was hesitant to abandon this position even after Lehman Brothers filed for bankruptcy on September 15, 2008, the largest such filing in US history. On the following day, at the regularly scheduled FOMC meeting, participants by and large downplayed the significance of the Lehman failure and the financial market turmoil it was causing. As Dennis Lockhart, president of the Atlanta Reserve Bank, explained in his briefing, "My view on the national outlook for the economy has not changed materially since our August meeting" (FOMC, 2008e: 29). In keeping with their macro-level indicators, committee members sought to deemphasize the implications of a single financial event for the real economy. Plosser explained the logic:

> While a lot of attention in the short run is being paid to financial markets' turmoil, our decision today must look beyond today's financial markets to the real economy and its prospects in the future. In this regard, things have not changed very much, at least not yet. . . . I agree that recent financial turmoil may ultimately affect the outlook in a significant way, but that is far from obvious at this point. (FOMC, 2008e: 38)

Richmond Reserve Bank president Lacker concurred: "Overall, I don't take what's happened in the last few days as changing much. It's not obvious to me what the implications are for the outlook for inflation and growth, at least at this point" (FOMC, 2008e: 48).

Many participants simply reasserted the inflation narrative of previous months. Indeed, they expressed concerns that the visibility of short-term financial events would distract the FOMC from its commitment to long-term price stability. For instance, Thomas Hoenig, Kansas City Reserve Bank president, implored the committee "to look beyond the immediate crisis, which I recognize is serious. But as pointed out here, we also have an inflation issue" (FOMC, 2008e: 31). Strikingly, the FOMC policy statement released on September 16, 2008, and presented at the beginning of this chapter continued to suggest that the risks to growth and inflation were roughly equal.

Not all reactions to the Lehman bankruptcy were so sanguine. Boston Reserve Bank president Eric Rosengren insisted otherwise at the September 16 meeting: "The failure of a major investment bank, the forced merger of another, the largest thrift and insurer teetering, and the failure of Freddie and Fannie are likely to have a significant impact on the real economy" (FOMC, 2008e: 30). Yet the extent of his alarm placed Rosengren in a distinct minority. Federal Reserve governor Donald Kohn, himself one of the more growth-focused participants during the lead-up to September, better captured the committee's central tendency with his projection that "activity is more likely to stagnate than to decline" (FOMC, 2008e: 58).

Of course, all of this would change in a matter of days (Abolafia, 2020). On September 29, 2008, the FOMC held an emergency meeting on the phone. At this meeting, Chair Bernanke announced that the Federal Reserve had taken three actions in the face of what was looking like a collapse of not only the US but also the world's financial markets (FOMC, 2008f: 1–4). He proposed to open the credit window to any bank that had a US presence, including foreign banks, in order to provide them with short-term liquidity. He also explained that he was expanding short-term credit swaps with most of the largest central banks in the world. He explained that the coordination of this effort was to give a signal to markets that the central banks would make sure there was sufficient liquidity in the markets that banks could borrow and survive. Finally, he reported on the first version of what became the Troubled Assets Relief Program (TARP).

The situation did not get any better in the next two weeks. Chair Bernanke called another emergency phone meeting of the FOMC on October 7, 2008. At this meeting, he explained to the members of the committee that six central banks had agreed to coordinate a 0.5 percent interest rate cut in order to display to banks around the world that the central banks were serious about providing credit for the world economy (FOMC, 2008g: 1–3). Chair Bernanke needed to persuade the members of the FOMC to go along with this tactic. After a short discussion, the committee voted unanimously to lower interest rates.

In their press release the next day, the FOMC explained,

> The Federal Open Market Committee has decided to lower its target for the federal funds rate 50 basis points to 1–1 / 2 percent. The Committee took this action in light of evidence pointing to a weakening of economic activity and a reduction in inflationary pressures.
>
> Incoming economic data suggest that the pace of economic activity has slowed markedly in recent months. Moreover, the intensification of financial market turmoil is likely to exert additional restraint on spending, partly by further reducing the ability of households and businesses to obtain credit. Inflation has been high, but the Committee believes that the decline in energy and other commodity prices and the weaker prospects for economic activity have reduced the upside risks to inflation. (FOMC, 2008h: 2)

By the next regularly scheduled meeting, on October 28–29, Janet Yellen was arguing that "we are in the midst of a serious global meltdown" (FOMC, 2008i: 68). Her fellow FOMC members agreed. The events that followed included the passage of the TARP and the reorganization of the largest banks. The main goal was to provide massive liquidity for banks that could survive and to march those who were insolvent into reorganization, merger, or bankruptcy in an orderly and rapid fashion. The actions of Chair Bernanke and the Federal Reserve to engage in these policies and aggressively lower interest rates and coordinate actions with international authorities probably prevented what would have been a much worse crisis. These policy decisions have been widely documented (see especially Blinder, 2013; Eichengreen, 2015).

Nonetheless, we can safely conclude that at no point prior to the last months of 2008 did the FOMC even remotely appreciate the depths or dangers of the financial crisis. Even after they came to grasp that housing and financial markets were intimately intertwined, they failed to recognize the extent of the risk that housing posed for financial markets and institutions. What is more, they failed to recognize the extent of the risk that financial markets and institutions posed for economic growth. In short, the FOMC continued to make sense of economic life in terms of two conceptually distinct and largely independent spaces: the "financial" and the "real" economies.

Conclusion

Framing suggests that groups will have a language to carry on their discussions but will tend to miss things outside of their primary frames. The existence of a frame coupled with a tendency toward positive asymmetry implies that groups often obscure or normalize discordant facts. The substantive content of the frames is a function of who the group is and how members are recruited. They reflect actors' experiences where they may have acquired them in prior contexts and through earlier professional training. In the case of the FOMC, the macroeconomic perspective informed many of the discussions of the committee. It also tended to not focus on the connection between what was going on in the housing market and what was going on in the financial markets. The tendency toward putting a positive spin on events meant that the FOMC minimized the problems that could have arisen as a result of the house price bubble.

Their focus on the fundamentals of the housing market using conventional economic theory made them doubt that there was a house price bubble in the first place. Their use of macroeconomic models to estimate the effects of a 20 percent house price reduction on the economy reassured them that if there was a problem, it was manageable. They did not see such a decline as having any impact on the large economy except through reductions in construction, some durable goods for housing, and the ability of households to consume as their net wealth declined. While they saw such effects as significant, they did not see them as creating systemic problems.

As foreclosures heated up in 2007, the FOMC did not see the link between this downturn and possible problems for the banks. Indeed, the house price decline and uptick in foreclosures was taken as a sign that the economy was rebalancing itself. From the perspective of the members of the FOMC, investment was going to move out of the overheated housing market and toward the economy.

It was not until the fall of 2007 and the winter of 2008, when the financial markets were in turmoil, that the connection between MBSs / CDOs and the foreclosures was finally a topic of conversation. The sense of crisis was heightened by the spring of 2008 when Bear Stearns collapsed in a matter of days. But the main worry at that time was the possible spillover effects of Bear Stearns's problems to other banks, not to the larger economy. These effects were framed as a concern with the liquidity problems of other banks. The actions the FOMC undertook were aimed at providing liquidity to banks by opening up the credit window, buying agency-backed MBSs, and lowering the federal funds rate substantially. The goal was to keep the supply of credit high and signal to the markets that the Federal Reserve was prepared act quickly to prevent more banks from becoming insolvent.

But as the Bear Stearns crisis abated, the FOMC became obsessed with a new set of events. There were price spikes in food and oil, and by the summer of 2008, the macroeconomic focus of the FOMC led more than half of its members to shift their focus from the financial crisis to a concern about inflation. This made many members of the FOMC interested in raising, not lowering, interest rates. Their argument was that the crisis playing out on Wall Street was going to be contained within the financial sector with little lasting spillover to the rest of the economy. The travails of that sector were not viewed as disruptive to the overall real economy. But a concern over potential runaway inflation meant that the overall economy was going to be worse off.

This conflict played out through the demise of Lehman Brothers on September 15, 2008, when members of the FOMC who thought inflation was still the big issue facing the economy going forward held their ground. But within two weeks, to their credit, the members of the FOMC shifted their focus to support Chair Bernanke's efforts to prevent an entire meltdown of not just the financial sector but the whole economy and with it the world economy (Abolafia, 2020). The FOMC under the leadership of Chairman Ben Bernanke aggressively pursued every effort to shore up the banks and the financial sector and prevent a meltdown reminiscent of the Great Depression. While they could not forestall a Great Recession, they were able to prevent an entire collapse of the banks and a rerun of the Depression of the 1930s.

9

THE BANKS DID IT
(WITH THE HELP OF THE GOVERNMENT!)

Since the Great Depression of the 1930s, states and market actors have codetermined the structure of financial markets (Preda, 2007). In the case of the market for home mortgages in the United States, the federal government played a critical role creating the modern version of that market by inventing the conventional mortgage, limiting interest rate payments on deposits, and creating depository insurance to make sure that banks were solvent. It actively policed banks and moved quickly to liquidate problematic banks. The federal government pioneered many of the tools of modern finance, including mortgage-backed securities, the financial instruments that were at the core of the financial meltdown of 2007–2010. In the 1960s, the federal government was so worried that the existing mortgage market could not handle the crush of baby boomers to buy houses that they created the government-sponsored enterprises to ensure the availability of mortgage loans. All of this has been very popular with the public, and as a result, politicians of both parties have supported these measures to support and increase homeownership.

One of the most dramatic aspects of the relationship between financial markets and the government has been around how the government responds to market crisis. Financial markets get set up to produce certain kinds of products. Inevitably, those markets produce some kind of market crash, and the government is there to pick up the pieces and help reorganize the market. In such crises, they have worked to stabilize banks that are illiquid by providing them with short-term funding. They push for those who were insolvent to be liquidated or merged. Usually after every episode of financial collapse, the government creates new rules and regulations to prevent what just happened from happening again.

The government can also act as an innovator of products and processes and the creator of new kinds of organizations. Then the cycle begins anew.

Financial institutions play a dominant role in creating their own conception of what the "new" market is and how to build product, process, and organization to aggressively pursue that opportunity. After all, this is capitalism. But government is always there, sometimes as regulator, but also as innovator and facilitator, and when the market fails, it is a stabilizing force. My long-run view of the run-up to the financial crisis of 2007–2009 shows that as circumstances in markets for financial products have changed, new opportunities have emerged. Financial institutions, particularly the largest and most influential, have not just been passive recipients of government carve-outs of particular protected markets.[1] They have worked to promote their conceptions of the market and operated to exploit new opportunities to produce new financial products. One of the key things they do is try to convince regulators that the old rules should be changed, and new ones come into existence to allow for innovation.

While this is sometimes self-serving, the conditions that created a market in the first place sometimes change so much that it entirely makes sense to try something new. Regulations put into place in the last crisis eventually run up against new challenges. For example, the high inflation and interest rates of the 1970s essentially destroyed the business model of the savings and loan industry. The industry convinced the federal government to let them try to save their business model by letting them pay higher interest on savings accounts that were now insured for larger deposits. This let banks make riskier loans. As we know now, it all turned out to be a disaster.

Financial institutions, particularly the largest commercial banks, lobbied beginning in the 1970s to have Depression-era restrictions removed. They argued that removing those restrictions would allow them to be larger and more efficient. This, they claimed, would expand new markets, create credit opportunities for borrowers and the providers of capital, and control risk by spreading it across participants with different risk profiles. By and large, the federal and state governments have listened to the largest banks and allowed interstate banking and the breaking down of the barriers between financial products and the firms that have delivered them (i.e., savings and loan, commercial, and investment banks). In spite of the savings and loan debacle, financial market expansion continued more or less apace in the 1990s and 2000s. Banks moved from being specialists in one kind of market to being participants in multiple markets.

Financial institutions have used these opportunities created by themselves and government to expand their businesses and find new and innovative ways to make money. But the effect of these product expansions and financial innovations can be to create speculative asset bubbles (Minsky, 2008). Unfortunately, it is difficult to tell as markets are zooming upward and expanding rapidly whether the exuberance is irrational or not. The line between being aggressive, predatory, illegal, or stupid is easy to see after the fact and hard to see while the party is raging. For example, was it irrational when banks shifted in 2003 from pursuing conventional to nonconventional mortgages as the conventional mortgage market dried up? One has to remember that for two years, this proved to be a very profitable strategy. We now know what happened next, but in the moment, it would have been harder to make the case that what was going on was simply irrational exuberance.

It is always difficult to see exactly how the problem of an asset bubble forming can have large and really negative consequences for the whole economy and the livelihoods and wealth of citizens. Asset bubbles can form in all forms of assets including stocks, bonds, houses, cryptocurrencies, commodities, and collectibles. This means that understanding how a particular asset bubble actually works is not a matter of theory but a matter of taking a deep dive into data that is often difficult to gather and hard to interpret. That data requires expertise, what might be called local knowledge, to see what is really going on and how what is going on might end up in disaster for all.

To make matters worse, such expertise is often tied up with the industry where the rapid expansion of the market is going on. This prejudices those experts to see the upside of financial innovation and to ignore the possible negative consequences. In the case of the financial instruments at the heart of the financial crisis, the economics profession universally agreed in the 1990s that financial innovation, particularly securitization, had generated impressive new products. These products not only made for good investments but helped everyone control risks. The basic idea was that such innovation meant that anyone who had risk could find someone else willing to help share it for a price (Merton, 1992).

The economics profession also agreed that barriers between financial services should come down and financial institutions should compete in any business they chose. The dominant theme for economists who studied banks in the 1990s was that the conglomerate bank was the future of banking. They argued that banks were well positioned to be in many businesses, and they would attain synergies from their participation in retail banking, loans, credit cards, mortgages, insurance, investment banking, and the trading of securities. By the time the government repealed the Glass-Steagall Act in 1999, the consensus among all economists was that financial services were about to enter a great period of innovation and positive ferment. Government oversight was unnecessary because the new financial tools allowed banks to control and diversify their risks and insure themselves against potential downsides.

By 2001 and the refinancing boom in housing, the consensus between the experts and the financial services industry was that all was good. The opportunities afforded by low interest rates and the ability to originate and securitize mortgages created a large, dynamic, and rapidly growing industry that produced products that both the buyers of homes and the buyers of securities found profitable. It would have been difficult in the boom days of 2001–2005 to find anyone who was seeing a "Minsky moment." As I have shown, the people in charge of looking for just such a bubble thought in 2005 that housing prices were not too high and that even if they declined 20 percent, the macroeconomy would suffer only marginally.

Finally, in any asset bubble, it is not clear how far the trouble will spread. So it may be the case that a few large and aggressive banks who might be thought of as "bad actors" are the ones who bear the brunt of the punishment when asset prices fall. This situation is the most manageable, as regulatory authorities can step in and make sure that an orderly reorganization occurs. The case of Bear Stearns shows this process. The Federal Reserve thought their fixing of the Bear Stearns problem worked, and the fact that financial turmoil briefly appeared to recede in the spring of 2008 suggests they were not entirely incorrect.

But the breaking of asset bubbles might become a systemic problem whereby the firms in an entire industry might be implicated and suffer huge losses. This kind of systemic failure is what happened in 2007–2009 in the mortgage securitization industry. The system was so overstretched in 2005–2007 that in order to keep their securitization machines going, as I have shown, almost all of the vertically integrated large financial institutions committed massive mortgage and securitization fraud. This systemic crisis is harder to observe and control. When banks doubled down and pushed for more mortgages, they relaxed lending standards and committed massive and systemic mortgage and securities fraud. This might have been the moment for intervention, but again, this is easy to see in hindsight.

The most difficult thing to perceive is whether a systemic crisis in part of the financial system is so interconnected with the rest of the economy that it creates a general economic crisis. The collapsing financial industry in the fall of 2008 made obtaining credit for anyone in the economy difficult. The unintended consequence of this was to choke off businesses and cause the stock and housing markets to collapse, thereby destroying a great deal of wealth and reducing household consumption. This resulted in mass layoffs and created a cycle whereby the economic decline spiraled downward.

It is easy now to see how the economy fell off a cliff as the credit markets seized up. But in the fall of 2008, after a summer of ominous financial institution failures and the day after Lehman Brothers collapsed, at least half of the FOMC still thought the trouble would be contained. They were prepared to recognize the deep stress in the financial mortgage securitization industry. But they still thought its spillover to the rest of the economy would be manageable. This shows how hard it is to recognize such a crisis even when you have the best data and up-to-date information in the world. It is indeed sobering.

With this in mind, I explore three themes. First, I want to describe briefly how the financial institutions have been reorganized since the financial crisis. The core of large banks has fulfilled the dreams of banking economists in the 1990s. The largest ten banks owned $12.2 trillion in assets in 2018, fully two-thirds of the assets of all US banks. These banks now participate in nearly every financial service market. Most of these banks were reorganized during the financial crisis, including buying or merging with scores of failed banks. My goal is not to consider what the last crisis was so much as to suggest what to look for in the next one. The next crisis will certainly not look like the last one. The nonconventional mortgage market has disappeared, and financial institutions have reduced their dependence on MBSs as investments. By looking at the potential issues involved with this high concentration of banking, one can get a glimpse of what issues might be relevant.

Then, I want to consider what regulators can do. The Federal Reserve responded aggressively and successfully to the systemic crisis that unfolded before them in 2007–2009. They took events as they came and met them with the tools that they had. When it became clear that a global financial meltdown was underway, Ben Bernanke and his colleagues showed remarkable foresight and acted aggressively (Abolafia, 2020). But their actions came very late in the game.

The events of the crisis undermined the economic consensus about financial innovation and the control of risk and the positive role of finance in the American economy. It is clear that the public's view of what happened shows little faith in the experts who all the way to the end were not sure such a crisis was actually unfolding. The problem of understanding systemic risk is really hard. It requires balancing the knowledge of experts whose main employers are the organizations involved in that risk with a deeper understanding of how such dynamics might end up in chaos. It is a deep and difficult problem. Here I have some optimism, as there is evidence that the Federal Reserve has rethought the relationship between finance and the economy and the role of regulators in that relationship. They appear to have learned the lesson that the financial system is systemically important to the rest of the economy, not just as a sector but as the provider of the basic infrastructure to business.

Finally, I want to consider how the financial crisis has opened up the politics of thinking about the relationship between government and business. The past forty years has been dominated by neoliberalism, the idea that government should not actively intervene in markets. This idea has animated American politics for both political parties and been at the core of policymaking since the late 1970s. This idea is now less politically popular at least partially because of the financial crisis. Neoliberalism was certainly one justification for the deregulation of the financial services industry, and because of the crisis, both financial innovation and neoliberalism have been discredited.

Now that the mortgage market has been reorganized by the government again, it is useful to consider how that should make us think of the role of government in the economy more generally. We need to recognize that government and markets are joined at the hip. But the crux of the matter is that market formation is often done at the behest of the largest and most powerful corporations. This means that analysts need to pay attention to who is helped and hurt by any set of state-market interactions. This recognition also undermines the idea that there is one and only one way to efficiently organize a market. Instead, it suggests that there may be alternatives, some that help incumbents and hurt challengers and others that might work differently. My goal here is to generalize some of the lessons that can be learned from this set of events to champion another kind of political economic analysis.

The Reorganization of the Mortgage Industry

It is useful to present some data on how the reorganization of the mortgage market after the financial crisis played out. In the wake of the meltdown and bankruptcy and reorganization of the largest banks, it is safe to say that the vertically integrated, mortgage-securitization-oriented bank no longer exists. The GSEs are now doing almost all mortgage securitizations (Government Accounting Office, 2019; Securities Industry and Financial Markets Association, 2019). Private banks have moved on from originating and securitizing mortgages. No one is producing subprime mortgages. Banks have instead expanded their activities in all directions and now operate as financial conglomerates with product divisions that participate in various financial markets. Banks continue to hold on to MBSs because those based on conventional mortgages are still a good investment. But this is only one of the investments in their portfolios. The ABCP market has returned to its more normal role in providing short-term credit for banks and nonfinancial companies.

To illustrate the role of private banks in the mortgage market, Figure 9.1 presents data on what happened to MBS production before, during, and after the financial crisis. The top panel presents data on the issuance of securities by non-

Private-Label Securities by Product Type

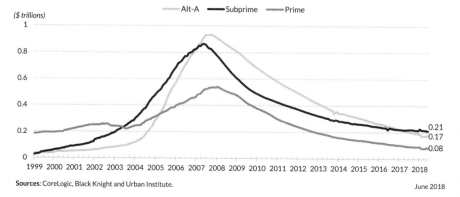

Sources: CoreLogic, Black Knight and Urban Institute.

June 2018

Agency Mortgage-Backed Securities

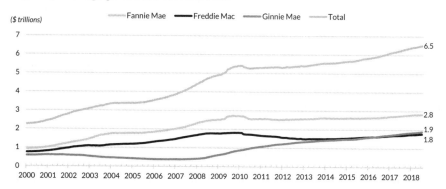

FIGURE 9.1 Production of MBSs by private-label securities (non-GSE financial institutions) and the total outstanding MBSs issued by the GSEs, 1999–2018. Source: Housing Finance Policy Center, "Housing Finance at a Glance," April 2018, p. 7. © Urban Institute.

GSE banks. As documented in an earlier chapter, most of the MBS production before 2000 was done by the GSEs. But beginning in 2000, one can observe an upturn in MBS production for banks and other financial institutions. Most strik- ing are the increases in Alt-A and subprime MBSs from 2003 to 2007. Subprime MBS production was less than $100 billion in 2000, and it peaked at around $900 billion in 2007. Alt-A production was close behind, going from about $100 billion in 2000 to $800 billion in 2007. One can also see that private banks began to compete more aggressively with the GSEs for securities based on convention- al mortgages. They securitized about $200 billion in 2002, which then rose to $575 billion in 2007. But in the wake of the financial crisis, private banks nearly exited the securitization industry. In 2018, their share dropped below what they were securitizing in 2000. Securitization is still a business for some of the private banks, but not the main one. The top half of the graph shows quite clearly the

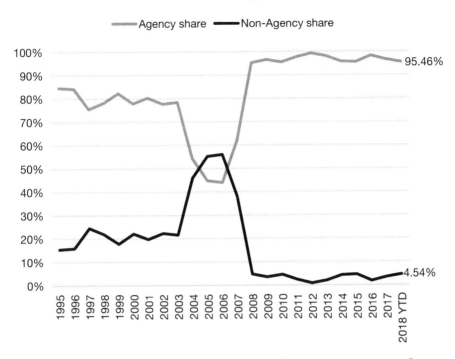

FIGURE 9.2 Agency and nonagency shares of residential MBS issuance, 1995–2018. Source: Housing Finance Policy Center, "Housing at a Glance," May 2018, p. 10. © Urban Institute.

rise and fall of the vertically integrated banks whose activities were centered on the production of nonconventional MBSs. Private banks simply have stopped producing MBSs.

The bottom half of Figure 9.1 shows the cumulative total of MBSs issued by the GSEs. From 2000 to 2007, one can see that the total amount of mortgage securities issued by the GSEs doubled, going from $2.2 trillion in 2000 to almost $4.4 trillion in 2007. Subsequently, this rose to $6.5 trillion in 2018. The dominance of the GSEs in issuing mortgage securities is clear. Even before the crisis, the GSEs were at the center of conventional mortgage securitization, and after the crisis, they were the only game in town. There is some interesting variation in the relative issuance of Fannie, Freddie, and Ginnie through the period. During the run-up of 2000–2007, Fannie and Freddie doubled the amount of securities they issued, while Ginnie actually fell in the total amount they issued. This implies that Ginnie was less active over this period. In the wake of the government takeover of Fannie and Freddie in August 2008, Ginnie has assumed the more dominant role in issuing mortgage securities.

Figure 9.2 presents the relative shares of GSE and private banks' issuance of residential MBSs from 1995 to 2018. From 1995 to 2003, the GSEs had about an 80 percent market share in MBS issuance. But as the market turned from conven-

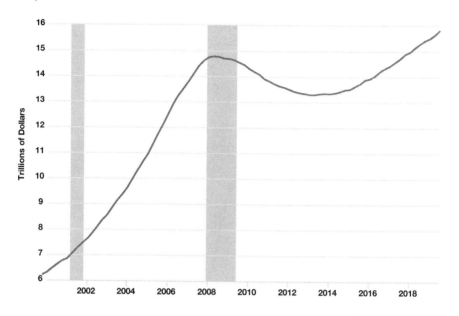

FIGURE 9.3 Mortgage debt in the United States. Source: Board of Governors of the Federal Reserve System (US), "Mortgage Debt Outstanding," retrieved from FRED, Federal Reserve Bank of St. Louis.

tional to nonconventional mortgages in 2003–2007, the roles of the two types of issuers shifted, and private banks had a majority of MBS issuance in 2004–2007. In the wake of the financial crisis, the pattern shifted dramatically. Private banks' share of the market dropped to under 5 percent and currently stands at less than 4 percent. Taken together, Figures 9.1 and 9.2 show the rise and fall of the vertically integrated mortgage securitization banks. For a couple of years, these banks dominated the production of MBSs because their share of nonconventional mortgage issuance was so high, and nonconventional mortgages dominated the MBS market. But after the crash, that market has disappeared, and now the GSEs, which are all owned by the government, dominate what is left of the industry, the securitization of conventional mortgages.

I next present data on the size of these markets and how they have changed over time. Figure 9.3 shows that mortgage debt rapidly increased in the United States from about $6 trillion in 2000 to a peak of over $15 trillion in 2008. This means that the amount of real estate debt in the United States increased by almost 250 percent in just eight years. This incredible spike in mortgage indebtedness is at the heart of the rise and fall of the mortgage securitization industry. There was a decrease during the financial crisis of about $2 trillion from 2008 to

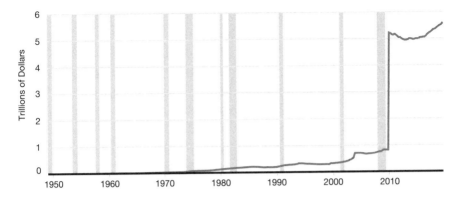

FIGURE 9.4 Government holding of MBSs, 2002–2018. Source: Board of Governors of the Federal Reserve System (US), "Mortgage Debt Outstanding by Type of Holder: Federal and Related Agencies," retrieved from FRED, Federal Reserve Bank of St. Louis.

2012 to $13 trillion as foreclosures rose and people lost their homes. This is about a 13 percent decrease. But since 2012, mortgage debt has been on the rise again and is about $15.8 trillion in 2018. This is an increase of $2.8 trillion in six years, about 20 percent. While the increase is not as dramatic as the increase earlier in the 2000s, it is still quite large.

One of the most interesting questions is, who now owns the huge amount of MBSs that exist? Figure 9.4 shows the amount held by the federal government. In 2000–2008, the federal government held about $1 trillion of mortgage debt. Most of this was in the form of conventional MBSs that were produced by the GSEs. In the summer of 2008, the federal government took over Fannie Mae and Freddie Mac and thereby got their MBS and loan portfolios. These totaled about $1.2 trillion. The Federal Reserve also began its asset-purchasing program in 2008 by buying agency securities from banks in order to provide them with liquidity and became a large holder of MBSs. Figure 9.4 provides graphic information about how this huge run-up in securities affected the federal government's ownership of mortgages. The total held by the government before the financial crisis was around $1 trillion. But beginning in 2008–2010, this increased to over $5 trillion dollars. In 2018, it stood at about $5.7 trillion. Given that all mortgage debt in the United States was about $15.8 trillion, the federal government owned about 36 percent of all mortgage debt in the country. One of the great ironies of what has happened is that the federal government created the GSEs in the 1960s as a way for them to not be directly involved in owning mortgages. But as a result of the financial crisis, the federal government is the owner of over a third of all mortgage debt in the United States. Most Americans are unaware that every month when they pay their mortgages, that money is going to the government.

Finally, I want to take up the issue of what happened to the banks. The forced reorganization of American banking in the wake of the financial crisis heavily increased the concentration of banking assets in the United States. In 2018, the five largest banks in the United States controlled 48.5 percent of assets, and the ten largest controlled almost 66 percent. These banks include JPMorgan Chase ($2,615.18 billion in assets), Bank of America Corp ($2,338.83 billion), Citigroup Inc. ($1,925.17 billion), Wells Fargo ($1,872.98 billion), Goldman Sachs Group Inc. ($957.19 billion), Morgan Stanley ($865.52 billion), U.S. Bancorp ($464.61 billion), TD Group US Holdings ($380.65 billion), PNC Financial Services ($380.08 billion), and Capital One Financial Corp ($362.91 billion). One of the persistent issues that have been expressed in the wake of the financial crisis is that these banks are now too big to fail. They are so large that their failure is likely to have the same kind of spillover into the rest of the banks and the rest of the economy that was witnessed in the downturn in 2008. If, for example, JPMorgan Chase went bankrupt, it would send ripples through the entire banking system and the whole economy.

One of the ways in which the federal government has tried to deal with this problem is the Dodd-Frank Act, which was passed in 2010. One part of the act allowed the Federal Reserve to define which banks were "systemically important"—that is, banks whose failure would potentially bring down the system. The Federal Reserve has the ability to force those banks to raise capital so that they can withstand a serious downturn. To judge where the banks are, the Federal Reserve has asked these banks to undergo a stress test to see what would happen to their balance sheets in the case of a serious downturn.

The basic idea is to consider how a severe economic downturn would affect the current holdings of the banks in order to determine whether the banks have enough reserves to control their losses.[2] It is useful to quote the conditions of what constitutes a severe downturn for the purposes of the test given in 2019:

> The severely adverse scenario is characterized by a severe global recession accompanied by a period of heightened stress in CRE markets and corporate debt markets. This is a hypothetical scenario designed to assess the strength of banking organizations and their resilience to unfavorable economic conditions and does not represent a forecast of the Federal Reserve. For the stress test, the U.S. unemployment rate climbs to a peak of 10 percent. In line with the increase in the unemployment rate, real GDP falls about 8 percent from its pre-recession peak, reaching a trough. (Federal Reserve, 2019: 4).

Applying this scenario to a complex balance sheet that differs dramatically across firms is a challenging prospect. Of course, the model about the potential impact of such changes is itself difficult to construct and relies on previous data. The Federal Reserve concluded in 2019 that all of the banks had the capital reserves to survive such a deep downturn (2019: 25). The adverse scenario results in an average decrease of about 25 percent in capital cushion and a $680 billion loss across banks. At the end, the average level of capital cushion is only 0.1 percent above what the Federal Reserve views as safe. Most of these losses were for investments they made that include residential and commercial real estate loans, personal loans, financial instruments (including government and corporate bonds and MBSs), and credit cards. The overall picture shows that the largest banks are no longer as dependent on MBSs and CDOs for investments, and they are no longer borrowing short term to fund those investments.

So, what does this all add up to? The mortgage securitization industry went through a huge expansion in the 2000s. When the downturn in conventional mortgages occurred in 2003, the market rapidly shifted to the production of nonconventional MBSs. These turned out to be a big problem, and all of the private banks involved in the production of MBSs underwent serious reorganization. As a result of the crisis, the federal government now owns the GSEs, and it controls mortgage origination and the production of MBSs in the economy. It is currently the largest holder of mortgage debt in the country. The private banks have moved on. They no longer are involved in the production of nonconventional MBSs (although they still hold mostly conventional MBSs on their balance sheets). The last crisis has passed, and the situation has stabilized (albeit with lots of government participation). The chance that the next financial crisis will be exactly like the last one is pretty remote. This raises the next question: what should the government be doing to be vigilant for the next crisis, one that will probably have entirely different causes?

What Could Policymakers Do Better?

The vertically integrated bank focused on mortgage origination and securitization using borrowed money is gone. It has been replaced by a small number of large conglomerate banks with their fingers in lots of pies. Banks will be wary of borrowing short to go long on mortgages they have originated and packaged into securities. They will be particularly sensitive to giving mortgages to people with impaired credit and little or no chance of paying loans back. Alan Greenspan thought that banks should not have done this in the first place. Now that they have, their organizations and leaders have moved on to other ways to make money. The mortgage market is no longer in their hands. It is controlled by the federal government and the GSEs. For the GSEs to continue creating MBSs, they need market actors to be confident that the underlying mortgages are not particularly risky. The GSEs have obliged in this regard. This makes MBSs a different and safer kind of product. Finally, regulators will be on the watch for any bubble, be they in house prices or the rapid expansion of credit instruments.

But there are some generic lessons to be learned from the crisis. One reason that this crisis was so severe is that the underlying market for mortgages was so large. The mortgage market is still a $2–3 trillion market. But it was not just its size but also the nature of the connections between it and the entire financial system. In the 2000s, the mortgage securitization market integrated the production of mortgages with financial instruments that were purchased mainly with money borrowed on a relatively short-term basis. The systemic nature of these connections and their large size should have sent off signals to regulators about the potential for trouble, particularly as the crisis unfolded in slow motion from 2006 to 2008.

This means that in the future, regulators should be vigilant for such large market movements and their interdependence with other important markets. Much discussion has focused on shadow banking as the culprit guilty for the crisis, as these were the markets that provided these funds. But as I have shown, shadow banking was only one part of the system. It had little to do with the vertical integration of those banks and how they made money. That success allowed them to borrow freely and in large amounts in the shadow banking markets. Shadow banking was only the conduit by which securities were produced and held.

There were other signs that should have concerned regulators. When any industry corners the profits in the economy the way that finance did in 2001–2007, regulators should be wary of potential problems. Understanding the business models of the largest firms in the largest and most profitable sectors and the risks inherent in their activities should be a front-and-center concern for regulators. No sector of the economy can sustain that level of profits for very long without running out of opportunities to make that kind of money. That banks had to turn to nonconventional mortgages to keep their high profits intact should have set of red flags for regulators. The 2005 FOMC meeting on whether there was a housing price bubble never even considered the role of the banks in making the market in nonconventional mortgages.

A more difficult set of issues to understand was interpreting the role of the increase in foreclosures and reports of mortgage and securities fraud. This should have alerted observers to the last gasp of the largest market in the country and the biggest profit center as well. Again, because the business models of the banks were not being observed, no one had any ability to connect the evidence of massive mortgage and securities fraud to the desperate attempt to keep the vertically integrated banks model going. To have done so, someone would have had to have the expertise to see the connections and enough distance to blow the whistle.

This brings me back to one of the most intractable problems in detecting the next crisis before it happens. People who have the expert knowledge to see the problem before it gets too big are frequently cognitively captured by the industry and often working in the industry. One cannot expect them to have any critical distance. In this case, the economics profession and those in positions of regulatory power was so enamored of financial innovation that few of them ever saw anything going wrong.[3] So who might be able to have this distance and be able to do something?

One candidate for the job is the Federal Reserve. It is the strongest of the regulators in terms of independence from finance and has lots of expertise and authority to manage the banks and financial markets. In this case, as I have shown, the Federal Reserve repeatedly downplayed the seriousness of the brewing crisis. This was partly because they believed in financial innovation. But it was mostly because they failed to see the systemic threat of the vertically integrated banks. Their focus on viewing the problem from the perspective of the macroeconomy meant they never saw the links between finance and the so-called real economy. They also never thought that the spillovers from the foreclosures would have a broad effect. It is here that some changes can be made.

A report by the Independent Evaluation Office (2010) at the International Monetary Fund agreed with my analysis of the cognitive biases of not just the Federal Reserve but central banks and regulatory authorities in general. They concluded that similar kinds of cognitive biases precluded that organization from seeing the dangers of the financial crisis as well. In the view of this study, "The *linking of macroeconomic and financial sector analysis* remained inadequate. . . . This reflected the lack of a suitable conceptual framework for analyzing such linkages within the economics profession at large" (Independent Evaluation Office, 2010: 18; emphasis added). The fact that the group of experts whose job it is to make sense of the direction of the economy at the Federal Reserve and at the International Monetary Fund were more or less blinded by their assumptions about how that reality worked is something to ponder. It is also something that someone can do something about.

It is useful to ask what such organizations might do to overcome the effects of culture, framing, and cognition to better identify crises. One can certainly argue that little can be done. The complexity of troubling events and the rapidity with which that complexity can produce dramatic outcomes make it especially difficult to overcome the blinders of any frame. Nonetheless, in our case, by September 2008, the FOMC did recognize that there was a crisis brewing in the housing market and that it had spilled over into a financial crisis. But as my analysis has shown, their macroeconomic perspective continued to convince them that it could be contained and that its negative effects would not spread dramatically across the economy.

This suggests that there are two important processes that would need to be counteracted. First, the existence of any frame facilitates group decision-making but also tends to push a group toward underplaying some disconcerting facts and putting a positive spin on them. Second, the cultural content of a frame plays a big role in what are considered facts and what kinds of explanations can be justified.

Organizational solutions would have to deal with both problems in order to help such decision-making groups see a crisis and its causes and consequences. One strategy is for decision-making groups to create independent work groups whose job is to study the potential pitfalls of any policy decision. These groups would need to have standard input into decision-making processes and become part of the policy discussions. Participation in these groups would have to be rewarded by ensuring that members were rotated in and out and that participation would be seen as a boost to one's career. This would reduce the penalties for having dissident views and potentially legitimate the ideas coming out of these groups in the more general discussion. It might also instill skepticism into future participants of decision-making groups.

While this might help undermine the effects of positive asymmetry, it would not solve the problem that all primary frameworks limit the types and forms of understanding involved in decision-making. This presents an even more difficult challenge. First, it comes into conflict with the fact that a primary frame serves a positive function for decision-making by allowing a consensus to emerge. Relatedly, giving legitimacy to multiple primary frameworks undermines the status and privilege of those who have power based on their use of the primary frame, in this case the macroeconomists.

This suggests that if a decision-making group were serious about bringing dissident voices into the discussion, an effort would have to be made to ensure that these dissident members had a substantial presence (see the review by Williams and O'Reilly [1998] for a discussion of the conditions under which such diversity can have positive or negative effects). In the case of the Federal Reserve, this would mean decreasing the presence of macroeconomists and increasing the presence of people with expertise relating to finance as a new and potentially dominant force in the economy. Members of the FOMC with a financial or banking background did speak up more on financial topics and clearly saw more danger in housing and finance than did the dominant macroeconomic perspective. Imagine what might have happened if the members who considered inflation to be the most serious problem in the economy in the spring and summer of 2008 had been replaced by members with significant finance and banking expertise. It is possible that the FOMC would have recommended different policies throughout the year and worked to mitigate the financial collapse.

To be clear, I am not advocating a revolving door between the FOMC and the financial industry or the "capture" of the Fed by financial interests themselves. Rather, I am arguing that the FOMC should couple the theoretical logic of its members' academic training with greater on-the-ground attention to the industry that the Fed actually regulates. In this regard, it is telling that on September 16, 2008, the single dissenting voice in the room (Dr. Rosengren) was himself an academically trained macroeconomist who also had extensive technical knowledge of banking. Dr. Rosengren was uniquely positioned to perceive and act on the risks because he was somewhat autonomous from financial industry interests yet simultaneously knowledgeable of the industry. In this context, however, he was isolated, and his perspective did not figure into the outcome of the meeting.

The financial crisis has already quietly shifted the way that regulators, particularly the Federal Reserve, think about financial innovation, risk, and regulation. We no longer hear how financial innovation controls risk and is the best thing to happen to American capitalism ever. Instead, skeptics wonder about the efficacy of financial products and the problems of asymmetric information between buyers and sellers whereby sellers make money because buyers remain uninformed about the riskiness of products. Instead of assuming that every financial product by definition makes the system work more efficiently, regulators worry about the possibility of rent seeking and fraud on the part of banks.

Even more important, regulators have learned that the financial system is a system that implicates not just the financial sector but the rest of the economy. This, of course, has been the main message of this book. Regulators have realized that banks and many nonfinancial corporations fund their activities through the shadow banking system (i.e., the repo, ABCP, and money markets). This means that to ensure that short-term financing is available throughout the economy for all corporations who want to be borrowers, regulators must be prepared to step in to provide liquidity to financial markets by buying assets and providing cash.

This policy shift has already been put into practice. In the spring of 2020, a large swath of the economy of the United States was shut down due to the coronavirus pandemic. As a result of the great uncertainty the pandemic presented, stock prices dropped about 30 percent in a month. Even more troubling, the repo and ABCP markets began to freeze up just as they had in the fall of 2008. Nonfinancial corporations found it difficult to borrow short term. Banks found themselves under some pressure to provide and receive credit. The Federal Reserve acted aggressively to ensure the flow of credit in the economy and helped stabilize the ability of everyone to continue to borrow to fund their current economic activities. They bought trillions of dollars of Treasury securities and conventional MBSs to provide banks with cash. They began buying corporate debt and other securities. They provided liquidity to the repo and ABCP markets. At a press conference on April 29, 2020, Jerome Powell, chair of the Federal Reserve, said,

> Let me say that we're committed to using our full range of tools to support the economy in this challenging time. We're going to use them, as I mentioned, forcefully, proactively and aggressively until we're confident that we're solidly on the road to recovery, and also to assure that that recovery, when it comes, will be as robust as possible. As you know, our credit policies are not subject to specific dollar limit. They can be expanded as appropriate, and we can do new ones.[4]

This worked spectacularly well, as the stock market rallied and lending resumed.

The shift in orientation toward viewing the financial system as part of the central circulation of the economy represents a break with the idea that it is just another sector. To invoke a metaphor, instead of a set of sectors that operate more or less independently of one another, the economy now looks much more like a living organism where the financial system operates as the heart, pumping blood to the rest of the system. Anything that dramatically limits that flow can bring the economy to its knees. Notice that the regulator of that heart now acts as a doctor (or maybe a brain), prepared to intervene to save the life of the patient by flooding the system with liquidity. The Federal Reserve has partially accepted that the economy is a system. But it needs to do this with greater insight on the interconnectedness of firms and markets.

A New Political Economy?

It is useful to consider more general lessons to be learned from my long-run perspective on the bank-government-mortgage nexus. The most important implication, for both scholars and policymakers, is that understanding any market requires making sense of the business models and practices of a market and how they came into being. This involves studying the history of the market, its crises, previous interventions by government, who has political power, and the role of corporations in pushing a particular set of understandings and a political program to organize the market. The role of ideas in this process is a matter of some contention. Policymakers (that is, experts in positions where they have to formulate and enforce policy) are influenced by their training, their experiences, what has happened, and what they think should happen. But the literature shows pretty clearly that policymakers matter to creating policies because of the active political support of citizens, elected officials, and business.[5]

During the Depression of the 1930s, in the face of a massive economic crisis, American voters were willing to consider more direct forms of government intervention into markets in order to restore economic health. In the case of financial markets, policymakers proposed radically changing the role of government in the economy by intervening to make sure that financial markets were stable. They forced banks to decide which markets to participate in, and they created regulators to make sure those markets were stable enough to provide products for consumers.

The economic crisis of the 1970s caused a rethink in how those relationships should be structured. Beginning in the 1970s, a critique evolved that too much government intervention was responsible for the stagnant economy in the United States, which was experiencing slow growth and high inflation. President Carter, a Democrat, began to experiment with changing government rules that controlled forms of competition in trucking, airlines, and the savings and loan banks. President Reagan, a Republican, came to power in 1980 with the agenda of pushing policies even more in favor of what business wanted, particularly the largest corporations. He ran on a political agenda to deregulate the economy and cut taxes. When he entered office, he followed through by giving business a huge tax cut, encouraging an all-out assault on what was left of organized labor, suspending the antitrust laws, and encouraging mergers. The economic landscape of the 1980s was transformed by these shifts in policy.

The policy community, mostly made up of economists, embraced this set of ideas, which came to be known as neoliberalism. Its basic position was that government should not try to regulate markets and choose winners and losers but instead should allow firms to compete however they chose and make investment decisions. The assumption was that the invisible hand of the market would always be more efficient than anything a government might manage. Neoliberalism has been used as a justification for relaxing labor standards, attacking unions, and reducing taxes for the wealthiest citizens.

As part of this neoliberal turn, powerful financial interests pushed change on the largest corporations in the reorganization of American industry during the

1980s merger movement. Institutional investors came to embrace the idea that the purpose of the corporation was to make money for them, the shareholders. It pushed managers to focus only on policies that would raise the share price and, in doing so, changed the relationships between management and employees. Managers that resisted this message found themselves the target of a hostile takeover. By the 1990s, shareholder value capitalism was in ascendance (Useem, 1996).

Economic growth and reduced inflation returned to the United States in the 1980s and 1990s, solidifying public support for these policies. Indeed, both the Democratic and Republican Parties came to embrace neoliberalism. Both parties, not surprisingly, were also in favor of financial deregulation and innovation. But since the financial crisis, there has been some political reconsideration of this view of the relationship between government and business both by the public and by those interested in policymaking.

This has been driven by several forces. First, while economic growth returned in the 1980s and 1990s, it was accompanied by an increasing concentration of income and wealth (Lin and Tomaskovic-Devey, 2013). Executives who ran corporations to maximize shareholder value declared war on unions in the 1980s, used technology effectively to displace the remaining organized workers, cut benefits and job security for those that remained, and outsourced and offshored jobs to increase profits in the past thirty years (Van der Swan, 2014). Those who have benefited the most from this, the richest 1 percent of the population, have gotten Republican governments to produce tax policies that have favored corporations and the wealthy over most citizens.

Second, government has also cut back its commitment to provide a social safety net for citizens and provide infrastructure and education for all. In the United States, this has caused an increase in poor health outcomes, drug addiction, suicides, and early deaths. One impact of these cutbacks was an increase in pressure on communities of color. These communities experienced the brunt of low wages and insecure employment. They were more likely to have gotten caught up in the prison industrial complex that also intensified in the 1980s in the "war on drugs."

The financial crisis played an important role in the increasing recognition that neoliberalism as a policy position needed rethinking. The financial revolution of the past forty years was the poster child for the good that deregulation could do. As a result of rewriting the rules by which financial activities were governed, the landscape of American banking was transformed. It increased the size of banks, their spread geographically, and the number of products they produce. The shift away from the highly regulated system where markets were fragmented by producer and place has undeniably increased the availability of credit to many citizens. But it has also allowed banks and the financial sector to capture a disproportionate share of profits in the economy.

Those profits, of course, have ended up mostly with shareholders and mostly with the wealthiest investors. The newest version of American banking, where ten systemically important large banks control two-thirds of all financial assets in the country, raises questions about the degree to which those banks compete and whether they will continue to try to provide credit to all who need it. Americans perceive that bankers did not appear to suffer in the financial crisis. Bankers continue to draw down outsized pay packages and offer an easy target for citizens disgruntled with a government that seems to favor the wealthy over its citizenry.

A new political economy would recognize that the government-firm relationship exists no matter what. The imagery of fettered versus unfettered markets is an illusion. The case of financial deregulation is often put forward as an unalloyed success of neoliberal policies. But as we have seen, when applied to the mortgage industry, the financial innovation of the past forty years depended a great deal on government. While the banks clearly did it, the government was there to help structure the market, invent new products (most importantly, securitization), and produce new rules and laws for banks to take advantage of the new system. Banks had to be coaxed into building the market for mortgage securitization. But once they realized how much money could be made, they quickly took advantage of how the market worked. They figured out how to build vertically integrated structures and incorporate the large pools of capital available in the repo and ABCP markets to fund their activities.

Scholars and policymakers also need to recognize that these arrangements always favor some and not others. The relative power of incumbent firms means that they can get regulators and the policy community to support their policy preferences. In this case, we can see that the preferences of the largest banks generally guided the changes in financial regulation. A different kind of political economy would incorporate this understanding into its analysis of any economic sector and its history and links to government. While this is not all necessarily bad, it can lead to negative outcomes. Current policies favor shareholders over stakeholders, capital over labor, and the wealthiest 1 percent of households over all other citizens. But if a different politics prevails, one can expect an interest in redressing these imbalances on the part of citizens. Taking a historical and system perspective on markets allows policymakers to make sense of why what exists is there and what might be done to fit different policy goals.

Finally, such a political economy does not start out with the assumption that there is one best way to organize markets. Neoliberal analysis suggests that market actors left to their own devices will find the best way to do things through market competition. But if markets are the historical product of government and firms and if incumbent firms are successful at getting the rules they want, it is not clear that this is because they are efficient. It may be because they are stable and powerful. The savings and loan model of mortgages increased homeownership from 43 percent to about 65 percent of households. Mortgage securitization increased that to 69 percent, but in its collapse, this has gone back to 64 percent. It is hard to argue that all of that financial innovation produced an efficient system that served the interests of consumers.

There is a huge irony to what happened to the market for mortgages and mortgage securitization after the crisis. The whole reason the federal government created the GSEs in the 1960s was so that they would not be the main lender of mortgage money in the country. The reason that they invented MBSs was to involve the private sector in the funding of mortgages. But fifty years later, the federal government, as a result of their having created the MBS market, now holds $5.7 trillion in mortgage debt, around 36 percent of all mortgage debt. It finds itself the main organizer of the mortgage market in the United States.

This appears to be a stable arrangement for now. Politicians of all political persuasions with the support of the American public have worked hard to increase homeownership in the country. When the bottom fell out in the 1930s, in the 1980s, and after 2008, the federal government rode to the rescue to rebuild the market. Each time it was different, but each time it came to pass. It is difficult to imagine that it will be any other way the next time. Politics will determine whether policymakers will come to use the principles I have elucidated here to make sense of varying sectors of the economy and their link to broader economic processes. The question of creating policies to govern markets requires public support based on some perception of what will be good for the economy. But just as neoliberalism reflected one political moment in responding to a substantial economic crisis, the financial crisis has provided us with another. Moving toward a more realistic political economy has already started among scholars and policymakers. It remains to be seen if the public and politicians will embrace it as a way to decide what to do next.

Notes

4. Financial Innovation and the Alphabet Soup of Financial Products

1. Of these, Ranieri (1996: 35) notes, "The CMO concept is very simple. Rather than look at a mortgage pool as a single group of thirty-year mortgages, the CMO concept approaches it as a series of unique annual cash flows each year for the next thirty years. It recognizes that cash flows are higher in the early years of the pool, and they can be carved up into separate tranches with a whole range of securities from one to thirty years. Each tranche can then carry a separate coupon priced at a spread off treasuries with the same maturity." Ranieri (1996: 36) also notes that after developing these structures, the deal makers realized that this technology had already existed in the form of serial bonds in the municipal bond industry. Thus, although this technique had already existed, it had been overlooked for these purposes.

2. While credit scores are a kind of financial instrument, I discuss them here because they are used as part of the processing of loans. While securitization also produces financial instruments, it is part of a general set of production processes by which banks take one kind of financial asset and turn it into another. It does not just create the output (i.e., financial instruments) but also creates a set of techniques to do so.

3. I do not mean to suggest that FICO scores do not come with biases. Since they were first invented, there have been critics of these scores and their biases against certain kinds of people, particularly racial and ethnic minorities (Capon, 1982; for a more recent critique, see O'Neil, 2016).

4. One can see that many of these mortgages were to individuals who were stretched financially and had relatively poor credit. These kinds of MBSs were at the core of the financial meltdown in 2007–2008.

5. The Subprime Moment, 2001–2008

1. The federal funds rate is the interest rate at which depository institutions (banks and credit unions) lend reserve balances to other depository institutions overnight, on an uncollateralized basis. As a result, it drives the level of other interest rates in the economy.

2. Many banks remained specialists in one part of the industry to the end in 2008. But the largest and most important financial institutions eventually were involved in both origination and securitization. I will provide evidence to this effect throughout this chapter.

3. There has been a debate about whether it was the repo market or the ABCP market that was more central to the financial crisis (Gorton, 2010; Acharya et al., 2013). The data in Acharya et al. (2013) convincingly indicate that the meltdown in the ABCP market was more substantial in size than that in the repo market, and hence it was the major site of the crisis.

7. Fraud and the Financial Crisis

1. Lenders may also conceal aspects of the origination process, such as commissions earned by brokers, thereby misrepresenting their impartiality.

2. For example, when the SEC in 2010 accused Goldman Sachs of creating and selling MBSs secretly intended to fail, the bank's initial defense amounted to claims of caveat emptor (Klapper et al. 2009; Davidoff et al., 2012).

3. In addition to the evidence presented in Figure 7.1, a US Senate investigation found evidence of widespread opportunism in lending practices by Washington Mutual. Residential Capital, Chase, Bank of America, and other banks have settled in major servicing-related suits. Finally, in March 2008, an internal memo from Chase's mortgage lending division was leaked that detailed procedures for circumventing safeguards on its automated lending software in order to get unduly risky loans approved (San Francisco Chronicle, 2008; Dash, 2011; de la Merced, 2012; Friesen, 2008).

4. The following account was based on an interview conducted by the Financial Crisis Investigation Commission on April 19, 2010 (Financial Crisis Investigation Commission, 2010b).

5. The following is based on Mary Haggerty's testimony to the Financial Crisis Investigation Commission on August 17, 2010 (Financial Crisis Investigation Commission, 2010a).

6. US District Court, Central District of California, case no. 2:09-cv-05438-SJO (JCx), filed July 24, 2009, accessed July 9, 2019, https://www.courtlistener.com/recap/gov.uscourts.cacd.449912.1.0.pdf.

8. Why Did the Federal Reserve Miss the Financial Crisis of 2008?

1. For more analysis of these texts both qualitatively and quantitatively, the reader should see Fligstein et al. (2017).
2. Many of the arguments in the transcripts rely on more generic forms of economic reasoning. But the attempts to decipher the direction of the overall economy use macroeconomic data and models.
3. The FOMC had access to a wide variety of economic indicators. These are gathered in what are called the "Green" and "Beige" Books. The Green Book contains the data gathered on the performance of the economy by the Federal Reserve staff. They also present their models of the economy and predictions about the future growth of the economy. The Beige Book contains the data gathered by each of the Federal Reserve Districts. Both books are circulated before the FOMC meeting.
4. The other major element of this disciplinary transformation was Lucas's (1976) critique, which attacked the practice of basing predictions of future developments in the economy on historical data, particularly macroeconomic aggregates. He argued that a more defensible approach was to make macroeconomic models consistent with microeconomic principles, basing predictions of aggregates on individual-, household-, and firm-level considerations. The FRB / US model incorporates these principles as well (Brayton et al., 1997).
5. Thus, Chari and Kehoe (2006: 4) applaud how general-equilibrium models have come to incorporate "financial market imperfections . . . *and other frictions*" (emphasis added). Borio (2011: 88), a critic of this approach, goes so far as to argue that "by construction, macroeconomic models could not incorporate financial instability."
6. A similar trend holds for related mortgage products: before mid-2005, the term *adjustable-rate mortgage / ARM* appears only twice, and neither *nonconforming* nor *Alt-A* appears at all.
7. Note that zoning ordinances are exactly the kind of rigidities that the macroeconomic synthesis postulates.
8. Alan Greenspan captured this spirit of optimism most succinctly on December 13, 2005: "It's hard to imagine an American economy that is as balanced as this one is" (FOMC, 2005c: 66).
9. In retrospect, the FOMC would date the start of the financial crisis to August 2007, which marked a severe and sustained round of financial market turbulence associated with a collapse of confidence in the ABCP market.

9. The Banks Did It (With the Help of the Government!)

1. Of course, banks and other financial institutions have also lobbied to keep their privileges. As I have shown, for a long time, banking was fragmented as state

regulators prevented out-of-state banks from doing business and regulated the branching activities of in-state banks. This protected locally owned banks and created a whole class of small banks. Financial deregulation has generally been advocated by the largest banks, which have convinced state and federal regulators that interstate banking would provide more capital to local areas. Financial deregulation was a project of those banks and has benefited them the most.

2. The eighteen banks include Bank of America Corporation, the Bank of New York Mellon Corporation, Barclays US LLC, Capital One Financial Corporation, Citigroup Inc., Credit Suisse Holdings (USA) Inc., DB USA Corporation, the Goldman Sachs Group Inc., HSBC North America Holdings Inc., JPMorgan Chase & Co., Morgan Stanley, Northern Trust Corporation, the PNC Financial Services Group Inc., State Street Corporation, TD Group US Holdings LLC, UBS Americas Holdings LLC, U.S. Bancorp, and Wells Fargo & Company.

3. The economics profession lost a lot of legitimacy with the public for their role in ignoring the crisis and appearing to be cheerleaders for whatever the banks wanted to do. The idea that all financial innovation is efficient, an idea that is core to much of financial economics, is one that many are now skeptical of.

4. The transcript of this press conference was accessed on July 30, 2020, at https://www.rev.com/blog/transcripts/jerome-powell-federal-reserve-coronavirus-press -conference-transcript.

5. In situations where experts have arcane knowledge and have been delegated decision-making power, they can have more influence. The Federal Reserve and monetary policy are a site where some have suggested this might be the case (Hirschman and Popp Berman, 2014).

References

Abolafia, Mitchel. 2004. "Framing Moves: Interpretive Politics at the Federal Reserve." *Journal of Public Administration Research and Theory* 14(3): 349–370.

———. 2010. "Narrative Construction as Sense-Making: How a Central Bank Thinks." *Organization Studies* 31(3): 349–367.

———. 2012. "Central Banking and the Triumph of Technical Rationality." In *The Oxford Handbook of the Sociology of Finance,* edited by Karin Knorr-Cetina and Alex Preda, 94–112. Oxford: Oxford University Press.

———. 2020. *Stewards of the Market: How the Federal Reserve Made Sense of the Financial Crisis.* Cambridge, MA: Harvard University Press.

Acharya, Viral, Thomas Cooley, Matthew Richardson, and Ingo Walter. 2009. "Manufacturing Tail Risk: A Perspective on the Financial Crisis of 2007–2009." *Foundations and Trends in Finance* 4(4): 247–325.

Acharya, Viral V., and Philipp Schnabl. 2010. "Do Global Banks Spread Global Imbalances? Asset-Backed Commercial Paper during the Financial Crisis of 2007–09." *IMF Economic Review* 58(1): 33–73.

Acharya, Viral, Philipp Schnabl, and Gustavo Suarez. 2013. "Securitization without Risk Transfer." *Journal of Financial Economics* 107(3): 515–536.

Adrian, Tobias, Brian Begalle, Adam Copeland, and Antoine Martin. 2011. "Repo and Securities Lending." Staff Report No. 529, New York, New York Federal Reserve.

Agarwal, Sumit, Amromin, Gene, Ben-David, Itzhak, Souphala Chomsisengphet, and Douglas D. Evanoff. 2013. "Predatory Lending and the Subprime Crisis." NBER Working Paper 19550. Accessed January 8, 2020. http://www.nber.org/papers/w19550.

Akerlof, George A., Paul M. Romer, Robert E. Hall, and N. Gregory Mankiw. 1993. "Looting: The Economic Underworld of Bankruptcy for Profit." *Brookings Papers on Economic Activity* 2:1–93.

Akerlof, George A., and Robert Schiller. 2009. *Animal Spirits*. Princeton, NJ: Princeton University Press.

Allen, Franklin, and Douglas Gale. 2007. *Understanding Financial Crises*. Oxford: Oxford University Press.

Alves, Marta Isabel Guerra. 2012. "Bank Failures in Europe during the Financial Crisis." Working Paper. ISCTE Business School Instituto Universitario de Lisboa.

American Banker. 1982a. "Longbrake to Join Washington Mutual." June 24, 1982, 3.

———. 1982b. "Washington Mutual, Broker Plan to Merge." April 26, 1982, 8.

———. 1983. "Seattle's Washington Mutual Blazes New Trail." May 17, 1983, 12.

———. 1988. "Citibank Appoints Head of Mortgage Securities." February 4, 1988, 4.

———. 2001. "Mortgage Rankings, 2001." April 5, 2001, 9.

———. 2007. "A Bet Vertical Integration Still Has Legs." September 13, 2007, 1.

American Securitization Forum. 2007. American Securitization Forum Newsletter. Washington, DC., January 2007, 4.

Anderson, Richard G., and Charles S. Gascon. 2009. "The Commercial Paper Market, the Fed, and the 2007–2009 Financial Crisis." *Review* (Federal Reserve Bank of St. Louis) 91(6): 589–612.

Ashcraft, Adam, Paul Goldsmith-Pinkham, and James Vickery. 2010. "MBS Ratings and the Mortgage Credit Boom." *Federal Reserve Bank of New York Staff Reports*, no. 449.

Ashcraft, Adam, and Til Schuermann. 2008. "Understanding the Securitization of Subprime Mortgage Credit." *Foundations and Trends in Finance* 2(3): 191–309.

Asset Securitization Report. 1994. "Countrywide Targets Home Equity and Securitization." February 7, 1994, 1–2.

———. 1998a. "Former Chase Head to Countrywide." June 29, 1998, 3.

———. 1998b. "Nonagency Market Best since 1994." May 4, 1998, 1-2.

———. 2001. "Can Mortgage Refinancing Save the American Economy?" October 15, 2001, 2–3.

———. 2004a. "ABS Researchers Ponder Supply, Spreads." June 14, 2004, 10.

———. 2004b. "U.S. ABS Supply Remains Slow, Autos Maintain Pace." May 17, 2004, 2.

Atlantic. 2010. "More Corruption: Bear Stearns Falsified Information as Raters Shrugged." May 14, 2010. https://www.theatlantic.com/business/archive/2010/05/more-corruption-bear-stearns-falsified-information-as-raters-shrugged/56753/.

Baez, Bien, and Mitchel Abolafia. 2002. "Bureaucratic Entrepreneurship and Institutional Change: A Sense-Making Approach." *Journal of Public Administration Research and Theory* 12(4): 525–552.

Barmat, Joan. 1990. "Securitization: An Overview." In *The Handbook of Asset-Backed Securities*, edited by Jess Lederman, 3–22. New York: New York Institute of Finance.

Barnett, Harold C. 2011. "The Securitization of Mortgage Fraud." In *Economic Crisis and Crime*, 65–84. Bingley, UK: Emerald Group.

———. 2013. "And Some with a Fountain Pen: Mortgage Fraud, Securitization, and the Subprime Bubble." In *How They Got Away with It: White Collar Criminals and the Financial Meltdown*, edited by Susan Will, Stephen Handelman, and David C. Brotherton, 104–129. New York: Columbia University Press.

Barnett-Hart, Anna Katherine. 2009. "The Story of the CDO Market Meltdown: An Empirical Analysis." Bachelor's thesis, Harvard College.

Barrett, Andrew. 1992. "Countrywide's Home Sweet Loans." *Business Week*, September 14, 1992, 86–87.

Barth, James R. 2004. *The Savings and Loan Crisis*. Amsterdam: Kluwer.

Barth, James R., and Philip R. Bartholomew. 1992. "The Thrift Industry Crisis: Revealed Weaknesses in the Federal Deposit Insurance System." In *The Reform of Federal Deposit Insurance*, edited by James R. Barth and R. Dan Brumbaugh. New York: Harper.

Barth, James, Daniel Brumbaugh, and James Wilcox. 2000. "The Repeal of Glass–Steagall and the Advent of Broad Banking." *Economic Perspectives* 14 (2): 191–204.

Baumer, Eric P., J. W. Andrew Ranson, Ashley N. Arnio, Ann Fulmer, and Shane De Zilwa. 2017. "Illuminating a Dark Side of the American Dream: Assessing the Prevalence and Predictors of Mortgage Fraud across US Counties." *American Journal of Sociology* 123(2): 549–603.

Bear Stearns. 2006. "Quick Guide to Non-agency Mortgage Backed Securities." September 2006.

———. Various years. *Annual Reports*.

Beck, Thorsten, Tao Chen, Chen Lin, and Frank M. Song. 2014. "Financial innovation: The bright and the dark sides." Available at SSRN 1991216 (2014).

Becketti, Sean. 1989. "The prepayment risk of mortgage backed securities." *Economic Review* February 1979: 43–57.

Beltratti, Andrea, and Rene Stulz. 2012. "The credit crisis around the globe: why did some banks perform better?" *Journal of Financial Economics* 105: 1–17.

Ben-David, Itzhak. 2011. "Financial Constraints and Inflated Home Prices during the Real Estate Boom." *American Economic Journal: Applied Economics* 3 (3): 55–87.

Benmelech, Efraim, and Jennifer Dlugosz. 2010. "The Credit Rating Crisis." NBER Working Paper. Cambridge, MA: National Bureau of Economic Research.

Bernanke, Ben S. 1983. "Nonmonetary Effects of the Financial Crisis in the Propagation of the Great Depression." *American Economic Review* 73(3): 257–276.

———. 2007. "The Subprime Mortgage Market." Accessed July 29, 2020. https://www.federalreserve.gov/newsevents/speech/bernanke20070517a.htm.

Bernanke, Ben S., Mark Gertler, and Simon Gilchrist. 1999. "The Financial Accelerator in a Quantitative Business Cycle Framework." In *Handbook of*

Macroeconomics, edited by J. B. Taylor and M. Woodford, 1341–1393. Amsterdam: Elsevier Science.

Bhagat, Sanjai, and Brian Bolton. 2014. "Financial Crisis and Bank Executive Incentive Compensation." *Journal of Corporate Finance* 25:313–341.

Bitner, Richard. 2008. *Greed, Fraud and Ignorance: A Subprime Insider's Look at the Mortgage Collapse.* Toronto, Canada: LTV Media.

Black, Deborah G., Kenneth D. Garbade, and William L. Silber. 1981. "The Impact of the GNMA Pass-Through Program on FHA Mortgage Costs." *Journal of Finance* 36(2): 457–469.

Black, William K. 2005a. *The Best Way to Rob a Bank Is to Own One: How Corporate Executives and Politicians Looted the S&L Industry.* Austin: University of Texas Press.

———. 2005b. "'Control Frauds' as Financial Super-Predators: How 'Pathogens' Make Financial Markets Inefficient." *Journal of Socio-Economics* 34(6): 734–755.

Bleckner, David. 1984. "Section 106 of the Secondary Mortgage Market Enhancement Act of 1984 and the need for overriding State Legislation." *Fordham Urban Law Review* 13: 682–723.

Blinder, Alan. 1998. *Central Banking in Theory and Practice.* Cambridge, MA: MIT Press.

———. 2013. *After the Music Stopped.* New York: Penguin Press.

Bord, Vitaly, and João A. C. Santos. 2012. "The Rise of the Originate-to-Distribute Model and the Role of Banks in Financial Intermediation." *Economic Policy Review* 18(2): 21–34.

Borio, Claudio. 2011. "Rediscovering the Macroeconomic Roots of Financial Stability Policy: Journey, Challenges, and a Way Forward." *Annual Review of Financial Economics* 3:87–117.

———. 2014. "The Financial Cycle and Macroeconomics: What Have We Learnt?" *Journal of Banking and Finance* 45:182–198.

Boyd, John H., and Mark Gertler. 1994. "U.S. Commercial Banking: Trends, Cycles, and Policy." *Federal Reserve of Minneapolis Quarterly Review* (Winter): 2–21.

Brayton, Flint, Andrew Levin, Ralph Tryon, and John C. Williams. 1997. "The Evolution of Macro Models at the Federal Reserve Board." *Carnegie-Rochester Series on Public Policy* 47:43–81.

Brendsel, Leland. 1996. "Securitization's Role in Housing Finance: The Special Contributions of Government Sponsored Entities." In *A Primer on Securitization,* edited by Leon T. Kendall and Michael J. Fishman, 17–30. Cambridge, MA: MIT Press.

Brumbaugh, R. Dan Jr., Andrew S. Carron, Dwight M. Jaffee, and William Poole. 1987. "Thrift Industry Crisis: Causes and Solutions." *Brookings Papers on Economic Activity* 1987(2): 349–388.

Brunnermeier, Markus K. 2009. "Deciphering the Liquidity and Credit Crunch 2007–2008." *Journal of Economic Perspectives* 23(1): 77–100.

Burrough, Brian. 2008. "Bringing Down Bear Stearns." *Vanity Fair,* August 2008. https://archive.vanityfair.com/article/2008/8/bringing-down-bear-stearns.

Calavita, Kitty, Robert Tillman, and Henry Pontell. 1997. "The Savings and Loan Debacle, Financial Crime, and the State." *Annual Review of Sociology* 23:19–38.

Callon, Michel, Yuval Millo, and Fabian Muniesa. 2007. *Market Devices.* Oxford: Wiley-Blackwell.

Capon, Noel. 1982. "Scoring Systems: A Critical Analysis." *Journal of Marketing* 46, no. 2 (Spring): 82–91.

Caprio, Gerard, and Daniela Klingebiel. 1996. "Bank Insolvency: Bad Luck, Bad Policy, or Bad Banking?" *Annual World Bank Conference on Development Economics* 79:1–26.

Carruthers, Bruce. 2010. "Knowledge and Liquidity: Institutions and Cognitive Foundations of the Subprime Crisis." In *Markets on Trial: The Economic Sociology of the U.S. Financial Crisis,* edited by M. Lounsbury and P. Hirsch, 157–182. Bingham, UK: Emerald.

———. 2013. " From Uncertainty toward Risk: The Case of Credit Ratings." *Socio-Economic Review* 11(3): 525–551.

Carruthers, Bruce, and Arthur Stinchcombe. 1999. "The Social Structure of Liquidity: Flexibility, Markets, and States." *Theory and Society* 28:253–282.

Cassidy, Harold. 1984. "A Review of the Federal Home Loan Bank Board's Adjustable-Rate Mortgage Regulations and the Current ARM Proposal." Federal Home Loan Bank Board, Office of Policy and Economic Research.

Cerulo, Karen A. 2006. *Never Saw It Coming.* Chicago: University of Chicago Press.

Chambers, Matthew, Carlos Garriga, and Donald E. Schlagenhauf. 2013. "Did Housing Policies Cause the Postwar Boom in Homeownership?" NBER Working Paper 18821. Cambridge, MA: National Bureau of Economic Research.

Chari, Varadarajan Venkata, and Patrick J. Kehoe. 2006. "Modern Macroeconomics in Practice: How Theory Is Shaping Policy." *Journal of Economic Perspectives* 20(4): 3–28.

Christensen, Clayton. 1997. *The Innovator's Dilemma.* Boston: Harvard Business School Press.

Citibank. Various years. *Annual Reports.*

Claessens, Stijn, Giovanni Dell'Ariccia, Deniz Igan, and Luc Laeven. 2010. "Cross-country Experiences and Policy Implications from the Global Financial Crisis." *Economic Policy* 25(62): 267–293.

Claessens, Stijn, Rudiger Dornbusch, and Yung Chul Park. 2001. "Contagion: Why Crises Spread and How They Can Be Stopped." In *International Financial Contagion,* edited by Stijn Claessens and Kristin Forbes, 19–41. Boston: Kluwer.

Claessens, Stijn, and Kristin Forbes. 2004. "International Financial Contagion: The Theory, Evidence, and Policy Implications." Paper presented at IMF's Roles in Emerging Market Economies, Amsterdam, the Netherlands, November 18–19, 2004.

Cohan, William D. 2010. *House of Cards: A Tale of Hubris and Wretched Excess on Wall Street*. New York: Doubleday.

Collins, M. Cary, and Peter J. Nigro. 2010. "Mortgage Origination Fraud: The Missing Links." *Criminology and Public Policy* 9:633.

Countrywide Financial. 1992. 10–4. Securities and Exchange Commission.

———. 1993. 10–4. Securities and Exchange Commission.

———. Various years. *Annual Reports*.

Covitz, Daniel, Nellie Liang, and Gustavo A. Suarez. 2013. "The Evolution of a Financial Crisis: Collapse of the Asset-Backed Commercial Paper Market." *Journal of Finance* 68(3): 815–849.

Crotty, James. 2009. "Structural Causes of the Global Financial Crisis: A Critical Assessment of the 'New Financial Architecture.'" *Cambridge Journal of Economics* 33(4): 563–580.

Cummings, J., and D. DiPasquale. 1997. *A Primer on the Secondary Mortgage Market*. Boston: City Research.

Currie, Anthony. 2007. "Buy or Build: The Vertical Integrator's Dilemma." *Mortgage Broker*, May 4, 22–26.

Dash, Eric. 2011. "F.D.I.C. Sues Ex-Chief of Big Bank That Failed." *New York Times*, March 17, 2011. http://www.nytimes.com/2011/03/18/business/18bank.html.

Davidoff, Steven M., Alan D. Morrison, and William J. Wilhelm Jr. 2012. "The SEC v. Goldman Sachs: Reputation, Trust, and Fiduciary Duties in Investment Banking." *Journal of Corporate Law* 37:529–553.

Davis, Gerald, and Mark Mizruchi. 1999. "The Money Center Cannot Hold: Commercial Banks in the U.S. System of Corporate Governance." *Administrative Science Quarterly* 44:215–239.

de la Merced, Michael J. 2012. "S.E.C. Investigates Residential Capital for Potential Fraud." *New York Times*, August 28, 2012. http://dealbook.nytimes.com/2012/08/28/s-e-c-investigates-rescap-for-potential-mortgage-fraud.

Delgadillo, Lucy M., Luke V. Erickson, and Kathleen W. Piercy. 2008. "Disentangling the Differences between Abusive and Predatory Lending: Professionals' Perspectives." *Journal of Consumer Affairs* 42(3): 313–334.

Dell'Ariccia, Giovanni, Deniz Igan, and Luc Laeven. 2012. "Credit Booms and Lending Standards: Evidence from the Subprime Mortgage Market." *Journal of Money, Credit and Banking* 44(2–3): 367–384.

Der Hovanesian, Mara. 2006. "Nightmare Mortgages." *Bloomberg Businessweek*, September 11, 2006. https://www.bloomberg.com/news/articles/2006-09-10/nightmare-mortgages.

DeYoung, Robert, and Tara Rice. 2004. "How Do Banks Make Money? The Fallacies of Fee Income." *Economic Perspectives* 28(4): 34–51.

Diehl, David, and Daniel McFarland. 2010. "Toward a Historical Sociology of Social Situations." *American Journal of Sociology* 115:1713–1752.

DiMaggio, Paul. 1997. "Culture and Cognition." *Annual Review of Sociology* 23: 263–287.

Eichengreen, Barry J. 2015. *Hall of Mirrors: The Great Depression, the Great Recession, and the Uses—and Misuses—of History.* New York: Oxford University Press.

Elsas, Ralf, Andreas Hackethal, and Markus Holzhäuser. 2010. "The Anatomy of Bank Diversification." *Journal of Banking and Finance* 34:1274–1287.

Engel, Kathleen C., and Patricia A. McCoy. 2001. "The CRA Implications of Predatory Lending." *Fordham University Law Journal* 29:1571–1593.

Engelen, Ewald, Ismail Erturk, Julie Froud, Adam Leaver, and Karel Williams. 2010. "Reconceptualizing Financial Innovation: Frame, Conjuncture and Bricolage." *Economy and Society* 39(1): 33–63.

Ewalt, Josephine Hedges. 1962. *A Business Reborn: The Savings and Loan Story, 1930–1960.* New York: American Savings and Loan Institute Press.

Federal Bureau of Investigation. 2007. "2007 Mortgage Fraud Report." Accessed January 10, 2015. http://www.fbi.gov/stats-services/publications/mortgagefraud-2007.

———. 2008. "2008 Mortgage Fraud Report." Accessed January 10, 2015. http://www.fbi.gov/stats-services/publications/mortgagefraud-2008.

———. 2010. "2010 Mortgage Fraud Report." Accessed January 10, 2015. http:// www.fbi.gov/stats-services/publications/mortgagefraud-2010.

Federal Deposit Insurance Corporation. 2006. "Challenges and FDIC Efforts Related to Predatory Lending." Report No. 06-011. Accessed January 10, 2015. http:// www.fdicoig.gov/reports06/06-011.pdf.

Federal Open Market Committee (FOMC). 2002. "Meeting of the Federal Open Market Committee on August 13, 2002." Washington, DC.

———. 2005a. "Meeting of the Federal Open Market Committee on February 1–2, 2005." Washington, DC.

———. 2005b. "Meeting of the Federal Open Market Committee on June 29–30, 2005." Washington, DC.

———. 2005c. "Meeting of the Federal Open Market Committee on December 13, 2005." Washington, DC.

———. 2006a. "Meeting of the Federal Open Market Committee on March 27–28, 2006." Washington, DC.

———. 2006b. "Meeting of the Federal Open Market Committee on September 20, 2006." Washington, DC.

———. 2006c. "Meeting of the Federal Open Market Committee on December 12, 2006." Washington, DC.

———. 2007a. "Meeting of the Federal Open Market Committee on March 20–21, 2007." Washington, DC.

———. 2007b. "Meeting of the Federal Open Market Committee on June 27–28, 2007." Washington, DC.

———. 2007c. "Meeting of the Federal Open Market Committee on September 18, 2007." Washington, DC.

———. 2007d. "Meeting of the Federal Open Market Committee on December 11, 2007." Washington, DC.

———. 2008a. "Meeting of the Federal Open Market Committee on January 29–30, 2008." Washington, DC.

———. 2008b. "Meeting of the Federal Open Market Committee on March 18, 2008." Washington, DC.

———. 2008c. "Meeting of the Federal Open Market Committee on April 29–30, 2008." Washington, DC.

———. 2008d. "Meeting of the Federal Open Market Committee on August 5, 2008." Washington, DC.

———. 2008e. "Meeting of the Federal Open Market Committee on September 16, 2008." Washington, DC.

———. 2008f. "Conference Call of the Federal Open Market Committee on September 29, 2008." Washington, DC.

———. 2008g. "Conference Call of the Federal Open Market Committee on October 7, 2008." Washington, DC.

———. 2008h. "FOMC Statement: Federal Reserve and Other Central Banks Announce Reductions in Policy Interest Rates."

———. 2008i. "Meeting of the Federal Open Market Committee on October 28–29, 2008." Washington, DC.

Federal Reserve. 2008. "Joint Statement by Treasury, Federal Reserve, and the FDIC on Citigroup." November 23, 2008. https://www.federalreserve.gov/newsevents/pressreleases/bcreg20081123a.htm.

———. 2019. "Dodd-Frank Stress Test." Washington, DC: Federal Reserve Board of Governors.

Fender, Ingo, and Janet Mitchell. 2005. "Structured Finance: Complexity, Risk and the Use of Ratings." *BIS Quarterly Review* (June): 67–81.

Ferguson, Charles. 2012. *Inside Job: The Financiers Who Pulled off the Heist of the Century.* Oxford: Oneworld.

Fetter, Daniel K. 2011. "How Do Mortgage Subsidies Affect Home Ownership? Evidence from the Mid-Century GI Bills." NBER Working Paper 17166. Cambridge, MA: National Bureau of Economic Research.

Financial Crimes Enforcement Network. 2008. "Mortgage Loan Fraud: An Update of Trends Based upon an Analysis of Suspicious Activity Reports." April 2008. Accessed December 23, 2019. https://www.fincen.gov/sites/default/files/shared/MortgageLoanFraudSARAssessment.pdf.

Financial Crisis Inquiry Commission. 2011. *Financial Crisis Inquiry Report.* Washington, DC: US Government Printing Office.

Financial Crisis Investigation Commission. 2010a. "Interview with Mary Haggerty, Bear Stearns." August 17, 2010. Rock Center for Corporate Governance, Stanford University. Accessed July 10, 2019. http://fcic.law.stanford.edu/interviews/view/162%200n%20July%2010,2019.

——. 2010b. "Memorandum for the Record: Interview with Tom Marano." April 19, 2010. Rock Center for Corporate Governance, Stanford University. Accessed July 7, 2019. https://fcic-static.law.stanford.edu/NARA.FCIC.2016-03-11/SCREENED%20Interviews/2010-04-19%20K%20Dubas%20MFR%20of%20Interview%20with%20Tom%20Marano%20(Bear)%20(copy)_1.pdf.

Fink, Lawrence D. 1996. "The Role of Pension Funds and Other Investors in Securitized Debt Markets." In *A Primer on Securitization,* edited by Leon T. Kendall and Michael J. Fishman, 117–128. Cambridge, MA: MIT Press.

Fligstein, Neil. 2001. *The Architecture of Markets.* Princeton, NJ: Princeton University Press.

Fligstein, Neil, Jonah Stuart Brundage, and Michael Schultz. 2017. "Seeing like the Fed: Culture, Cognition, and Framing in the Failure to Anticipate the Financial Crisis of 2008." *American Sociological Review* 82(5): 879–909.

Fligstein, Neil, and Adam Goldstein. 2010. "The Anatomy of the Mortgage Securitization Crisis." In *Markets on Trial: The Economic Sociology of the U.S. Financial Crisis,* edited by M. Lounsbury and P. Hirsch, 29–70. Bingham, UK: Emerald.

——. 2012. "A Long Strange Trip: The State and Mortgage Securitization, 1968–2010." In *The Oxford Handbook of the Sociology of Finance,* edited by K. Knorr Cetina and A. Preda, 339–357. Oxford: Oxford University Press.

Fligstein, Neil, and Jacob Habinek. 2014. "Sucker Punched by the Invisible Hand: The Spread of the Worldwide Financial Crisis, 2007–2010." *Socio-Economic Review* 12(4): 1–29.

Fligstein, Neil, and Doug McAdam. 2012. *A Theory of Fields.* New York: Oxford University Press.

Fligstein, Neil, and Alexander F. Roehrkasse. 2016. "The Causes of Fraud in the Financial Crisis of 2007 to 2009: Evidence from the Mortgage-Backed Securities Industry." *American Sociological Review* 81(4): 617–643.

Forbes, Kristin. 2004. "The Asian Flus and the Russian Virus: The International Transmission of Crises in Firm Level Data." *Journal of International Economics* 63:59–92.

Forbes, Kristin, and Roberto Rigobon. 2001. "Measuring Contagion." In *International Financial Contagion,* edited by Stijn Claessens and Kristin Forbes, 43–66. Boston: Kluwer.

Follain, James R., and Peter M Zorn. 1990. "The Unbundling of Residential Mortgage Finance." *Journal of Housing Research* 1:63–89.

Forrester, Julia Patterson. 2005. "Still Mortgaging the American Dream: Predatory Lending, Preemption, and Federally Supported Lenders." *University of Cincinnati Law Review* 74: 1303–1347.

Fortune Magazine. 2007. "America's Most Admired Companies." Accessed January 6, 2020. https://archive.fortune.com/magazines/fortune/mostadmired/2007/snapshots/2835.html.

———. 2008. "The Last Days of Bear Stearns." March 31, 2008. https://archive.fortune.com/2008/03/28/magazines/fortune/boyd_bear.fortune/index.htm.

———. 2010. "How the Roof Fell in on Countrywide." December 23, 2010. https://fortune.com/2010/12/23/how-the-roof-fell-in-on-countrywide/.

Fourcade, Marion. 2009. *Economists and Societies: Discipline and Profession in the United States, Britain, and France, 1890s to 1990s*. Princeton, NJ: Princeton University Press.

Frame, W. Scott, and Lawrence J. White. 2004. "Empirical Studies of Financial Innovation: Lots of Talk, Little Action?" *Journal of Economic Literature* 42 (March): 116–144.

———. 2010. "The Federal Home Loan Bank System: Current Issues in Perspective." *Reforming Rules and Regulations: Laws, Institutions, and Implementation* 22:255–274.

———. 2012. "Technological Change, Financial Innovation, and Diffusion in Banking." In *The Oxford Handbook of Banking*, 2nd ed., edited by Allen N. Berger, Philip Molyneux, and John O. S, 262–285. Wilson. New York: Oxford University Press.

Frieden, Terry. 2004. "FBI Warns of Mortgage Fraud 'Epidemic.'" CNN. September 17, 2004. http://www.cnn.com/2004/LAW/09/17/mortgage.fraud/.

Friesen, Mark. 2008. "Chase Mortgage Memo Pushes Up Cheats and Tricks." *Oregonian / Oregon Live*, March 27, 2008. http://www.oregonlive.com/business/index.ssf/2008/03/chase_mortgage_memo_pushes_che.html.

Furfine, Craig H. 2014. "Complexity and Loan Performance: Evidence from the Securitization of Commercial Mortgages." *Review of Corporate Finance Studies* 2(2): 154–187.

Furletti, Mark. 2002. "An Overview and History of Credit Reporting." Federal Reserve Bank of Philadelphia Occasional Paper.

Gans, Kale. 2011. "Anatomy of a Mortgage Meltdown: The Study of the Subprime Crisis, the Role of Fraud." *Idaho Law Review* 48:123–158.

Gennaioli, Nicola, Andrei Shleifer, and Robert W. Vishny. 2010. "Neglected Risks, Financial Innovation, and Financial Fragility." NBER Working Paper 16068. Cambridge, MA: National Bureau of Economic Research.

Gerardi, Kristopher, Harvey S. Rosen, and Paul Willen. 2010. "Do Households Benefit from Financial Deregulation and Innovation? The Case of the Mortgage Market." *Journal of Finance* 65(1): 333–360.

Gilber, R. Anton. 1986. "Requiem for Regulation Q: What It Did and Why It Passed." Federal Reserve Bank of St. Louis, February 1986, 22–37.

Goffman, Erving. 1974. *Frame Analysis: An Essay on the Organization of Experience.* Cambridge, MA: Harvard University Press.

Goldstein, Adam, and Neil Fligstein. 2017. "Financial Markets as Production Markets: The Industrial Roots of the Mortgage Meltdown." *Socio-Economic Review* 15(3): 483–510.

Goodfriend, Marvin. 2007. "How the World Achieved Consensus on Monetary Policy." *Journal of Economic Perspectives* 21(4): 47–68.

Goodfriend, Marvin, and Robert G. King. 1997. "The New Neoclassical Synthesis and the Role of Monetary Policy." In *NBER Macroeconomics Annual: 1997,* edited by Ben S. Bernanke and Julio J. Rotenberg, 231–283. Cambridge, MA: MIT Press.

Goodman, Peter S., and Gretchen Morgenson. 2008. "Saying Yes, WaMu Built Empire on Shaky Loans." *New York Times,* December 27, 2008. http://www.ny times.com/2008/12/28/business/28wamu.html?sq=GRETCHEN MORGENSON &st=cse&scp=2&pagewanted=all.

Gorman, Elizabeth H., and Rebecca L. Sandefur. 2011. "Golden Age, Quiescence, and Revival: How the Sociology of Professions Became the Study of Knowledge-Based Work." *Work and Occupations* 38(3): 275–302.

Gorton, Gary. 2010. *Slapped by the Invisible Hand.* New York: Oxford.

Gorton, Gary, and Richard Rosen. 1995. "Corporate Control, Portfolio Choice, and the Decline of Banking." *Journal of Finance* 50(5): 1377–1420.

Gorton, Gary, and Nicholas S. Souleles. 2005. "Special Purpose Vehicles and Securitization." NBER Working Paper 11190. Cambridge, MA: National Bureau of Economic Research.

Government Accounting Office. 2019. *Prolonged Conservatorships of Fannie Mae and Freddie Mac Prompt Need for Reform.* Washington, DC: US Government Printing Office.

Grebler, Leo, David M. Blank, and Louis Winnick. 1956. *Capital Formation in Residential Real Estate: Trends and Prospects.* Cambridge, MA: NBER Books.

Green, Richard, and Susan Wachter. 2005. "The U.S. Mortgage in Historical and International Contexts." *Journal of Economic Perspectives* 19(4): 93–114.

Greenwood, Robin, and David Scharfstein. 2013. "The Growth of Modern Finance." *Journal of Economic Perspectives* 27, no. 2 (Spring): 3–28.

Griffin, John M., and Gonzalo Maturana. 2016. "Who Facilitated Misreporting in Securitized Loans?" *Review of Financial Studies* 29(2): 384–419.

Halliburton, Robert A. 1939. *The Real Estate Bond House.* Franklin: Indiana University.

Harriss, C. Lowell. 1951. *History and Policies of the Home Owners' Loan Corporation.* Cambridge, MA: NBER Books.

Haveman, Heather A., and Hayagreeva Rao. 1997. "Structuring a Theory of Moral Sentiments: Institutional and Organizational Coevolution in the Early Thrift Industry." *American Journal of Sociology* 102(6): 1606–1651.

———. 2007. "The Winds of Change: The Progressive Movement and the Bureaucratization of Thrift." *American Sociological Review* 72:117–142.

He, Jie, Jun Qian, and Philip E. Strahan. 2012. "Credit Ratings and the Evolution of the Mortgage-Backed Securities Market." *American Economic Review Papers and Proceedings* 101:131–135.

Hendershott, Patric, and Robert VanOrder. 1989. "Integration of Mortgage and Capital Markets and the Accumulation of Residential Capital." NBER Working Paper 2847. Cambridge, MA: National Bureau of Economic Research.

Hendrickson, Jill. 2001. "The Long and Bumpy Road to Glass-Steagall Reform." *American Journal of Economics and Sociology* 60:849–874.

Herzog, Thomas. 2009. *History of Mortgage Finance with an Emphasis on Mortgage Insurance.* New York: Society of Actuaries.

Hess, Christopher M., and Chris F. Kemerer. 1994. "Computerized Loan Origination Systems: An Industry Case Study of the Electronic Markets Hypothesis." *MIS Quarterly* 18, no. 3 (September): 251–275.

Hirschman, Daniel, and Elizabeth Popp Berman. 2014. "Do Economists Make Policies?" *Socio-Economic Review* 12:779–811.

Holmes, Douglas. 2014. *Economy of Words: Communicative Imperatives in Central Banks.* Chicago: University of Chicago Press.

Huffington Post. 2014. "Financial Crisis Villain Doesn't Understand Why Everyone Is So Mad at Him." Accessed January 3, 2020. https://www.huffpost.com/entry/angelo-mozilo-lawsuit_n_5752152.

Immergluck, Daniel. 2010. *Foreclosed: High-Risk Lending, Deregulation, and the Undermining of America's Mortgage Market.* Ithaca, NY: Cornell University Press.

Independent Evaluation Office. 2010. *IMF Performance in the Run-Up to the Financial and Economic Crisis.* Washington, DC: International Monetary Fund Press.

Inside Mortgage Finance. 2009. *Mortgage Market Statistical Annual.* Bethesda, MD: Inside Mortgage Finance.

Jacobides, Michael G. 2005. "Industry Change through Vertical Disintegration: How and Why Markets Emerged in Mortgage Banking." *Academy of Management Journal* 48(3): 465–498.

Jaffee, Dwight, and Kenneth Rosen. 1990. "Mortgage Securitization Trends." *Journal of Housing Research* 1:117–137.

James, Christopher, and Joel Houston. 1996. "Evolution or Extinction: Where Are the Banks Headed?" *Journal of Applied Corporate Finance* 9:8–23.

Jarrow, Robert. 2011. "The Role of ABS, CDS, and CDOs in the Credit Crisis and the Economy." Working paper, Johnson School of Management, Cornell University.

Jiang, Wei, Ashlyn Aiko Nelson, and Edward Vytlacil. 2014. "Liar's Loan? Effects of Origination Channel and Information Falsification on Mortgage Delinquency." *Review of Economics and Statistics* 96(1): 1–18.

Johnson, Simon, and James Kwak. 2010. *13 Bankers: The Wall Street Takeover and the Next Financial Meltdown.* New York: Pantheon.

Johnston, Jarrod, and Jeff Madura. 2005. "Valuing the Potential Transformation of Banks into Financial Service Conglomerates: Evidence from the Citigroup Merger." *Financial Review* 35(2): 17–36.

Jones, Oliver, and Leo Grebler. 1961. *The Secondary Mortgage Market.* Los Angeles: University of California, Los Angeles.

J.P. Morgan. 2010. Loan Performance. New York: J.P. Morgan Research.

Kaufman, Gerald. 1993. "The Diminishing Role of Commercial Banking in the U.S. Economy." In *The Crisis in American Banking,* edited by L. H. White, 139–159. New York: New York University Press.

Kaufman, Henry. 2009. *The Road to Financial Reformation.* Hoboken, NJ: John Wiley and Sons.

Kendall, Leon T. 1962. *The Savings and Loan Business: Its Purposes, Functions, and Economic Justification.* Englewood Cliffs, NJ: Prentice Hall.

———. 1996. "Securitization: A New Era in American Finance." In *A Primer on Securitization,* edited by Leon T. Kendall and Michael J. Fishman, 1–16. Cambridge, MA: MIT Press.

Kendall, Leon T., and Michael J. Fishman, eds. 1996. *A Primer on Securitization.* Cambridge, MA: MIT Press.

Kennedy, Jane, and Robert Bowen. 2008. *WaMu's Option Arm Strategy.* University of Washington Business School Case Study, October 2008.

Kersnar, S. 2001. "Who Gains from Fannie's and Freddie's Internet?" *Mortgage Technology* 8(7): 18–23.

Klaman, Saul B. 1959. *The Postwar Rise of Mortgage Companies.* Cambridge: NBER Books.

Klapper, Richard H., Michael T. Tomaino Jr., and Christopher J. Dunne. 2009. "Submission on Behalf of Goldman, Sachs & Co." Securities and Exchange Commission. File No. HO-10911. Accessed January 10, 2015. http://online.wsj.com /public/resources/documents/GSWellsSubmission.pdf.

Klee, Kenneth N., and Brendt C. Butler. 2002. "Asset-Backed Securitization, Special Purpose Vehicles and Other Securitization Issues." *Uniform Commercial Code Law Journal* 35(2): 23–68.

Kochen, Neil. 1996. "Securitization from the Investor View." In *A Primer on Securitization,* edited by Leon T. Kendall and Michael J. Fishman, 103–117. Cambridge, MA: MIT Press.

Koester, Genevieve. 1939. "Chicago Real Estate Bonds, 1919–1938: I. Corporate History." *Journal of Land and Public Utility Economics* 15(1): 49–58.

Koller, Cynthia A. 2012. *White Collar Crime in Housing: Mortgage Fraud in the United States*. El Paso, TX: LFB Scholarly.

Kramer, Bruce, and Gyan Sinha. 2006. "Bear Stearns Quick Guide to Non-agency Mortgage Backed Securities." Bear Stearns, September 2006, 7. https://quant labs.net/academy/download/free_quant_instituitional_books_/%5BBear%20 Stearns%5D%20Bear%20Stearns%20Quick%20Guide%20to%20Non-Agency %20Mortgage-Back%20Securities.pdf.

Kroszner, Robert, and Philip Strahan. 2005. "Bank Regulations in the United States: Causes, Consequences and Implications for the Future." In *Economic Regulation and Its Reform: What Have We Learned?*, edited by Nancy Rose, 485–543. Chicago: University of Chicago Press.

Kurland, Stanford, and Eric G. Flamholtz. 2005. "The Transformation from Entrepreneurship to Professional Management at Countrywide Financial Corporation." *International Journal of Entrepreneurship Education* 3(1): 1–18.

LaCour-Little, Michael. 2000. "The Evolving Role of Technology in Mortgage Finance." *Journal of Housing Research* 11:173–201.

Laeven, Luc, and Fabien Valencia. 2008. "Systemic Banking Crises: A New Database." IMF Working Paper No. 08 / 224. Washington, DC: International Monetary Fund.

Lea, Michael J. 1992. "Sources of Funds for Mortgage Finance." *Journal of Housing Research* 1: 390–421.

———. 1996. "Innovation and the Cost of Mortgage Credit: A Historical Perspective." *Housing Policy* 7(1): 147–174.

Lerner, Josh. 2006. "The New New Financial Thing: The Origins of Financial Innovation." *Journal of Financial Economics* 79:223–255.

Lerner, Josh, and Peter Tufano. 2011. "The Consequences of Financial Innovation: A Counterfactual Research Agenda." *Annual Review of Financial Economics* 3(1): 41–85.

Levine, Jonathan. 2007. "The Vertical Integration Strategy." *Mortgage Banking*, February 1, 2007: 58–65.

Levine, Ross. 1997. "Financial Development and Economic Development: A Review and Agenda." *Journal of Economic Literature* 35:688–726.

Lewis, Michael. 1990. *Liar's Poker*. New York: Penguin.

———. 2010. *The Big Short*. New York: Norton.

Leyshon, Andrew, and Nigel Thrift. 2007. "The Capitalization of Almost Everything." *Theory, Culture, and Society* 24:97–115.

Lin, Ken-Hou, and Donald Tomaskovic-Devey. 2013. "Financialization and US Income Inequality, 1970–2008." *American Journal of Sociology* 118:1284–1329.

Lipman, James. 1984. "Home Buying Process Is Changing Rapidly because of Technology." *Wall Street Journal*, January 25, 1984, 1.

Lipuma, Edward, and Benjamin Lee. 2004. *Financial Derivatives and the Globalization of Risk*. Durham, NC: Duke University Press.

Lo, Andrew. 2012. "Reading about the Financial Crisis: A 21-Book Review." *Journal of Economic Literature* 50:151–178.

Longstaff, Francis A. 2010. "The Subprime Credit Crisis and Contagion in Financial Markets." *Journal of Financial Economics* 97:436–450.

Lounsbury, Michael, and Paul Hirsch. 2010. *Markets on Trial: The Economic Sociology of the U.S. Financial Crisis*. Bingham, UK: Emerald.

Loutskina, Elena. 2011. "The Role of Securitization in Bank Liquidity and Funding Management." *Journal of Financial Economics* 100:663–684.

Loutskina, Elena, and Philip Strahan. 2006. "Securitization and the Declining Impact of Bank Financial Condition on Loan Supply: Evidence from Mortgage Acceptance Rates." Working paper, Carroll School of Management, Boston College.

Lowenstein, Roger. 2010. *The End of Wall Street*. New York: Penguin.

Lown, Cara S., Carol L. Osler, Philip E. Strahan, and Amir Sufi. 2000. "The Changing Landscape of the Financial Services Industry: What Lies Ahead?" *FRBNY Economic Policy Review* (October): 39–54.

Lucas, Robert E. 1976. "Econometric Policy Evaluation: A Critique." In *Carnegie-Rochester Conference Series on Public Policy*, 1:19–46. New York: North-Holland.

MacKenzie, Donald. 2011. "The Credit Crisis as a Problem in the Sociology of Knowledge." *American Journal of Sociology* 116(6): 1778–1841.

Malone, Thomas, Joanne Yates, and Robert Benjamin. 1987. "Electronic Markets and Electronic Hierarchies." *Communications of the ACM* 6:485–497.

Markus, M. Lynn, Andrew Dutta, Charles W. Steinfield, and Rolf T. Wigand. 2005. "The Computerization Movement in the US Home Mortgage Industry: Automated Underwriting from 1980 to 2004." In *Computerization Movements and Technology Diffusion: From Mainframes to Ubiquitous Computing*, edited by Kenneth Kraemer and Michael Elliott, 115–144. Medford, NJ: Information Today.

Martin, John Levi. 2010. "Life's a Beach, but You're an Ant, and Other Unwelcome News for the Sociology of Culture." *Poetics* 38:228–243.

Mayer, Christopher. 2011. "Housing Bubbles: A Survey." *Annual Review of Economics* 3:559–677.

Mayer, Christopher, Karen Pence, and Shane Sherlund. 2009. "The Rise in Mortgage Defaults." *Journal of Economic Perspectives* 23:27–50.

Mayo, Justin, and Melissa Allison. 2005. "WaMu Has Stake in Risky, Sub-prime Arena." *Seattle Times*, November 13, 2005, 24.

McConnell, John J., and Stephen A. Buser. 2011. "The Origins and Evolution of the Market for Mortgage-Backed Securities." *Annual Review of Financial Economics* 3:173–192.

McGarity, Mary. 2006. "Subprime Mortgages." *Mortgage Banking,* December, 2–4.

McGrath, Ben. 2010. "The Movement: The Rise of Tea Party Activism." *New Yorker.* https://www.newyorker.com/tag/tea-party-movement.

McLean, Bethany, and Joe Nocera. 2010. *All the Devils Are Here.* New York: Penguin.

Megbolugbe, Isaac F., and Peter D. Linneman. 1993. "Home Ownership." *Urban Studies* 30(4–5): 659–682.

Merrill Lynch. 2006. "Merrill Lynch Announces Agreement to Acquire First Franklin." Press release, September 5, 2006.

Merton, Robert C. 1992. "Financial Innovation and Economic Performance." *Journal of Applied Corporate Finance* 4(4): 12–22.

———. 2015. *House of Debt: How They (and You) Caused the Great Recession, and How We Can Prevent It from Happening Again.* Chicago: University of Chicago Press.

———. 2017. "Fraudulent Income Overstatement on Mortgage Applications during the Credit Expansion of 2002 to 2005." *Review of Financial Studies* 30, no. 6 (June): 1832–1864.

Miller, Merton. 1986. "Financial Innovation: The Last Twenty Years and the Next." *Journal of Financial and Quantitative Analysis* 21, no. 4 (December): 459–471.

Minsky, Herman. 2008. *Stabilizing an Unstable Economy.* New York: McGraw Hill.

Mishkin, Fredric. 2007. "Housing and the Monetary Transmission Mechanism." Accessed July 29, 2020. https://www.kansascityfed.org/publications/research /escp/symposiums/escp-2007.

Moench, Emanuel, James Vickery, and Diego Aragon. 2010. "Why Is the Rate of Adjustable Rate Mortgages So Low?" New York Federal Reserve. Accessed January 7, 2020. https://www.newyorkfed.org/research/current_issues/ci16-8.html.

Morgan Stanley. 2006. "Morgan Stanley to Acquire Saxon Capital for $706 Million." Press release.

Mortgage Banking. 2002. "Housing." June 1, 2002, 36–37.

———. 2004. "Editorial." May 1, 2004, 7.

———. 2005. "Transition and Vertical Integration." September 1, 2005, 3–4.

Mortgage Servicing News. 2005. "Nontraditional Loans Responsible for 85% of Profits." July 2, 2005, 1093.

Morton, James E. 1956. *Urban Mortgage Lending.* Princeton, NJ: Princeton University Press.

Moser, Thomas. 2003. "What Is International Financial Contagion?" *International Finance* 6:157–178.

Muniesa, Fabian, Yuval Millo, and Michel Callon. 2007. "An Introduction to Market Devices." *Sociological Review* 55:1–12.

Muolo, Paul. 2005. "Nervous Times." *Mortgage Strategy,* October 17, 2005, 43.

Nadauld, Taylor D., and Shane M. Sherlund. 2013. "The Impact of Securitization on the Expansion of Subprime Credit." *Journal of Financial Economics* 107:454–476.

National Mortgage News. 1982. "New Law Changes Products." May 13, 1982, 4.

———. 1986a. "Bear Stearns Conduit Will Securitize Jumbos." March 31, 1986, 2.

———. 1986b. "MBS Issuance High." October 13, 1986, 1.

———. 1986c. "Year Ends Financing Rush." December 22, 1986, 1.

———. 1987a. "Thrift Debt Gets Strong Pricing." February 16, 1987, 3.

———. 1987b. "Washington Mutual Is Successful Small Financial Supermarket." May 25, 1987, 3–4.

———. 1988. "Second Tier Issuers Advance." January 11, 1988, 2.

———. 1989a. "Washington Mutual Going Back to Its Roots." September 11, 1989, 4.

———. 1989b. "Washington Mutual Is 100 and Going Strong." October 23, 1989, 10–11.

———. 1990a. "Bear, Gruntal Launch CMO Investment Fund." November 12, 1990, 3–4.

———. 1990b. "Mortgage Rankings." December 31, 1990, 16–17.

———. 1991a. "Analysts Like Stock of Washington Mutual." September 30, 1991, 23.

———. 1991b. "Countrywide Raises $160MM." September 30, 1991, 4.

———. 1992. "WAMU Stock Draws Raves from Analysts." February 10, 1992, 7.

———. 1993a. "Countrywide Explores Alternative Products." November 8, 1993, 5.

———. 1993b. "Countrywide Has Conduit." February 13, 1993, 3.

———. 1994a. "Citibank Committed to Grow MBS Business." October 10, 1994, 1.

———. 1994b. "Countrywide Buys Title Company." March 14, 1994, 6.

———. 1994c. "Countrywide Has Outsourcing for Brokers." May 23, 1994, 7.

———. 1994d. "Financing Is Available through Prodigy." March 22, 1994, 3.

———. 1996a. "Commercial Paper Option for Lenders." January 22, 1996, 23.

———. 1996b. "Countrywide Ads Target Retail Share." January 29, 1996, 6.

———. 1997a. "Issues Getting Magnified." March 3, 1997, 4.

———. 1997b. "Two CEOs Seek to Dominate Organizations." August 25, 1997, 1.

———. 1999. "WAMU Buys Long Beach Financial." May 29, 1999, 1.

———. 2005. "Nonconventional Market Booming." March 10, 2005, 1–2.

New York Times. 2007a. "Trading Blame for Implosion in Subprime Mortgages." May 8, 2007. https://www.nytimes.com/2007/05/08/business/worldbusiness/08iht-subprime.1.5613647.html?searchResultPosition=1.

———. 2007b. "Fed Chief Addresses Foreclosures." May 18, 2007. https://www.nytimes.com/2007/05/18/business/18fed.html.

———. 2007c. "Stopping the Subprime Crisis." July 25, 2007. https://www.nytimes.com/2007/07/25/opinion/25rosner.html.

———. 2008a. "Greenspan Shocked That Free Markets Are Flawed." October 23, 2008. https://www.nytimes.com/2008/10/23/business/worldbusiness/23iht-gspan.4.17206624.html.

———. 2008b. "Investment Banking Leader at Citigroup Is Leaving." July 22, 2008. https://www.nytimes.com/2008/07/22/business/22citi1.html.

———. 2008c. "Citigroup Saw No Red Flags Even as It Made Bolder Bets." November 22, 2008. https://www.nytimes.com/2008/11/23/business/23citi.html?_r=1&hp =&pagewanted=print.

Nguyen, Tomson H., and Henry N. Pontell. 2010. "Mortgage Origination Fraud and the Global Economic Crisis." *Criminology and Public Policy* 9(3): 591–612.

O'Neil, Cathy. 2016. *Weapons of Math Destruction*. New York: Crown Books.

Opelka, Frederick G. 1994. "Toward Paperless Mortgages." *Savings and Community Banker* 3(1): 39–40.

Origination News. 2006. "FBR: Market Paying Up for Payment Option ARMs." August 2006, 44.

Palgrave Dictionary of Economics. 2008. Online ed. Accessed October 15, 2015. http://www.dictionaryofeconomics.com/article?id=pde2008_M000370&edi tion=current&q=macroeconomics&topicid=&result_number=1.

Park, Yoon-Shik. 2009. "The Role of Financial Innovations in the Global Financial Crisis." *Seoul Journal of Economics* 22:187–202.

Passas, Nicos. 2005. "Lawful, but Awful: Legal Corporate Crimes." *Journal of Socio-economics* 34(6): 771–786.

Patterson, Laura A., and Cynthia Koller. 2011. "Diffusion of Fraud through Subprime Lending: The Perfect Storm." In *Economic Crisis and Crime*, edited by M. Deflem, 25–45. Bingley, UK: Emerald.

Peek, Joe. 1990. "A Call to ARMs: Adjustable Rate Mortgages in the 1980s." *New England Economic Review* (March): 47–61.

Piskorski, Tomasz, Amit Seru, and James Witkin. 2015. "Asset Quality Misrepresentation by Financial Intermediaries: Evidence from RMBS Market." *Journal of Finance* 70(6): 2635–2678.

Plosser, Charles I. 1989. "Understanding Real Business Cycles." *Journal of Economic Perspectives* 3(3): 51–77.

Poon, Martha. 2007. "Scorecards as Devices for Consumer Credit: The Case of Fair, Isaac & Company Incorporated." *Sociological Review* 55:284–306.

———. 2009. "From New Deal Institutions to Capital Markets: Commercial Consumer Risk Scores and the Making of Subprime Mortgage Finance." *Accounting, Organizations and Society* 34:654–674.

Post, Mitchell. 1992. "Evolution of the Commercial Paper Market since 1980." *Federal Reserve Bulletin* 78(12): 879–892.

Pozsar, Zoltan, Tobias Adrian, Adam Ashcraft, and Hayley Boesky. 2011. "Shadow Banking." *Federal Reserve Bank of New York Policy Review* 8:1–17.

Prasad, Monica. 2012. *The Land of Too Much: American Abundance and the Paradox of Poverty*. Cambridge, MA: Harvard University Press.

Preda, Alex. 2007. "The Sociological Approach to Financial Markets." *Journal of Economic Surveys* 21:506–528.

Purnanandam, Amiyatosh. 2011. "Originate to Distribute Model and the Subprime Mortgage Crisis." *Review of Financial Studies* 24(6): 1881–1915.

Pyburn, Allison. 2005. "CDO Machine? Managers, Mortgage Companies, Happy to Keep Fuel Coming." *Asset Securitization Report,* May 23, 2005.

Quinn, Sarah. 2019. *American Bonds: How Credit Markets Shaped a Nation.* Princeton, NJ: Princeton University Press.

Ranieri, Lewis. 1996. "The Origins of Securitization, Sources of Its Growth, and Its Future Potential." In *A Primer on Securitization,* edited by Leon T. Kendall and Michael J. Fishman, 31–44. Cambridge, MA: MIT Press.

Reinhart, Carmen, and Kenneth Rogoff. 2009a. "The Aftermath of the Financial Crisis." *American Economic Review* 99:466–472.

———. 2009b. *This Time Is Different: Eight Centuries of Financial Folly.* Princeton, NJ: Princeton University Press.

Renuart, Elizabeth. 2004. "An Overview of the Predatory Mortgage Lending Process." *Housing Policy Debate* 15(3): 467–502.

Romer, Thomas, and Barry R. Weingast. 1991. "Political Foundations of the Thrift Debacle." In *Politics and Economics in the Eighties,* edited by Alberto Alesina and Geoffrey Carliner, 175–214. Chicago: University of Chicago Press.

Rona-Tas, Akos, and Stephanie Hiss. 2010. "The Role of Ratings in the Subprime Mortgage Crisis: The Art of Corporate and the Science of Consumer Credit Rating." In *Markets on Trial,* edited by M. Lounsbury and P. Hirsch, 115–156. Bingley, UK: Emerald.

Rose, Andrew, and Michael Spiegel. 2010. "Cross Country Causes and Consequences of the Crisis." NBER Working Paper 16243. Cambridge, MA: National Bureau of Economic Research.

Rose, Peter, and Richard Haney Jr. 1992. "The Players in the Primary Mortgage Market." *Journal of Housing Research* 1:91–116.

Rosen, Harvey, and Kenneth Rosen. 1980. "Federal Taxes and Home Ownership: Evidence from Time Series." *Journal of Political Economy* 88(1): 59–75.

Rugh, Jacob S., Len Albright, and Douglas S. Massey. 2015. "Race, Space, and Cumulative Disadvantage: A Case Study of the Subprime Lending Collapse." *Social Problems* 62(2): 186–218.

Ryback, William. 2010. "Case Study on Bear Stearns." University of Toronto Leadership Centre.

Ryder, Nicholas. 2014. 'The Global Financial Crisis and Mortgage Fraud—the Untold Story." *Financial Regulation International* 6:14–16.

Sabry, Faten, Sungi Lee, and Linh Nguyen. 2017. "Trends in Credit Crisis Settlements." NERA Consulting, September 18, 2017. https://www.nera.com/content/dam /nera/publications/2017/Trends%20In%20Credit%20Crisis%20Settlements%20 -%20Law360.pdf.

San Francisco Chronicle. 2008. "Washington Mutual Rewarded Issuance of Risky Loans." March 22, 2008. http://www.sfgate.com/business/article/Washington -Mutual-rewarded-issuance-of-risky-loans-2374992.php.

Sanders, Anthony. 2008. "The Nonconventional Market and Its Role in the Financial Crisis." *Journal of Housing Economics* 17:254–261.

Sbordone, Argea M., Andrea Tambalotti, Krishna Rao, and Kieran James Walsh. 2010. "Policy Analysis Using DSGE Models: An Introduction." *FRBNY Economic Policy Review* 16(2): 23–43.

Scharfstein, David S., and Adi Sunderam. 2013. "Concentration in Mortgage Lending, Refinancing Activity and Mortgage Rates." NBER Working Paper 19156. Cambridge, MA: National Bureau of Economic Research.

Schiller, Robert. 2015. *Irrational Exuberance.* Princeton, NJ: Princeton University Press.

Schorfheide, Frank, Keith Sill, and Maxym Kryshko. 2010. "DSGE Model-Based Forecasting of Non-modelled Variables." *International Journal of Forecasting* 26(2): 348–373.

Securities Industry and Financial Markets Association. 2019. "U.S. Agency Debt Outstanding." Accessed October 20, 2019. https://www.sifma.org/resources/research /us-agency-debt-outstanding/.

Sellon, Gordon Jr. 1990. "The Role of Government in Promoting Home Ownership: The U.S. Experience." *Economic Review* (July–August 1990): 37–44.

Sellon, Gordon Jr., and VanNahmen, David. 1988. "The Securitization of Housing Finance." *Economic Review* (Federal Reserve Bank of Kansas City) 73(7): 3–20.

Sherman, Mathew. 2009. "A Short History of Financial Deregulation in the United States." Center for Economic and Policy Research, Washington, DC.

Silber, William L. 1983. "The Process of Financial Innovation." *American Economic Review* 73, no. 2 (May): 89–95.

Smith, Yves. 2009. *Econned: How Unenlightened Self Interest Undermined Democracy and Corrupted Capitalism.* New York: Pantheon.

Snowden, Kenneth A. 1995. "The Evolution of Inter-regional Mortgage Lending Channels, 1870–1940." In *Coordination and Information: Historical Perspectives on the Organization of Enterprise,* edited by Naomi Lameroux and Daniel Raffe, 209–256. Chicago: University of Chicago Press.

———. 2010. "The Anatomy of a Residential Mortgage Crisis: A Look Back to the 1930s." NBER Working Paper 16244. Cambridge, MA: National Bureau of Economic Research.

Solow, Robert. 2008. "The State of Macroeconomics." *Journal of Economic Perspectives* 22(1): 243–246.

Starbuck, William H., and Frances Milliken. 1988. "Executives' Perceptual Filters: What They Notice and How They Make Sense." In *The Executive Effect: Con-*

cepts and Methods for Studying Top Managers, edited by Donald C. Hambrick, 35–66. Greenwich, CT: JAI.

Stigum, Marcia. 1989. *The Repo and Reverse Markets.* Homewood, IL: Dow Jones-Irwin.

Stiroh, Kevin J., and Adrienne Rumble. 2006. "The Dark Side of Diversification: The Case of US Financial Holding Companies." *Journal of Banking and Finance* 30:2131–2161.

Stone, Amey, and Mike Brewster. 2002. *King of Capital: Sandy Weill and the Making of Citigroup.* New York: John Wiley and Sons.

Straka, John W. 2000. "A Shift in the Mortgage Landscape: The 1990s Move to Automated Credit Evaluations." *Journal of Housing Research* 11(2): 207–232.

Swan, Peter L. 2009. "The Political Economy of the subprime Crisis: Why Subprime Was So Attractive to Its Creators." *European Journal of Political Economy* 25:124–132.

Swedberg, Richard. 2010. "The Structure of Confidence and the Collapse of Lehman Brothers." In *Markets on Trial: The Economic Sociology of the U.S. Financial Crisis,* edited by Michael Lounsbury and Paul Hirsch, 371–414. Bingley, UK: Emerald.

Terris, Harry. 2007. "Citi-ACC: A Bet Vertical Integration Still Has Legs." *American Banker,* September 13, 2007, 18–19.

Tett, Gillian. 2009. *Fool's Gold.* London: Little, Brown.

Thakor, Aanjan V. 2012. "Incentives to Innovate and Financial Crises." *Journal of Financial Economics* 103(1): 130–148.

Tillman, Robert, and Henry Pontell. 1995. "Organizations and Fraud in the Savings and Loan Industry." *Social Forces* 73(4): 1439–1463.

Time. 2010. "25 People to Blame for the Financial Crisis." April 20, 2010. http://content .time.com/time/specials/packages/0,28757,1877351,00.html.

Tufano, Peter. 2003. "Financial Innovation." In *Handbook of the Economics of Finance,* edited by George M. Constantinides, M. Harris, and Rene M. Stulz, 307–335. Cambridge, MA: Elsevier.

Turner, Ralph H. 1976. "The Real Self: From Institution to Impulse." *American Journal of Sociology* 81:989–1016.

Urban Institute. 2019. *Housing Finance at a Glance.* Washington, DC: Urban Institute.

U.S. Department of the Treasury. 2007. *Annual Report on Foreign Holdings in the U.S.* Washington, DC: Government Printing Office.

Useem, Michael. 1996. *Investor Capitalism: How Money Managers Are Changing the Face of the World.* New York: Basic Books.

Vaisey, Stephen. 2009. "Motivation and Justification: A Dual-Process Model of Culture in Action." *American Journal of Sociology* 114(6): 1675–1715.

Van der Swan, Natasha. 2014. "Making Sense of Financialization." *Socio-Economic Review* 12(1): 99–129.

Van Horne, James C. 1985. "Of Financial Innovations and Excesses." *Journal of Finance* 40(3): 620–631.

Van Order, Robert. 2000. "The U.S. Mortgage Market: A Model of Duelling Charters." *Journal of Housing Research* 11:233–256.

Vanguard. 2013. *The ABCs of MBS.* Vanguard Corporation.

Vaughan, Diane. 1996. *The Challenger Launch Decision.* Chicago: University of Chicago Press.

Wall Street Journal. 1970. "Ginnie Mae Offers First Mortgage Backed Bond." April 24, 1970: 22.

———. 2009. "Inside the Fall of Bear Stearns." May 9, 2009. https://www.wsj.com /articles/SB124182740622102431.

Wallison, Peter. 2015. *Hidden in Plain Sight: What Really Caused the Financial Crisis and Why It Could Happen Again.* Washington, DC: AEI.

Walsh, Carl. 1993. "What Caused the 1990–1991 Recession?" *Economic Review* (Federal Reserve Bank of San Francisco) 2:33–48.

Washington Mutual. Various years. *Annual Reports.*

Wang, Xia, and Kristy Holtfreter. 2012. "The Effects of Corporation- and Industry-Level Strain and Opportunity on Corporate Crime." *Journal of Research in Crime and Delinquency* 49(2): 151–185.

Weick, Karl. 1988. *Sensemaking in Organizations.* Los Angeles: Sage.

Weick, Karl, Kathleen Sutcliffe, and David Obstfeld. 2005. "Organizing and the Process of Sensemaking." *Organization Science* 16(4): 409–421.

Westhoff, Dale, and Bruce Kramer. 2001. "Can Mortgage Refinancings Save the U.S. Economy?" *Asset Securitization Report,* February 2001, 3–7.

White, Lawrence. 2009. "The Credit-Rating Agencies and the Subprime Debacle." *Critical Review* 21(2–3): 389–399.

———. 2010. "The Credit Rating Agencies." *Journal of Economic Perspectives* 24(2): 211–226.

Williams, Katherine, and Charles O'Reilly. 1998. "Demography and Diversity in Organizations: A Review of 40 Years of Research." *Research in Organizational Behavior* 20:77–140. Oxford: JAI.

Willis, Lauren E. 2006. "Decision-Making and the Limits of Disclosure: The Problem of Predatory Lending Price." *Maryland Law Review* 65:707–840.

Wilmarth, Arthur E. 2009. "The Dark Side of Universal Banking: Financial Conglomerates and the Origins of the Subprime Financial Crisis." *University of Connecticut Law Review* 41(4): 963–1045.

———. 2013. "Citigroup: A Case Study in Managerial and Regulatory Failures." *Indiana Law Review* 67:69–137.

Woodford, Michael. 2003. *Interest and Prices: Foundations of a Theory of Monetary Policy.* Princeton, NJ: Princeton University Press.

————. 2009. "Convergence in Macroeconomics: Elements of the New Synthesis." *American Economic Journal: Macroeconomics* 1(1): 267–279.

Yates, Joanne. 2005. *Structuring the Information Age.* Baltimore: Johns Hopkins University Press.

Zerubavel, Eviatar. 2015. *Hidden in Plain Sight: The Social Structure of Irrelevance.* New York: Oxford University Press.

Zweig, Philip. 1995. *Wriston.* New York: Crown.

Acknowledgments

When the financial crisis first really hit in the summer and fall of 2008, I became obsessed with what was going on. It was like a giant train wreck happening. No one seemed to have predicted it or had a handle on it. It was clear that the main government officials were scrambling to make sense of what was going on as events were overtaking their actions. I know I was not the only one who was riveted by these events. I had conversations with many people who, like me, were stunned as every day the crisis unfolded in unexpected and devastating ways. Its size, breadth, and rapidity were overwhelming.

I was teaching an undergraduate class on economy and society at the time. It was impossible not to bring to class everyday materials from the newspapers and talk about what was going on and what they meant. I first of all thank that class for providing me with the opportunity to follow the facts, talk about them, and begin to grapple with them myself. Subsequent iterations of that class have found me developing many of the materials that appear in this book. Many classes of undergraduate students never realized the important part they played as guinea pigs in my figuring out what happened and working to present it to a smart but not necessarily informed audience. As such, my goal is to write a book that is not only technically interesting to scholars and specialists but also accessible to educated readers. I have in mind those undergraduates who after listening to me lecture on these materials for five weeks or so showed a remarkable grasp of what happened. I hope that I can reproduce that understanding in this book.

I had the great fortune to have a number of amazing graduate students who were interested in the crisis and worked with me on various parts of this project. I would like to especially thank Adam Goldstein, who began to work as a research assistant with me on the topic. From the beginning, Adam was more a coauthor than a research assistant. He amazed me with his insight, his ability to find data, and his deep grasp of the industry. We worked through lots of this stuff together and collaborated on the papers that are the basis of this book. Jacob Habinek also worked on parts of this project. He has made substantial contributions, particularly to understanding how the crisis spread from America to Europe. Alex Roehrkasse worked with me as a research assistant and coauthor on a paper that is part of Chapter 7. Jonah Stuart Brundage and Michael Schultz worked with me as research assistants and coauthors on how the Federal Reserve's Open Market Committee viewed mortgage securitization and the housing market from 2001 to 2008. Finally, Nataliya Nedzhetskaya went through the manuscript to prepare it for review and Emily Ruppel prepared the index.

Chapter 7 builds on ideas first discussed in "The Causes of Fraud in the Financial Crisis of 2007 to 2009: Evidence from the Mortgage-Backed Securities Industry," *American Sociological Review* 88, no. 4 (2016): 617–643. Portions of Chapter 8 were first published as "Seeing Like the Fed: Culture, Cognition, and Framing in the Failure to Anticipate the Financial Crisis of 2008," *American Sociological Review* 82, no. 5 (2017): 879–909.

Over the years, I have gotten great feedback from a variety of audiences who listened to various versions of these chapters. They are sufficiently numerous, and this has been going on for such a long time that I am embarrassed to try to reconstruct them. I thank everyone. Over the years, I have had many great conversations with many people about the topic of this book. I would like to thank a few of them: Bruce Carruthers, Frank Dobbin, Marion Fourcade, Mike Lounsbury, Donald MacKenzie, Sarah Quinn, Akos Rona-Tas, Marc Schneiberg, Richard Swedberg, and John Williams. I got great feedback from two anonymous reviewers of the book manuscript. They helped shape the final version of this to make it more coherent as well as, hopefully, more accurate. I would like to thank James Brandt, my editor at Harvard Press. He offered many useful suggestions in making this book more readable and coherent. I would also like to thank Eric Mulder, Design Specialist at Harvard University Press, for his help in producing the figures and graphs in the book.

Finally, I would like to thank Heather, who has been with me throughout my obsession with the financial crisis. She has asked me good questions, humored me, and gotten me to occasionally forget that I was doing any of this. This book is dedicated to her.

Index